THE FAST STUFF

MAT OXLEY

Twenty years of top bike racing tales from the world's maddest motorsport

Haynes Publishing

First published in May 2008

A catalogue record for this book is available from the British Library

ISBN 978 1 84425 496 5

Library of Congress catalog card no 2007943101

Published by Haynes Publishing,
Sparkford, Yeovil, Somerset BA22 7JJ, UK
Tel: 01963 442030 Fax: 01963 440001
Int. tel: +44 1963 442030 Int. fax: +44 1963 440001
E-mail: sales@haynes.co.uk
Website: www.haynes.co.uk

Haynes North America Inc., 861 Lawrence Drive, Newbury Park, California 91320, USA

Designed and typeset by James Robertson
Printed and bound in Britain by J.H. Haynes & Co. Ltd., Sparkford

CONTENTS

'I still can't ride and just have fun. I've got to ride it to where it's skiddin' the front and the rear. I'm not at the point where I can ride around slowly. That's why when I first came to Europe I knew I would die if I did the Isle of Man. And it's still my problem. Someone watched me ride a motocross bike the other day and said "What the fuck, you're going to kill yourself, crank it down!" But that's the way I ride, I can't crank it down.'

King Kenny Roberts, aged 52½,
August 2004

'I have this theory that many years ago some world government conspiracy had the bright idea of creating this sport to encourage as many psychos as possible to spend their weekends in the same place, surrounded by 10-feet tall wire fences, to keep normal society safe from these crazies.'

Mat Oxley, aged 43¼, July 2002

For all the good people who didn't make it through: brother Julian, Conor Brennan, Dave Chisman, Kevin Clementson, Mark Farmer, Steve Hislop, Rob Holden, Kenny Irons, David Jefferies, Howard Lees, Mez Mellor, Jonny Opie, Gus Scott, Ronnie Smith.

INTRODUCTION

Some kind of extreme

I first discovered that I like going fast on motorcycles when I got my first bike aged 17. Riding motorcycles (even now, at much more sensible speeds) is one of the big joys of my life – I would never want to live without that feeling – and I've always got a huge kick out of watching other people ride bikes fast. Motorcycle racers are fascinating people, they live their lives at some kind of extreme, which makes them fascinating people to talk to, mostly, anyway.

That's what this book is really about – it is a collection of stories and interviews that live and breathe on the words of the sport's towering greats, like Wayne Rainey recalling his pre-race psych-up routine: 'I'd be dancing around my motorhome, kicking my leathers, or I'd sit there, focusing on the feeling of being excited and wanting to spit nails and rip the handlebars off the bike'. That's what I love about motorcycle racing, it's not just the bikes and the speed, it's the gladiatorial heroes and the nutters who'll do just about anything to win. It is a violent, vicious sport, but at these extremes you can easily discern the difference between the good guys and the bad guys. Like Orwell said, it's war, without the shooting.

The pages of this book are filled with the words of incredible people like Rainey: my thanks to all of them for allowing me to take up their time.

Mat Oxley

London, Spring 2008

My thanks to Arie Blokland, Adil Jal Darukhanawala, Mark Forsyth, Mark Graham, Mark Hughes and Darryl Reach of Haynes, Magnus Johansson, Mick Matheson, Rupert Paul, Marc Potter, Steve Rose, Matthias Schröter, Michael Scott, Tim Thompson, John Ulrich, John Westlake, Hugo Wilson, Ken Wootton, Gunther Wiesinger and all the other editors who've been kind or foolish enough to publish my crazed rants.

CHAPTER 1

OUT THERE WITH THE

BIG BOYS

August 1989

What's it like racing with Rainey, Schwantz, Doohan and Gardner? I got to find out in the 1989 Suzuka Eight Hours, the most hyped race in the world

The weather is typical of Japan in July – so steamy hot the air you breathe feels second hand and rivulets of sweat run down every part of your body.

I shouldn't care though – I am lying on a couch with two girls draping nicely chilled towels across my legs and torso. I have an ice-cold drink in one hand and a bowl of sliced orange and banana within reach of the other. A Japanese doctor massages my body and an electric fan blows a cooling draught on my face, rustling the leaves of the nearby palms.

Heaven surely couldn't be a much more delightful experience – but the pleasure of this visit through the pearly gates is tainted by the knowledge that I soon have to return to the fiery torment of hell.

Hell in this case is the Suzuka racetrack, designed back in 1962 by some fiendish Japanese, obviously intent on giving racers sleepless nights well into the next millennium.

The circuit is tough enough in itself but it's the viscous Japanese summer which makes the Suzuka Eight Hours bike racing's Dante's Inferno. As you get deeper into the race, the ogres of physical and mental exhaustion grow like monsters before you and devils dance around, laughing hideously at the sight of a mere mortal venturing so far into their terrible territory.

The exhaustion may not be tangible but the devils certainly are – they are dressed in colourful suits, mounted on evil 145 horsepower motorcycles and their names are Rainey, Schwantz, Gardner, Doohan, Sarron, Magee and Kocinski. They fly past, taunting you with daredevil deeds that would mean inevitable disaster if you were foolish enough to attempt to emulate them.

Sharing the track with these men is indeed like moving through a door into another world where the laws of physics mean more to some people than others. You can no longer smugly announce 'I could do that' and walk away from the spectator area safe in the knowledge that, if someone put a million dollars in your hands and sat you on a factory race bike, you could cut the same lap time as these guys.

I can only watch through my visor in wonder as Mick Doohan slips by me into Suzuka's first gear hairpin aboard his RVF750, lays the bike on its side until both tyres must surely exceed their traction limit, cracks open the throttle as he progressively moves his body weight to the front of the machine and lays a streak of scorched rubber on the tarmac. The thick black arc curves outward towards the kerb and continues unfalteringly through the shift to second for another 20 yards until Doohan hits third, then the tyre hooks up and the RVF's power finds another way of showing itself – the front wheel jumps two feet in the air before slamming back down onto the deck, just in time for Doohan to snatch fourth and lay the bike into the next, fast right-hander.

'I'm still close enough to see what's happening as Doohan's rear tyre breaks traction, this time at very high lean, and lays another wild trail of rubber'

Since the hairpin Doohan has been climbing a shallow rise but after the brow halfway through the fast right, the track drops away. I'm still close enough to see what's happening as his rear tyre again breaks traction, this time at very high lean, and lays another wild trail of rubber, thicker and darker than the hundreds of others already etched on the tarmac. As the rear tyre gets more and more out of line Doohan turns the handlebars onto opposite lock to control the slide, shifts into fifth and lifts the bike momentarily before laying the RVF into the next, even faster right that leads into Suzuka's famous Spoon Curve.

I'm given similar exhibitions of what it takes to be a superhero on a million dollar factory contract by the other stars. I don't emulate them, I can hardly learn from them – all I know is that they are going a lot faster and I know that if I try to go as fast – I'll crash. That's why they're rich boys and I'm not.

But for one week I'm a factory rider – well, almost. I've got just about everything I need: a mega-trick RC30 prepared by Honda's Hamamatsu boffins (including forks machined from solid), flash leathers created specifically for this race and emblazoned with the logo of our sponsors Kawai Steel (motorway bridge builders), a pit bristling with Japanese mechanics, a PR man, a doctor, two assistants and even three bikini-clad girlies who are trained to smile for the cameras, presumably to save me the effort of doing so.

My team-mate in this expensive lark is French bike journalist turned TV commentator, Gilbert Roy. We're both part-time racers pretending to be pros in what is arguably the world's most important race. I hear that the team's budget for the race is £80,000. And I know there's room for 60 bikes on the grid. Fifteen of those will be full factory bikes from Honda, Kawasaki, Suzuki and Yamaha, the rest will be semi-factory missiles and massively-funded privateer teams piloted by pros imported from Down Under, Europe and the USA. Names like Graeme Crosby, Carl Fogarty, Rob McElnea, Paul Lewis, Hervé Moineau, Malcolm Campbell litter the programme. The pressure is on.

There's already an air of growing tension when we arrive at Suzuka six days before the race with five days of practice scheduled (that's how seriously people take this race – at GPs you get three days). Right away I am anxious to pick up any tips from the stars who fill Suzuka's in-house hotel and restaurants. On the first night I dine with Wayne Gardner but all he wants to talk about is his new 1700 horsepower motor yacht. Practice starts next morning, so I'm a little surprised when he orders the biggest beer in the house. If this is how the pros do it, then I better have one too. I discover too late that Gardner is not practising until Wednesday.

Next morning the pits are already swarming with Japanese factory staff, with inscrutable race bosses keeping an inscrutable eye on their teams. By race day there will be 250,000 fans here and that's why winning the Eight Hours comes a close second to a 500 world title in the Big Four's sales battle. The hype in the Suzuka pit lane easily matches the intensity of racing on the track. Each team has its own 'Race Queen', and each pit includes its own prefabricated rider and hospitality lounge which vary from the simple to the exotic – ours is very much the latter with palm trees and a neat little bar, where journalists can have a drink while watching Gilbert and I go through hell.

Qualifying begins and we know we're going to have to cut something like a 2 minute 24 second lap to qualify. Rainey (teamed with Magee on a Yamaha YZF750 Genesis), Gardner (with Doohan on a Honda

RVF750), Schwantz (with Doug Polen on a Yoshimura GSX-R750) and Co are expected to battle for pole at around 2m 16s on their factory rocket ships.

In untimed practice I kick off with 2m 28s laps, which I whittle down to a 2 26. Over the next two days I have a further two 45-minute timed sessions to slice off at least another two seconds, or suffer humiliation at the hands of the stars who I have to interview at every GP in my position as GP reporter for *Motor Cycle News*. The trouble is that it's three months since I last sat on a race bike. That's enough time to lose the confidence you need to flick into turns and slide out of them. Not only that, it's not easy setting up a race bike when you do it so infrequently. It's like speaking a foreign language a few times a year – you forget the vocabulary you need to make things work.

In the first timed session I manage a 24.371 – which might just get us on the grid. I come across Rob McElnea scrubbing in a new set of tyres on his RC30. I follow him, hoping for a tow – a trick that riders employ to great effect in GP qualifying. He signals me to tuck in behind him but he's doing 21s and I can't hack it. He drags a few hundred yards on me in a lap, snatches a look at me over his shoulder and I can almost see his mocking grin behind the blackout visor. I pit again with ten minutes qualifying and get a fresh soft rear Michelin radial.

This time I have to get a fast lap in. I try to give chase to Dominique Sarron on a factory RVF but halfway through the lap that I feel is going to be The One, the RC30 springs a water leak, forcing me into the pits. I have to wait until my final Saturday session to get us on the grid.

At dinner Rainey asks me how things are going – and he's managing not to be too patronising. I tell him I've gone two seconds faster every time I've been out and I feel I can go quicker. 'Hey, I can go faster,' he says. 'You sound like a real racer, I'll have to come over and interview you guys sometime,' he grins. 'Anyway, just get into the low 20s and you'll be okay.' Rainey manages to make 'low 20s' sound so easy, and lying in bed thinking my way round Suzuka's 18 corners I reckon I can make a 2m 22s lap on Saturday. But I haven't taken Japan's freaky climate into account – when I wake up there is a typhoon outside. The rain is lashing down. I don't even bother going out but I give up all thought of slashing my wrists when the final grid sheet arrives – we're 57th on the grid – five short of disaster.

Race day dawns a little sunnier but a few clouds keep the temperature down to a 'cool' 30 degrees. Normally Suzuka can be 35 degrees with stifling 85 per cent humidity.

The hype fuels the tension as the 11.30am start approaches. I was faster than Gilbert in practice so I'm doing the Le Mans start. And from where I stand it's a long, long way to the front of the Le Mans-style grid where Doohan stands on pole. After a few mouthfuls of electrolyte 'energy' drink I line up for the sprint. My mouth is parched, my heart racing and my legs nervy like jelly as Suzuka's electronic grandstand info board flashes up 'GO!' I make a good getaway but within two seconds all hell breaks loose. Two bikes collide in the getaway melee, I swerve wildly to avoid the exploding debris and I can't believe it when another bike alongside me ploughs into the wreckage. The last I see, the rider is two yards in the air hanging on to his motorcycle – upside down.

Incredibly the marshals have cleared the mess by the end of the first lap and the Eight Hours isn't going to be stopped. The next lap brings more crashes as the banzai locals get carried away with the occasion. I soon discover that riders who had qualified in front of me can't keep up at that kind of pace for more than a few laps. I'm steadily making up places.

But after five laps or so the heat is getting to me already, sweat from my forehead is splashing like rain on the inside of my visor and stinging my eyes, I begin to wish I could crash and get it all over with. A few laps later the heat begins to take its toll on the tyres too. Another rash of crashes proves that some riders haven't prepared themselves for this – it's so hot and slippery at Suzuka that you have to slide the rear tyre to keep going at a decent pace.

My only worry is getting in the way of Doohan and his fellow GP stars when they lap me – and my pet nightmare is bringing down Rainey, currently locked in a duel with Eddie Lawson for the 500 crown. I can see the headlines – 'RAINEY BREAKS LEG AND RUINS WORLD TITLE CHANCE IN JOURNALIST SMASH'. So I take a few glances over my shoulder as the session draws on. Doohan is way ahead when he effortlessly swoops by me followed by Rainey. Kocinski comes past at the rapid Turn One, puffs of smoke coming off his right knee scraper as he chases the leaders.

By the end of the first hour we're up to 24th. The bike is flying, revving hungrily to 13,000rpm and handling well through Suzuka's twists. There were no less than 28 RC30s on the 60 bike grid – that's nearly 50 per cent of the bikes and adequate proof that the RC is as near as any normal human being can get to a factory motorcycle.

In between sessions I am given the full treatment by the team doctor. I've got wrist problems so he gives me acupuncture. Every hour off the bike – while Gilbert is out there doing his bit – is spent on a bed being massaged and rehydrating. There's even a canister of oxygen on hand if I need it. And the two girl assistants who help me dress and undress give me a new pair of socks for every session.

Doohan is receiving similar treatment in the next door pit but he doesn't look as knackered as I feel – he doesn't get new socks either. The awesome pace begins to tell at the front of the pack. Doohan and Gardner are stretching their lead but Doohan collides with a backmarker and goes to hospital with a badly mangled hand, putting fellow RVF pilots Dominique Sarron and Alex Vieira into the lead.

Despite the massage and acupuncture, I feel more drained each time I get on the bike and I can't maintain my early pace. Joker Schwantz comes past me on the back straight, wildly waving both legs at me. In the next session he powers underneath me out of a fast left-hander, shaking his head mockingly. Earlier I had passed him pushing his Yoshimura GSX-R after he'd run out of fuel and I begin to wish I'd slowed right down and had a good laugh at his predicament.

Rainey and Kocinski's teams go out too – after five hours we're 16th, one place out of championship points. In the later hours of the race the temperature cools but my wrists weaken. My last two sessions are not enjoyable at all but we're 12th at the flag as darkness falls. The relief of the finish is both breathtaking and frightening – the last lap is lit by a massive, booming firework display and as we arrive back at the finish the track is invaded by the frenzied crowd. We just get the bike back into the pits when we're engulfed by the seething masses who snatch whatever they can as a Suzuka souvenir – I feel they'd be quite happy to have one of my arms, or legs.

The team celebrations begin with huge bottles of Moët & Chandon. We all shake hands, Mr Kawai beams, the two girl assistants burst into tears. Next morning we pick up £1000 prize money each. My head hurts and every bit of my body aches but I could get used to being a pro racer.

CHAPTER 2

RIDING THE NSR WAS

LIKE DEATH…

November 1989

'…every time you flicked into a turn you didn't know if you were going to make it out'. That's what Eddie Lawson said of the evil sonofabitch Honda NSR500 with which he miraculously won the 1989 500 crown. So what was I going to make of the thing at a chilly Suzuka, just a few weeks after he'd secured the title and hightailed it back to Yamaha? I've ridden a lot of Honda GP bikes, from Ron Haslam's 1983 NS500 triple to Mick Doohan's awesome 1992 big bang NSR to Valentino Rossi's last-of-the-line 2001 NSR but Lawson's '89 bike stands out as the most terrifying thing I've ever ridden in my life. Pure malevolence on two wheels

Mondai nai, as they say in Japan: no problem. It is, after all, only another motorcycle. No reason why I shouldn't ride the bitch to the limit, flick the 'bars and stick it into the turn, jump on the throttle and steer it with the wheelspin.

This is a psychological battle. I'm trying very, very hard to work myself into a state of mental superiority over Eddie Lawson's Rothmans Honda NSR500 which looks plain evil standing there in pit lane, waiting to do terrible things to me.

And if the NSR looks horribly menacing, it sounds even worse. When the HRC mechanics bump the beast into life in Suzuka's pit lane its strident rrrrinnnng, rrrrrinnnng unleashes a flood of adrenalin into my veins.

My legs turn to jelly, I'm not winning the battle. It's November, it's damned cold and blood runs thickly through my veins; pain is also more painful when it's cold and fat slick tyres don't warm up so well either. But I've come a long way for this. I've bought my own air ticket, spent 12 hours on a Jumbo next to a couple of professional ballroom dancers, come within one molecule of oxygen of suffocation on the

Tokyo subway, remortgaged my flat for a seat on the bullet train and watched my dinner being cooked alive in front of my very eyes.

The motorcycle is not going to be a problem.

Lawson's NSR is not only evil, it is also deceitful. Dawdling out of the Suzuka pit lane the motor crackles though its carbon-fibre cans and sounds pretty harmless. It drives from nowhere, making a tuned RD350LC seem unrideable. Thirteen corners later I hit Suzuka's back straight, which curves gently left and uphill over a rise, and I let the NSR do its very worst for the first time.

'The front wheel hardly makes contact with the tarmac all the way down the 190mph back straight'

Revs rise in a remorseless rush, I'm shifting gears faster than I've ever shifted gears before, the motor shrieking out more than 160 utterly intimidating horsepower at 12,500rpm. The acceleration freezes my brain and paralyses my senses which struggle to cope with the speed at which the scenery turns to a blur. The front wheel hardly makes contact with the tarmac all the way down the 190mph back straight, skimming from ripple to ripple and grabbing left, right, left, right with a scary violence. The 115 kilo NSR makes an early Suzuki GSX-R feel mighty stable. The only way to keep the thing going straight is to lock my arms around the petrol tank and hold on for grim life, just like the death-cheating heroes of the 1970s on the Daytona banking. Surely Lawson didn't ride his NSR like this all year?

Indeed he did not. After a frankly worrying (nope, make that terrifying) first few laps, I pull into the pits ashen faced and feeling my respect for Lawson raised to new heights. I mime a nasty tankslapper to the waiting HRC mechanics who descend upon their pride and joy, turning the handlebars from side to side and chatting furiously. They soon find the problem – they'd set the steering damper on minimum. Thanks guys. With a cheery laugh they wind the damper up to its 21st and last click (FULL!!) and usher me out of the pits once more. I'm beginning to wonder if this is their idea of a joke.

If you've ever ridden a motorcycle with almost solid steering you'll know what it's like – in slow corners you just topple over – and I have visions of myself crashing at Suzuka's dead-stop chicane. Incredibly, Lawson rode the bike like this for much of his championship-winning season, fighting to get the thing into turns at more normal racing speeds. The NSR does indeed require serious physical input to overcome the chassis' inadequacies. Lawson and his pit-lane guru Erv Kanemoto used 12 different chassis during '89 as they tried to tame the NSR but the bike still goes where it wants to, rather than where you aim it. At the end of Suzuka's main straight all it wants to do is keep going straight, and the only way I can get it to take the third-gear left-hander is by wrenching hard on the handlebars to overcome the gyro-effect. Even so, I never manage to hit the apex. God only knows how Lawson raced the bike, let alone won the world title on the thing.

Two weeks before I scared myself on the NSR I had ridden Kevin Schwantz's 1989 Pepsi Suzuki RGV500 in the less exotic surroundings of Snetterton, Norfolk. The RGV consumes the straights with almost as much voracity as the Honda, melting the scenery, dragging the horizon towards you at jet-like speed.

There's no doubt that the Honda has more power – Lawson needed all the top speed he could get to compensate for the bike's nightmare handling – but the NSR engine isn't the vicious beast that racing legend would have us believe. The theory goes that the Suzuki has smooth, controlled power, while the Honda is the tyre-shredding sonofabitch. In fact the Honda has the smoother power curve, even if it runs out of puff 500rpm sooner than the 13,000rpm RGV. Both motors have gaping wide powerbands and are much more tractable than you'd believe possible. But the RGV's power curve is much steeper, so much so that it tries to loop the loop in the first three gears, which is why Schwantz must resort to his rodeo riding stunts when he gets on the throttle, moving his body weight as far forward as it'll go, so he doesn't have to turn off the throttle to keep the front under control. The NSR wheelies for sure, but its flatter power curve means the front lifts more controllably.

If you watched Lawson take on Schwantz and Wayne Rainey during the 1989 season you'll know that it was always a problem for Lawson to put the NSR where he wanted it. While Rainey's Yamaha and in particular Schwantz's Suzuki proved nimble enough to hog the tight, fast line, Lawson had to use every bit of the track to stay in the hunt. He had to use his body in a different way to subdue the NSR, hanging his torso as far off the inside as he could to drag the bike through the turns.

The NSR's behaviour is a puzzle because the textbooks dictate that its chassis dimensions should make it turn better than the Suzuki.

The NSR has steeper steering geometry, a shorter wheelbase and a smaller front wheel (Lawson ran a 16-inch Michelin front through much of the season, while Schwantz stuck with the older and more popular 17 inch).

At Snetterton the Suzuki mostly did what it was told through the corners. Just a spark of mental input was enough to flick the bike on its side, at the very most it needed just a tickle of the handlebars to get it through the faster curves on precisely the line you'd intended. But the Suzuki's light-headedness became hard work on the gas. Schwantz may be happy exiting a turn cranked over with the front tyre lifting and the rear spinning, but I wasn't about to go there.

Adapting one's brains to the way these 500s shrink wide open racetracks into slender ribbons of tarmac isn't a rapid process. Neither is reprogramming one's brain to their stopping power. The Suzuki's carbon AP Lockheeds explode so violently into action when you grab a handful that it's hard just staying on board. The Honda's Nissins aren't so dramatic but you still need to lock your arms to maintain control during braking.

At Suzuka I managed three outings on the NSR, about 40 minutes on the bike, before I was a physical wreck: my wrists and arm muscles ached from braking and turning, my leg muscles ached from shifting my body around the bike and my brain ached from total mental overload. No doubt about it, Lawson is no normal human being.

CHAPTER 3

An audience with King Ted

February 1990

This interview, conducted shortly before the start of the 1990 GP season, doesn't reveal much about Eddie Lawson but in not doing so it reveals quite a lot. Eddie's dryness, his taciturnity, his distaste for wasting time doing interviews with hapless journalists are all here in bucket loads.

Lawson had only recently stunned the world with his second shock team transfer in as many winters – after winning his third 500 crown with Ago's Marlboro Yamaha outfit in 1988, he defected to Rothmans Honda (prompting some fans to call him 'The Anti-Christ'), won the 1989 title against all the odds and then returned to Marlboro Yamaha, then under new management with King Kenny Roberts. Honda lost Lawson at the end of '89 for the same reason they lost Valentino Rossi a decade and a half later – they treated him like just any other employee – and because the NSR was a motorcycle racer's nightmare.

Lawson is a highly intelligent man, so you need to read between the lines to find out what he really thinks. When he says that adapting to the Yamaha after a sometimes terrifying but ultimately successful season aboard the fiery NSR500 is straightforward, 'it's easy to go back this way', he's really telling you what a nightmare he had getting used to the NSR500 a year earlier.

And I like the way his answers are so clipped, so disinterested, then when I tickle his ego by asking him about getting out-braked by the up-and-coming John Kocinski, he revs up for his longest answer of the whole interview.

Racers are funny people and Lawson was funny as hell – he used to really take the piss out of us journalists – he

**loved winding us up and wasting our time. He liked racing
motorcycles, he hated talking to journalists. And who could
blame him for that?**

Standing in the Marlboro Team Roberts truck at Jerez, Eddie Lawson
pops a couple of small white pills into his mouth and sweeps them
down his throat with a gulp of water.

'Hey, Eddie, are you on drugs?' I ask idly.

'Nope, they're aspirin. I gotta headache. It must be looking at you
journalist guys all day.'

Lawson names the interview as the thing he most hates about being
a four-times world champion. A Honda calendar, recently printed to
celebrate his 1989 title success aboard its NSR500, quotes him thus:
'I'm not looking for fame but for self-satisfaction.'

This man does not need praise and glory to motivate him.
His motivation to win, to be the best, year after year, comes wholly
from inside.

When Lawson talks his words are as dry as dust. And the man is a
master of ultra-understatement.

*How does it feel to be back on Yamaha's YZR500, which has already taken you
to three world titles?*
Pretty familiar, it's real easy to ride and I already feel comfortable. I'm
not having trouble adapting – it's easy to go back this way.

*After one day here at Jerez, you've already lapped faster than you did last year on
the Honda.*
Yeah, but if Kevin [Schwantz] was here we'd be doing 1m 47s. I never
get cocky, I know what happens when you do.

How's the YZR's straight-line speed?
That's come up, the engine feels better than in '88, much better. I don't
know, it might be a little weaker than the Honda.

You started last season injured, you should be at full fitness this year.
I hope, you know that's what I thought last year. Then a week before
the first GP you get hurt...

Last year Erv Kanemoto helped you to the title, this year he's working with Wayne Gardner. Will that make Gardner a bigger threat?
Erv's going to be a big help to him, that's for sure. Wayne'll still go well, be a big threat. The only problem is that Gardner has to race Wayne Rainey, Kevin Schwantz *and* Eddie Lawson – it's pretty tough odds against three guys like that.

What threat will Schwantz pose – has he put the crashing behind him?
It all depends on how he goes under pressure if he's leading the championship, we'll have to wait and see.

When you joined Honda you said 'I've always wanted to race for Honda'. So what motivated your move out of there?
Riding for Honda!

One year was enough?
Yeah.

What was the problem?
We just couldn't come to terms. Their offer was far below what the other teams had offered. They wanted me to do four-stroke testing and do the Suzuka Eight Hours and this and that and the other. You know, there was no way of even discussing the contract, so there was nothing I could do. I wanted to stay with Erv but no way could I stay with Honda with what they were offering.

So, as world champion you wouldn't race for less than what you knew riders like Rainey were getting?
No, it was a question of what the market was offering. I had Suzuki and the Marlboro team offering me far, far more than Honda, and Rothmans seemed to show no interest at all, And so, shoot, if basically you're not wanted, it's time to go.

Have you always wanted to race for Kenny Roberts?
Yeah. I have wanted to do that for a long time. But this way it's worked out really nice, cos I'm back with Marlboro and I never had a problem with Marlboro.

How's it going to be racing for the title with Rainey as a team-mate? You usually try to distance yourself from your main rivals.
Not really. I think you have to race these guys no matter where they are at, what they are riding or anything else, so it makes no difference what team or anything else. You know, I know I have to race Wayne Rainey and I have to race Kevin Schwantz and possibly Wayne Gardner if he comes back and maybe Kevin Magee if he's on the gas. I mean, you have to race these guys whether they're your team-mate or not.

The arrival of John Kocinski in your team must be pretty exciting. Will you be a teacher to him?
I don't think there's anything we can teach him. You know, if he has competitive equipment, he'll do his own thing and he'll be competitive.

How did you feel at last year's [1989] Spa GP when he outbraked you and passed you in the wet?
Yeah, he rode really well and I think if I'd been on a Yamaha, on Dunlop rain tyres and had nothing to lose whatsoever, I think I could have gone pretty fast too. But no one seemed to bring that up. You know, I was on a bike that was a little bit hard to ride in the wet and maybe I didn't pick the right tyres and I had everything to lose if I went fast, so there was no reason to chase him down at all. But he rode really well and he's capable of riding a 500 really well. But where was he in the dry? Nobody seemed to mention that. I think he is capable of winning world championships. He will. But he's not God and we shouldn't build him up to be that because it'll only hurt him.

'I wouldn't go to Cagiva and try to win on a Cagiva'

Would you say you don't race for fame but for self-satisfaction?
Sure, yeah, that's where I'm at. I'm not looking to be famous, that's for sure.

When you were talking with Suzuki, did the idea of winning three world titles on three different bikes appeal?
All I wanted to do was be on a team that works well for me – that's all I thought about – I wouldn't go to Cagiva and try to win on a Cagiva.

To me the Suzuki deal was interesting cos they wanted me so badly and that was nice. But it's not where I wanted to go. It's nice when people want you, you feel good about doing a job for them. It's like Marlboro and Kenny. When I went to them and asked them about it, they were interested, they wanted to do it. Where I was at, no one seemed to be interested so it was time to go.

Epilogue: Lawson did indeed go to Cagiva and not only did he try to win on the Italian V4, he did win, taking victory at the damp 1992 Hungaroring. He retired at the end of that year. As he walked out of the paddock for the last time, Schwantz shouted after him 'Good riddance and don't come back'. They weren't great mates in those days but time has healed old wounds.

CHAPTER 4

YEN AND THE ART OF

MOTORCYCLE DESTRUCTION

August 1990

And this is when motorcycle racing goes wrong. If our 1989 Suzuka Eight Hours ride had been a good weekend for a couple of wannabe racers, the 1990 event was an unmitigated disaster

The final qualifying session for the 1990 Suzuka Eight Hours: ninety thousand spectators have come to watch this because they fully understand it's time for banzai tactics, death or glory, that kind of stuff.

So far we're two seconds off the pace, and two seconds in roadracing is an age, an epoch. Which is why the red mist has already descended by the time I climb aboard our Honda-prepped Honda RC30 and accelerate down pit lane. I should know that the mist (which prompts the belief that a quick burst of heroism is enough to overcome incompetence and conjure up the magical lap time we need to get to the grid) will inevitably lead to disaster. And I am not wrong.

Already bathed in sweat, I decide lap four is going to be the first lap I really go for it. Top gear down the straight and I've got a bit of a tow off one of the factory Yoshimura Suzuki GSX-Rs. Ahead lies the slightly daunting Turn One. In the Suzuka circuit guide, this corner is described thus: 'One of the typical points for riders to overtake others, gives you a great chance to see a hot battles.' (sic)

I've already decided my battle isn't hot enough through Turn One. It's already fourth gear, 90mph plus, and it's already pretty scary. The approach is downhill, off-camber, with ripples and bumps at the apex. I nearly crashed there the day before, but as the Japanese say: 'Necessary faster'.

I brake a few millimetres later than usual, shift back a couple of gears and have to hold the front brake a little deeper than usual into the corner. It's all happening so fast but I can already feel the front end getting pretty washy on the bumps as I lay the bike into the corner. I need to get off the brake quick but, if my memory serves me correctly, my fingers unfurl from the lever a little too fast. The forks rebound from full compression too rapidly, taking too much weight off the front tyre, which loses grip and tucks under.

Life moves in Fast Forward mode but I'm picking up every little detail as I realise This Is A Crash. The sickening front tyre slide ends with the bike on its side. The hellish noise of the murderously over-revving engine and expensive carbon-fibre scraping against tarmac fill my helmet as I am thrown forward onto the track. I'm spun around so I'm sliding backwards, helmet first, lying on my front, limbs akimbo to scrub off some speed as I skip and bounce through the gravel trap towards the barriers. My main worry is where the bike is – I don't want 150 kilos of Honda to land on top of me.

'My RC30 is 20 feet in the air, what's left of its bodywork exploding off the main structure, like a fighter plane being blown out of the sky by anti-aircraft fire'

I catch a glimpse of the RC out the corner of my right eye. It's about 20 feet in the air and what's left of its bodywork is exploding off the main structure. In that instant it appears rather like a fighter plane being blown out of the sky by anti-aircraft fire.

I plough through the gravel, finally coming to rest amid a cloud of choking, boiling dust which subsides to reveal the RC naked and contorted. I hobble over to the wreck. The forks are so bent the front wheel is stuffed through the lower radiator. The rear subframe does not exist anymore. The remains of the seat and fairing lie scattered all around. The damage is not yet complete though: flames leap out from beneath the fuel tank, blackening the paintwork and commencing the final work of destruction.

A bunch of jabbering, helmeted marshals arrive on the scene, their voices rising several octaves when they see the fire. Extinguishers attack the blaze and within seconds the bike has once again disappeared from view in a cloud of fire-quenching white powder.

This is what happens when a hobby racer tries to get up there with the professionals.

The qualifying pace at the Eight Hours is lunatic. Up-and-coming GP youngster Mick Doohan and four-time 500 world champion Eddie Lawson clash in the battle for the much-prized pole position, which in Japan carries almost as much kudos as race victory, because pole is all about ultimate speed. Doohan, aboard the amazing Honda RVF750, wins the encounter at 2 minutes 13.427 seconds, just one hundredth of a second ahead of Lawson's Yamaha YZF750. Doohan's pole time is just two seconds off his best 500 GP time at the track. British GP star Niall Mackenzie qualifies 36th fastest at 2m 19.664s, endurance world champ Thierry Crine is 51st fastest at 2m 21.210s and 1990 Assen Formula One victor Kees Doorakkers is seeded onto the rear of the grid, by virtue of the championship points he scored at Le Mans.

The Eight Hours is what you might call pretty competitive. The race is like an out-of-control steam train running even faster downhill while team managers throw great heaps of money at it, encouraged all the while by Japan's booming economy, which is also spiralling out of control, soon to go into full-on meltdown. Most national race teams in Europe could race for a whole year on what a good private team throws into the Eight Hours. And then there are the factories – 19 full factory bikes line up at the start of the race and half the remainder of the 65 bike grid are semi-factory machines.

Despite my high-speed accident we just make it into the race, but we're right at the back of the grid with Doorakkers. Our bike has been miraculously reincarnated overnight by our Japanese mechanics who await the start bleary eyed but bursting with pride at their work.

I'm grateful that my team-mate Gilbert Roy is taking the Le Mans start because I know he's going to crash the bike again. Five laps during the pre-race morning warm-up convinced me that the frame, the swingarm or both are bent. The team assures me that they are perfectly straight, but sure enough, six laps into the race Gilbert goes down in a big way. I pray he will leave the wreck languishing in the dirt. But minutes later I hear our very sick motorcycle rumble into the pits. Curse him. The mechanics throw it back together and send me out again. I do two laps and return to the pits.

'Look guys,' I say, 'The bike is fucked.' They suggest adjusting the suspension. Great idea. Gilbert does another couple of laps and isn't impressed. They adjust the suspension again. 'Look, the frame's bent, the bikes unrideable,' I repeat.

'Ah, but Mr Kawai, your sponsor, is very important man,' the team boss replies. The inference is that Mr Kawai (who, and I jest not, builds motorway bridges for a living) has ploughed a lot of money into this venture and while the bike might be bent, I am expected to go out and ride it until I, too, crash. Then if the bike is really broken, or if I have a broken leg, we can retire from the race with honour.

I may be a wretched coward, but today I prefer dishonour to pain. I insist we retire. Chief mechanic Chichan-San bursts into floods of tears. As is the Japanese custom he is taking all the blame on his shoulders. Gilbert and I offer Chichan our ripped-up leathers to placate him – as a rider's second skin, a racing suit holds mythical value in Japan.

I metamorphose from racer to race watcher and swell spectator attendance from 159,999 to 160,000 (310,000 over three days). It's around 40 degrees and 80 per cent humidity and reclining by an air-con unit in the pits I consider the insanity of sitting on top of a red-hot motorcycle in such conditions. No doubt about it, they're all mad.

About the time we retire, Wayne Gardner crashes the leading RVF he's sharing with Doohan, which hands the lead to Lawson and Tadahiko Taira. Gardner gets back into the race and is riding like a man possessed as he closes the gap on the YZF.

Honda pours crazy amounts of money into the Eight Hours. It means almost as much to the factory as winning the 500 world title and since they have no chance of doing that this year, the 1990 Eight Hours has become a desperate crusade in which the money and resources involved mean nothing so long as victory is secured. Cash is of little consequence to the other teams too. The sponsorship yen come from all quarters to encourage the Japanese to consume yet more consumables: Cup Noodle snacks, Nescafe coffee, Kawai Steel girders, Tech 21 men's hair mousse, Pentax cameras, Swatch watches, Seed department stores. You name it, they're flogging it.

Gardner is burning rubber out of just about every turn and the RVF is taking up to a second out of the YZF each lap, so Honda reckons they'll be ahead as darkness falls and the chequered flag comes out. But in their eagerness to save time, the Honda crew mess up a fuel stop and just before halfway, the RVF runs dry around the back of the track and all the zillions of yen thrown into the RVF mean utterly nothing.

Late that night, in Suzuka's notorious Log Cabin, the riders' bar, veteran comic, TT, Daytona and Eight Hours winner Graeme Crosby presents Gardner with a bottle of beer labelled, 'Honda Gasoline – one litre: 10 million Yen.' That's how much prize money Gardner lost.

And that's how much Lawson won. The reigning 500 world champion hates racing four-strokes and he would much rather have been back home on the Colorado river in between the French and British GPs than racing in a sauna on the other side of the world. Rumour had it that Yamaha paid King Ed $200,000 to help them beat Honda. In the event, whatever they paid him was worth it.

Lawson was his usual mysterious self at Suzuka. Rarely seen, he would materialise out of the ether just before it was his turn to take over from Taira. Obviously unused to the concept of endurance racing, he began the last stint wearing a black visor on his Shoei helmet (equipped with battery-powered neon Shoei logos!) but as dusk turned to darkness he didn't seem to mind too much.

Right after his most gruelling race ever, Lawson was bound for the British GP at Donington where he met his recently retired father who'd flown in from California for a rare GP visit.

'Hi son,' his father said.

'Hi dad,' Lawson replied.

'What you been up to son?'

'I was racing in Japan last week.'

'How'd you get on son?'

'Oh, I won the race dad.'

'Well done son.'

CHAPTER 5

ON A WING AND A PRAYER –
RIDING SECRETS OF THE GODS

January 1991

The late 1980s and early 1990s were a new age in GP racing, when technological advances turned 500s from motorcycles into missiles. Speaking with Kevin Schwantz, Wayne Rainey and Mick Doohan after 1990 – the year of the highside – revealed the violently acrobatic riding techniques employed by this legendary breed of new rocket jockey

A cloudy, depressing day at Misano is enlivened by the arrival of Mick Doohan, his Rothmans Honda singing through the down changes into the tight, first gear Cattolica left-hander.

Body hunched apparently awkwardly over the front of the machine, hunting for front tyre grip, Doohan slams the NSR onto its side so violently that he will surely crash. But the bike is only cranked over for an instant before the Australian wrenches it upright and turns on the throttle.

In first gear the rear Michelin immediately breaks traction. The revs rise wildly as the rear end cocks at least 20 degrees to the right, the rear tyre etching a black mark right out to the kerb. The tyre keeps spinning, the revs remain skyward as Doohan shifts up a gear with the rear end still well out of line.

Yet all this time the front wheel is pointing dead ahead and the bike is driving hard towards the next, faster left. Doohan eases off the throttle just enough to bring the Honda approximately into line before he keels her over once again. Out of that curve Doohan grabs another gear and the warbling exhaust note signals that the rear tyre is still scrabbling for grip as he shifts up again and takes aim at the daunting, sixth-gear left that leads onto Misano's back straight.

Rear-wheel steering is nothing new. The craft has been around in GP racing for a decade or more, but every year its execution becomes more conspicuous and more incredible to witness.

Each season, the true 500 elite (you can count them on your hands with fingers to spare) develop their skills further as machine development allows them to achieve things which a year ago, or even a month ago, would have been impossible. It is the rider who is able to use his riding talent and physical strength to harness each step forward in GP technology who ultimately wins the day. Those who don't keep rolling on that learning curve get left way behind to fill the lower placings.

The art of controlling a 170 horsepower 500 two-stroke V4 entails superhuman powers of co-ordination and the ability to analyse machine behaviour minutely through each millisecond at speeds of up to 190mph. It also requires immense physical strength to resist the forces imposed by modern tyres and chassis.

This fact is strangely neglected by just about everyone except the riders and a growing coterie of paddock quacks. Old-timers who censure today's superstars for failing to emulate the three-GPs-in-a-day performance of Mike Hailwood and other old-school racing legends are blind to the advances of science. In the 1950s, 1960s and 1970s, g-force was something only jet fighter pilots worried about. It's different these days.

And yet the New Age stars talk of their craft with mind-boggling matter-of-factness: scrubbing the front tyre sideways to supplement braking power, deftly controlling the crucial rear-wheel slide with foot pressure and throttle opening, steering the bike by body positioning and weighting of the footrests. All this has become just another part of their workaday racing lives.

Simply staying on a 500 is a major feat. Leading brake manufacturers AP Lockheed calculate that riders hit about 1.5g during heavy braking, which means the weight of rider and machine is amplified one and a half times. Thus a rider has to work against 300 kilos or thereabouts as he hurtles towards a corner.

At this point the rear wheel is probably off the ground, such is the weight transfer during braking, and the combined weight of rider and machine is thrown onto the front wheel and the rider's wrists. The tendency for anyone unused to such vicious forces is to be thrown over the handlebars. I know this because it happened to me while testing Doohan's NSR. A few laps and my arms could no longer resist the braking g-forces, so they folded while I was braking into a fast right-hander and I ended up flopping over the 'bars and headbutting the front number plate. Not nice.

The 500 stars are able to brake so violently because they are brave, strong and skilful enough to take advantage of the extraordinary power of carbon brakes and the immense grip of the latest slick tyres, which don't lock or skid during braking.

Now the problem is simply holding on – not easy when all four fingers are require to haul on the front brake lever. It's a happy coincidence that the leverage required to induce that level of deceleration has decreased as stopping power has increased. Most riders brake with two fingers, some only use a single finger, allowing the rest of the hand to concentrate on holding on.

The roadracer's version of tennis elbow and other physical peculiarities are the downside of this progress. Tendonitis (constriction of the nerve tissues caused by overdevelopment of the arm muscles, leading to loss of feeling in the hands) is a common paddock malady. Check out the stars' wrist scars for evidence of corrective surgery.

And the sport's latest demands are creating a new breed of racing mutant. When Doohan clenches his right hand, as if to grip his NSR's handlebar, a gruesome lump of muscle protrudes from the underside of his forearm. The overdeveloped tissue is nicknamed a 'throttle bump' and is the result of resisting 1.5g while simultaneously juggling brake lever, throttle and handlebar pressure.

The throttle bump won't be the end of GP rider evolution. And while the arm and thigh muscles do the greatest share of the work, the rider's whole body is at fever pitch during a race, fighting the negative forces and working to take advantage of the positive forces. GP racing produces the kind of heart bpms and breath rates experienced by Olympic athletes. Which is why today's GP stars are a (relatively) clean-living bunch whose daily routine is built around their physical training programmes.

Enough of the medical thesis. To examine the details of GP riding technique we will assume a rider is attacking a generously proportioned 180-degree right. He's heavy on the front brake, while his right foot strokes the rear brake lever. But with the rear tyre likely to be an inch or two in the air, there's no braking power to be gained there, so it's all about control, as Wayne Rainey says: 'On a 500 you've got no engine braking. When you backshift it's like the chain's come off, so I just use the rear brake to settle the suspension and to stop the rear end from going crazy.'

As the machine approaches the corner, the complications really begin. The lion's share of the braking is done in a straight line but the

time comes when the rider must set in motion the chain of events that
will take him through the corner. His eyes are already lining up the
entry point as he begins to ease off the front brake and apply handlebar
and footrest pressure to steer the bike.

Although the tarmac takes a smooth U-turn onto the next straight,
rider and machine don't describe such a graceful arc. That style may
have been the only way round a corner in the days of slippy tyres, dodgy
suspension and bendy frames, but modern GP machines permit a faster,
more aggressive route through the turn.

The object is to minimise the time the machine is cranked over,
because in that situation neither brake nor throttle can be applied.
Nowadays the rider keeps the bike relatively upright deeper into the
corner, accomplishing the actual turning in an instant and then firing
the bike out on the throttle. In effect he describes a 'V' line through the
turn, not the classic and graceful 'U' of olden times.

Getting the turning over and done with as rapidly as possible
demands violent measures. The rider doesn't just lean the bike into the
corner – he knocks the machine onto its side, applying aggressive
counter-steer by pushing heavily on the right handlebar to turn the
front wheel to the left and drop the machine to the right. Body weight
and feet inputs also play their part, the pilot's backside shifting to the
right and his extra weighting of the right footrest help to pull the
machine over. The transition from upright to full lean is accomplished
in such a dramatically short time that it seems certain that the rider
won't be able to arrest the descent before it's too late.

Of course, this time he does avert disaster, and yet as the bike leans
deep into the corner the rider is still fingering the front brake lever,
scrubbing off excess speed as the disc pads gently bite on the decelerating
rotors. From now on, applying any more brake really can spell disaster,
for the average rider at least, because this is where Mr Average and the
elite go their different ways. Instead these elite riders happily induce
front-tyre slides, either with a touch more brake, a tweak on the 'bars or
a fraction more lean angle. The tyre then begins to slide and scrubs off
the speed which couldn't be safely lost with a more drastic pull on the
brake. This is indeed treading the fine line between glory and disaster.

Rainey explains how it works: 'I usually only scrub the front tyre
when I get into a turn too hot but this is how it goes: you're in fourth
gear and jetting down to this U-turn. You brake and flick it in. You can

feel the brake and then you pick up the feel of the tyre and it starts moving a little bit. Just from racing so long I know what it's going to do most of the time, so I can adjust the pressure on the handlebars and know how hard I can drive it into the pavement. You just lay it over a little bit more, it slides and scrubs off that much more speed.'

Easy enough, but how does Rainey prevent the slide translating into a crash when he has only milliseconds to react to the signals of impending doom? 'That's the tricky part! I'm using everything. I use the rear brake, I'm using my knee and I'm using a lot of upper body weight to keep my weight at a certain angle to the bike.'

Rainey and most of his peers learned the complex and risky art of scrubbing the front tyre aboard more forgiving four-strokes. The natural engine braking and extra weight of a 'diesel' (the GP racer's mocking term for a four-stroke) make it easier for riders to control just how much input they put into the front tyre. On a 500 they have to rely partly on delicate dabs of the rear brake to shift weight off the front tyre, though this technique is only possible in left-handers because the rear brake lever isn't accessible when the bike is cranked over through right-handers.

> 'When the front slides it's kind of like "OH!" and you dig in your knee and it's a bit of a moment'

Doohan, who speaks disarmingly about his riding technique ('Really I don't know what I'm doing!'), employs the front-end slide technique to a monster extent on heavier, lazier four-strokes. And yet because he served his novice years on two-stroke proddie bikes he doesn't like the feel of engine braking, so when he races Honda's RVF in the Suzuka Eight Hours he enters corners with the clutch disengaged!

'On a four-stroke I can slide the rear even before the apex and I can slide the front good too,' says Doohan. 'At the Suzuka Eight Hours I had the front skidding in the second part of the Spoon Curve. I'd come around the next lap and see the black line I'd just laid. I couldn't do that on the 500. On the 500 you're only really washing a bit of speed off with the front. You don't slide it like the rear. It's more just to slow the thing up, when it does slide it's kind of like "OH!" and you kinda dig in your knee and it's a bit of a moment.'

With the bike into the corner and turned, the rider is thinking of one thing and one thing only from now on – getting on the throttle as soon as possible. Increasing corner exit speed is THE most important aspect of racecraft because you retain the speed advantage all the way down the next straight, hence the hurry to get the turning done to allow more time and space for playing with the throttle.

The turning point is the slowest stage during cornering but mid-corner speeds saw a significant increase in 1990. Before then tyres had provided the predictability to ride the bike deep into the turn and sideways on the exit, but they hadn't given enough side grip to allow riders to maintain real corner speed. That changed with Michelin's 1990 front and rear radial slicks, but there was a sting in the tail for riders who tried to abuse the extra grip they discovered at maximum lean. No doubt about it, 1990 was the year of the highside – Doohan, Schwantz, Wayne Gardner and Niall Mackenzie all discovering the terrifying, bone-crunching up-and-over flip.

'Suddenly we all found we had a lot more grip when banked over, more grip from all parts of the tyre,' says Mackenzie, Schwantz's Lucky Strike Suzuki team-mate during 1990. 'At the point where they used to slide they kept on gripping and some riders were giving it more and more throttle at bigger and bigger leans angles until eventually they got spat off.'

It was some time before riders had realised that you abused the extra grip at your peril, and by then the 500 GP injury list had grown critically long, to the point where the sport seriously discussed banning 500s and replacing them with 375cc two-strokes or 600cc four-strokes.

The 1990 world champion, Rainey, came within an ace of falling victim too, smashing several fairing screens at early GPs, as he wrestled to control the early stages of a highside.

'The bikes have been throwing everybody off because now you're at maximum lean angle with so much grip that when it does step out it throws you a long way,' says Rainey. 'That's what I try and stay away from in the middle of the corner when you've got max pressure on the tyres. I always try to hold it there. It feels so good that you think you can get on the gas but the consequences are terrible. I always hold it, hold it, pick it up, turn it and then nail it.'

The increased grip – even once he had learned its limitations – wasn't wholly good news for ex-250 rider Mackenzie, whose biggest talents are corner-entry speed and mid-corner speed. With his ex-dirt-tracking, rear-wheel-steering rivals finding new confidence in the latest radial front slicks, Mackenzie found his superiority in the early part of corners undermined. Nevertheless his high corner-speed style worked well at some tracks, like Yugoslavia's sinuous Rijeka circuit, where his fluid progress had him lapping within a tenth of Schwantz's best.

The art of rear-wheel steering – born of necessity on the slick dirt tracks of the US national circuit – is the showpiece of 500 GP racing. The theory and reality of the form are simple enough, it is the exercising of the art which only the few can muster, especially in low-gear corners.

Our rider is now safely through the transient mid-corner stage and aims to complete the last part of the turning routine literally by spinning the back of the machine around. This action will tighten his corner-exit line and give him more room than he would otherwise have had to unleash as much power as possible as soon as possible.

Rainey again: 'There's a certain point where you see the inside of the track, you can see the outside of the track and you know you are not going to make the corner, so you give it more throttle. You just need the bike to turn a little bit and as soon as it's spinning it turns just enough to where you can pick the bike up and then you nail it off the corner.'

This squirt of wheelspin which initiates the final turning phase is barely visible; the turning is all over and done with by the time the rider completes his acceleration out of the corner with a spectacular broad-slide. 'Where you really see us sliding around coming out, that's mostly power-wise,' continues Rainey. 'Usually the turning is all done right when it first spins, we're doing that only to help turn the bike.'

Doohan is probably the most spectacular and sustained of the rear-wheel steerers. Although a newcomer to 500s, the Aussie reckons the Honda gives him no other choice (Doohan sometimes uses lower-than-usual gearbox ratios to encourage the bike to wheelspin to aid turning). 'It's partly the way the power comes in,' he explains. 'But at the moment it's also one of the only ways I can steer the bike, especially in faster corners. If it's not spinning, it's not turning. On the Yamaha you don't have to do that. But I've noticed that whenever I'm sideways on the Honda, Schwantz is sideways on the Suzuki, but my suspension seems to work better in the slide than his.'

Rainey reckons to have between 8000 and 10,000 rpm on the rev-counter when he first begins to work the twistgrip. At those revs – with more than 3000rpm still to go – the 500 is already producing plenty enough power and torque to spin the rear tyre with only the most delicate increase in throttle opening. A fraction too much throttle and the rear tyre will spin out, most likely causing a highside crash.

The art therefore is to get the rear tyre spinning just enough to execute the turn, and then maintain forward drive as the tyre struggles to hook up. Doohan once again: 'I'm just feeding the throttle in, winding it back and forth, trying not to put down too much or too little. I just keep it spinning until it gets to a point where it's not making any more power and then I shift gears. I'd rather have it doing that than lifting the front and shaking its head.'

Throttle control isn't enough on its own to do this and riders play a treacherous and delicate juggling act, weighting the footrests and shifting body weight to increase or decrease rear tyre grip as required.

Sometimes the rider will find too much grip and he can loosen the rear tyre's hold on the tarmac by shifting his body weight forward, away from the tyre contact patch. As ever he relies on phenomenally rapid reactions to check any sudden loss of grip before the point of no return is reached. And just as the rider uses his inside knee as a lean-angle sensor, his outer foot plays a crucial part as an early warning system and can then provide the extra grip required to avert disaster. By forcing down on the upper, outside footrest the rider obtains exceptional feel for rear tyre grip. Weighting the footrest further increases grip by counteracting the tyre's tendency to sideslip and crucially helps move the machine upright where the tyre contact patch is larger, once again offering more grip and predictability.

Rainey believes he couldn't make a corner at GP speed if he merely sat on the bike without pushing down – hard. 'You'd actually fall off. You've got to push down on the bike to get your seating right so when you're on the throttle it's all hooked up together. Going through a right you're using your right side to feel for traction and your left to give you traction. You can feel the grip more and you can control the bike a lot better by forcing down on the 'peg when the rear steps out.'

Schwantz, less of a dirt tracker than his American contemporaries, acquired his footrest-weighting techniques from another two-wheel discipline. 'I learned a lot about how to keep traction from riding trials. You lean out of a corner on a trials bike to keep the tyre biting. On a roadracer, if you keep your weight on the outside 'peg as you throw the bike into a corner you stand much less chance of having the rear end step out. Then you go over the seat and hang off the inside, but you still keep a lot of weight on that outside 'peg and you put some more on if the tyre starts really sliding.'

As the rider begins his corner exit he works to lift the bike upright as soon as possible to get on to the fatter, grippier part of the rear tyre, so he takes a straight trajectory, rather than a curved trajectory to complete the corner.

Schwantz is the master of wrenching the bike upright onto the fatter part of the rear tyre, jumping on the gas and pulling the tightest, quickest line out of a corner. It is this ability that has often given him a crushing advantage over his rivals, who talk jealously of the Suzuki RGV's capabilities. But while the RGV may be a nimble machine, Schwantz's team-mate Mackenzie believes that the Texan's physique – his long, gangly legs in particular – is a crucial factor in the Schwantz/ RGV combination.

'Kevin's got a unique style – it's the way his body is,' says Mackenzie. 'His legs are so long that when the rear breaks away he can pick the bike up so quickly because he's already on it. I'm right off the side of the bike, so it takes much longer for me to get back on it and control the slide.'

As body weight is transferred back to the centre of the machine, lifting the bike still further, the rider heaves himself forward over the front. Today's 500s wheelie out of most corners and lift the front even when the rider still needs the front tyre's grip while arcing out of turns. So the turn will almost certainly be completed with the bike hard against the kerb, front wheel off the tarmac, the rider still using body weight to steer (with the front wheel airborne he doesn't have a lot of choice) as the rear tyre continues to lay down its tell-tale smear of hot rubber.

Even down the straight the rider is working to use every trick he can muster to get to the next corner as quickly as possible. Especially exiting faster corners he may try to keep the bike cranked over longer than necessary. This keeps the bike on the smaller diameter section of the rear tyre, thus lowering the final gearing ratio and thus increasing rpm and power.

Of course, not all corners are straightforward U-bends. Modern racetracks are infested by chicanes, which demand a complex cocktail of all kinds of riding techniques. The purpose of these tight esses is to keep speeds at safe levels, invariably at corners made unsafe by the speed of modern cars and bikes. In general, riders don't like chicanes, especially the really slow kinks, because they break up the flow of a racetrack and demand a less gung-ho, more confined approach.

'In chicanes you're basically doing everything except rear-wheel steering,' says Rainey. 'It's kinda like jumping your body around the bike and counter-steering – you go right if you flick the 'bars left, and you go left if you flick the 'bars right.'

Chicanes require massive amounts of counter-steer as a rider heaves the bike from full lean on one side down to full lean on the other in a fraction of a second. But only a certain amount of this can be directed through the handlebars because the front end will only take so much input before the 'bars turn towards full lock, and the rider crashes.

Footrest weighting, throttle control and movement of body weight again play a vital role here. The rider enters the first part of the chicane pretty much how he enters a normal corner, but at the very moment he achieves maximum lean the bike is forced upright and laid down in the other direction. The change of attitude is achieved far quicker than in a normal turn, and this is where rider strength and stamina really tell.

'You don't realise you use your feet so much until you hurt one of them,' affirms Doohan. 'Even if I just get one of my feet in the wrong position when I'm on the bike it really messes me about and it's easy for that foot to just flick off the 'peg.'

To initiate the change of direction, the rider stands hard on the outside footrest to force the bike upright, also using the 'peg to lever his body weight up and over to the other side. At the same time he also uses counter-steering to help flip the bike in the other direction. And as he lifts the bike in the middle of the chicane he gives the throttle a gentle tweak which raises the front end to assist the up-and-over motion. If the front wheel lifts a few inches off the tarmac at this point you may see evidence of counter-steer – the airborne wheel momentarily pointing one way as the bike steers the other.

The forces transmitted through the footrests is more difficult to ascertain – until you check out the soles of a GP rider's boots – which invariably feature great holes gouged out by the footrests. Some top riders ruin a pair of boots in a single GP weekend.

Each season, physical strength becomes more crucial in the bid for 500 GP glory. Today's 500 riders are serious athletes, constantly developing their physique and technique to fit the ever-growing demands of a two-stroke V4 on big, fat slicks. And as the technicians discover ways for the machines to accelerate faster, brake harder, corner deeper and grip better, those riders have to keep working their arses off to keep up – or jump off the rollercoaster.

CHAPTER 6

JK: YOUNG GOD OR DARK STAR?

June 1992

A lot of bike racers are strange people, but John Kocinski was one of the biggest weirdos I ever found in the paddock. He drove team boss King Kenny Roberts half round the twist with his bizarre antics, which did make him the most fascinating of subjects for shit-stirring journalists

They say genius and madness are near allies but what is John Kocinski all about? From his lucky holey racing underpants to his maverick racing lines, Kocinski is a man out on his own. His mentor and spiritual father King Kenny Roberts is sometimes moved to wonder whether his protégé does indeed come from this planet. 'He's on Moonsville,' the living legend was once moved to say.

Be this as it may, human beings don't get to be extra special by being extra normal. Kocinski certainly isn't quite normal but is he good guy or bad guy, madman or genius?

Whatever, JK is the new life force in 500 GP racing, the freckly 23-year-old who wasn't afraid to bust into 1991's exclusive 500 GP winners' club – apart from Wayne Rainey, Mick Doohan and Kevin Schwantz, Kocinski was the only man to win a 500 GP in the summer of '91.

His ebullient disrespect for his elders has won him an army of young fans who delight in youth triumphing over experience – you see more Shoei Kocinski replicas on the roads of Europe than any other 'wannabe' lid.

But the Marlboro Team Roberts pilot's brash young style has also won him enemies. Kocinski's older rivals don't like getting beaten by raw youth and his maiden 500 victory at Shah Alam in September '91 bit deep into vanquished Aussies Doohan and Gardner. The Rothmans Honda pair found the American's victory euphoria too much to bear, so they took him aside and told him to cool it in the post-race press conference.

Kocinski has had to get used to ruffling feathers since he made his first appearance on the GP circuit in 1988. Then just 20 years old he turned up at Suzuka and battled bravely for the lead with 250 stalwarts Sito Pons, Toni Mang and Jacques Cornu. From that initiation Kocinski has shown fear for no one.

Two years later he was a GP full-timer, destroying the cosy world of 250 grands prix as he whipped Europe's best on what was usually a below-par motorcycle. The 1990 season firmly established the Kocinski enigma. The Midwest American, who at 17 left his parents back home in cotton-picking Arkansas to live close to Roberts in California, was like none of his rivals. He seemed a bit of a recluse but maybe this was natural for an all-American boy, living in a strange land for the first time.

'I don't ever give up – I'll be sliding that cocksucker like you've never seen'

His rivals mistook his self-imposed isolation for snobbishness, but Kocinski simply preferred to keep himself to himself. 'I just don't rap with them,' he said at the time. 'I'm not gonna say why. It's private and no one knows except me. The people who know me, know me, and the people who don't, don't.'

When Kocinski wasn't in his motorhome (the same model as 1987 500 champ Wayne Gardner's but a crucial few centimetres longer) he was either firing shots at the opposition or getting fired at himself. The verbal warfare raged this way and that like a gangland shootout.

His 250 Honda rival, Helmut Bradl: 'Kocinski has a brain the size of a pea…' Kocinski: 'If you ain't American you ain't shit…' Another of his Honda rivals, Carlos Cardus: 'The only thing educated about Kocinski is his asshole…' Kocinski: 'Honda riders are a bunch of crybabies…'

Of course, Kocinski got the last laugh when he won the title. And he couldn't resist getting in the final word: 'Bradl said I had a brain the size of a pea. I think that's funny. But I kicked his ass every week – I mean I really laugh. Maybe it'd be a different story if he was beating me.'

In 1991 the tone changed when Kocinski graduated to 500s with Team Roberts. He was no longer the new boy in town, he'd learned the ways of the continental circus and now he was racing against the men he'd always wanted to race against. The 250 world title had just been a minor diversion.

But the first half of his debut 500 season suggested that ambition may finally have got the better of him. He crashed out of three races as he tried to ride his YZR500 faster than it wanted to go. 'I can't even get close to the speed I want through the corners,' he said midseason. 'Try and ride it fast and it goes YEEEAAKKK – right out into the sand trap.'

But though he whinges and moans when things aren't going right, it's only because he wants perfection so he can do his best. And if he's hard on others, he's even harder on himself.

Later in 1991 Kocinski began to get what he needed from his motorcycle and he was transformed – once again the excitable kid with the cute smile. 'My team think I'm going fast around that first corner,' he grinned at Donington. 'Man, I could ride my bicycle faster around that corner.'

As his confidence grew on the 500, the talk got taller. 'I don't ever give up. I'll be sliding that cocksucker like you've never seen, but to ride as fast as I want to ride it's going to take a mean motherfucker to hang on to that thing for a full race.'

Kocinski has always been a man of extremes. His motorhome is undoubtedly the cleanest in the paddock because Kocinski suffers from OCD. Ask Wayne Rainey where his team-mate is and the champ jokes: 'Try down at the dry cleaners!'

You will never see Kocinski line up on the grid blemished by a single microdot of dirt. He spends hours meticulously cleaning his riding gear, folding his T-shirts with miraculous precision, picking the lint out of his socks, fussing over his kit like a street-riding kid bursting with pride over his first-ever set of leathers.

It's the same back home on King Kenny's ranch – his motocrosser is always spotless – so Roberts and Rainey never miss an opportunity to bury the kid in dirt when they're off-road training together. Kocinski's schooling with Roberts was never easy. The triple world champion gave Little John a hard time, all the time – a tough upbringing for a tough world.

Like many youngsters, his conversation is liberally scattered with expletives and like any twentysomething, primed with testosterone and ready to go, Kocinski loves talking about girls. He likes talking to them too – a pretty female walking through the paddock is about the only thing that'll distract him from his work. Shame that his chat-up lines are like car crashes.

In some ways the kid is just misunderstood, and his constant companion, sports psychiatrist Ed Conboy (that's got to be a joke shrink's name, surely?) would agree. Conboy was signed up by Roberts to transform Kocinski from volatile genius into a full-time GP-winning machine. But the long-term therapy session ended when Conboy fell out with the team's physio Dean Miller [see *Zen and the Heart of Motorcycle Racing*, page 214].

Get Kocinski on a good day and he'll chat and joke for ages. Get him on a bad day and he won't even know you. The unlucky people who meet him at the wrong moment will go away convinced he's arrogant and pigheaded. And they wouldn't be totally wrong.

There's no doubt Kocinski has a few issues but what really screws him up – and this is the case with a fair number of racers – is his total and utter commitment to being the fastest racer on earth. He allows nothing to get in the way of his lofty ambitions, so if you try chatting to him while gear ratios and steering geometry are occupying his thoughts, bad luck, dude.

Life is never dull when JK is around – either in the paddock or out on the racetrack – because he doesn't give a toss how many people he rankles. In little more than two seasons Kocinski has generated more column inches than most riders do in half their careers. Now he is poised to achieve the success he's dreamed of ever since his hero King Kenny was 500 world champion. And like always, Kocinski's not taking prisoners. As he says: 'I ain't afraid of nobody.'

Epilogue: Kocinski and Roberts split at the end of 1992. King didn't need him, thinking he still had a good few seasons left in Wayne Rainey. After that JK couldn't even get a job with another 500 team and ended up joining Suzuki's 250 outfit which sacked him halfway through '93 for deliberately over-revving his RGV. So Cagiva snapped him up, the Italians lavishing love and attention on the kid, who won two GPs on the blood-red V4s. When the Cagiva team folded at the end of 1994 JK took a year out, then came back in World Superbikes, first for Ducati, then Castrol Honda, with whom he won the title in 1997. After a troubled return to 500s in 1998 and 1999 he faded into retirement. Last time I saw him he was testing Yamaha's M1 four-stroke in 2001, boasting about his hand-crafted Bentley Azure Mulliner. At £170,000, it sounds like JK is still having the last laugh. Hope he's found happiness.

CHAPTER 7

WAYNE AND KEVIN: 'THERE'S A BIG EGO THING BETWEEN US'

July 1993

The Rainey versus Schwantz rivalry was bubbling towards boiling point when the pair sat down to discuss their astonishing career-long rivalry in the summer of 2003, just months before Rainey's career-ending accident

They've been at it for over six years now. From Daytona's 'salad bowl' banking all the way to Donington's lawn-edged curves, Wayne Rainey and Kevin Schwantz have duked it out, no quarter asked, and never any given.

Between them the Californian and the Texan have dominated the GP scene since the late 1980s, winning more races than everyone else put together, stealing the headlines and entertaining millions with some unforgettable do-or-die battles. So far they have won 23 500 GPs each.

Rainey has come through it with the most world championships, taking three crowns on the trot and earning the nickname 'Mr Perfect' for his unerringly consistent displays of controlled aggression. Meanwhile Schwantz has been the crowd pleaser, building an unenviable reputation as a win-or-crash merchant. But he's lived and learned.

The real beginnings of their rivalry go back to Daytona, March 1987, the start of a season-long fight for the US Superbike title. The results read like a trailer for their GP contests – Rainey won the crown, Schwantz won more races and twice fell while leading.

In those days Schwantz was the mercurially talented up-and-comer, plucked from obscurity by Yoshimura Suzuki, while Rainey was the deadly skilled, established star with a US Superbike title (with Kawasaki in 1983) and a full 250 GP season (with Team Roberts in '84) already behind him.

'I didn't even know who he was,' says Rainey of those early days. 'He had this big thing to prove – to beat Wayne Rainey, and I wasn't going to let that happen. We were like kids who hated each other at school.'

Ironically their most vicious duels were acted out when they were team-mates. 'It was the '87 Transatlantic Match races, and we were pretty close to knocking each other down a few times,' remembers Schwantz of their Honda VFR versus Suzuki GSX-R brawls which astonished the British crowds. 'I don't think we've ever raced each other quite so bad since.'

Most GP spectators would disagree, for when the pair were snapped up for full-time 500 GP duties in 1988 – Schwantz by Pepsi Suzuki and Rainey by Team Roberts Yamaha – they took their bitter rivalry worldwide. Since then they've bumped and barged their way around the GP circuits, dazzling fans with their skill, bravery and total trust for each other. Few other GP racers have got so close, so often, without ending up in a big heap.

'When we first got to GPs the big thing was who could win a GP first, who could be the fastest. There was a big ego thing between us,' says Schwantz, who went out and won the opening race of the '88 season, riding the woefully underpowered Suzuki with a recently broken wrist.

'I was really pissed off about that, but I beat him on points that year,' declares Rainey, who's finished ahead of Schwantz in each of their five GP seasons. 'Kevin thought he was going to smoke us after that first win, but I was more consistent. I guess I go about it a different way.'

Consistency indeed. Since that first GP, Schwantz has crashed out of 11 races. The super-aggressive but always precisely controlled Rainey has fallen down just three times, two of those while chasing Mick Doohan's exceptionally good big-bang Honda NSR in 1992.

'Kevin always used to ride balls out even if he didn't have a chance, he'd be out of the saddle more,' explains Rainey, who has scored 24 per cent more points since they started GPs. 'He'd hit the ground whereas I'd ride for a position. I sometimes wondered if he liked crashing. I know I don't.'

Rainey hasn't won any more GPs than his constant opponent but the secret of the triple champ's success is going for safe points when he can't win. 'Fifth's okay for me, so long as he's sixth! Kevin's the guy I'm always looking at beating. We kinda gauge ourselves off each other. I hate getting beat by him more than anyone else.'

Schwantz has managed a best of second overall only once (in 1990), but the big zero on his world title score isn't all his own fault.

'Wayne is just consistent,' he says. 'A lot of that is himself, but he gets a lot of it from his team – he's always had a real strong team behind him. In the past I've had a bike that works good at three or four tracks. The Suzuki always used to be on the edge, you had to ride it risky if you wanted to win.'

As well as their different approaches to winning titles, Rainey (who's three years Schwantz's senior at 32) believes there's a big contrast in their riding styles.

'Kevin is really, really good on the brakes. He's got a lot of feeling for the tyre going into the corners, but that's often why he falls down. I'm easier going in, and I work harder mid-corner and on the exit. Some tracks his style works best, other tracks it's mine. I guess it levels out. About the only thing we do the same is the way we get on the bikes.'

Schwantz puts it all down to machinery: 'The way you ride depends a lot on the bike you're on. On the Suzuki you always had to ride it into turns, stop it, turn it and get it out. That was the only way to ride it, and it's easy to jump off when you have to ride that way.'

All that changed at the start of 1993. Suzuki have finally built an RGV500 that works everywhere, while Yamaha seem to have taken a giant step backwards.

'Kevin's on the best bike this year,' Rainey affirms. 'We've beat Suzuki every year since '88, it was only a matter of time before they got it right. We always used to have a bike which worked pretty well right from when you loaded it out of the truck. This year the Yamaha chassis has been a real struggle at every racetrack, and we're not sure why.

'We both know you can get hurt real bad on a racetrack'

'Kevin's grown up a lot this year too. He's thought about what it takes to win a world championship. Sometimes it takes finishing fifth to be world champion, I realise that.'

Although Rainey and Schwantz have clashed every year since they started sharing GP starting grids, they've only once gone head to head for the 500 title. That was in 1990 and it was Schwantz's *Annus Horribilis*. He chased Rainey hard for much of the season, then crashed out of three of the final four GPs.

There was a lot of tension between them that year. But both are older and wiser now. 'I'm not saying that ego thing is totally out nowadays,' says Schwantz. 'But we've grown up a bit. We realise that we're both at the top of the sport, and all that petty stuff between us when we were racing Superbikes and stuff is well behind us now.

'Sure we may have a problem, but when we do we iron it out. We settle our differences and race clean – we both know you can get hurt real bad on a racetrack. When we're off the track I'd say we're good friends now.'

Rainey echoes Schwantz's feelings of mutual respect and friendship: 'When you see each other for eight months of every year it would be hard work if we hated each other. We'd probably end up taking each other out. We respect each other's talents, we know the pressures and it's good we can get on and have a beer after the race. 'But when you're racing for the world championship it's hard to be best buddies, but if I can't win it, I'd like Kevin to, because he's American.'

Despite the friendship, the rivalry for biking's biggest gong has taken its toll this season. 'It's already getting a bit tense,' says Schwantz. 'Normally when Wayne's leading the championship, he's easier to find. He keeps to himself more nowadays. I guess neither of us likes losing.'

Epilogue: I wrote this story just before the 2003 British GP, where Schwantz was taken out on the first lap by a brakeless Mick Doohan, putting Rainey back in title contention. Then Rainey won at Brno to take the points lead. Everyone knows what happened next – Rainey was leading the Misano GP on 5 September when he crashed and broke his back, paralysing him from the chest down. And that was the end of one of the most enthralling rivalries ever witnessed by GP fans.

CHAPTER 8

How to ride a motorbike, by Mighty Mick

August 1993

Mick Doohan won five 500 world championships in a row and was the towering talent of the mid-1990s, so not a bad guy to explain the art of motorcycle riding. We did this interview in the summer of 1993, a year after he broke his right leg at Assen. The leg was still mangled – somewhat bent and very weak – but he had just started winning GPs again.

As usual, this interview was conducted in Mick's motorhome, between morning and afternoon practice sessions, Mick sitting there, eyes aflame, studying the morning time sheets, observing his rivals' splits to see who was fast where, wearing nothing but a pair of stubbies and eating his usual 'lunch of champions', an unbuttered French stick and some fruit. Mate and then full-time 500 rider Niall Mackenzie was in on this interview too, perhaps hopeful of picking up a few tips

No one rides a motorcycle better than 500 GP magicians Wayne Rainey, Kevin Schwantz and Mick Doohan. These guys ride sideways out of 100mph turns, rear tyre spinning and smoking, like it's all part of an ordinary day's work, which is exactly what it is for them.

When I first talked to Doohan about his riding style he said 'I don't really know what I'm doing,' and that's still the way he likes to talk about it. There are three possible reasons for this: either he's lying, or he doesn't want others to learn his secrets, or he's just got a sickening amount of natural talent. Or a bit of all three. Here's what he said:

How to brake
'When I start braking I sit up pretty sharpish, which helps weight the front end so I've got more grip for hard braking with the front brake. With slicks you're not really going to lock the front, you're more likely to

go over the 'bars if you overdo it. That's why I use the rear brake, initially, and then getting into the turn, but not in the mid-part of braking. At first it's to pull the rear end down to squat the bike, so it doesn't stand on its nose. As I get into the turn I use the rear some more so the bike's not loaded up on the front, and that helps get you turned.

'If I'm getting into a turn too hot I use the rear a lot more, just to try and slow the bike, or maybe I just go in there sideways. I use the rear brake coming out of corners sometimes too. If it's a real peaky point of a gear, like a first-gear corner, I just stay on the rear brake to ride through it and keep the front wheel on the deck, rather than shut the throttle.'

How to get into a turn

'As I go into the corner I release all the brakes – not in a big rush, otherwise the suspension rebounds too quick and goes kinda crazy. Then I crack the throttle just a touch, not to give it power, but just to get the engine firing so the bike doesn't slow itself up too much. That's just before or just on the apex but well before I accelerate for real. I do it at a constant throttle, not even an accelerating throttle, so it doesn't break away the rear tyre when I really get on it. I guess it also takes a bit of weight off the front tyre mid-corner, which is good.

'If the front starts to go I dig my knee into the tarmac even harder'

'I dig in my knee pretty heavily as I go into and through a turn. When the front tyre gives me a good feeling I really drive the knee into the ground. I wear out scrapers pretty quick. It sounds funny, but if the front end's not feeling good then I'm not really scraping my knee but just skimming it across the tarmac – I'm not getting the feel to really bend the bike over. If the front starts to go I dig the knee in even harder – it's just a reaction to save some bark [Aussie for skin] but maybe it takes a bit of weight off the tyres too.'

How to push the front

'It's not something I do on every corner – it depends on the circuit. Some places, like Eastern Creek, I push the front quite a bit. A lot depends on the front tyre too. Back in 1991 I was riding the bike sideways on the front, but now it's just skimming across the tarmac, almost like understeer, without the tyre actually tucking under. Some guys just stick it in there, get to a point and drop it in without really turning, so they're still going straight ahead with the bike leant over, but scrubbing off speed.

'You can do it more on a four-stroke because you can feel a lot more. I guess 500s are a lot lighter and more precise, so everything's a lot more sensitive. A four-stroke is like a sponge – it just absorbs everything and you can get away with it a lot more. A few years back on the RVF750 endurance bike I used to be able to lay black lines with the front tyre mid-turn, and in 1991 I was leaving a lot of black marks with the 500's front tyre. But the tyres are a lot better now, and they don't scrub so much as skim across the tarmac. You don't really get the front tucking under either, because you can feel them losing grip before they really tuck, so you've got time to do something about it.'

How to steer

'I guess you're using opposite lock to steer all the time – pushing on the right 'bar to turn the 'bars left and make the bike go right. But you notice it more when you're changing direction. That's how I bagged it at Eastern Creek in December '92 when my right leg was still pretty weak. I wasn't using my feet much to steer the bike, I was putting too much force through the 'bars. You do a lot more steering with your feet than you realise – I reckon it's pretty much a 50/50 thing between your feet and your hands.'

How to change direction

'In real slow-speed changes of direction, like the chicanes at Suzuka and Assen, you probably use more feet than hands. At Assen it's a right, left, right chicane, and after a few laps doing that my right foot gets tired. You're on the 'pegs a lot – you can tell because the 'pegs are always making big holes in the soles of your boots. If you just used the handlebars you wouldn't get through a chicane.'

Niall Mackenzie chips in here: 'When I'm riding on the road I just sit on the bike because I'm so scared! But if I start riding properly I feel ten times safer. If you're just flopping about using a bit of body weight, you don't feel anything. You feel a lot better if you brake to weight the front tyre, accelerate to weight the rear, and keep weight on the 'pegs. You've got to go into every corner properly: brake to get the front down and change the geometry, so the bike steers better.'

How to slide

'I'm not sure really. If it snaps out quick the instant thing you do is shut the throttle down, but sometimes when it snaps out quick it feels all right, so you just keep feeding throttle into it and the bike pulls itself straight. Once the rpm goes past the power peak, it starts to tone off, so the back wheel stops spinning and pulls itself back in.

'When you're getting on the gas – just feeding it in – I guess it's just like a dirt bike. Once it starts sliding I don't give it any more throttle. I just keep a constant throttle with a little opening, and wait until the rpm has gone into the over-rev, then I click another gear so the tyre doesn't get a big surge of horsepower halfway through the slide. It's the same thing with a four-stroke – I let the RVF over-rev a bit and it pulls itself straight again.

'Also, when you're sliding, say coming out of a left, you put pressure on the right footpegs and that gives you a lot more feel and a lot more control. It just feels out of control if you don't put any force through the 'pegs.

'Once the tyre starts to spin you don't really keep the bike leant over and keep gassing it. You start to pick the bike up, and, as the contact patch gets bigger, you're accelerating harder so it keeps spinning.

'If I want it to spin some more I move my body weight forward to take some weight off the rear tyre. In some places it's quicker to spin it up and get to the rpm where you can hook another gear, rather than shut the throttle. Basically, a 500 will spin no matter what gear you're in. Like at Phillip Island there's a fifth gear left, and as soon as you bend it over the bike picks up revs and starts to step out sideways.

'I even used to slide my TZR250 when I was proddie racing, but that was just because the tyres weren't good enough. It wasn't a power thing. It was just the corner speed breaking the tyres away, but it was the same thing. I didn't shut it down, I just kept it in there, and I guess keeping it sliding is the same principle on a TZR250 as it is on an NSR500.'

CHAPTER 9

THE HYPOTHALAMUS PAPERS –
THE SCIENCE OF SPEED

September 1997

Speed is the biggest buzz in biking and you're probably only here, reading this, because you love the stuff, same as most racers. But what's speed all about – why do we love it and what does it do to us? Time to investigate the facts behind frighteningly fast

Okay, so you like going fast. But have you ever wondered why? Is it for the sensation of speed or do you love the risk factor? And what makes you different from people who hate going fast? How does speed affect your brain, what biochemical reactions take place when you give it some?

Almost certainly, you go fast for the buzz, wherever it may come from. When you race down some strip of tarmac faster than you've ever been before, you get the buzz and your body undergoes an amazing transformation, heightening your mental awareness, increasing your physical capabilities and minimising risk of injury in case you crash and burn. It's adrenalin city: your heart pumps, your mouth goes dry, you're buzzing. You know the feeling…

As you wind open the throttle and tuck down behind the screen, your body and brain need energy, so you produce hormones to convert fats and proteins to sugar, and your liver releases extra sugar to fuel your muscles. Your metabolic rate increases in anticipation of expending energy, as do your heart rate, blood pressure and breathing rate. Your spleen releases extra red blood cells to help carry more oxygen, your muscles tense, and inessential bodily functions, like digestion, are halted to save energy. Saliva and mucus dry up, increasing the size of the air passages to your lungs (hence the dry mouth).

These functions help you perform better, so you can ride faster and more safely, but at the same time your body prepares for disaster: you secrete natural painkillers called endorphins, constrict your blood vessels to minimise bleeding, increase your blood's clotting rate, while your bone marrow produces more white blood corpuscles to fight infection in case you go down big style.

All this happens because you're in a high-stress, high-risk situation. Your brain's stress centre, the hypothalamus, kicks in to control your fight-or-flight response. It's the adrenalin thing – the hypothalamus looks after your brain's neuroendocrine systems (the adrenal-cortical and sympathetic nervous systems), which pump out the hormones epinephrine (adrenalin), norepinephrine (noradrenalin) and ACTH (the adrenocorticotrophic hormone) to trigger the drastic physiological responses already mentioned.

It all adds up to the sensations that speed freaks know and love: pounding heart, dry mouth and a state of hyper-consciousness. Some racers will be aware of a particularly acute form of this condition, which moves you into a state of apparent hyper-reality. Psychologists call it 'flow', and some racers liken it to meditation, or moving into a fourth dimension, where despite the world rushing past at 180mph, you feel a Zen-like inner peace.

I experienced this feeling a few times in my racing career: you're going faster than ever and your subconscious takes over, it's like you're driving without interference from your conscious self. The world seems to shift into slow-mo, and things go quiet, except your breathing rate has gone sky high and you are riding better than ever before, seemingly correcting mistakes before you've even made them. Five-time 500 world champ Mick Doohan knows the feeling: 'Riding fast is a subconscious thing – you go quickest, you're most in control and least likely to make mistakes when you don't have to think about anything.'

This is the biggest high that a racer or speed freak can ever have: it's a transcendental moment. But it can just as well go the other way. Your brain can reach overload if you become over-aroused – too excited, too angry or too scared. Instead of that state of hyper-reality, you just get hyper, your brain absorbs too much information and you end up thinking and reacting more slowly. It's like an adrenalin OD. As a racer you have to learn to control your adrenal flow. When I started racing I used to almost puke on the grid, and a friend of mine sometimes used to wet himself waiting for the green light. You see, it's a myth that racers have to psych themselves up for a race. If anything it's the other way around, they work to calm themselves down. Former 500 champ King Kenny

Roberts – possibly the hardest speed-meister in history – used to chill out listening to country 'n' western before going out to kick Barry Sheene's arse. You should do something like that – you should never be in a state of high excitement when you climb on a bike.

The adrenalin fix delivered by high-speed riding is certainly a drug; it alters your state of mind like an illegal substance might and a lot of riders get seriously addicted – they're adrenalin junkies, they want that rush coursing through their veins.

'Going fast is a big thrill for many people,' says psychologist Dr Richard Cox. 'A lot of that comes from your feeling of control over the machine. Then there's the perceptual thing – if you focus on the periphery the world's whizzing past in the opposite direction at a very high rate.

'The risk doesn't appeal to me now, but years back I liked crashing and cheating injury on the road or the track'

'People learn to love speed – they don't ride a bike for the first time and do 140mph, they do 50, then 80, then the magical ton. It's a journey into the unknown. Man is a naturally curious animal; some of us love to do things we've never tried before, go where we don't know what's going to happen.'

The element of risk is part of the rush and is also attractive to many people – the theory goes that we like to get close to death because it makes us feel so alive. And the quality of a life lived at the extreme is more important to some than a longer lifespan. Multiple British champ Niall Mackenzie admits that he used to enjoy crashing!

'The risk doesn't appeal to me now, but years back I liked crashing and cheating injury on the road or the track,' he says.

Generally, racers won't admit a conscious attraction to risk. They may acknowledge risk but they put it to one side, having convinced themselves that they won't suffer death or some appalling injury: 'It won't happen to me'. What they really like is controlling the risk – riding fast, right on the edge, knowing that their own skill is keeping them on the brink. In such a situation they are in control of their own destiny, close to death, but not too close.

Of course, not everyone gets off on the speed buzz – most humans seek pleasure and want to avoid pain. They may enjoy sitting in front of the telly watching racers do their stuff, but no way would they want to get out there and do 180mph. Some people crave speed and danger more than others, just as some people enjoy skydiving, nicking cars, popping pills or even the thrill of unprotected casual sex. They all give off some kind of a buzz, and they all have that element of risk about them.

By the same token, many so-called fearless racers are worried by stuff that wouldn't worry most people: WSB champ Carl Fogarty is scared of water, three-time 500 king Wayne Rainey has vertigo and Mackenzie is claustrophobic.

The question is why do some people crave speed and excitement more than others? Like everything else, it's part nature, part nurture – the mix of your genetic make-up and how you were brought up. A lot of racers come from racing families and were brought up surrounded by bikes and speed – your dad does it, so you end up doing it, that's nurture.

'Everyone has a different pathway to this kind of thing,' adds Cox. 'Maybe you get into speed from some experience in your youth – you may have seen a bike going fast on the road, or even on TV, or you were taken to a racetrack and you fell in love with the noise, the speed, the smell.'

Then there's the nature aspect: the genetic configuration of your brain and its neural circuitry. The reticular system is another area of the brain that plays a major role in controlling your state of arousal, and research shows that some people's reticular systems demand more excitement than others – making the difference between thrill-seekers and couch potatoes, extroverts and introverts.

Mackenzie obviously isn't aware of how his reticular system is configured, so he sees it more simply. 'You either like speed or you don't,' he says. 'You're either into going as fast as possible or you're not interested at all.'

Like most adrenalin junkies, Mackenzie remembers loving speed from his earliest years – his surroundings nurtured a desire for speed. 'I lived in this village on a hill and I used to go down that hill as fast as I could. I got so many bloody noses from crashing at the bottom – my Raleigh Chopper wasn't built for speed, it always got out of control. I've got so many memories of mates pushing the bike home, with me staggering behind them. The fact that I kept doing it means I must've liked it.'

I still remember pedalling like crazy down hills when I was a kid. It was the biggest thrill, more exciting than anything else I could do. And, like Mackenzie, that lust for speed got me into bikes. Back in my own hoodlum days, I used to love busting speed limits. I'd be well pleased if I could treble a 30mph speed limit: wow, 90mph past the post office. Moron, I know, but it all made perfect sense at the time, it was a big macho thing: the thrill, the risk, the ego trip, the rebellion. Mackenzie says: 'You do it because you're not supposed to. When I was young all I wanted to do was 100mph. It was a magical figure back then, not many cars or bikes would do the ton.'

However, racers see speed very differently from your average speed freak. Their childhood love of speed in its own right is overtaken by the competition. The speed is no longer the buzz per se, it's beating other guys by being faster and crazier than they are. Mackenzie again: 'Once you've done 100 or 150 a few times it's no big deal. Going down that hill on my Chopper was a big thrill, the wind in my face and all that, but the big thing became beating my mates, that's why I wanted the speed.'

Racers are barely aware of the sensation of speed. Ask a racer how it feels to do 190mph and he'll just shrug his shoulders: the straights are the easy part, they're not thinking about riding in a straight line, they're thinking about the next few corners, that's the fun part. Michael Schumacher reckons that 'straights are boring' in an F1 car, but of course it's slightly different on a GP bike, you're nudging the double ton, head and shoulders stuffed under the screen, fingers delicately gripping the handlebars, hoping the bike doesn't break into a terminal speed wobble. I've done it on Doohan's Honda NSR500 and it is kinda scary, but you're so focused on the next corner that you don't have time to savour the sensation. The scenery doesn't even dissolve into a blur, because you're looking dead ahead, not to the side. It's just hellishly noisy, and pretty uncomfortable.

I once asked Rainey what's the fastest he's ever been. 'Three hundred and twenty three kays at Fukuroi,' he said. (That's 201mph at Yamaha's main Japanese test track.) So, how did that feel? 'It felt like it needed another tooth off the rear sprocket,' he replied. The speed itself meant diddly squat, his only concern was the gearing. Not a hint of a buzz and certainly no fear. 'It doesn't matter if you're doing 150 or 205,' Rainey adds. 'You don't feel the sensation.'

There's also anecdotal evidence that it isn't the actual miles per hour that are the buzz, but the effort required and the actual sensation – I get more of a speed thrill riding my little Typhoon scooter at 60mph than riding a Super Blackbird at the same speed.

So, is speed an irrelevance, something that doesn't matter nearly as much as we think it does? Just a cheap adrenalin fix, a manifestation of man's inability to leave anything alone, of his desire always to go bigger, better, faster, higher, deeper, louder? Or am I asking too many questions, rather than just getting on with it and having a blast? Maybe. There's just one thought I can't get out of my mind, that suggests the whole miles per hour deal is indeed a big joke: the world motorcycle speed record is held by a Harley. Work that one out...

MotoGP Mutterings: November 1998
Crash, bang, ha ha ha! In praise of MotoGP's own little book of schadenfreude

There's a book published at the end of each GP season which will gladden the hearts of all crash perverts. It's produced by GP organisers Dorna, and the 1998 edition was simply entitled 'Falls 98'. This thick tome is a ridiculously exhaustive record of every single crash during the 1998 GP season; it's a statistician's wet dream and it runs to 170 pages.

That's 170 pages packed with pain, agony and suffering, and the most expensive repair jobs in history (a race-ready Repsol Honda NSR500 fairing costs £10,000). The book is also a record of hopeful world championship careers ending in the misery of failure, of million-dollar dreams of stardom disappearing amidst clouds of dust, flailing limbs and disintegrating motorcycles.

'Left hand little finger dislocation/ ring finger fracture-dislocation/fracture of right extra-malleolus/right hip strain/fracture of right astralagus'

And it's great! You can find out who crashed the most last season and which class had the most tumbles, you can find out which is the most crashed-at GP and what is the most crashed-at corner. And you can use the neat little bar charts to compare all these figures against numbers from every season back to 1994, when some sick bastard decided to start these records. Then you can get really macabre and read Dr Costa's spooky medical reports for each and every get-off, like this entry for French 500 nutter Regis Laconi at the Japanese GP: 14.33hrs, Friday 3 April, marshals' post 2, left hand little finger dislocation/ring finger fracture-dislocation/

fracture of right extra-malleolus/right hip strain/fracture of right astralagus. Ooch, fucking ouch. Or how about Max Biaggi in Germany: 15.00hrs, Saturday 18 July, marshals' post 21, lacerated-contused wound in middle finger right hand with avulsion of ungula phalanx and consequently little fracture of unguinal phalanx, left heep contusion. (Presumably heep is Italian for hip? And contusion is bruising, in case you wondered). This kind of stuff sounds even more scary in real Italian – this is Nobby Ueda going to hospital in France: 'Frattura omero dx. con paralisi del nervo radiale, operato dal Dottore Prost'.

The stats are top stuff: during 1998 a total of 132 riders fell 486 times, making for an average of 34.7 crashes per GP, 1.6 per cent up on 1997. Put it another way and every rider crashed an average of 6 times, the second worst year on record (in '94, riders crashed a mere 5.1 times each).

King crasher of '98 was Japanese 125 loon Youichi Ui, the man with the shortest name in GP racing. He fell 13 times during the 14-race season, just beating 250 kamikaze Yasumasa Hatakayama by one tumble.

The most crashed-at GP was Germany's new Sachsenring (51 falls), followed closely by Donington (on 48). This fulfils a well-known racing axiom, 'the safer the circuit, the more the crashes'. The Sachsenring is slow and safe, and Donington's gravel run-offs and neatly clipped lawns look so inviting it seems churlish not to give them a go.

The most crashed-at corner in GP racing is the last left before the pits at Ricard in France (17 tumbles), followed by Turn One at Jerez (14), then the chicane at Johor, venue for last year's Malaysian GP, and Degner Curve at Suzuka (both on 13), then the exit of the Donington's Melbourne hairpin (12) – highside central – and a good place to watch the British GP if you're a real sicko.

The figures also show us that the most crashed-on day is Sunday, which just goes to show that GP riders haven't learned that old racing maxim: 'Always get your crashing done in practice'. The most dangerous practice session is Saturday afternoon's final qualifier – no surprise there since this is the moment when every rider has to lay it on the line to produce his fastest-possible lap to get a good grid position.

As well as telling us how many riders crashed in 1998, Falls '98 also tells us how many didn't crash: precisely zero, which just goes to show how hard these bastards are trying.

Of course, there is a real purpose to this blood-soaked document. Serious analysis of all this data will help make GP racing even safer. For example, the Ricard corner that claimed more victims than any other is one of the circuit's few left-handers, so riders arrive there with the left side of their tyres too cool. Armed with hard facts of life like this, GP bosses might stand a better chance of persuading track bosses to spend some cash on a circuit redesign.

Only one bad thing about the book – it's not in the shops, so readers who enjoy a bit of *schadenfreude* will have to stick to *EastEnders*...

MotoGP Mutterings: December 1998
Bike racing is meant to be fun, so why's everyone getting more serious and boring?

Why are modern-day sportsmen so boring? No, let's narrow the focus: why are modern GP racers so boring? Compare your Crivillés and Schumachers with your Mike Hailwoods and James Hunts and you're talking a breed apart.

Maybe they're not exactly boring, but they're hardly a bundle of laughs. In TV interviews they stare at the camera, mouthing weary platitudes because their minds are fixed on some hi-tech conundrum: data-logging graphs, high-speed rebound damping and transient engine behaviour.

Back in the good old days, GP racers were fast-living, up-for-a-laugh daredevils, apparently able to win races with inspired, risk-taking heroics. Back then racing was an art and racers behaved accordingly: out on the piss, sniffing and snorting their way through ranks of glamorous shags.

Sadly, it ain't like that any more. Racing at 500 GP level is a science and racers are the front-line laboratory troops, they just wear leathers instead of white lab coats. Talk to Doohan of racing concepts like bravery, risk-taking and heroics, and he stares at you like you're nuts. It's not about that any more, nowadays racing is a cold and precise science – a giant, globally televised physics experiment. Sure, racers need balls just as much as they ever did, but only as much as they need to understand computer data-logging, kinetic traction or the intricacies of transient engine behaviour.

Hailwood was happily technophobic. Someone like Mick Doohan ain't no rocket scientist, but he can talk deep technical concepts.

There is a parallel here with the USAF's jet-fighter test pilots, as described in Hunter S. Thompson's book *The Great Shark Hunt*. The gun-totin' acid casualty author talks of how a few decades back the USAF developed 'a computerized version of the legendary, hell-for-leather test pilot', banishing the old 'kick the tyre, light the fire and away we go' heroes of old. He goes on: 'the best pilot in the world – even if he could land a B-52 on the number eight green at Pebble Beach without taking a divot – would be useless on a test-flight project unless he could explain, in a written report, just how and why the landing could be made'.

It's the same with modern GP aces – 500s are so hi-tech that riders must describe machine behaviour in acute detail, then check it and cross-check it with their technicians and computer read-outs.

There's another link between old fliers and GP racers. Thompson describes how test pilots used to get their kicks in the Mojave desert: 'Back in the good old days, when men were men and might was right and the devil took the hindmost, the peaceful desert highways were raceways for off-duty pilots on big motorcycles. Slow-moving travellers were frequently blown off the road by wildmen in leather jackets and white scarves, human torpedoes defying all speed limits and heedless of their own safety.'

'The survivors pushed on, treating death like a churlish, harping creditor, toasting their own legend with wild parties to ward off the chill'

Not any more: when he revisited this base in '69, he found the USAF appalled at the idea of anything as fun and as dangerous as a motorcycle. 'Today's pilots go to bed early, and regard big motorcycles with the same analytical disdain they have for hippies, winos and other failure symbols. They take their risks, on assignment, between dawn and 4.30pm.' So the big brass weren't impressed when he rolled up and shook hands with his left hand because he'd broken the other in some crazy bike crash.

Of course, there is another reason for your modern-day GP racer to get all serious and scientific: money. Modern 500 GP racers get paid big money, with enough noughts to command anyone's total commitment. If you were on five mill a year, you'd stop partying and become boring for a while, wouldn't ya?

You may wonder why I've only mentioned 500s so far, and not Foggy and Superbikes. Well, WSB has still got that ol' barnstorming thang about it – those heavy, wobbly streetbikes can still be made to do things they don't want to with some seriously inspired heroics. And the stakes aren't so high – hundreds of thousands, not millions. The Supers paddock is old skool too – there's still riders staying up late larging it, shagging other riders' girlfriends, getting into punch-ups and trashing hotel rooms. Which is great. It's just that 500s are that much more serious – too many computer screens to stare at, too much money and the meanest sonofabitch motorcycles that don't take any shit from anyone.

Finally, there is one other reason why Mr 1990s Racer man takes his game seriously (regardless of what bike he's racing), and that's DEATH. Those old-time racers may have partied non-stop, but they spent way too much time at the funerals of mates who'd broken themselves in half on a trackside telegraph pole. Just like their soul brothers in the 1950s USAF: 'the survivors pushed on, treating death like a churlish, harping creditor, toasting their own legend with beakers of gin and wild parties to ward off the chill. Live fast, die young, and make a good-looking corpse.' The list of racing casualties is too long and illustrious for any modern racer to want to add his own name at the bottom.

CHAPTER 10

'I'VE CRASHED BIKES AT 300MPH ... TWICE'

April 1999

For several decades Californian Don Vesco was motorcycling's king of speed, roaring across the Bonneville Salt Flats in Utah, breaking speed records on both two and four wheels. I interviewed him in the spring of 1999, three years before he died of prostate cancer at the age of 63. At the time he was working on his Turbinator streamliner, designed to be the first wheel-driven vehicle to crack 500mph. Nutter!

Don Vesco was the first man to do 300mph on two wheels and he held the bike land-speed record for 12 years from 1978 at 318.598mph, running a streamliner powered by two turbocharged Z1000 motors on the Bonneville Salt Flats. Before that he had used two TZ750 two-stroke race engines.

In 1990, fellow American Dave Campos broke Vesco's record by a few mph, touching 322.87mph in a seven-metre streamliner powered by two Harley-Davidson motors (I kid ye not!), but Vesco is now considering a new attempt in a streamliner powered by two supercharged Vincent engines. A famed tuner, Vesco builds most of his own machines. He also roadraced successfully in his younger years.

How does it feel to go 300mph-plus on a bike?
I'd probably compare it to being in a jet-liner on the runway, just before take-off. The acceleration isn't amazing, speed-record bikes don't accelerate that hard, though my car goes pretty rapidly after 140mph, when it takes around 20 seconds to reach 470mph.

With the bikes it probably takes a minute and a half to do a six-mile run, but you cover the last mile in about ten seconds. They've got these markers that are one mile apart – you can do six so fast you don't even realise you're there. Where I really see the speed is with this black line they put down to guide you. The line is straight, but where you're going fast it gets wiggly. When the speed picks up it seems to get darker too, but maybe that's because you're concentrating so hard.

'You cover the last mile in about ten seconds'

You don't get a lot of vibration because the track's smooth. And the engine noise tends to get carried away. A lot of the time you don't hear nothin', but only because you're not paying attention.

And what's the fastest you've been?
About 437 on four wheels, 333 on two. I did it twice with my twin-engine Kawasaki in 1978. I was just messing around. I ran 330 and then 333, but I didn't back them up because I figured the record was pretty safe. [Official records must be two-way.]

What's the fastest you've crashed?
About 350mph. That was with a bike made into a car – it had four wheels at the back and one at the front and I got a flat. I saw it coming, but I probably knew it was going to happen for only 100th of a second. There's nothing you can do, you just hang on. I broke a collarbone one time.

I've crashed bikes a couple of times at 300mph, but I got the parachutes out before I hit the ground, so they took care of everything. One time I did crash sideways and, wow, that's not good because the thing can pencil roll.

Apart from flat tyres, what makes you crash?
If you get a crosswind, it tries to tip you over like a boat, but you don't have a keel. You try to correct it by steering, but if the wind is bad and you run out of lock, you're gone.

Why do you like speed so much?
It's a kind of thrill, I guess. I just feel the desire to do it; I certainly don't like the risk part of it. I like beating people; I like the competition. It's the ego thing and the adrenalin rush.

How come you're still breaking records at 60?
I never grew up, I guess. If I'd baled out for a few years I wouldn't be up with what's going on, but I've always stayed around.

What are you up to at the moment?
I've been working on my Turbinator – a gas-turbine, four-wheel drive, powered by a helicopter engine. I've run 439 miles and hour with it so far.

Any bike action?
I haven't ridden my two-wheeler but I've tested another guy's twin-engined Vincent.

Isn't the Vincent a strange motor to use?
Yeah, but they make good horsepower and they're supercharged. It doesn't make any difference what engine you've got, you've just got to have the right power. The Vincent makes 500 to 600 horsepower, but that's too much… things break or don't work right. Also, it's difficult when you've got one guy building the thing and another guy driving – I ride them and build them.

How fast should the Vincent go?
The builder is thinking of going 400 with it, but I told him you've got to do 322 first.

So how long are the straights at Bonneville?
They vary from seven miles to eleven, and you need about ten miles for a run – five to go, five to stop. The last couple of years we've been lucky to get nine, because of the salt mining.

As a tuner, you compete in the workshop too…
Right, I have my own ideas and I do my own stuff; I've always been that way. Everyone has their own ideas about how to break a record, you've got to challenge it your own way. But nowadays when you go racing you can just buy everything you need – Yoshimura's got it or Honda's got it. In the beginning you had to do it all yourself.

How much power do you need to do 350mph?
I'd say about 300bhp. I only had 160 when I went 280mph with my twin-engined TZ750. It was a bit weak compared to my Kawasaki streamliner, which ran two turbocharged Z1000 motors and made around 260bhp. With turbochargers you can compensate for altitude.

How did you first get into speed?
I grew up around it – my dad was racing cars. I got into motorcycles because it was less expensive. I started out drag racing, that was real easy because it'd cost you three dollars to go drag racing at the weekend.

Do you do anything else dangerous?
I don't bungee jump, I don't jump out of airplanes, I don't hang-glide and I don't fly ultralights. I like being on the ground, with wheels. I tried boats but I don't like them.

Do you ever get scared?
I don't think so. Sometimes I get a little concerned. When you crash you don't have time to be scared. All of a sudden you're crashing and you just have to wait for it to stop.

MotoGP Mutterings: *August 1999*
Who's that bustin' through the pain barrier? Must be Metal Micky D, Man of Steel

In our wonderful modern world of all-powerful anaesthetics, it is sometimes difficult to remember what true pain is all about. Not for top GP racers though.

These guys may live pampered five-star lifestyles with helicopters, speedboats and personal masseurs, but boy, do they know the meaning of the word 'ouch'. Men like Doohan and Biaggi race when normal people like you and me would beg for a big, fat syringe up the bum. Good night nurse.

Trouble is, no one ever raced that well on a general, so these guys have something called mesotherapy inflicted upon them – a special local anaesthetic applied via multiple injections. Let's say you broke your wrist a couple of weeks ago and can't risk missing the next race because your team might give you the sack; you hobble down to Dr Costa's Clinica Mobile where they inject the wrist 20 or 30 times. Yup, that's 20 or 30 spikes in your arm. Guys come out of Costa's House of Pain looking very grey after treatment.

An ultra-high pain threshold is a fundamental qualification for anyone seriously wanting to make it to the top in racing, as opposed to retiring the first time they get properly hurt. On the road to the big time, lots of stuff like this will happen...

A few years back I got young British hopeful Jamie Robinson a ride with Team Roberts in the Spanish Open series at Calafat, a few hours south of Barcelona. His TZ250 seized flat out in fifth and flicked him into a rocky run-off area. He was badly battered and one of his fingers swelled up purple, he was in agony. So Sandy Rainey (Wayne's dad and the team's mechanic) says: 'Son, you gotta relieve the pressure'; he grabs a Black & Decker and drills through the finger nail until blood gushes out. Trying hard to look cool, I tell Jamie: 'Better get down the medical centre and get that sterilised.' 'Hell no,' barks Sandy. 'Stick it in some gasoline, that'll fix it up.' So Jamie did, then went out, led the race... and fell off again.

Then there's American Superbike racer Dale 'Cut it Off' Quarterly, who wrecked a finger some years back at a US meet. Surgeons gave him a choice: 'We can fix the finger and you'll be racing in three months or we can cut it off and you can race next Sunday'. No choice for a racer.

But the hardest motherfucker of them all is Metal Micky Doohan, Man of Steel, the man who lost a finger in his debut GP season, nearly lost a leg in '92 and has more broken bones and scar tissue than a gridful of WSB racers.

'The man's resistance to pain astounds his surgeons who treat American footballers and other so-called ruff 'n' tuff sportsmen'

A few days after his sickening career-ending crash at Jerez 1999 I called the great man at his hospital in the States, where he was waiting to be screwed back together. 'How are you Mick?'

'Aww, not so bad, 'cept when I got here they filled me up with drugs to kill the pain, so I didn't feel too good. I told them to take me off that stuff except one painkiller and I feel better – I'd rather have a clear head and deal with the pain than a fuzzy head from all the drugs.'

So the guy's flat out in hospital with a paralysed arm and a broken leg, wrist and collarbone and he's telling the nurses 'no thanks'. Mick, you got it wrong man, try the morphine. No really, try the morphine, you'll like it.

The man's resistance to pain astounds his surgeons, who regularly treat American footballers and other so-called ruff 'n' tuff sportsmen. Even now, when he must have 10 to 20 million in the bank and five

'Doohan says racing
is 90 per cent
psychology'

NSR500s sitting in his lounge in Oz (Honda gave him one for each world title), he is still determined to come back and race again.

Why? How come he doesn't give up and slip into a paradise retirement of mucking about in boats down on the Great Barrier Reef? Because he's a devout pupil of racers' logic, that's why. Racers' logic is a kind of divine madness, the ability to stare reality in the face and still disbelieve. So when someone asks Mick if he's scared of jumping back on his NSR, he replies: 'No, because I know I can crash and I know I can hurt myself.' Fine.

GP racing lost its edge the moment he was stretchered away at Jerez. However good guys like Crivillé and Okada may be at racing bikes, they just don't grill my burgers. Mick has a superb attitude to his sport. The man doesn't give a flying fuck about anything but going fast. He's a real racer, not an image-obsessed, TV-pleasing PR tart like some of your modern stars. He's often blunt, curt, even rude, but who cares? His job is Hard Bastard Racer Who Doesn't Know When To Give Up. That's what he's good at.

Even Mick doesn't realise how much we're going to miss him. When I told him that, he replied: 'You'll get used to it.' Maybe, but not for a while.

MotoGP Mutterings: *September 1999*
Racers are strange people, so you've got to delve deep into their psyches to find out what makes a GP winner

So, what's the most important part of a GP rider's anatomy? His right wrist, his balls or his brain?

It's his brain, or to be more specific, his psyche. Going fast is above all a mental thing. Five-time 500 king Mick Doohan will tell you that – he says racing is 90 per cent psychology.

In which case, a rider's state of mind is more important than anything else when it comes to winning races, more important than engine, tyres and suspension, because if he doesn't feel right, he won't go fast.

That's why team managers and engineers – the guys who get closest to riders – invest a huge amount of effort in making sure that their men feel confident and comfortable. In the most extreme cases this may mean treating the rider like a kid: patting him on the back, telling him he's the greatest, wiping his bottom, just generally making him feel big, bad and dangerous and the most important geezer on the planet.

Look at John Kocinski. When he's in the right team, working with people who know how to get the best out of him, he goes superfast. When he's not in the right team, it all tends to go wrong. Castrol Honda won his confidence by doing stuff like fitting his RC45 with his own handlebar grips. And he won the world championship. During 1998 he raced 500s for Sito Pons, and the Spaniards hadn't a clue how to deal with him, so he flunked.

It sounds daft but it works. What you have to remember is that fast motorcycle racers are very weird people. Treat them like normal human beings and you don't stand a chance, treat them like weirdo psychos, and you're there.

So how do you do that? Well, start off with a bit of straightforward psychoanalysis: understand that most of these guys are driven by something very deep but very simple: personal insecurities. In that respect they're probably no different from anyone else who makes it big in this world: people who dedicate their lives to climbing to the top are usually desperate to prove themselves; well-adjusted, self-confident people see no need to risk life and limb to show everyone they're bigger and tougher than the next guy.

As Mike Sinclair – the engineer who guided Wayne Rainey to his three titles and now fettles Max Biaggi's bikes – says: 'The fastest riders are usually the most insecure people.' In other words, these guys gain strength from their weakness – using their insecurities to push them to victory.

Sinclair is amazed that sports psychologists – already widely used in pretty much every other big-money sport – have hardly made it into the paddock. 'It's a huge area we've not got into,' he adds. 'But in some ways us guys do the same job – what you do to the bike can affect the rider's head. I had times with Wayne when he really struggled in practice, so I made a change on Sunday morning and he went out and won the race, and I'm sure what I changed didn't make any real difference, he just thought it did. It's like a placebo.'

That's the engineer's job: to give his rider the confidence to help him push deep into the danger zone – and if that means fitting the back wheel in the front because the rider reckons he'll feel happier that way, so be it.

World 500 number two Biaggi emphasises the crucial part played by psychology in 500s. 'I think you have to be very strong in your mind to ride a 500 – that's the most important thing of all,' he says. 'I remember something Rainey once said – he said you can race a 500 all season and your bike will work perfectly for two or three GPs at best. That's why 500s are so different from other motorcycles. At every other race your bike might not be steering exactly the way you want it to, so you have to use your mental strength to overcome any deficiencies, to make the bike do what you want it to do. If you really want to do something, you can, but it's like a mental sacrifice, and it's tough.'

Beyond the rider/bike relationship, the overall team environment is also crucial to a rider's mental well-being. Kocinski didn't only shine at Castrol Honda because they fitted his RC45 with the right grips, he felt good because it's a hyper-organised Anglo-Saxon outfit, as is Marlboro Team Roberts, with whom JK won the 1990 250 world title. As everyone knows, Kocinski has a cleanliness/tidiness obsession, so he likes his team to have schedules and programmes and timetables. When he rides for the Latins – like Pons in '98 and Ducati in '96 – he struggles because they don't get all anal about doing things by numbers. Carl Fogarty's the opposite – he much prefers the laid-back but hot-blooded way Ducati do things. Foggy and the Italians operate on passion, not precision.

It's thus the team manager's job to understand his rider's personality, so he can build the right environment around him. Hervé Poncharal, boss of the French Tech 3 team that runs Olivier Jacque and Shinya Nakano in 250 GPs, puts a huge emphasis on building relationships with his riders. He tried, and failed, with JK, with whom he had an acrimonious split mid-way through the '93 250 GP season.

'With John I thought I could give him something, he seemed lonely, like he needed some support or friendship, but that doesn't always work,' he says. 'Generally, the more you get to know a rider, the more you know about what he needs. If you spend time with him away from the racetrack and talk about non-racing things, you'll find out different aspects of his character. Some riders want to be your friend, some like to be alone, some need compliments, some don't. Racing is not an easy life, especially when things aren't going well – it's quite easy for the rider to blame the team or vice versa, or maybe the rider will start doubting himself. But you can't push your rider too much or he'll start crashing; then again, you mustn't make him feel too secure or he'll go to sleep – you've got to keep him hungry. Like everything in life and in racing, it's a compromise.'

CHAPTER 11

'I BELIEVE I CAN OUTRIDE ANYBODY FOREVER'

March 2000

Back at the start of 2000, Kenny Roberts Junior had yet to win the 500 crown, but he already knew he was the best rider in the world – he just didn't want to admit it

You can tell Kenny Roberts is a seriously dedicated motorcycle racer. At the climax of his team's glitzy launch night in Spain, Roberts emerges on stage amidst a sweat of PVC-clad dancing girls and the first thing he squeezes is the throttle grip of his freshly painted number-two RGV500. Then when his index finger reaches out a few moments later, it is to stroke the RGV's front-brake lever. That's what you need to be 500 world champion – focus.

Later that evening the grinning hostess stumbles across the stage and topples into his Movistar Suzuki, so Roberts dives forward to save not the girl, but the bike. That's something else you need to be 500 world champ – a certain disregard for the comfort of others.

The rider formerly known as Kenny Roberts Junior (he dropped the Junior suffix at the start of 2000, then reintroduced it a couple of years later, then dropped it again, then… oh, I've lost interest) has pretty much got everything it takes to be king of bike racing's toughest class. All he lacked in 1999 was a fully competitive bike. Many GP insiders now consider him to be the best 500 rider in the world, better than Alex Crivillé, the hugely experienced Spanish Honda rider who beat him to the '99 crown.

Kenny knows that too, but just try getting him to admit it. Unlike his mouthy dad, the former triple 500 champ who is (quite rightly) never afraid to voice his opinions, King Kenny's son is polite, reticent, a speaker of sponsor-speak.

So Kenny, are you better than Crivillé?

'There is no better or worse. Alex is a great champion, I feel really happy for him and it's great for Spain. The question I ask myself is "Could I beat him if he was my team-mate, if I was riding the same motorcycle?' At no time last year did I ever feel less superior to him on riding ability."

No better or worse? Hang on, ain't that what it's all about, proving you're faster than the next guy, than the rest of the whole goddam world? So come on Kenny, are you a better rider than Crivillé?

'Whether I think that or not is irrelevant; it's too basic to say I'm better or worse. If you were to ask me whether I could take a motorcycle that shouldn't beat him and then go out and do that, well yes, I believe I can do that.'

So you must be a better rider.

'No, that's for you and the fans to decide, that's not for me to say. Of course I'm going to think that, I wouldn't be a grand prix rider if I didn't. I thought that when I was riding the Modenas. To make you see it, that's a different thing.'

So you obviously believe you are better, why don't you just say it? (He's getting wound up now).

'No! I want *you* to say it, I want *other people* to say it, because it doesn't matter what I say. I believe I can outride anybody forever, because that's the way racers think, that's the way world champions think. But my goal is for everyone else to think that.'

Okay, okay, point taken. We're sitting and chatting on the Jerez pit wall, Spanish spring-time sunshine beaming down while the Marlboro Yamaha crew works on a YZR500 belonging to Max Biaggi, the man many rate as Roberts' most dangerous rival for the 2000 crown.

Biaggi is widely reckoned to be bike racing's biggest earner, now that ten-million-a-year Micky D is drawing his pension. Popular estimates have Biaggi on four mill plus, and while Crivillé maybe earns similar wedge, no one else comes close, not even Roberts. Does this worry him?

'Sure, I'd love to earn more money, make no mistake. If I made Max's money I could probably afford to burn what I earn. It's just because of where I was born, Max and Alex come from countries where bike racing is popular. If I was Spanish I'd probably be making double what I make, because I'd make good money off sponsors. But Mick Doohan was the highest-paid racer ever and he made money from winning races and world championships; that's my goal too. If I can do that my life will be content. Right now I'm content with my ability but I'm not content because I've not won a world championship.'

Biaggi, of course, works on his image. He hangs out with models and TV stars, lives in Monaco, drives around in flash motors and is in love with the camera. Roberts lives in Modesto, California, is engaged to a local girl he first met at school, drives a Toyota pick-up and couldn't care less if he's famous or not. Perhaps he could boost his star rating, and thus his dollar-earning potential, by following the example of GP racing's big stars, Biaggi, Valentino Rossi & Co. Like, how much would he want to dye his hair orange, $200,000?

'No, I wouldn't do it for a couple of hundred grand but maybe for a million or more. In my job I'm always concentrating on something else. You have to work on an image and I guess my image is not working on an image. Anyway, I believe cameras have a way of seeing through that stuff. Being the one with the loudest hair, the biggest mouth and the wildest lifestyle, it's a game you never win.'

If you wanted to give Roberts a tabloid-friendly nickname, it would have to be something like Mr Clean. No, make that Mr Squeaky Clean: never a hair out of place, never a rude word. Well, not until a Jerez marshal strides over and orders us off the pit wall. Kenny refuses to budge, then calls to one of his mechanics to 'kick that guy's ass'.

'The party fliers said bring hard alcohol, bring shotguns and bring motorcycles'

Roberts hails from America's conservative west, old cowboy country where men are men, 'good' Christian values still hold true (or are certainly supposed to) and the unconventional is regarded with deep suspicion. As his dad says: 'There's only two kinds of music worth listening to: country... and western.'

Of course, them cowboys have their own way of partying and it ain't all Willie Nelson. Dad Roberts' birthday is on New Year's Eve and his Modesto ranch parties are legendary, usually involving plenty of serious racing – dirt track, motocross and the climax event, a four-wheel demolition derby. Last NYE little Kenny planned a special millennium bash for dad, and printed invites for family friends.

'The fliers said bring hard alcohol, if you want, because we were providing beer, bring shotguns for clay shooting and bring motorcycles and karts too. Well, our lawyers got a hold of the fliers and went apeshit. They said that in Californian law this thing was just an open letter of sin

– bring booze, bring guns, bring bikes and cars. They said the insurance company wouldn't insure the ranch. It was my fault. None of that stuff happened but we had a party and it was a great party, no one got out of control, though my dad was disappointed because none of the girls took their tops off, which has been an occurrence once in a while.'

Despite his Jerez pit-lane outburst (hey, he was only jokin'), Roberts really is a softly spoken, normal kind of a nice guy. Back in '96, midway through his first 500 season, I asked his dad how this could be, when dad's got such a mouth? 'Well,' replied the King. 'He's still got time to become an asshole!' What Kenny Senior meant was this: 'As Kenny gets better, he'll get harder to please. That's what I want, I never want him to be satisfied with a result or with his bike. You don't win championships like that.'

Roberts Senior had every faith in his first-born back then. 'Junior has what it takes to be world champion,' he said. 'He has natural talent. So long as everything happens right I see no reason why he shouldn't be champ.'

Ironically, what happened right was Kenny defecting from his dad's struggling Modenas team at the end of '98 to ride Suzukis. Even in '96 (when he was riding Yamaha 500s for his dad) Junior knew he had what it takes. 'I know I can run top three, mentally I don't have a problem with the speed,' he said then. 'It's just a matter of learning to get the set-up right.' He proved he'd learned that the moment he got back on a V4 in 1999, whupping everyone including Doohan at the first two races.

Roberts has been bred for 500 glory. Back in '96, he also told me this: 'For me, sliding a bike is like a streetbike rider turning on the ignition key, I just do it.' He grew up sideways, spending his childhood racing guys like Wayne Rainey, Eddie Lawson and the King himself around the dirt oval at his dad's ranch; wheelspinning a 500 is in his nature and in his nurture.

Now working with genius Australian engineer Warren Willing, he's trying to develop the Suzuki into a Honda-beating motorcycle. This is where what dad was saying about never being satisfied comes in, and when you realise that within the nice guy is a control freak, determined to bend the Suzuki factory to building the bike he wants.

'Some people in the team probably say I'm outspoken. I try not to be derogatory, but I try to make my team and engineers see what we can achieve with this modification or this improvement. I like to control the situation in that I want to know what's happening. And I pay attention to the other motorcycles, a lot of attention. I never stop thinking about our motorcycle, how we can improve it and what the other teams are doing. Because racing isn't just about racing the other guys, it's about giving input to help Suzuki build the ultimate motorcycle.'

Willing's target was always to build that bike for the 2000 season. He joined Suzuki alongside Roberts at the end of '98 and knew there wasn't time to develop a Honda-beater in their first year with the factory. No surprise then that Roberts complained that the '99 RGV was 'out-gunned in all departments'.

'Now we've got more horsepower,' he says. 'We haven't gained what we needed to achieve but we've got a better connection between the throttle and the rear tyre, which means I'll have the feel to accelerate better. The bike is lighter, too, I could feel the difference right away. The team wants to be able to get under the minimum weight, so they can move ballast around to change the way the bike handles.'

His other big worry in '99 was burning tyres, a problem blamed on excess weight and lack of power, because Roberts had to ride the throttle harder to compensate for those deficiencies. 'It was worse if I was running with someone who uses less corner speed, so I had to run through turns slower, and accelerate harder. But the huge benefit for me now is being on the same motorcycle for a second year. Your input level is enhanced because you're feeling the same kind of things, so you can compare what's better and what's worse.

'As a rider you're always learning until you quit. I try riding different ways and that's helped me win some races. You do stuff like change your style and your appearance to the guy behind halfway through a race. Then you change again, to give them some confusion, so everything changes, where they'd planned a pass or felt they had an advantage. You camouflage yourself until the end of the race.'

Then he goes and contradicts all that stuff about building the 'ultimate motorcycle', which isn't much of a surprise, since, hey, we're all a mass of contradictions. And racers especially. What Kenny really wants is a bike that's worse than the rest, or only just as good! He may spend millions of Suzuki's money and devote his every waking moment to improving his RGV, but then he says, 'for me it's no fun to have the best equipment, the best team and the best engine. It's no fun because it's not a level playing field. The best feeling in the world is to take something that is lesser or the same and ride it harder than anyone else, that's what it's all about. All I want is a level playing field.'

You don't need to be a fully qualified shrink to understand the psychology behind that – Roberts wants everyone to have absolutely no doubt that he's the best rider in the world, then perhaps people might stop bugging him, asking him if he really is the greatest. Or maybe it goes a bit deeper than that. Roberts' dad is rated as one of the top two or three bike racers of all time, so does Kenny have a burning desire to escape the patriarchal shadow?

'I've never thought of it that way. What he did has no reflection on what I do. The thing that drives me is doing the best I can on the equipment I have. That's what my dad accomplished and that's what Wayne and Eddie did too. When it was their time they were the best in the world, now I have the chance to be the best guy in my era.'

Epilogue: KRJR did indeed win the 2000 500 title, beating rookie Rossi. He drifted into apparent retirement in 2007, but he'll be back if he finds the right bike.

CHAPTER 12

'DOOHAN'S A BIT GERMAN, I'M DIFFERENT, I'M EASYGOING'

November 2000

Garry McCoy burned bright and burned short in 500 GPs – his super-sideways style smokin' him to five wins in 2000 and 2001 before injuries and the dastardly four-strokes ended his time at the top

Never believe a journalist. The week after Garry McCoy won his debut 500 GP victory at Welkom, South Africa, in March 2000, a German mag screamed this headline: 'McCoy – Der Neue Doohan!' (That's 'The New Doohan!')

Wrong. Garry McCoy is not the new Micky D, never will be, never could be. It would be hard to imagine two more different racers: Doohan was the psycho, burning up inside, scarred and broken outside. He was a phenomenon, determined, driven and focused like no other. As a racer he had an aura that crackled with electric intensity; he wasn't easy to be around.

Gazza is the total opposite: no superhero aura, no withering stares and gritted teeth, just a big toothy grin and plenty of laughs. Gazza is a normal geezer who doesn't stand out from the crowd. He soon got used to the Doohan comparisons but never understood it. 'I reckon Mick's a bit German, like he's got a bit of German blood in him!' he laughs. 'I'm very different, I'm easygoing and I don't believe I'll ever change. I've won a race as I am, so why do I need to be different to win more?'

Fair enough. What does make the tiny Aussie stand out from the crowd is his riding style – a lunatic, crossed-up-on-the-brakes, full-lock-on-the-gas rodeo ride. 'Ferret tied to a rocket!' cry some. 'Monkey tied to a greyhound!' say others. McCoy gets more sideways than Kevin Schwantz ever did and his tyre-smokin' antics have raised eyebrows. Apparently you're not supposed to ride 500s like that any more. Sideways used to be the way to ride a 500 back in the days of Wayne

Gardner, Wayne Rainey and Schwantz, when horsepower exceeded chassis and tyre performance. Australians and Americans ruled, because they'd grown up sideways on dirt tracks, while Europeans couldn't translate their 125 and 250 roadrace technique to those fiery old-school 500s. But later advances in chassis and tyre design allowed men like Valentino Rossi, Alex Crivillé and Max Biaggi to ride 500s like they once rode 125s and 250s. Then along comes McCoy, sliding and spinning his YZR500 and disappearing into the distance.

After that first win at Welkom, Doohan wasn't even sure Gazza had got it right. 'He doesn't really look in full control of the thing when it's snapping sideways,' said the former grandmaster. However, McCoy's further victories at Estoril and Valencia proved that the boy does know what he's doing, even though he looks like he's heading for the straw bales.

On the other hand, former champ Rainey reckoned that McCoy was the only man who impressed him during 2000. 'He rides the bike sideways and that's where 500s are happiest,' said the American. 'They're okay until the tyres go off halfway through a race, then you gotta ride them sideways.'

You see, McCoy needs the bike to snap sideways. 'When it snaps mid-corner, that allows me to get the bike turned a lot quicker,' he says, laughing, as he does most of the time he's talking about giving his factory YZR heaps, giving it the guts, to coin a couple of his fave Aussie phrases. 'People forget that everyone rode like that seven years ago and some guys have told me I should pull the bike back into line but that's not what I'm used to. It's difficult to change your style, a lot of thought has gone into it, plus I'm pretty light, so the rear spins up easy.'

McCoy's style does cause him some problems but only because it's different from everyone else's. 'If I'm behind someone they hold me up a hell of a lot because they're not really on the gas until their bike is upright, so I have to run through a corner at their speed, spending more time turning the bike. If I'm on my own I can get on the gas a lot earlier, steer the bike with some wheelspin, then stand it up and away we go. I learned most of that through riding speedway ten years back. To me, it's the same thing.'

McCoy hasn't raced speedway for a while. Nowadays he hones his sideways style on a 600 trail bike. 'I've got a 600 on knobbie tyres and that's good for learning powersliding on tarmac. You snap it on through roundabouts and get big slides, the tyres are just jelly. It's scary, but good fun.'

The man obviously has a startling amount of talent, so how come no one's really heard of him until now? His GP career is a convoluted story of hard knocks, tough luck and a few lucky breaks. He started in 125s in '92, then graduated to an uncompetitive Honda 500 twin in '98, when a badly busted ankle seemed to have ended his GP career, until a middle-of-the-night call from Red Bull Yamaha in June '99.

McCoy made his GP debut at Eastern Creek '92, subbing for an injured rider. Barry Sheene got him the ride after watching him win a 250 proddie race a few weeks earlier. He'd been roadracing just four months. Typically Aussie, Gazza wasn't fazed. He ran eighth at the Creek until the bike broke, even though this was his first ride on a real race bike.

He started speedway in '89, at tracks near his Camden home outside Sydney and was all set for a professional career on the shale until mate Mat Mladin (who went on to rule the US Supers championship) started earning good money on tarmac. McCoy was friends with wild child Anthony Gobert too, though he admits 'it's always been a bit difficult to hang onto Goey's rope!

'I'd saved up to buy some speedway bikes, a van and an air ticket to England. But Mat had just got a ride with Kawasaki Australia after one season on a 250 proddie bike. Everyone thought he was a hero and they were throwing him into this factory team. I thought maybe that's the way to go – there's more money in it, though I'd have been more than happy to struggle away doing speedway in England.'

So McCoy canned speedway and blew his cash on an RGV250. After his promising GP debut – a week after his 20th birthday – he got a full-time GP deal for '93, riding an Aprilia RS125, soldiering on in 125s for six seasons, even though it wasn't where he wanted to be. 'Smaller bikes don't relate to my riding style. I wasted a lot of years. I did slide 125s but it's not the way to go because you're washing off speed. The idea was to prove myself then move up but I got stuffed around by a couple of teams.' One German outfit abandoned him in the Jerez paddock, leaving him with just his suitcase for company. Gaz had refused to ride after they'd offered him joke wages, 50 dollars per championship point.

There were good times too – his first GP win at Shah Alam '95 and another at Eastern Creek '96. Finally, at the start of '98 he got a 500 ride, albeit on a Honda NSRV500 twin, giving away 50 horsepower to the dominant V4s. He scored one top-ten finish that summer before crashing big time at Brno, clipping the back of Doohan's NSR, tumbling horribly and shattering an ankle. On crutches all winter, he got passed over for a '99 ride and had resigned himself to working with his uncle, fitting garage doors.

'I'd kind of had enough of racing. You put your life on the line and the teams don't want to pay you, you're busting your ass for nothing. I guess I wanted to ride again, though with who and what on I didn't know. I thought about racing in the US – you get paid there and it might've been a happy life.'

Then the phone rang at 3am on 22 June 1999. It was Peter Clifford, race director of the Red Bull Yamaha WCM team, who'd just split with Kiwi Simon Crafar. He wanted to put Gazza on Crafar's YZRs.

'I even tried riding with the wheels in line but it didn't work for me, the lap times suffered'

'I was a little iffy. I still wasn't 100 per cent fit and I'd never ridden a four-cylinder 500 before. Peter made me an offer, hung up and said he'd ring back in two hours, I'd have to get on a plane that afternoon. I had nothing else to go for, so I just had to do it.'

McCoy turned up at the Dutch GP two days later looking like cannon fodder. You couldn't think of a worse place to get to know a V4 – Assen is super fast and super narrow. He was out of control through the awesome right–left kink that leads onto the back straight, the YZR wheelspinning, tank-slapping, Gazza hanging on for dear life. Hugely entertaining but frightening too.

He finished the race 15th, alive, at least, and continued relatively unnoticed at the next few GPs. It was at the Valencia GP a few months later that McCoy first got noticed. He was getting the hang of the YZR, starting to treat the thing with some serious disrespect, smokin' the rear tyre and finishing third. 'After about four races I was into it, I found my style on the bike and got comfy with it. I even tried riding with the wheels in line but it didn't work for me, the lap times suffered.'

Over the winter McCoy and his amiable Scottish crew chief Hamish Jamieson worked at adapting his YZR500 to suit his manic style. 'When I first rode the thing it was like a raging bull but it's a lot better now, just through riding it more and getting it set up to suit my style. Hamish has been one of my supporters. He was around in the days of Schwantz and Rainey so he's happy to see the sideways thing again. He says if it worked in them days, why shouldn't it work now.'

Jamieson is indeed delighted with his new man. GP engineers generally have a rough life these days – mega-serious, mega-stressful – but happy-go-lucky Gazza holds an obvious joy for his riding.

'Racing is fun again,' says Jamieson. 'I can't wait for Sundays to come around because he's a real racer. These are the wildest bikes in the world and though he's got little upper-body strength he's in control. He's riding it, he's not scared of it.

'The thing with Garry is that he doesn't have much baggage. He's not earned a few million dollars over the last couple of years like a lot of the other guys, so he's not worried about spending it, about his house, his toys and so on, like a lot of the others. He's very focused on the bike. He goes away between races and thinks about it and he'll be straight back into it at the next race. A lot of guys aren't like that, you have to remind them what you were talking about at the last race. He's bright. And he's not had many races on the 500, so he'll get better, and as he gets better he should get a bike and tyres that work better for him.'

McCoy is the man who started the whole 500 pack switching from Michelin's 17-inch rears to 16.5s. At the beginning of 2000, he was the only rider using the smaller tyre, but pretty soon everyone was using it. 'The 16.5 has more edge grip mid-corner, which is where I like to get on the power. The 17 is a lot flatter on the top of the tyre, so there's not enough rubber on the ground when you're cranked right over.'

It's no coincidence that McCoy is generally strongest after half-distance, once his Michelins really start sliding around. He even changes his riding style mid-race to compensate for the change in tyre behaviour.

'The rear starts sliding more easily and it can stop driving forward, so I either short shift, get easier on the gas or stand the bike up sooner when I'm coming out of the turns.'

Some observers are amazed that McCoy's tyre-smoking antics don't destroy his tyres way before the chequered flag. But he explains that his apparently reckless style is, in fact, good for the tyres. 'Spinning the tyre doesn't really hurt it. What really chews the rubbers is getting maximum drive out of the turns without spinning, because that puts so much load on the tyre.'

Michelin has had much to do with McCoy's success. In 1999, the French tyre brand accelerated development of its 16.5in rear slick, first used successfully by Schwantz in the mid-1990s. McCoy soon found he preferred the tyre to the 17in used by his rivals, because it puts more rubber on the road at max lean, giving him the kind of grip he needs to throw it sideways.

When McCoy won his first 500 race, the season-opening South African GP back in March, he used the 16.5in. But because he was the only man regularly using the tyre, Michelin only had a limited range of compounds and constructions and it took until mid-season to get the choice he wanted to suit every racetrack. That's why his results apparently slumped after that great start to the year. 'They always make tyres available to everyone, so it took time because they couldn't just make them for me. I started getting the tyres I wanted in July.'

With Michelin and Yamaha well behind him he undoubtedly looked like a major contender for the 2001 title. But you have to wonder whether McCoy is just too nice to be world champ, like fellow former Aussie 500 winner Kevin Magee and Niall Mackenzie – hugely talented but lacking that psychotic killer's instinct. Then again perhaps his musical tastes reveal a rougher side. 'Iron Maiden and Megadeath are two of my favourites, just something to relax with at the end of the day.' Megadeath for relaxation? Nutter!

How to corner the Gazza way
Ever wanted to rear-wheel steer? No worries, just follow Garry McCoy's easy instructions…
'Coming into a turn I tend to get the rear end a little washy, so the bike tends to want to back in there. Sometimes I've had it backing into a corner sideways and before the bike's got straight again, I've fed on the gas and kept the rear end out there all the way around the corner. That's a good feeling, you think "Shit, that was excellent!"

'After you've got the bike backed into the corner you pretty much lay it on its side, then you start feeding in the gas just before mid-corner, picking up speed. You get on the gas hard from there and the bike may start to wheelspin, that's when you weight the outside footpeg to get a bit of extra grip. So you're hard on the gas and getting into a slide and if it looks like you're going to run off the track you just keep the throttle nailed to keep the thing steering in the right direction. That's rear-wheel steering.

'If you oversteer, so you're going to come out on the inside of the corner, you just back it off and weight the outside peg to let it drive a bit more and run out back to where you want to be. The way I see it, you've just got to get on the gas as early as possible and let the thing drift out to the white line.'

MotoGP Mutterings: January 2001
How to discover Britain's next world champion

Eureka! I reckon I've discovered the richest-ever source of future British world champions! So much so that I feel justified in guaranteeing you, the reader, a 21st century of glorious Sunday-afternoon TV viewing, watching gangs of Pommie racers annihilate Johnny Foreigner while you sit there submerged in half-chewed pizza crusts, crumpled tinnies and a sense of overwhelming wellbeing. Paradise, or what?

The answer lies right outside my front door. Quite literally, mate. On any Saturday night (or any other night, for that matter) it's like Brands bloody Hatch around my gaff. It's all wet cobblestones and dark alleys and gangs of kids thrashing around on nicked scooters. Yip, crack's not the big buzz in London no more, it's scoots, and these kids can't be assed to wait until they can afford the things, so they just nick them. From then on it's chaos: they're careering around on crashed-to-fuck Piaggio Typhoons, getting totally sideways on the cobbles and (sometimes) executing perfectly controlled two-wheel drifts. They have no fear because they've nothing to lose. In other words, they'll make great racers.

'On any Saturday night it's like Brands bloody Hatch around my gaff'

I've been studying form over the past few weeks and there's a couple of the little fucks who are pretty trick. I have a plan: sign them up on ten-year contracts, guide them up the racing ladder, all the way to GPs, and take a cool 50 per cent of whatever they earn along the way. Mr Big, that's me.

But I'm planning one final test before I get them to sign (will they be able to write, I wonder, or will it just be a thumbprint?). I'm going to lay an oil slick at the end of my street. No, no, no, I'm not going to shriek with laughter when they highside into a double-decker, I just want to give them one final test of their ability before I risk getting involved.

Of course, we don't like people who nick bikes but the fact is that most top racers are hard nuts with dark and dodgy pasts, racing around on the roads and getting into all kinds of trouble with the feds. Mick Doohan, for example, was an incorrigible truant who got banned five times before he was 20, for pulling wheelies and displaying unfriendly hand signals to the Gold Coast constabulary, amongst other things. And he did nick a bike once, well, it was his bro's Z650. No doubt about it, bike racers are hooligans with a licence to misbehave and, if they're real animals, they earn millions doing it.

The tricky part is to maintain these kids' loony psychology all the way to the top. When they're young, they're full of hunger and bursting with the joy of thrashing around on race bikes. But with every step they take, the pressures and rewards can kill the joy and take away the hunger. All of a sudden, they ain't the men they used to be.

The pressures on top racers, especially those doing 500 GPs, are huge. When they're off the bike, their days are filled by debriefing with their engineers and tyre technicians, meeting and greeting sponsors and VIPs, and getting interviewed by idiots like myself. Boring, boring, boring. Valentino Rossi seems to be one of the few 500 guys who has got this sorted. By keeping the joy, he rides at his very best. He rides fast because he wants to, because it's a blast. Most of his rivals have let the serious shit get to them, so they've stopped having fun and they struggle to be quick enough. Racing has become a chore.

Money is another problem. Once a rider earns his first few million he can easily mislay his youthful nothing-to-lose craziness because now he has got something to lose. He's got a nice house or two, a flash motor or three, a tasty bird or four, and a garage full of toys. All of a sudden he's thinking he doesn't want to get hurt, he wants to enjoy his success, so he starts taking it a tad easier on the throttle and a tad easier on the brakes, doing just enough to keep his job for another year or two. Then he can retire with a couple of mill in the bank and cruise through the rest of his life. Nice.

Many pit-lane engineers reckon their best-paid riders get lazy, so they implore their team managers to offer results-only contracts, but, of course, most riders won't go near those deals. Somehow I've got to make sure that success doesn't turn my kids into sloths; it could cost me a lot of money.

MotoGP Mutterings: *March 2001*
How to find the limit, then fatten it

Goin' fast, and we don't mean on-the-road fast, we mean racetrack fast, is all about finding the limit, bumpin' right up against it but not going beyond it. Sounds easy but, of course, isn't.

First of all, you've got to find the limit, that point where gravity takes over and dumps you in the dirt. Anyone who's raced will know that the only way to find the limit is by tripping right over the bastard thing, repeatedly, until you start getting the hang of what where it is (or retire with several broken legs). Yet where the limit is at changes pretty much every time you race. If you change bike or tyres, or even if the track temperature or weather conditions change, the limit won't be where you left it last time. So you've got to find it all over again, hopefully not the bone-crunchin' way.

'Anyone who's raced will know that the only way to find the limit is by tripping right over the thing, repeatedly'

This is true whether you're doing a track day at rainy Cadwell on a shagged CBR, or whether you're Valentino Rossi on his peerlessly prepped factory NSR500 at sunny Jerez. Getting it just right is what racing is all about, the buzz of rockin' on and bending those laws of physics just as far as they'll go, keeping the bike skating on the edge of disaster. As a mere mortal you need to make the limit as wide as possible, so you know you're there before you're out the other side and on your arse. You need to transform that knife-edge into a big grey area, a transition phase where you can feel the tyres running out of grip. You can do this several ways: by becoming aware of the transition phase, by smoothing out your riding to improve feedback from tyres and suspension, and by working on bike settings and tyre choice to optimise feel and feedback.

Inevitably, the faster you're going, the narrower the grey area becomes, so your shagged CBR on street tyres should have a much wider transition phase than Rossi's slick-wearing NSR. I started racing on street-tyred proddie bikes and found it difficult to adapt when I moved on to racers on slicks. A proddie bike starts getting out of control long before it actually goes out of control. The tyres are squirming, the chassis is flexing, it's like an early warning system, you see the limit coming, so you ease off just in time (at least that's the idea). GP bikes aren't like that, the chassis is rock steady, the tyres are gripping, everything seems totally cool. Then, whacko, you're flying through the air wondering what the fuck happened. The grey area was so narrow that it came and went before you even saw it, but as you're hurtling towards pain city, you remember that maybe the rear did start sliding 0.0001 seconds before it let go.

Obviously the skill required to survive as the grey area narrows increases exponentially. And, just to complicate matters further, the really greatest riders can find extra speed by actually shrinking that grey area. They are the only ones able to use a tyre that offers more grip but less feedback.

Michelin, who have dominated 500 GP racing for years, spend vast resources on widening that transition phase just as wide as it'll go, because that's what all but a handful of the world's riders need.

'To slide like they do, 500 riders need a huge amount of feel and feedback,' explains the firm's racing boss Nicolas Goubert. 'They need to sense exactly what the tyre is doing, and from experience, know what it's going to do next. Tyre compound and, to a lesser extent, construction are the crucial factors in offering excellent feedback.

'The more grip a rider has at his disposal, the more feel and feedback he needs. What most riders want is a period of warning as they approach the limit. It's no good having massive amounts of grip if the limit is reached without any warning, because the rider won't have the confidence to approach that limit. Most riders will go faster with slightly less grip and more feedback. Only the very best riders can go fastest with a huge amount of grip and minimal feedback, because their skill allows them to cope with less of a transition phase.'

Mick Doohan is the man Goubert is talking about, and I only mention him because Michelin's tyre engineers are still in awe of the bloke, their eyes rolling in the back of their sockets when they recall what he could do with their tyres. He was so familiar with them that he reckons he always knew what the tyres were going to do *before* they did it. With that kind of knowledge (and faith), ain't no one going to touch you.

MotoGP Mutterings: April 2001

The most basic racing question of all – why do people race? For the adrenalin rush, you say, but maybe it's way more complex than that

People race for the buzz, of course, which comes from riding the edge of disaster. But the risk itself isn't the real deal, it's the feeling of controlling that risk which is what really gets you going. The risks are there, of course, but as Martin Luther King said: 'If a man hasn't discovered something that he will die for, he isn't fit to live'. Now bike racing might not be the kind of worthy cause that King died for, but it's still something you go into eyes wide open, knowing you are putting yourself in the line of fire. And by bringing yourself closer to death, you make living all the more vivid.

A friend of mine, appalled by some racing injury, suggested that racers must suffer from low self-esteem if they're willing to get themselves so beat up on a regular basis. There's probably some truth in that; certainly, the desire to prove yourself is an element in every racer's make-up, it's like a rite of passage, part of becoming a man. Looking back I now know that was one of the forces that got me racing, plus the deeply mistaken belief that it'd get me girls.

People also race to challenge themselves, the sport attracts characters who don't want an easy life, who want to have to work at things, then look back and feel rewarded. Take Ducati star Ben Bostrom. Bike racing isn't enough for him, so in between World Supers rounds he goes rock climbing. 'Climbing is a different kind of scary from bikes but it's the same adrenalin rush,' he says. 'When you find yourself somewhere difficult you've got to push yourself and dig deeper, otherwise you'll be stuck out there on the mountain. It's the same with lap times, if you knock it back a fraction and run half a second a lap slower, you won't win the race.'

Every racer has his own way of forcing himself to ride the limit, to dangle over the precipice. I used to play the hunted, convincing myself that the guys chasing me would kill me if they caught me (this was way back in the early 1980s when I was winning club races on a 250LC, pushing out, ooh, at least 42 horsepower). It was a striking act of self-delusion but I remember the feeling being strangely vivid and very effective. I suppose it triggered some basic, primeval save-yourself reaction which opened up another dimension of perception and reaction that helped me dig deeper and scrape a few more tenths per lap.

Racing is also an escape from the pressures of the day-to-day world, as Steve McQueen once said: 'Speed has a kind of affinity to me, it's the time God and I have our little talks.' Riding on the road isn't quite the same, but it's a few steps down the same road: slip on your lid, shut down the black visor and get away. Once you're moving you've no choice but to zone in on the road ahead and forget the world around you, so your mind starts working in a different way and things become clearer. In a car you read ad hoardings, check out miniskirts, send text messages and read the backs of CDs, trying to find out who mixed track nine.

'Speed has a kind of affinity to me, it's the time God and I have our little talks'

I think that's another reason I started racing. It was the only thing that demanded everything of me, totally consumed me, gave my lazy-assed mind no room to wander uselessly, though having said that, I did crash a few times in my first few seasons because I wasn't concentrating on the job. I'd find myself cartwheeling through the gravel trap aware that my mind had been somewhere else. Idiot. Even off-the-track racing demands all of you, so small wars in faraway big countries and romantic bust-ups don't hit so hard. You're too busy on your knees in the workshop, thinking about the next race, and even if there is some bad shit going down, you just channel all your angst and aggression into the next race. Racing zoned me out of everyday life for a few years to the extent that I have huge blank spots in my pop memory, like I've not got a clue what happened on *Top of the Pops* between 1981 and 1985. Only now, watching ancient music vids, do I realise how lucky I was.

CHAPTER 13

COMPUTER HACKER, SHOE COLLECTOR, FUTURE WORLD CHAMP

May 2001

Daijiro Kato was only halfway through his second GP season when we had this little chat, but the world already expected him to become Japan's first-ever MotoGP champion. Sadly, it wasn't to be

It's meet the media time at Planet Kato. I'm among a group of GP journalists crammed into Honda's PR bus in the Le Mans paddock at the 2001 French GP, the little man squeezed into the corner looking slightly bemused, for he's a shy man surrounded by sweaty hacks – hangover eyes, pens and notepads at the ready.

Someone suggests we should drive to Skegness for the weekend; there's a few laughs and Kato giggles politely, even though he hasn't a clue what we're on about. We're speaking to him through an interpreter girl from Shoei, whose lids Kato wears. The atmosphere is a little uneasy – Japanese GP riders are notoriously difficult to talk to. The language problem makes communication difficult at best and they very rarely say much, largely because most of them are factory riders, unwilling to let loose their employers' jealously guarded secrets. Most interviews with Japanese stars of the GP scene rarely offer much more than: 'Yes', 'No', 'Coming better' and 'I will try my best'. We are determined to try our best at squeezing something more out of this ridiculously talented 250 bladerunner, but his first words are: 'I don't speak much, not only because I can't really speak English. I don't say a lot anyway, that's my character.' You can almost hear the clichés clanging around the brains of the assembled hacks: 'Kato – the man who lets his riding do the talking'.

Which is true. No one in racing history has ridden a 250 as fast as this waif-like 24-year-old, who looks more like 12 in the flesh. Kato clocks lap times that make 500 riders weep and he rewrites the history books pretty much every time he jumps on his Honda NSR250 – a jewel of a motorcycle that trips out 102 horsepower, tips the scales at 96 kilos and is good for over 170mph. How trick is that?

The day after we spoke to him, Kato became the first man to win the opening four rounds of a 250 world championship since Mike Hailwood in 1966. And since most experts rate Mike the Bike the greatest racer in the world ever, that's a big deal. Kato's French GP win also took him past Mick Doohan's phenomenal win rate, and not only that, his current win rate of 41.7 per cent puts him ahead of men like King Kenny Roberts, Freddie Spencer, Wayne Rainey, Eddie Lawson, Kevin Schwantz, Valentino Rossi and Max Biaggi. To complete the statistics overload, Kato already rates as Japan's fourth most successful GP rider of all time, even though he's only halfway through his second world championship season. And by the end of 2001, unless something goes horribly wrong, he'll be Japan's best ever.

'My dad tried to put me on a pocketbike when I was three, I was so scared I ran away'

Scary-quick Japanese riders are nothing new on the GP scene but 20 years back there were few around, because they found life on the road too unbearable, too different from Nippon. Some would have a go in Europe but after a few weeks of unfamiliar food and surroundings, their spirits would plummet and their results would follow. Homesickness would strike too deep and they'd return to Japan craving raw fish, sushi, green tea and more familiar surroundings. It's perhaps understandable therefore that the first Japanese in GPs were mad bastards, fitting the kamikaze stereotype almost too well. Takazumi Katayama became Japan's first world champ in 1977, three years after his GP debut when his banzai riding style triggered a barrage of complaints from European rivals, used to a more gentlemanly style. He later turned to Buddhism to improve his riding.

Kato belongs to a very different Japanese generation. The globalisation of east/west culture has changed everything. Kato and his peers eat Big Macs and pasta in Tokyo, so Europe doesn't seem so different. And the Japanese paddock community is so large now that he hardly has time to feel homesick. Technology has also played its part in making people feel more at home wherever they are, and like every GP star, Kato has a laptop and GSM communications in his motorhome. 'I spend a lot of time on the net, in on-line chat rooms, and I'm a bit of a computer

hacker. Sometimes I even speak to other Japanese r'
though they're also in the paddock!' Kids these days, e.

During the GP season Kato, wife Makiko and six-month
Ikko base themselves on the east coast of Italy, close to his tea...
workshops in the seaside resort of Rimini and just down the road from
Rossi's home town. Ever since 125 nutter Nobby Ueda – the first of the
modern generation of Japanese GP riders – moved there during the
early 1990s, Japanese and Italian GP people have had a special affinity
for each other. As the Telefonica-sponsored team's press officer says:
'It's an explosive mixture – the passion and typically fancy nature of
the Italians, joined with Japanese scrupulousness and devotion.'
Yes, quite.

Kato, who rides full-factory Hondas in an outfit run by former 125
champ Fausto Gresini, loves living in Italy. 'I love it, I love the climate
and I love Italian food, maybe too much,' he smirks, though he's hardly
got a pizza problem. At seven stone and five foot four Kato is the perfect
shape for 250 racing, not a knee or elbow poking outside the bodywork
of his tiny NSR.

Kato started riding at the tender age of three after one false start.
'My dad was into bikes and he tried to put me on a pocketbike, I was so
scared I ran away. He ran after me, I tried again and my fear went.'
Kato has been riding Honda's rapier-edged NSR250s since '95, first in
a Honda Racing Corporation satellite team, and since '97 with the
official HRC outfit, when he won his debut GP, contesting Suzuka as a
wild card. He also won that year's All-Japan 250 title and last season
finished third in his debut world campaign, winning four GPs, two of
them at tracks he'd never even seen before. The man and his bike have
grown up together, recording god knows how many thousands of laps,
HRC adjusting every aspect of engine and chassis performance to
exactly complement his riding style. 'The bike was almost perfect last
year,' he says. 'This year it is perfect.'

The rider/machine combination is so devastating that even Tetsuya
Harada (currently Japan's most successful GP rider) is falling into a
deep depression because he's fed up with getting his butt well and
truly kicked by the young upstart. When Kato can't run away with a
race, he seems to delight in torturing the '93 world champ, running
just ahead, then letting Harada pass, before finally nailing him on the
last lap. That's what he did at Le Mans anyway, and Harada's

body language said it all; as they crossed the line, the Aprilia man bowed his head in despair and his wife Miuki burst into tears in the pits. You can understand her being upset – it can't be much fun living with a beaten man.

Kato admits he prefers a bit of fairing bashing, even though he's making a habit of winning races by a mile. 'I enjoy racing with other riders. When you're on your own, it can be difficult to keep concentration, my mind starts wandering; I start thinking about my team's PR girl, Michaela!' he says, giggling at his own joke. Ah, the man's loosening up, spreading out on the sofa, looking us straight in the eye and revealing a bit of a sense of humour.

Of course, the question everyone wants to ask little Kato is when will he graduate to 500s, or rather GP1, as next year's new 990cc four-stroke class is likely to be christened. And will his artful 250 style translate to bigger bikes?

He's already answered that one. While 250s are his day job, Kato earns extra bucks by riding big lairy four-strokes at Japan's huge Suzuka Eight Hours event. He won last year's race, riding a factory SP1 with fellow NSR250 rider Tohru Ukawa, whom Kato quickly demoralised in last year's 250 GP series. And he's already tested a 500.

So which does he prefer racing, the 250 or the SP1? 'I like the 250 more because my feet don't touch the ground on the four-stroke.' More giggles.

Of course, the chat gets more serious when we start talking about money. Has he already agreed terms with HRC for 2002? 'Not yet, I have no contract with HRC for 2002. And if I don't get a lot more money, I'll quit and go somewhere else.' Fighting talk for a man from Japan, where job-for-life loyalty was once the cornerstone of the nation's economy. Not any more. Nowadays people get sacked and made redundant in Japan just like anywhere else, and workers are only as loyal as they want to be. Five years ago Harada caused a sensation when he quit long-time employers Yamaha to ride for Aprilia, but nowadays it'd be no big deal if Kato spat his dummy and moved on from Honda.

So what does he spend all his money on? When he first came to GPs, his PR profile named shoe collecting as his favourite hobby, which must make him the Imelda Marcos of GP racing. The Japanese trainer obsession is a well-documented national phenomenon but Kato has now kicked his footwear habit, thanks to sterling support from the missus. 'I used to have too many shoes, so my wife started throwing them away, now no more shoe collecting.' Ah, the lifestyles of the rich and famous.

Kato may be a bit kooky but he's also fast as fuck. So fast in fact that he may be the man to take on and beat current 500 dominator, the self-styled Doctor Rossi, when he graduates to the big class. The pair have only shared the same racetrack on a few occasions – on 250s and four-strokes – and so far Kato has always come out on top. Watch out Dr Rossi, your time may be at hand.

Epilogue: Kato did indeed go on to win the 250 world title in 2001 and he had Rossi worried a few times when he moved up to MotoGP in 2002. Named the man most likely to steal Rossi's crown in 2003, Daichan died after receiving massive injuries in a horrific high-speed crash at the season-opening Suzuka GP.

CHAPTER 14

NUTTER'S DELIGHT – THE CULT OF ELSIE

June 2001

A dewy-eyed retrospective of the Cult of LC, the lunatic two-stroke twin that helped give us the supersport bikes of today

There've been plenty of legendary machines in biking history: Ducati's 900SS and 916, Honda's RC30 and the original CB750, Norton's Manx single and Yamaha's R1. All these bikes hold their place in history for pushing the limits of performance to new levels, but however impressive they once were or still are, they'll never be as great as Yamaha's RD250 and 350LC.

While the 900SS, 916, RC30, CB750, Manx and R1 have changed motorcycling forever, they aren't bikes of the people, they're exotic, costly machines owned only by the lucky few, unlike the LC. No other humble, small-capacity motorcycle ever had such an effect on biking as did Yamaha's first water-cooled sports bikes, descended directly from the marque's ridiculously successful TZ250 and 350 GP racers. And the LC was the touchpaper for today's four-stroke superbikes, as R1/R6 project leader Kunihiko Miwa says: 'With the R family we wanted to re-create the RD sensation'.

Between 1980 and 1985 Yamaha sold almost 30,000 LCs in Britain, and the LC was much more than just a runaway sales success, more even than a milestone in sports bike history. The LC was a cultural phenomenon, provoking the Cult of Elsie that tore up racetracks, dual carriageways and town centres all over Britain throughout the 1980s. For years, LCs dominated Britain's sports bike scene and ruled club and national racing.

The LC hit the streets at a volatile moment in modern British history. Punk rock and new wave had swept all before them in the preceding two or three years, Maggie Thatcher and the Tories had got in the previous summer and the country was a seething mass of disaffected

youth, half of them on the dole, all of them angry. Unemp.
riding out of control and the kids were revolting. There was a ιc.
that something big was gonna happen, that a revolution was just
around the corner. Perhaps it was mere coincidence, but within a year
of the launch of the LC, Britain was burning up. From Brixton to
Liverpool and from Bristol to Nottingham there were riots, torching
and looting, thousands of youngsters venting their fury against a
government that had cut public spending by £1000 million in its first
budget. It's hard to credit 20 years on, but the country
was teetering on the brink of anarchy.

You couldn't imagine a motorcycle better suited to
such a seductive climate of mayhem. The LC was the
do-anything-you-want-to-do motorcycle (as punk
band Eddie and the Hot Rods had sung a year or two
earlier): buy one cheap, learn to wheelie, get pissed,
outrun the cops, crash out at the squat, crawl out of
bed next afternoon to collect the dole. It was about
as anti-establishment as you could get in an age
when just about every kid hated the establishment.

*'The LC was the
touchpaper for
today's superbikes,
as Yamaha says:
"with the R1/R6 we
wanted to re-create
the RD sensation"'*

And because LCs weren't R1 expensive, it didn't matter if you
crashed. In fact the cult of lunacy demanded you ride like an idiot and
fall like a fool. LC owners wore their dinged fuel tanks and scraped
spannies with pride; after all, a scratch-free LC could only belong to a
wimp. Anyway, the things were made for crashing and became more so
as aftermarket manufacturers created all kinds of crash protectors, like
special handlebar kits that covered the all-too vulnerable clocks console,
allowing owners to jump off more often for less money. Once again,
these bolt-on extras were a symbol of hoodlum cred, but counted for
nothing if they too didn't bear telltale scars of excess speed and
insufficient judgement. After all, the early 1980s weren't all about track
days and advanced riding techniques, it was just nail the throttle and
wait for something scary to happen.

It was, of course, the LC powerband, that seven-grand kick up the
arse, that got kids whipped into a frenzy. The original 250LC, launched
some months before its bigger-bored big brother in the spring of 1980,
didn't make outrageous horsepower, it just felt like it did. What really
mattered was that it was the world's first true ton-up 250, and this in
the days when novices could walk into a shop, buy a 250 on credit,

attach a couple of L-plates and wheelie off down the road, probably straight into an oncoming Ford Escort. Without doubt Yamaha's hooligan creation played rather a large part in the government's introduction of new learner laws the following year that restricted beginners to 12bhp, 65mph 125s. That'll learn ya.

The 350 turned up in the autumn of 1980, visually identical except for a second front disc brake and 350 stickers on the sidepanels. In standard form it wasn't the loon tool everyone had expected, but with a bit of judicious work with a riffler file and lathe, it rocked. The 350's arrival only accelerated the establishment of a countrywide cottage industry dedicated to turning LCs into insane streetbikes, nutty proddie racers or full-blown open-class race bikes. Tuners like Stan Stephens, Rob Farnham and Dave Swarbrick became legends in pubs and paddock cafés across the land, their names dropped whenever an owner felt the need to impress: 'Yeah, I just got a Stephens stage-three done on me 350, it wheelies in third now, no problem.' 'Nah, mate, you wanna get some Swarbrick pipes innit, really sort the powerband they do.'

It was perhaps inevitable that this LC-evoked infatuation with speed would lead a lot of owners to take to the racetrack, many of them not through choice, having lost their licences through repetitive madness on the streets. Club racing throughout Britain became an LC fest, battered, rusting Transit vans arriving in paddocks from Brands Hatch to Knockhill, each disgorging two or three LCs and their spotty, dishevelled owners (me amongst them), who would race in just about every class going: production, formula and open-class events. Clean up in them all too. But proddie racing was the big deal – with gridfuls of LCs and nothing else. These were the years when British club racing collectively removed its brain, placed it in a toolbox and went out to race. The 250 and 350 proddie classes were the big entertainment at every club meet, nicknamed Demolition Derby, Headbangers, anything that suggested brain-dead, elbow-to-elbow racing with not a thought for your own, or anyone else's, safety.

The racing was totally insane. I know because I spent my second and third seasons racing a 250LC. Six lap, 12 mile races at Snetterton would start with 40 riders and end with less than 20 crossing the finish line. First corners would claim five or six victims – I remember having tyre marks on my bike's fuel tank, and across my leathers and helmet after one turn-one mass pile-up. And it was rare for a race to go its full course without getting red flagged to allow fallen bikes and riders to be dragged out of harm's way before the action, and further carnage, resumed. Weekend meets got wilder and wilder, huge Saturday night piss-ups in the Snetterton paddock bar were followed by Sunday's first race at 10am, still pissed. No one really seemed to care – if you tipped off, LCs were cheap to fix and you could always blag spares off some other LC owner in the paddock. Or nick a street bike. Various police raids in the late 1980s established that a large proportion of proddie LCs were stolen; and no one seemed very surprised. Serious physical injuries seemed to be remarkably few and far between. Mere scabs and broken bones were things to be admired and laughed at, and anyway, the nurses at Norwich hospital were just the cutest.

My first LC, bought on hire purchase in the spring of '81 (I didn't tell my bank manager what I was going to do with the bike), never did the business. The squish band was too big, or the exhaust port too low, something like that, but my '82 250 was a rocketship. That summer I won 40 races on the bike, and a 350 borrowed from a mate, set a few lap records at Brands and Snett and used one front tyre all season. I think I may also have changed the piston rings at some point, but I'm not sure.

The cult of Elsie spawned some pretty serious racers too. Mick Doohan won five 500 world titles, ending up earning ten million a year, after a typical mid-1980s entry to the sport, on an LC. He had bought a 250 (called an RZ250 Down Under) for the street and lost his licence five times before he was 20 for speeding, pulling wheelies, the usual LC lunacy. He also crashed the bike a lot – pretty much totalling the thing on a trip to Australia's infamous Bathurst races in '83, looping the bike after a wheelie went wrong, then riding into the side of a car in a gas station. He replaced the wreck with one of the just-out YPVS RZ350s, persuading his dealer to affix 250 stickers to the sidepanels because he didn't have a full licence.

Doohan was a typical LC hoon – fast as you like and not giving a flying fuck about anything. He'd fool around on the street and occasionally fork out a few bucks to hustle around his local Surfers Paradise racetrack, as elder brother Scott remembers. 'He never used to check the tyre pressures or anything. He'd be sliding around with 15psi in the tyres, with his shirt hanging out between his two-piece leathers. He was a bit loose in those days – it was just all good fun.' Exactly.

Doohan only started racing because a mate had borrowed his RZ and stacked it. His local dealer – having witnessed Micky D's talent on dirt trackers – offered to fix the bike for free if he could be bothered to enter a race. The rest, as they say, is history.

Multi-British champ Niall Mackenzie also started his career on an LC. 'My first road bike was a 350. I'd read about them a few months earlier and reckoned they were the most gorgeous bikes ever built, so I scrimped every penny to get one. Within a few months I was racing.

'I was 19 with a death wish. I didn't care about anything – crashing, argy-bargy on the track, everything was fine. LCs were hooligans' bikes for young kids, not born-again bikers. You could throw them around, they were easy to ride and pretty safe.'

Mackenzie's LC career ended with the Pro-Am championship, a berserk, televised one-make series introduced in 1981 that perfectly encapsulated the sheer madness of the LC era. Pro-Am had been designed for mass-appeal armchair entertainment and provided exactly that: full ITV coverage (in an age when bikes never made it onto TV), serious prize money (£500 for a win was serious money back then) and, most of all, bikes loaned (and fixed) free by the Yamaha importers. A recipe for serious trouble.

The Ams were riders in their first year of international racing, the Pros were a bit, but not much, more experienced. Competitors were allocated bikes by lucky dip, picking keys out of a hat minutes before practice got under way, thus preventing any sneaky tuning. The racing was never less than terrifyingly close and though Mackenzie never won the series, he had plenty of laughs.

'It was wild and it couldn't happen nowadays because it wouldn't work with all the different sponsors and teams. We were mental, we didn't care if we crashed. It was free racing – free bikes, wreck as many as you liked and no one complained, and brilliant prize money. So you could really put it on the line and, if you got away with it, you'd win. I didn't care what happened, if I crashed spectacularly it was on TV so that was a big result and if I won I was a hero; it was a no-lose situation. There were always lots of spectacular crashes and you'd just pick yourself up and get back on; you don't get injured the same when you're 20 as you do when you're 30 plus.

'There'd be ten different leaders every lap. I was the original left-hand-on-the-fork-leg, both-feet-up-on-the-seat merchant. The antics got pretty crazy, hitting each others' kill buttons and so on. Everything seemed to happen in slow motion and pretty much anything went. A fair amount of kicking went on – that was fairly serious and malicious, a lot of it instigated by Alan Carter (who went on to win the 1983 French 250 GP). The Yamaha importers sometimes got a bit concerned that it could all go a bit pear-shaped but luckily it never did.'

Mackenzie's final race on an LC was the '83 Euro final at Hockenheim – by then the LC cult had spread far beyond these shores. Mackenzie, Kenny Irons (who also went on to race GPs but got killed in '88), and a few others, including myself (I'd finished top Am in that year's UK series), made up the British team. Mackenzie and Co blazed a trail of chaos through Germany that autumn, crashing hire cars, doing runners from bars (no doubt confused by the continental system of not paying for your drinks round by round) and terrifying the foreigners.

They had the number-one French hope in tears after ganging up on the guy during practice and running him off the track at 100mph-plus. And they dealt with the threat of super-quick Brit Steve Chambers – who was being dead serious, going to bed every night at a sensible time – by calling up whores from the local brothel and sending them round to his hotel room in the early hours. Irons lucky-dipped a dog of an LC and compensated for its lack of speed by pulling himself past anyone ahead by hauling on the leading bike's pillion grabrail, then swerving violently, forcing Johnny Foreigner to back off or risk a high-speed endo. Manxman Graham Cannell won the race by a gnat's from Chambers, and the defeated continentals shuffled home, struck dumb by the Brits' full-on aggression. But it was only what Cannell and Co had been doing at home for years.

That LC madness is still going on today, there's LC nutters out on the track and at large on the streets, though in much diminished numbers. While the machine's status as a race-winning phenomenon may have withered somewhat, there's now a special class for LCs. Formula LC is a cheap, fun way of getting into a fun, not-so-cheap sport. Bikes go for a few hundred and beginners can even rent an LC racer for £150 per meet. Just don't ask how many times your bike's been crashed.

On the streets, the LC's signature chain-saw massacre exhaust wail is a rare sound and owners are so few and far between that they have to communicate on the net, logging onto sites like rd.linefeed.com. But good to hear they keep the 'Sod you all!' punk spirit alive with angry discussions on the site's packed message board.

'Was last night's Chelsea run any good? Couldn't make it meself,' asks one LC idiot. 'The run was good – glad you weren't there!' comes the reply from some other loon. 'It must be hard being a moron,' comes back number-one LC geezer: 'It's a good job your parents gave you a name with only three letters or you'd have been struggling with any more than that.' Morons one and all, just the way it should be.

LC history lesson
The original RD250LC – descendant of the air-cooled RD250, itself descended from Yamaha's original sports twin, the 1959 YDS1 – appeared in Britain in the spring of 1980. It was a true milestone machine and stayed on sale for six years, undergoing just a handful of minor changes during that period; the bike was that good from the start.

The fully square 54 x 54mm motor employed technology learned from Yamaha's range of TZ250 and 350 racers but was nevertheless a fairly straightforward piston-ported two-stroke with reed-valve induction. Bullet-proof – until club-race owners started doing dodgy home-tuning jobs – the stock motor made over 30bhp, with well-tuned versions exceeding 40bhp.

The 108mph 350, with 10mm bigger bore, turned up half a year later, looking identical to the 250 but for an extra disc. Yamaha claimed 47 horsepower from this engine and, like the 250, it responded well to simple but clever tune-up jobs. And, also like the 250, the chassis needed few modifications for the track: fit some KR124 Dunlops (KR124 front/Michelin TG22 rear were the go later on), stick spacers in the forks and you're winning races and setting lap records.

Unlike the 250, the 350 did undergo a major revision. The much-changed mark two version appeared in 1983, with handlebar and belly fairing, uprated chassis and YPVS exhaust control. The motor was undoubtedly more powerful and easier to use than the original, with a smooth 59bhp and 115mph top speed. Full-race versions could be tweaked to a genuine 70bhp plus. The new chassis was appreciated by road riders though racers weren't so keen on the handling. Nevertheless, it came to rule the 350 and 500 proddie classes, just as its predecessor had done.

Later versions of the YPVS were given unpretty full sports fairings and, as sales faded in the mid-to-late 1980s, production was moved to Yamaha's Brazilian factory, where the last RD rolled off the line in 1995. It seems only right that such a mad motorcycle should end its days being built by Brazilians, people who know how to have a mad time.

CHAPTER 15

THE EMPEROR WHO WANTED
TO BE KING

July 2001

Max Biaggi had a horrible job in 2001 – trying to beat Valentino Rossi for the last 500 title and fighting his nemesis for the love of the Italian fans. There was only ever going to be one winner

It's not easy being Max Biaggi. You're racing Valentino Rossi, everyone's favourite GP rider. Beat him and everyone hates you, get beaten by him and everyone thinks you're a wuss. Win or lose, you lose. You're the bad guy, he's the good guy, end of story.

Then you go and have a punch-up. No one really knows who won, but everyone just hates you some more, or at least, that's the theory. And yet Max Biaggi seems to have come out of the infamous scrap at the 2001 Catalan GP winning respect. Mostly, the self-styled Roman Emperor courts unpopularity for his apparent arrogance but the feud has uncovered a possibly surprising streak of dignity.

The notorious fracas, which followed the pair's one–two at Catalunya, demands deeper examination of their relationship and individual psyches. For years it's been known that they don't get on; they're irreconcilable. Biaggi's background is black-and-white different from Rossi's, which surely goes some way to explaining their very different attitudes to life – Rossi the laidback, sometimes shabby young liberal who likes to get messy in nightclubs, Biaggi the intense thirtysomething with the painstakingly crafted goatee who once had tea with the pope and a rumoured romance with supermodel Naomi Campbell (with the emphasis on 'rumoured').

To be fair, Biaggi hasn't had the fairytale life that his nemesis has enjoyed; his road to the top has been altogether tougher. While Rossi grew up in a loving family environment (his parents divorced but stayed neighbours and friends), racing minibikes from the age of four, coached by his GP-winning dad, Biaggi was brought up by his father after his mother deserted her husband and young child. He didn't go near a racetrack until he was 18. As such he's probably the latest starter in MotoGP, surrounded by rivals who were mostly riding or racing by the age of four or five. Rossi rode his first bike race in 1990 at the age of ten, one year after Biaggi started his career aged 18. On top of that, they're rival suitors for the love of the Italian fans, and the millions of euros that come with that devotion.

Looking back over the years, it's always been Rossi who's wanted to make something out of their rivalry. 'It's simple,' Rossi told me a few summers back. 'I don't like Max and he don't like me.' And he rarely misses a chance to mock, whether he's riding a victory lap with a blow-up doll to diss Biaggi's alleged affair with Naomi Campbell, or tipping him a contemptuous wink on the podium.

Biaggi never even publicly acknowledged his long-running feud with Rossi until after the fisticuffs. 'My only defence is to say nothing,' he nods. 'By getting involved I have everything to lose and nothing to gain.' All he will say is that Rossi only whacked him once someone had Biaggi's arms behind his back. 'That wasn't nice,' he says, face flecking with hurt. 'It was unfair.' No one really seems to know exactly who did what in that chaotic melee, but the roles of bad guy, good guy don't seem so clear any more. There's a new and darker side to The Doctor.

'Rossi is clever, he gets energy from all this, but I think people get tired of it'

According to one witness of the contretemps, Biaggi managed to headbutt Rossi's team manager while the guy had his arms behind his back, giving Rossi's boss a black eye. Then he managed to fight free, clocking Rossi in the face. If you were looking for a points decision in the absence of a knockout, you'd have to give the fight to Mighty Max. Even better was his answer to someone who asked him what had caused the graze on his face. 'Oh, a mosquito bit me,' he replied, exhibiting that skill for lightning-quick put-downs possessed only by the very proud, like Romans and the British aristocracy.

Biaggi insists he's baffled by the whole rivalry, which started in a Suzuka restaurant back in 1997 after Rossi had taken a pop at his elder on Italian TV. 'We only started racing together in 2000 but it feels like Rossi's been racing me ever since he was in 125s. It's not normal to have a go at another rider when you're not even in the same class. It's like me saying Troy Bayliss [then riding in World Superbikes] is an idiot; why would I want to fight him if we're not racing together? Rossi is clever, he gets energy from all this, but I think people get tired of it.'

Eight years Rossi's senior, Biaggi was first on the GP scene, though he only started racing a year before his arch-rival. While Rossi was raised on bikes by his GP-winning dad, Biaggi had nothing to do with them until a visit to a racetrack in his 18th year. Now 30, he came to GPs four years later, and won four back-to-back 250 titles from '94, the first three with Aprilia, the fastest 250s of the era. But then he fell out with his Italian employers and made an apparently ill-judged switch to Honda for '97, winning the title again, against all the odds. That success secured Honda 500s for the following year, when he had Mighty Mick Doohan rattled, an achievement of which he's still proud. 'Mick had an easy life until I came to 500s, I put some fire on his back!'

While Doohan stayed at Honda, Biaggi wasn't going to get full-factory support, so he moved again, joining Yamaha, even if that meant he was back to riding second-best machinery. The Yamaha YZR is good now, though not as perfect as Honda's NSR, and that's something Biaggi never lets anyone forget.

'Rossi is lucky, he's always in the right place at the right time, he had the best bikes in 125s and 250s and now he has the best 500, the Honda has some magic. At the end of '98 it was obvious Honda would never put me in the HRC team, so my destiny was elsewhere. I'm not a magician, how could I have known Doohan would stop in '99?' So Biaggi is used to the underdog role. 'In '97 I proved you can win if you really believe you can do it – I have a strong mind.'

Since 1999 Biaggi has worked ceaselessly to improve his YZR500s, committing to a gruelling test programme that few other riders would even contemplate. 'In '99 the Yamaha was nowhere. I'm proud because we've made the bike better, and if we make another step forward it'll be hard for Honda to win. I just hope they don't make another jump. The Honda's strongest point is its engine, it brings a big benefit to the bike. In 1999 the Yamaha was nowhere, Honda was winning everything. To start off in '99, the Yamaha's crankshaft was too light, so I asked for a heavier crank to improve throttle-to-tyre connection. The next year all the Yamaha riders had the same crank, and that was better for everyone. My job isn't just to fight for the championship, it's to be a test rider.

'Even at the start of the 2001 season we didn't have the right set-up, we went the wrong way at the first two races. I've also changed my style to better suit the 500. I'm trying to go in deeper, then stand the bike up, so I can get on the throttle sooner. Riding the 500 like a 250 doesn't make sense, you can only be fast until the rear tyre starts sliding, then you struggle.'

The contest for the last-ever 500 crown is drawing into its final stages. Rossi has been ahead since the start but the upcoming tracks suit the Yamaha, and Biaggi is one of those rare people who gets off on stress, the kind that buckles normal minds. 'I won three of my four 250 titles at the last race, I respond well to pressure.' He was also the highest-scoring rider in the final phases of both the 1999 and 2000 series, and there's every reason to expect he'll have an even stronger finish to this season.

This title fight is going to be a close call, scarily close probably, because the pair have already ridden into each other at 120mph. It's a bit of a worry, really, but it's going to be great watching history unfold.

Epilogue: Biaggi went on to get soundly beaten for the 2001 500 title, crashing out of several crucial races as he vainly tried to stay with Rossi. Things didn't get any better when MotoGP went four-stroke in 2002 – Biaggi was on the hopeless Yamaha, Rossi on the awesome Honda. Biaggi got a Honda ride for 2003 but still couldn't win. His ignominy was complete when Rossi switched to Yamaha in 2004 and won the title again.

CHAPTER 16

'HOLY FUCK, THESE GUYS ARE DOIN' SOME REALLY SCARY STUFF'

July 2001

Former 500 legend Kevin Schwantz talks about 500 GPs, crashing Porsches and having fun on his 200mph 'Busa streetbike

Kevin Schwantz was the Valentino Rossi of the late 1980s and early 1990s. Hugely popular, he won fans for his give-it-everything-you-got riding style and a dogged determination to have a ball, whatever he was doing, wherever he was doing it.

Revvin' Kevin first made it big in the States, muscling Yoshimura GSX-R750s into submission while commencing a bitter and career-long rivalry with Wayne Rainey. The two took their fight to GPs in 1988 and pretty much dominated the world championship scene until Rainey's crippling accident in 1993. Following Rainey's hat-trick of titles, Texan Schwantz won the crown that year, but, with the man he loved to beat the most in a wheelchair, he was never the same again. Having built a reputation for ridiculously brave (or foolish) comebacks from injury, Schwantz retired from racing midway through '95, suffering major problems with a much-battered wrist and hip. He took the last of his 25 GP wins at Donington '94.

After he quit, Schwantz didn't go near a motorcycle for a year or so. He tried his hand at car racing, without much success, and is now back into two wheels in a big way. He is now rider adviser to Suzuki's US Superbike team, dispensing wise words to factory Yoshimura GSX-R riders like US champ Mat Mladin. He also runs a GSX-R race school at Road Atlanta. In other words his life revolves around GSX-Rs, just like it did in the mid-1980s.

Mostly, anyway. When we met up during the 2001 Italian GP at Mugello he'd been riding – of all things – an R1100RS in a BMW Boxer race. This was his first roadrace since he quit GPs and it was hardly a spectacular return. Riding purely for fun, the outing failed to re-ignite Schwantz's famous will to win, and there's no GP comeback on the cards.

'It'd be fun to come back but I'd only want to do it when the weather's perfect, when it's a track I like and when we've got the set-up, otherwise I don't want to know!' he smiles, that famous ear-to-ear grin still firmly in place. 'It's like when I went to Phillip Island last year and it really started raining. Kenny (Roberts Junior) offered me his gear and said "Hey, you go ride". I just said "I'm off for a coffee and doughnut, I'll see you later". All it takes is for me to come here and watch one guy hit the ground and it's "Uh oh, it's not worth it".

'Anyway, every now and then Suzuki say "come ride this or come ride that", and I still get a huge buzz from riding top-level machinery. I rode Mladin's bike at Road Atlanta and I rode Kenny's bike at Phillip Island. The 500 was a kick in the ass!'

Having been away from GPs for a while, Schwantz admits he was stunned at Mugello. 'I never question why I raced but I look at these guys now and think "holy fuck, they're doin' some really scary stuff". As a kid growing up, I'd ridden and ridden and ridden and the bikes have gotten bigger and speeds have gotten greater, and it's all kinda worked into itself. Now I play around on dirt bikes and ride a street bike occasionally, and to come back and watch the 500s, it's a huge difference from anything you'd ever imagine. It's a whole different mindset. I'm sitting there watching some 500 guy goin' around a corner and riingggggg [he does a very passable imitation of someone having a big sideways moment] and it's like "fuck, I'd pull in and stop right now, that would've scared the living shit out of me!"'

Schwantz used to have the same effect on people watching him. He'd have a wince-inducing highside on Saturday, crack a few bones, get pilled up at Dr Costa's, then win the race on Sunday. But he was paid well for the pain. 'The year I won the championship I made five million dollars. That's bonuses and everything said and done.' At 15 GPs a year, that's $333,333 a ride. Riders like Rossi and Max Biaggi make more but Schwantz wouldn't want to have been born later. He reckons he raced in a golden age, when riders could earn millions and still party.

'Back then Sunday nights weren't about worrying where the next race was or the next test was, it was "where we all gonna meet, have beers, tell stories, lie about the race and whatever else?"' Everybody who raced in that era raced as hard as they possibly could the entire time. So on Sunday evenings we needed to go do something that made us realise we were still havin' fun because it was nuts on the line 99 per cent of the time, though I'm not saying that's not the case now.'

But things are very different now. Crashing still hurts just as much and bike racing is still a vicious way to earn a living but the technology has changed everything. Twenty-first century racing is all about 'the set-up'. 'Yeah,' he continues. 'It's [adopts whingeing voice] "we don't have the set-up right". You know how many times I rode a 500 that was set up right? I could count them on one hand and have some fingers left over. A 500's never gonna be perfect.'

Another thing Schwantz has noticed is that GP racing has got a lot more corporate, just like the rest of the world. 'The paddock probably needed to do that, but you don't get so many of those happy-go-lucky, fun-to-be-around people that used to be involved.'

Schwantz always made sure he was having fun when he was racing, to the point that things inevitably got out of control. Like when Porsche loaned three 944s to him, Eddie Lawson and Randy Mamola. They stacked the lot of them. 'I came around this totally blind corner where there's this little lady stopped. I just get stopped but I'm thinking "I know who's comin' up behind me," so I'm rolling forward, thinking I need to give these guys some space because this is dangerous. Eddie gets through, then we hear Randy comin'. I look in the mirror and Eddie's hunched in his seat, waiting, and Randy comes round the corner, hits Eddie and Eddie hits me. So we've got three wrecked Porsches and it's getting dark so we have to stop at a gas station and borrow some tyre irons to pry open the pop-up headlights.'

'We'd probably had just a little bit too much to drink, and Eddie stuck his Porsche in the ditch, with my coaching'

It didn't end there either. 'After the race in Austria, Eddie and I decided to do a lap and honest to God, we didn't do it fast. We just drove around and talked about the race, but when we were done there was this security guy, about eight feet tall, and he's like "What are you doing? You're not supposed to do that." He goes to pull me out the car but I had the seatbelt on, so he couldn't. Eddie's laughing now and that pissed the guy off, so he's slammed my door, shattered the window and the glass cuts my face. There's blood gushing out, so we both unclip and go after this guy. He's running, because there's two guys half his size out to kick his ass and Eddie kicks him in his nuts as hard as he can. After that we went into town. We came back to the paddock at three in the morning, we'd probably had just a little bit too much to drink, and Eddie stuck his Porsche in the ditch, with my coaching.'

Despite a good few years of jackassing around the world, there's not much that Schwantz regrets having done in his career. The single world title he won certainly wasn't reasonable recompense for his astounding talent, and there's plenty of so-called experts who reckon he would've done better if he'd ditched Suzuki's fickle RGV to ride a more user-friendly 500 from Honda or Yamaha. But despite an eye-opening ride on Mick Doohan's NSR a year after he limped into retirement, he thinks he did the right thing.

'Mick's NSR was intimidating, but then any 500 would've been after a whole year of not riding. I'm happy I stayed at Suzuki. I had an opportunity to go ride Yamaha at the end of '89. All I wanted was the same exact shit that Wayne had, because I wanted to beat him on the same stuff. When Yamaha couldn't promise that, I stayed where I was. I also talked to Erv (Kanemoto, Honda GP guru) midway through '92 but that never really got close.

'If I regret anything it'd be what I did to my wrist in '94 to fix it quick. I should've taken time, got it fixed right, taken a year or two off and realised at that point, "Shit, I'm still only 32".'

Of course, Schwantz's career-long association with Suzuki has opened up some cool retirement options; he seems to enjoy his new role as rider training guru. 'I go watch the Yoshimura Suzuki guys practise. Then I come in and say "Hey, some other guy is out a little bit from where you are at that corner, and they're not hitting that bump, so the front's not unsettling, so the whole bike's not getting messed around". That seems to work good with the young kids. If their mechanic tells them this and that, the kids are like "What does he know about riding?", where hopefully I can come from a different perspective.'

Although his prime duty is to coach up-and-comers, Schwantz is also an invaluable go-faster aid to Mladin and Suzuki's older riders. 'I'll see some guy from another team using a gear higher to get through a corner, not having to make a shift and not unsettling the bike. But sure, you can't just say "Hey, you're doing this corner wrong". It completely depends on if he's comfortable doing it your way and if the bike set-up will let him.'

At Daytona 2000, Schwantz's track-spotting skills helped Mladin win the 200 miler, America's biggest race. 'Mat said "My bike's working real good through the infield but it's not getting up on to the banking as good as I'd like it to. But I know that if I adjust it to get on to the banking better, I'm gonna give away the advantage I've got through the infield, so tell me what it looks like to you, is it that much worse on to the banking than everyone else's?" I went out and watched him and his bike didn't look any worse than anybody else's, it actually looked one of the better ones getting up there. I said "You're not giving anything away," so he raced it that way.'

Two of Schwantz's biggest GP rivals – Rainey and Doohan – have also tried their hand at trackside coaching. Rainey gave it up as a bad job, realising it'd take forever to find a rider who matched his staggering commitment. Doohan still dispenses advice to Honda riders like Rossi and Chris Walker, but never begins to pretend he can instil anyone with world title-winning skills.

Schwantz agrees, adding: 'It's just keeping their minds open to different ideas. When guys get to this level they don't need to learn how to do stuff, they just need to be reminded there's more than one way to do it. Maybe they get too focused, a bit of tunnel vision about some corner, so they're going "I gotta make this work", so they hit that same bump and bang! [He shouts a passable impression of a race bike crashing to earth.] Whereas if they'd made a later or earlier entry, they wouldn't even have hit that bump. It's like at Mid-Ohio, they've got big concrete patches right through the apex of some corners, with only so much on the inside that's asphalt. So Mat asks me "Where's everyone running, on the patch or inside the patch?" I went and watched and all the people who were getting around good were riding right on the edge of the asphalt, where there was like a little berm, where the cars had pulled up the asphalt to the edge of the concrete, so they were on rails.'

Schwantz's closeness to Suzuki also guarantees a well-stocked garage. 'I got a Hayabusa, a GSX-R1000 and a 750. I like riding the 750 and the 1000 when we do the school, and the Hayabusa is a neat streetbike. I've gotten better, I've gotten to where I can ride it sane 75 per cent of the time. Any time I got on a streetbike when I was racing, it was like "how fast will it go and how quick will it get there?", that's all I cared about. Now I can ride for fun, I stop and look at things and enjoy the scenery.' Jeez, he'll be buying a Harley next.

MotoGP Mutterings: July 2001
Spending too much time in the GP paddock can make you a bit nuts. Here's the proof

A few nights before the 2001 GP season kicked off at Suzuka I had a dream, one of those pre-season anxiety dreams I have before most seasons. I dreamt that all the riders had had head transplants with each other. I was rushing around the paddock searching for riders I needed to interview, but I kept speaking to the wrong guys. I walked over to Kenny Roberts Junior and started talking to him, then realised it was Rossi; the pair of them had swapped heads. I tracked down Leon Haslam, only for him to tell me he'd exchanged with Jezza McWilliams (that'll be the old head on young shoulders, then). I tell you, I was getting a little confused, a little panicked, and a long way behind my deadlines.

'I dreamt all the riders had had head transplants with each other. I was rushing around searching for riders, but kept speaking to the wrong guys'

The GP paddock can have that effect on you. It's a weird environment, populated by some of the most extreme people you'll ever meet. And not only the riders, everyone at GPs has a hint of the psychotic about them (yeah, I'm including the media in this) because they're ultra-ultra serious about what they're doing. The riders, for starters, have one of the weirdest jobs on earth: flying around the world, employed as mobile advertising hoardings and occasionally hurling themselves into Armco barriers. Their mechanics are no less obsessed with what they do; most of them only get to return home for six weeks in a year. And then there's the team managers, the PR people, the cooks and the gofers, the medics and the media, the hangers-on and the floozies, almost a thousand people in all – and stress monkeys, the lot of them. As Randy Mamola said recently, if a bunch of Martians started monitoring bike racing from space, they'd worry for humanity.

It's my job as a journalist to wander through the paddock and make sense of the madness. But like life itself, it doesn't quite work out like that. 'The more I see, the more I know, and the more I know, the less I understand,' sang that geezer from The Jam and he was pretty damned right. However, we have some fun along the way, trying to suss out this travelling circus of semi-lunatics.

Years back I used to work with John Kocinski's Yamaha team and it was my job to speak to the unpleasant little man every time he got off his motorcycle. When he wasn't downright rude he was often hilarious, though he probably didn't realise it. Spitting venom one Sunday morning after pre-race warm-up, he snarled at me: 'I could do more with the turd that was floating in my toilet bowl this morning than with that motorcycle'. I had hazy visions of the former 250 champ, later World Supers king, lining up on the grid astride a big pile of steaming shit, the commentator shrieking: 'And heeeere's the little shit on a big pile of shit'. I now hear that Little John has become a real estate magnate, selling multi-million dollar plots of land in Beverly Hills to Hollywood stars like Eddie Murphy. Congratulations, mate, I always knew you'd make a really good estate agent.

Of course, you can't really expect the riders to be anything other than slightly crazy: it is, as I've already pointed out, part of their job description. And as some team bosses occasionally say, with only a hint of irony in their voices, they're only cannon fodder. You only really see the truth in that statement when you've been hanging around in the paddock for a decade or two, watching riders come and go, arriving fresh-faced and enthusiastic, leaving gnarled, slightly broken and (occasionally) very rich.

The cleverest people in the GP paddock are the team managers and the riders' personal managers. They're around forever, like us journalists, and they don't have to hurl themselves at the Armco barrier to make a few quid. You've got to get up early in the morning to catch out a manager, way too early for me. A few years back I caused a bit of a paddock furore by writing something about Max Biaggi. I wrote that there was a rumour going around the paddock that he was gay (it transpired that this was indeed only a rumour), and I'd only mentioned it because some other magazines had started writing puerile, vaguely homophobic stuff about 'pole positions' and 'coming from behind', oh how very funny. My angle was that if he was gay, it was everyone else who seemed to have a problem. Wandering along the back of the pits one morning I was accosted by a couple of Suzuki mechanics (behind the pits at GPs is like behind the bike sheds at school, everyone hanging out, 'aving a fag), who wanted to know why I'd written that Max was gay. Nah, I said, I only wrote that there was a rumour going around the paddock that he was gay. 'Well,' replied their team manager Garry Taylor. 'There's a rumour going around the paddock that you're a cunt.' To which there is no reply.

CHAPTER 17

BEST BEFORE...

August 2001

British Superbike dominators Steve Hislop and John Reynolds were approaching their sell-by dates but still kicking arse in a major fashion when we got together for this interview in the summer of 2001. In the light of what happened to poor old Hizzy, it's full of poignant moments

Born-again bikers dominate the British biking consciousness – scoring more bike sales and hospital visits than anyone – so it's perhaps fitting that two knocking-on-40 racers are dominating the 2001 British Superbike series.

Steve Hislop and John Reynolds are the Chris Walker and Neil Hodgson of 2001, duking it out way ahead of the pack and getting involved in some seriously hairy paint-swapping. At their age, these two dads should know better.

But, of course, they don't. Hizzy and Gentleman John just keep getting faster and faster, this final flourish to their careers powered by near-factory-spec 996s and bankrolled by rich patrons Paul Bird and Ben Atkins. Hislop, backed by Bird's MonsterMob crew, is the older of the two, just five months away from the big Four-0 and with 19 seasons of roadracing behind him. His career has been mostly British championship with a heap of TT successes and a few endurance wins thrown in. Reynolds, three years younger but more touchy about his age, has been racing 15 years. He's done 500 GPs and World Superbike, returning to the British scene for the past few years with ever-faithful benefactor Atkin's Red Bull outfit, even winning a Brands WSB race last autumn. And both did schoolboy motocross before they hit the tarmac. In other words these old gits have an extraordinary amount of race experience within them and there's nothing that beats experience on the racetrack.

'The only way you can tell how you're riding is by results and lap times, and every year we're going quicker,' says Reynolds, who first won the British Supers crown in 1992. 'That tells me I'm still learning and I feel I still ride aggressively. You know when you're riding on the limit – you just get the bike stopped for a turn, just scrub off enough speed, so the front's moving around as you tip in, then the rear's moving when you tap on the power. The whole bike is just floating.'

Yes, nothing beats experience on the racetrack, except experience. 'That's the thing,' says Hislop, who was British 250 champ way back in 1990. 'We've both got 15/20 years of knowledge and gamesmanship, so it's "Where am I gonna try him on the last lap?" I'm digging deep and the problem is that John's been racing almost as long as me.'

Reynolds adds: 'When you first start racing you're ten feet behind the bike, that's the dangerous part, where all the learning and hurting comes in. Then as time goes on, you get level with the bike, so you're sort of happy. Now I feel like I'm ten feet ahead of the bike, so I'm predicting what it's going to do, and that's where you want to be at.' Then he thinks for a moment... 'Having said that, you still make mistakes.'

Reynolds is right though, it's all about using brains rather than bravery to go fast. But does that mean that racing gets easier the longer you go on? 'No way!' he answers. 'Nah,' adds Hizzy. 'Maybe it's easier riding because your knowledge is greater, but the racing never gets easier; in a way it gets harder every bloody race.' Reynolds chips in again: 'It bloody well does with him about!'

Out of Walker's and Hodgson's shadows, both men know they're riding harder than they've ever ridden in their lives, so they bristle when people suggest they should pack it in and give the kids a break. 'We're enjoying it and putting on a good show, so why should we call it a day?' says Hizzy. 'People expect you to hang up yer boots and let a youngster take over yer job, but I've got two kids to think of and I don't know what I'm going to do after racing. I've not made enough money to retire, I've screwed up with a few teams and been used a bit, so it's a proper job for me if I call it a day. Jamie Whitham's the funniest guy ever, he says "I'm scared, scared of getting a real job".'

Which brings us to fear. Racers never lose their skill, they just lose the will to use it, and until they reach that point they keep getting faster. That's Hislop and Reynolds for you; they've not yet reached that moment when fear begins to creep around their psyches, stealing a

tenth of a second here and a tenth of a second there, until they're no
longer competitive. Or maybe they're just better than most at keeping
the fear at bay. Ask Reynolds whether he gets more scared now than
when he was a youngster and he sounds like he's trying to convince
himself: 'Scared doesn't come into it,' he says. 'Once you're scared it's
time to pack it in.' But doesn't he find himself getting more sensible
with age? 'No, and that's sometimes a worry to my wife Shelley. She'd
like me to stop tomorrow, but why would I do that when I love doing it
and I get paid pretty well?'

Reynolds puts his own sell-by date a couple of years down the line.
'You've got to take every weekend as it comes,' he says. 'But I'd like to
go for another two or three years.' So has he got a pension sorted? 'I've
a few things in the pipeline,' he says mysteriously, politely refusing to
reveal his earnings after Hizzy tells us his pay packet is knocking on
100K, though Reynolds almost certainly earns more. For Hislop, the
proverbial gold carriage clock looms a little larger. 'I said at the start of
this year that I'd ride this season and see how it goes
but probably do at least another year beyond that.
You never know, why quit when you're riding good?

*'The only thing that
really scared me was
when I broke my
neck at Brands last
year'*

'The thing that worries me is the thought of an
injury, I can't cope with the thought of being beat up
every weekend. Some of the younger guys seem to
jump off, get beat up and jump straight back on. I did
that ten years ago but now it takes longer to get
better. A bit o' age and bringing up kids, you start
thinking a bit, you're more aware of the details in life. I drive a bit
steadier on the road these days.

'The only thing that really scared me was when I broke my neck at
Brands last year. We never found out it was broke for a couple of months
and it wasn't the broken neck that scared me, it was my left arm which
had stopped working. We got the neck scanned and they found two
broken vertebrae and loads of gunge and shit which had jammed in a
nerve port. I knew something was wrong and I'd been scared I was
going to end up with a withered arm for the rest of m'life.'

I know what he means. The only things that really worried me when
I was racing were head and spinal injuries. I first started getting proper
scared a couple of years before I stopped, and I can pinpoint the exact
moment when fear found a foothold in my psyche. I was eating

breakfast after early morning TT practice on the Island, the news crackling out of the café's tinny little radio, telling us that a rider I knew had been killed that morning. From then on, this thought would creep into my mind on race mornings: 'Is this my last breakfast?' As a racer, I was fucked from that moment.

Although he won't admit to fear, Reynolds still feels something on race mornings: 'I get sick as a dog, not physically sick but I don't feel well.' Hislop is more laid back about it all, though maybe only because short circuits seem so safe after years of cheating death on the Island, where he won 11 TTs. 'I used to get really wound up before the TT, that was terror butterflies. These days I just get a little bit butterfly-ish before we go up pit lane, but I watch my 250 team-mate, little Stuart Easton, get dead wound up at British meets.'

Hislop, now an Island resident, hasn't done a TT in seven years and even though he still rates it his favourite circuit (and considered doing the 2000 TT: 'I thought it'd be a good idea to get some wedge'), the terror of the place is still with him. 'Every year on the last lap of the last race, coming out of Ramsey and up the mountain, I always used to say to myself, "Just one more time over this mountain and that's it, thank fuck, for another year". By the end of '94 I was like, "I've had enough of this".'

Reynolds raced the TT just once. A chance meeting with Hizzy during practice, as they tackled the terrifying Baaregarroo section, was enough to convince him never to return. 'Jesus Christ, Steve came past like I was stood still, and I wasn't hanging about. He bounced through the bottom of Baaregarroo, sparks flying off the bottom of the bike, and wobbled off to Kirkmichael. I thought "If that's what you've got to do to win a TT, you can flippin' keep it".'

Since then Reynolds has had his fair share of scary moments on short circuits. 'I got a ride with a Japanese team in the Suzuka Eight Hours in '92 which was going to make me quite a bit of cash. First thing they did was take us to see this spiritualist. She wanted a bit of my hair, a bit of each fingernail and a bit of toenail which she wrapped up, said a few words over, and gave to me. Fuckin' hellfire, we had to hang it over the pit door so we'd go under it whenever we went out. First time out, my first lap, I went into Spoon curve and saw something fly out the front of the bike, then when I hit the brakes for the next turn, nothing happened. I looked down and saw one of the brake callipers swinging in the breeze. Don't know how I stayed on.'

If Hislop is mostly more frank about feeling fear, he's used that very weird thing called racers' psychology to convert the negative into a positive. 'Getting my arm fixed was what gave me the sheer determination to come back this year. People wrote me off, "Oh, he's a half-season special, he'll go fast for a while but his head'll go, he's a fuckin' fruitcake". Everybody's wrote me off that way for the past four or five years. I've had problems in teams but there's been reasons for that, which is why I'm so determined to come back and do well. The arm scared me but it's given me real determination since then. It's like Doohan in '92, he wrecked his leg and came back from that. Fantastic!'

And here's another dose of racers' psychology, from Hizzy again. 'I was panicking a few weeks back because I hadn't crashed in ages, so I was thinking, oooh nooo, I'm in for a big one. Then I went and lost the front in practice at Oulton. That's the way to do it, lose the front, go down nice an' easy. I felt a lot better after that.'

Despite a bit o' fairing bashing this year, at Oulton and elsewhere, the pair remain friends, though they're not sure how long that'll last as their title fight approaches the final round. 'I enjoy racing Steve,' says Reynolds. 'You can pretty much rely on what he's going to be doing, but sometimes you can't, and that's what racing's all about. We all do it – you try and pull off a move and you end up colliding.'

Hislop knows what he's talking about: 'I know, I know, two years ago I did a do or die on John at the Old Hairpin at Donington, taking him and Bayliss out. On the way back to the paddock, John said to me "If there was one guy in Britain I trusted not to wipe me out it was you, I'll just have to watch you now." That was a rare moment of madness for me. John is fast and aggressive but safe – I can almost work out what he's going to do, just like he said about me. We're the old school of riding, we've got a bit of mutual respect here, whereas some of the younger guys just run into you and wipe you out.'

Speaking of young guys, does it worry the pair that there doesn't seem to be much young British talent around? 'I think there are some good guys coming through,' says Reynolds. 'But the problem is that it costs so much to race Superbikes. A team like ours costs a million a year, so you can't afford to take a gamble on some kid.' Hislop reckons that proposed regulations changes for 2002 will make a crucial difference. 'There's already a few guys like Shane Byrne coming on strong, he's mega, but the change to semi-Supersport rules will allow some of those wilder young guys to stick on some slicks and see what they can do.'

Until then it's likely that the Old Gits will have it all their own way. And while they may be approaching their sell-by dates, Hizzy and Reynolds are a long way from being that carton of rank, stinky milk at the back of your fridge.

Epilogue: JR went on to win the 2001 BSB crown after Hizzy got hurt at the dreadful Rockingham racetrack. Hizzy got his revenge the following year, then lost his life in a helicopter crash in July 2003. Reynolds won his third BSB title in 2004, then quit racing the following year after two bone-shattering accidents.

CHAPTER 18

WHO WANTS TO BE A
MILLIONAIRE?

September 2001

**Not Leon Haslam, well not much anyway. Back in the summer
of 2001 the Pocket Rocket was getting paid £150 a week by his
mum for racing a Honda NSR500. Not greedy, our Leon**

Little Leon and me are chatting in his motorhome, parked at the end of
millionaires row in the Brno paddock. A few doors up from Haslam's
humble(ish) abode are those of multi-millionaires and fellow factory
500 riders Max Biaggi, Noriyuki Haga, Valentino Rossi and Loris
Capirossi. This is the poshest part of the paddock, 100 grand Ferraris
squeezed in amongst the rolling palaces, hired drivers spending their
days scrubbing and polishing motorhomes until the chrome hurts
your eyes.

Guys like Biaggi know how to blow their millions – private jets,
Monaco apartments, $600,000 motorhomes and armies of personal
flunkies. So far, 18-year-old Haslam's fiscal concerns aren't quite in the
same league. Son of Ron may ride factory 500s just like the rest of
them, but while his colleagues stash millions in offshore bank accounts,
the Pocket Rocket™ gets by on £150 a week pocket money from his
mum, Ann.

So far the high-roller lifestyles of Haga and Co hold no interest for
Haslam. 'It's nice to look at but for me money's not the thing, so long
as I can get from A to B and do what I like,' he says. 'I give all the
sponsorship to my mum and she pays me £150 a week, plus expenses
and bonuses, like last year I got a car bought for me. I don't go short on
anything.'

A factory 500 star working for the minimum wage, pretty bizarre,
eh? Not really. Haslam's career is a family thing, racing is what the
Haslams do and they're not exactly skint, so money really isn't the
deal. Leon has lived his life in the paddock and on the racetrack, and

his career so far has been a breathless, meteoric rise to the premier division. Not that you'd know it; considering where he's at, he's remarkably down to earth and ungobby.

Haslam was on the GP trail from six weeks old, travelling through Europe with his dad, once the wild man of British racing, who was riding Honda NS500s alongside world title-winning team-mates Freddie Spencer and Marco Lucchinelli in the early 1980s. Leon won his first race, a kids' off-road event at the '87 Argentine GP, when he was four, 'I can remember that, I got a nice little trophy,' and he was national schoolboy motocross champ at 12. A year later he switched to tarmac and walked the British scooter title. That success made him the youngest-ever winner of a national roadrace crown, the first of a whole run of youngest-ever achievements.

The following year, 1998, Haslam graduated to 125s and became the youngest-ever winner of a British championship race. He made his GP debut the same summer to become, you guessed it, the country's youngest-ever GP rider. He contested his first world championship season in 2000, still on 125s, and commenced 2001 riding Honda NSRV500 twins for the Shell Advance squad, scoring points in two of the first seven GPs. But when senior team-mate Chris Walker was sacked after falling out with Aussie team-owner Jeff Hardwick, Haslam was given the Stalker's NSR V4s. The surprise promotion makes him Honda's youngest-ever 500 GP rider and completes a giant leap from 45 horsepower to 190 horsepower in less than a year. Oh yes, and Leon just got voted a top-ten pin-up by teen girls' mag *Bliss*.

All giddy stuff, but racing has also been hard on Haslam. He lost two uncles to the racetrack, broke his left leg when he was 12, his right leg when he was 13 and his first GP season with the shambolic Italjet team was a nightmare that would've finished some riders. He's come a long way, baby, and now he faces the toughest challenge of his career – taming the bikes that ate Walker alive.

Haslam has until the end of 2001 to prove he's worthy of factory support into 2002 and beyond. That's serious pressure for an 18-year-old, especially when the NSR appears less than willing. Walker spent his five months with the NSR crashing his brains out and Haslam didn't get off to a much better start, tumbling out of his first two GPs on the bikes. One can't help but wonder whether Shell's NSRs are cursed...

'My theory of racing was always that if you can ride a bike, you can ride any bike but these things have opened my eyes,' he says, like a teenager who once thought he knew it all. 'They're not normal bikes, they're different, and if you don't understand them, you'll never get on with them. It's not so much riding to go faster, it's sitting down and thinking about it to go faster. I always wondered why Chris was struggling because I know he's a good rider, now I know it's not so much whether you're a good rider, it's more a case of thinking and understanding.

'The Honda is hard because it's reckoned not to turn so well [Haslam's NSRs aren't latest-spec bikes like Valentino Rossi's], and coming from 125s I've always rode heavy on the front, doing all my steering off the throttle, all through the front end. Plus the four has got so much power, so you've got to steer it off the rear more, concentrating on not running so much corner speed and getting it out of the corner. It's totally different for me, I've got to get my head sorted not to go into corners putting all the weight on the front. It's hard; guys like John Kocinski never got on with the Honda 500, but I'm learning the set-up and the style.'

Despite all the scary losing-the-front moments, the NSR does, of course, have its good sides. 'It's a full-on bike, and it's mega spinning it up. First time I rode it, I was spinning it up every corner and loving it. But you've got to be precise. I could get away with a lot more on the 500 twin, you could run wide, square off the corner by spinning it all the way to the white line and fire it out, but if you're a foot off line on the four, the lap's finished. That's what I've learned from looking at Mick Doohan on videos, he was so smooth. When you try harder on the four, you go slower.'

'Mum and dad tried to put me off and get me into football'

So Haslam is discovering that the process of adapting to life in the fastest lane of all isn't easy, even though his whole life has been working towards this moment. 'All I know is that from four years old I've always been riding. We've got a motocross track at my dad's farm and all I can remember is riding every day, from morning till it got dark, spending whole days with my dad working on one aspect of my riding. I wouldn't be where I am now without him. What he gives me now, more than anything, is reassurance. As a newcomer there's always doubts in your mind, so if you've got someone there who understands what you're saying, it gives you so much more confidence.'

But Haslam Senior, who scored nine 500 podium finishes in an eight-year GP career with Honda, Suzuki and Cagiva, hasn't always been behind Leon. 'When I broke my legs doing motocross, mum and dad tried to put me off and get me into football. I nearly lost my right leg in Ireland, I had compartment syndrome like Doohan. My dad knew some good doctors in England, so he rang them and they airlifted me straight home. They cut open the side of the leg and the muscle jumped on to the table; they said I'd have lost the leg in another couple of days. After that I asked my dad for one more go, and that's when he realised I was 100 per cent dedicated, so he's been behind us ever since.'

With or without his dad's help, the final month of the 2001 season will be the most crucial period in Haslam's career so far. And he knows he's got it tough, though 14 years of racing helps him handle the pressure with admirable cool. 'The 500 twin was good for me because there wasn't any pressure. The twin was only capable of so much, and I was already doing that but now I'm on a bike that's capable of much more than I am, at the moment. I've got a lot more to come from myself, simply from more track time, but I've been struggling with fitness. I did a wrist at Le Mans in May, a finger at Assen in June and I dislocated my collarbone in Germany, they've all knocked me. But I'm where I want to be. I turned 18 this summer, Valentino Rossi is 22, so I've got four years on him and I feel confident that I won't be far away with a year of learning. If I can get V4s for next season, and so far Honda Japan seem very interested, I see that as a learning year, then hopefully the year after that I'll be on a four-stroke, then the next season I can go for the title. And if I make it then, I'll be the youngest-ever premier-class champ.' And hell, you never know, he may even get a pay rise, too.

Epilogue: Haslam didn't get the Honda GP job in 2002, everyone knows that. Instead he came home to race BSB and WSB.

CHAPTER 19

HANGIN' WITH HAGA

November 2001

Noriyuki Haga may have flunked his debut 500 season in 2001 but the so-called Sultan of Slide still rocked as a super-cool paddock dude when I caught up with him in his Liberace-style motorhome

I never thought my life would come to this. It's race morning at the 2001 Valencia GP and we're huddled in a paddock hospitality unit haggling over the price of laydeez. Things are starting to get seriously embarrassing. We want four and we're ready to pay them fifty quid each for ten minutes work. Seems like a fair deal to us, and the girls seem up for it, until their screaming harpy of a pimp sticks her nose into the deal.

She's not a nice lady and she's not being reasonable, at all. She wants more than her pound of flesh for her girls and she can sense she's got us cornered. The problem is we've only got £250 cash on us and we don't want to make a scene. Eventually she nails us down to two girls for the price of five, or £250 for two for ten minutes. We hand over the cash, feeling seriously fucked over.

But it's not what you think. The girls aren't for us, they're for Noriyuki Haga, and once we've chosen the sweetest two, we walk them over to Haga's motorhome. You can't miss the thing, it's the biggest, baddest in the MotoGP paddock, which is as it should be because Haga-san is the biggest, baddest dude in the paddock.

Haga is racing's Mr Boombastic. While most 21st-century racers stash a good whack of their multi-million earnings into pension funds and investments, Haga prefers to live life for the moment and live it very large indeed. His £450,000 13-metre motorhome packs acres of white leather and a 1300-watt sound system, enough to keep a club-full of pill-heads rocking. And it's the man's love of phat hip hop beats that explains the two young laydeez getting their kit off in the trailer behind his 'home. We're setting up a booty babe shoot for the man, because he's the P Diddy of the paddock, the Roots Manuva of the racetrack: nuff booty, nuff beats, nuff said.

Haga's livin' it large attitude is old skool, a blast from the past when racers counted their days like WW1 soldiers in the trenches. 'Racing life maybe not as long as you expect,' he says. 'So whenever you have money you must spend it, otherwise maybe it will be too late. If you want something and you have the money, buy it. This is racing life. And if you need money, you have to win it, ha ha ha!'

Of course, Haga didn't do much winning in 2001, in fact he did none at all. A year after he'd come within one drugs test of winning the World Supers title on an R7 (nothing fun, just ephedrine, from a cold-cure, he insists), he struggled so badly on his Red Bull Yamaha YZR500 that he pretty much gave up and just rode around. Cynics reckon he backed off because he couldn't be arsed to learn the art of 500 riding, preferring to wait for the factory's more user-friendly YZR-M1 four-stroke GP bike to show, though there's rumours he may even return to Supers.

'Racing life maybe not as long as you expect, so whenever you have money you must spend it, otherwise maybe it will be too late'

For a man who needs to enjoy his racing, the 2001 season must've been tough. But what's more important to Haga, winning or having fun? That may sound like a daft question to ask a pro-racer, but years back I asked Kevin Schwantz what meant more, winning the 500 world title (which he hadn't done at that point) or making wads of cash. 'About the same,' he answered, which was weird: I always thought winning had to be the main deal. Haga is the same. 'For me, first priority is enjoyment. For sure it's important to win, but first priority is to enjoy racing.' And what about the money? 'Money depends on results, so if I get a lot of money it means I am winning, ha ha ha.'

Haga spends most of this interview laughing and cracking jokes; not very Japanese. When we move on to the subject of girls and sex ('Jiggy, jiggy,' in Haga speak), I ask if he's got a girlfriend. 'No, unfortunately I have wife,' he says, slapping me on the shoulder like some downtrodden hubby male-bonding with me at the bar. 'After this race I must go home and make marriage.' At this, his personal assistant nearly falls off his chair, shrieking questions in Japanese. 'No, no, it's joke,' replies Haga. Yeah right, it is. He's not the funniest man in the world but Haga's got to be the Vic Reeves of Japanese GP racers.

Anyway, it's nice to see him in a good mood, because he's spent most of 2001 looking dead miserable, and not only because he's bombed out on results. 'One problem is I don't have so many friends in GP, this is my first time. But everyone so serious, I don't think that's necessary. For sure Superbike paddock is more funny and people more friendly.'

Such is the curse of modern corporate-funded sport – more money equals more pressure equals more stress equals less fun. Football's the same, everything's the same. There are far greater rewards available in GPs than World Supers, so there's no time for charging around getting wrecked on Sunday nights. Haga finds this hard to cope with. 'There's always so much thinking about riding the bike, so there's much tension. If I think too much, for sure coming stressed.'

Haga copes with stress the same way as most normal folk: he gets pissed. Okay, so he's cut down since his pre-2000 fat-boy days, but he still likes a beer and he's happy to front up to his vices. 'Basically I like alcohol, I like drink beer. But now I'm 26 so when I take a lot of beer, next day not possible wake up!' Haga has partied with the legendary Anthony Gobert on occasion, most recently after July's Suzuka Eight Hours, where racing's most renowned pissheads shared a factory R7. Incidentally, it's interesting that Goey and Haga have stopped doing all that crazy colour shit with their hair; as Haga says, they're getting old.

'After race Yamaha make party and we party a bit, but he's unbelievable. I ask him "What alcohol do you drink", and he say (Haga adopts very loud and totally bizarre Asian Ocker accent) "For me always only beer!" He drank about ten litres in four hours, too much! But when he drunk, he very funny, very funny!' [Haga enunciates 'very' like many Japanese who struggle with their Vs and Rs, so it comes out 'belly'.] And what about Haga, does he get funny when pissed up? 'I don't remember!' More guffaws.

Eventually we move on to serious stuff, like why hasn't he ripped up the tarmac in GPs the way he did in Supers? Of course, we already know the answer – an R7 on Dunlops is a cosy armchair ride compared to a 500 on Michelins. As former Supers champ Scott Russell once said: 'You better take your time with 500s or you'll be pulling straw out ya ass and having Dr Costa shoot Novocaine in ya feet.'

Haga likes to ride out of shape, sideways on the brakes, sideways on the throttle and he's not been able to translate that style to the less-forgiving YZR. But he's not keen to go into detail, so he mostly just shrugs and grunts. Asked whether he prefers four-strokes to two-strokes, his eyebrows arch and he replies: 'What is two-stroke? No, basically I like four-stroke. Sometime I like two-stroke but normally four-stroke. I know what is problem but I cannot say, because after there will be problems for me. But for sure Superbike is more easy, more easy to control.'

Haga has also struggled to make the move from Dunlop to Michelin, after eight years on the Anglo-Japanese tyres, but again he avoids detailed questioning. 'I don't know. Yeah, yeah, I think so,' is his only reply to persistent interrogation on the subject. You see, Japanese riders are not renowned for making revelations – they maintain a corporate loyalty way beyond that of most round eyes.

But there's good reason for Haga to keep his lips zipped. Despite his miserable performance during 2001 (mostly qualifying on the third or fourth rows and finishing 10th or worse), Yamaha still rate him as a favoured son, and they'd be mad not to give him a YZR-M1 for 2002 because however shite he is on a 500, he's the bomb on big, lairy four-strokes. There's only one problem. Carlos Checa recently destroyed lap records on the M1 so there's others after this particular 200 horsepower ride and Haga's got to join the queue with Checa, Biaggi and Co.

Not surprisingly he avoids all talk about 2002; indeed we'd been told that this subject was out of bounds. We ask him anyway. 'Maybe I stay house, in Japan.' he replies. 'Maybe my father and mother come to GPs instead.' Thanks Nori, you've been most helpful.

Epilogue: Haga returned to WSB in 2002 and has been there ever since. At the time of writing, however, he still hadn't won the title.

CHAPTER 20

THE BOY WONDER'S
LONGEST INTERVIEW

November 2001

**These days, all media interviews with Valentino Rossi are
restricted to ten minutes, give or take a minute or two for good
behaviour (on the journalist's part). Back at the end of 2001,
soon after he'd wrapped up his first premier-class crown, Rossi
agreed to a one-on-one interview which ended up going on for
an hour, in his team's office within the Sepang paddock. As the
clock ticked, Rossi's white-haired manager Gibo Badioli began
to pace the room impatiently, but Vale was happy chatting, so
Gibo let him be. This might just be Rossi's longest-ever interview
with a non-Italian journalist...**

*You were incredibly dominant throughout 2001, were you surprised by how
many races you won?*
I was surprised to win the first three in a row because I'm usually not
so fast at the start of the season. But we had some very good tests
during the winter, so we arrived at the first three GPs in good shape. I
knew we had the potential to win some races and the world
championship, but I thought it would start more slowly.

Max Biaggi always talks a lot about you having the better bike...
Who? Max who? Ha, ha!

But could you beat him if you were on a Yamaha?
For me, I think yes, because we're not talking about Biaggi winning six
races and me seven, or me scoring just ten points more than him. Of
course, I think my bike is very good. Me, my team and HRC had worked
hard on this bike since October 2000, we did some fantastic work and
we made a fantastic bike, but I also think that I was the fastest rider in
2001, usually. I won 11 races, Biaggi won three and he only won Assen

because the race was stopped early because of rain. And when he won at Le Mans and Sachsenring, his team-mate Carlos Checa was second, so for sure those tracks were not so bad for the Yamaha; at Sachsenring there were five Yamahas in the first six! Sometimes Loris Capirossi also said he'd beat me if he'd had a 2001 NSR like me. He had the old bike this year but I still beat him in 2000 when I was riding the same bike for most of the season. I ended the season second overall, he arrived in seventh.

You seemed to make a big jump forward after the midseason break, which halted Biaggi's title charge; how did you do that?
We had a few better parts from HRC, but it was the team that made the difference because they changed their way of working to suit me. Mick Doohan had a different riding style from me, he didn't use so much corner speed, so he had less of a problem with settings. He used to slide and go, like a real 500 rider. But I came from 250s so I had to change my style to go into corners a little slower and though I learned to understand slide control and started to slide like Mick, I'm still faster in the middle of the corner, not because I'm a better rider, just because I have a different technique. And to ride with this style, using more corner speed, you have to have more accurate settings.

But the team also started working my way. Germany was a very hard race for us and a very bad result [Rossi was seventh, his worst dry-weather result of 2001], but it was also very good because Jeremy [Burgess, Rossi's ex-Doohan crew chief] understood that it was necessary to follow me more and to make more changes. From Germany on he changed a lot and we tried many different things with settings. Before that I would sometimes say I want to try this or that and he would say 'No, for sure it won't work', but now we try everything.

So how did the bike change?
All the suspension settings, to give me more front tyre grip, but most of all the bike now turns better. The Honda 500 had always had a turning problem, it would always run wide; now the bike is better from that point of view.

[At this moment, Rossi's HRC team manager Carlos Fiorani chips in: 'I'm saying this because I know Valentino can't. When Valentino came to 500s, Jeremy would only let him test one or two things at a time, because Mick was like that, Mick would never test more than two or three things at a time. But now Jeremy says that Valentino has an incredible system, he can test many different things at the same time, without getting confused. He has some kind of amazing link system which allows him to think "I like this" and "I don't like this".']

Do you think Max hasn't changed his style from 250s?
Yes, absolutely. Biaggi is a very hard 250 rider, he won four 250 championships, so he's very good on 250s, and of course, he's also very good on 500s. But he never slides the rear, never, you never see him sliding because he uses the front so much. Riding like that it's possible to win three or four races a year, because with that style it's necessary to have the settings 100 per cent correct. When I started 500s I also used the front very much, and I crashed many times because I was using the front too much. Biaggi also uses the front too much.

Does Biaggi's Yamaha YZR have any advantages over your Honda NSR?
Yes, the Yamaha is easier to use than our bike on acceleration, it's easier to open the throttle early because the engine character is softer. We have good braking stability but the Yamaha has a very good corner speed.

You rode your best race of 2001 at Donington, coming from 11th to win; how come you're so good at overtaking?
I'm very used to coming from the back because I've never been a very good starter; it was the same in 125 and 250. Like at Barcelona this year, I started from pole but I was almost last at the first corner because I collided with Alex Crivillé or Sete Gibernau. Maybe other riders would have thought 'Oh fuck, we're lost', but I did the same in the 250 race there in '98. I started from second on the grid, and I'd had a good pace in practice, but I started very bad and I was 20th at the first corner, so it was necessary to stay calm and just go. It's always been quite easy for me to overtake everywhere, but I don't think that's because I'm better than the other guys, just because I try. Many other riders say that it's very hard to overtake at the Sachsenring, okay so it is, but if you try, maybe it's not very hard.

During 2001 the 500 pace was much faster than before, why?
With Michelin's 16.5in rear for sure it's possible to have a faster rhythm all the way through the race. Also, there were three Italians fighting for the championship, so there was lots of rivalry and we all gave 120 per cent to be the fastest. Plus I've always had a good pace in races, so if the others want to chase me and beat me, they've got to push.

During 1999, when I was doing 250s, and during 2000, the 500 pace was sometimes the same as the 250s and I hated that. It's not right that the pace should be the same because 500s have double the horsepower, so it was time to raise the pace. After Mick stopped in early 1999, the 500 pace was very calm and sweet, the lap times were always slower than the lap record.

So if Mick was still racing, could you beat him?
Ha ha! I think I'm now quite good on 500s, but I've seen some of Mick's data readouts and, fuck, he was very fast. It was him that made the difference, not the bike. He was able to make the difference because he'd always been fighting with Rainey, Schwantz, Lawson and Gardner, and when all the 'Old Dogs' stopped, it was easy for him to beat Crivillé, Roberts, Okada and all. If I was to race Mick, I think I could fight with him, but I don't know who would win. Nobody knows, ha ha!

When Biaggi crashed right in front of you at Motegi, for the second time in four races, are you sure you didn't smile?
No, I didn't smile. When Biaggi crashed at Brno and Motegi he was going so quick. I had my mind on other things, like 'Ah, maybe it's possible to overtake him here on the last lap', or 'Here I'm faster, there I'm slower', and when he crashed I thought 'Oh fuck, now it's necessary to change my plan', so it was 'What do I do now?' For sure it was easier to win after he crashed at Brno and Motegi but I didn't smile either time.

Will beating Biaggi to the title change your relationship with him?
It won't change my relationship with him, because we don't have a relationship, ha!

Tell us what happened when you had the punch-up at Catalunya.
What happened wasn't very big and it wasn't important. It was like being at school: 'He started it!', 'No, he started it!', 'No, he started it!' Biaggi

said that I started this fucking shit but it's necessary to think about what happened before. I started the race from last position and I arrived first at the flag, I made the fastest lap and I made a fantastic victory, so why would I want to make all that shit? That's all I'm saying.

Max says you use the rivalry for energy to help you ride faster; do you agree?
When I was racing for the 250 title in 1999 my main rival was Tohru Ukawa but I always knew in my mind that I could beat him. For sure, Biaggi is stronger because he's so fast. To beat me he gave 120 per cent, so the fight was fucking hard. In the past in he never rode the 500 like he did last season, maybe '98 but in '99 and 2000 he wasn't so fast.

In '99, when I was fighting with Ukawa, he had a 40 point lead after my chain broke at Paul Ricard. It was a strange situation because I knew I was faster than him but I knew I couldn't afford one mistake because the gap would go to 60 points and I'd be fucked.

You want to choose between the RCV and NSR for 2002, but do you really think Honda will let you make the choice?
It's a difficult situation but I think it's necessary for me to try the RCV because although Honda think this bike is very much faster than the 500, I'm not so sure. Before I speak any more I think I need to try the RCV again because so far I've only ridden it for eight laps at Suzuka in the rain.

You seem to think the four-stroke won't give you as much riding satisfaction as the 500…
Yes, the satisfaction of riding the 500 is a very, very big motivation for me, because when you're riding the most difficult bike in the world, it's necessary to have a perfect set-up if you're to be able to ride fast, and you've also got to ride perfect all the time. I think it's necessary to have big balls to ride the 500. I think the four-stroke may be faster but for sure it won't give the same sensation.

You have achieved a huge amount of success, and wealth also, but is the price of fame too much?
There is a price, but for sure fame has more good points than bad. The first bad thing is the stress. Now I can't go anywhere in the world without being recognised. Very many people recognise me and want

'He's very clever, he's sly, foxy. On the track he's pretty vicious!' Valentino Rossi's rivals and pit-lane mates reveal what makes him so great. Chapter 53 (Gold and Goose)

ABOVE: *Oxley and team-mate Gilbert Roy at the 1989 Suzuka Eight Hours, racing with Rainey, Schwantz, Gardner and Doohan. Well, kind of. See chapter 1. (Gold and Goose)*

BELOW: *'Everyone was shouting and cheering, they all got sucked along by the Norton' – clever Trevor Nation won British hearts and minds and lots of races on Britain's awesome rotary superbike. See chapter 44. (Phil Masters)*

'If the tyre wasn't spinning, I didn't feel right.' Three-time 500 king Wayne Rainey devastated rivals with his mastery of the rear-tyre slide. He tells us how, chapter 29. (Gold and Goose)

ABOVE: 'When people talk about riders losing confidence it's just that scary feeling affecting you, it's chemicals in your brain.' The lowdown on crashing, chapter 35. (Gold and Goose)

BELOW: 'Mainlining the greatest drug known to mankind' – Oxley gets high at Ballaugh Bridge on his way to the first 100mph 250 proddie TT lap in 1986. See chapter 42. (Phil Masters)

ABOVE: *King Kenny Roberts, Randy Mamola and a can of Watneys Pale Ale. A winning combination in 1980. Roberts talks sliding in chapter 29. Mamola talks failure in chapter 25. (emap)*

BELOW: *'Makes an NSR500 feel like a bag of nails.' Oxley rides Rossi's MotoGP-winning Honda RC211V, the greatest bike of MotoGP's 990cc era. See chapter 27. (Waldemar da Rin)*

ABOVE: *'Barry Sheene wasn't merely a world-title-winning bike racer, he was a 1970s icon along with Pele, Muhammad Ali, George Best and James Hunt.' Bazza, the coolest rider ever, chapter 34. (emap)*

BELOW: *'We behaved disgracefully, getting drunk, crashing hire cars and devising ever more mendacious ways of dealing with rivals.' The UK team at the '83 Pro-Am Euro final: Niall Mackenzie, Graham Cannell, Kenny Irons, Oxley and Steve Chambers. See chapter 51. (Phil Masters)*

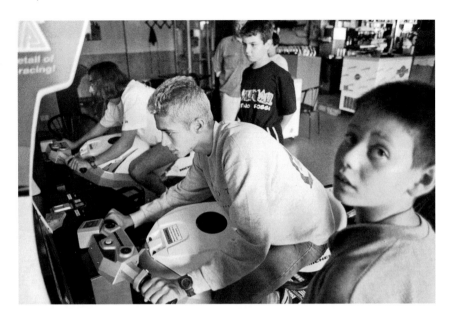

ABOVE: *'After the racing is finished he's impossible to find, no one knows where he goes, maybe he's in a disco with some friends.' Or down the local amusements. The year that changed Rossi, chapter 37. (Claudio Vitale)*

BELOW: *'We had high 'bars cos proddie racing was big at home – all clanging handlebars, scraping side covers and lots of crashes, that's what the audience liked.' Graeme Crosby hassles Ron Haslam in '79. See chapter 45. (emap)*

ABOVE: 'It probably takes a minute and a half to do a six-mile run, but you cover the last mile in about ten seconds.' Don Vesco slips into the tube for another 300mph ride on the Bonneville salt flats, chapter 10. (emap)

BELOW: 'The acceleration paralyses my senses which struggle to cope with the speed at which the scenery turns to a blur.' Oxley rides Honda's '89 NSR500, the scariest race bike ever built. See chapter 2. (Koichi Ohtani)

autographs and photos. The situation is a little better in London, but now I've won the 500 championship, Italy is a nightmare, a nightmare. I will never be able to live a normal life there, never.

You seem to cope very well with fame, especially the attention you get from the media.
Until 2001 I was most famous when I started 125s because I was new, and I started to win very much and I made some big shows at the end of races. At that time my popularity increased and it changed my life, because before then I was normal! Now I don't know when I'll dare to return to Italy. But fame affects you in different ways; when you have many fans waiting outside your motorhome who follow you like a slipstream, yes, it's heavy, but it's good. But it's worse with the Italian journalists because they only follow me for one reason, they're waiting for a mistake. If I say one word wrong or if I crash, it's 'Ah fuck, he's stupid.'

'Rossi won very many 125 races in 1997 but now he makes mistakes, he's stupid'

After you won the 125 title, you went to 250s and your popularity slipped, why?
When I started 250s my results were, well, not shit, but during the first half of the season I only won one race. I made some mistakes, had some crashes and sometimes I finished behind Tetsuya Harada and Capirossi, who were also riding Aprilias. I think that was normal because Harada and Capirossi had ridden 250s for many years, while it was my first season, so it was difficult to beat them with so little experience.

But very many people, who I thought were my friends, said 'Ah, 250s aren't the same as 125s. Rossi won very many 125 races in 1997 but now he makes mistakes, he's stupid'. This was really bad for me, but also really good because I found out who my real friends were. Before then I thought I had more friends than I actually did.

So who are your real friends, celebrities or old mates?
For sure, in my position I know some famous people, singers, actors and whenever I'm in Milano or Roma, I see these people and say 'Ciao!' But my best friends are old friends. We have a group of eight or nine people who have been friends for 15 or 20 years, since pre-school.

You seemed less open and more serious during 2001, have you changed?
The way you see things, your view of the world, changes between the age of 18 and 22. I'm older now, so I think I understand more, and for sure my life has changed. Whenever I leave my motorhome there are always very many people and unfortunately I don't have enough time to do every autograph and photo because we have work to do. If I never say stop, I don't get a minute to myself.

When you're 16 or 17 you don't have problems, unless it's something really big like family problems. Life is different when you're young, you only think about having fun. All that changes when you get more responsibilities, especially in my case because I have so much to do.

Tell us about your alter egos: Rossifumi, Valentinik and the Doctor…
Before I started racing in the world championship I was a big fan of GP racing, it was my passion. I watched all the races on TV, knew all the riders' numbers, all their helmet design, the whole circus. Rossifumi was for Norifumi Abe because I really liked him and all the Japanese riders.

We changed to Valentinik in 1999 because we needed a superhero to come back from the bad situation of '98. At the end of '98 I changed my riding style a little, won the last four races and became very strong on the 250. After that I prepared to win the championship in '99, so we chose this superhero based on an Italian comic hero called Paparinik. Paparino is Donald Duck in Italian and Walt Disney has a duck superhero called Paparinik, who wears a mask and a cape, but he's not like Superman, he's a little bit unlucky, he makes some mistakes, some casinos [Italian for chaos], but at the end of every story he's always the superhero. Paparino becomes a superhero and becomes Paparinik, so Valentino became a superhero and became Valentinik!

After that we changed to the Doctor for 2001 because with 500s you don't need a superhero, you need to be quiet, calm and thoughtful, more like a doctor. Also, because in Italy there are very many doctors called Dr Rossi, so I became Dr Rossi.

So what's next?
For 2002 we stay with the doctor for sure, and after that I don't know, we've no ideas yet.

And what do the words 'Tribu dei Chihuahua' on your visor mean?
It means 'The Chihuahua Tribe'. The Chihuahua were a tribe of North American Indians, and our gang of friends is called the 'Tribu dei Chihuahua'!

And WLF on the collar of your leathers?
WLF stands for 'Viva La Figa' which means 'Long Live Pussy'!

Tell us how your post-race victory celebrations started.
Usually in a bar in Tavullia at two in the morning! They're just a game, just some fun with my fan club. When I started winning GPs, we decided we should try to make some big fun because back then all the riders were very, very serious. We just wanted to do something new to show the big emotion of winning races.

So why did they finish?
Because I don't think a lot of people really understood the whole thing, so they don't deserve it. It's like last June at Mugello, we had my bikes in that Hawaiian paint scheme, they looked great. But when I crashed out of the race some people said I'd only crashed because I'd been up all night painting the bikes!

In '98 at Mugello I finished second and arrived on the podium wearing beach gear and people said bad things. It's like if you win every race of your career you're a genius, but if you finish second you're a fucking clown, or stupid! So I decided it was better to stop all this and just wave like other riders, then have a big party on Sunday night with my real friends.

The problem with many journalists who write bad things is that they are too conformist, so if you make a rude sign for fun, you're a piece of shit, or a criminal, so you should go to jail. I don't understand all that.

Where did the Hawaiian paintjob come from?
It was an old idea. In '99 we had two different ideas for my Mugello paintjob – the 1970s-style Valentinik peace and love thing, which is what we used, and the Hawaiian thing. So we already had the idea, and I think it was a very, very beautiful bike.

Tell us about your sleeping habits, JB has had to wake you a few times for practice…

I never go to bed before one o'clock, and there's no limit on when I go to bed, but even when I go to sleep very late I always wake up at 8.30, though when I do wake up I always have a big confusion for the first five minutes, then after that I remember: 'Oh fuck, I'm at world grand prix!' So I have a shower and then I'm okay. I never get up too close to riding time because the 500 is a dangerous bike so it's necessary to be awake when you climb aboard. Maybe in the afternoon after practice at four or five o'clock I'll sleep for another hour.

How much time do you spend in London now?

Most of the time. I have very many Italian friends there, who work in restaurants. There's one near my home, all the chefs and waiters are Italian, and when they finish work we go dancing, to clubs like China White.

What's the girl situation?

I split up with Eliana last October, so I've been single for a year, one year of freedom, ha!

You're 22 years old and you've already won everything in bikes; how are you going to stay interested?

Now we have a new fight with the four-stroke. It's like starting from zero, like changing classes again. But if I win with the four-stroke maybe it will be necessary to change sport. I know myself very well, and once I've won, I don't find it very interesting to stay on to win again. Breaking records isn't important to me. Once I've won the 250, I've won it, same with 500. Now I have the four-stroke, which is a new bike to develop, a bit like having a baby. If we win with the RCV, it will be very satisfying. And after that, bo, I don't know…

What about rally driving?

I like driving cars very much. My first dream when I was young was to become a car racer. I started racing in karts because I very much liked Formula One, Senna, Prost and Mansell, I was a big fan, so I started go-kart racing. I also started riding minibikes, but that was just for fun. But the problem with go-karts is that they cost too much money. Just to do the Italian championship needed very much money, so I said to my father, 'Maybe it's better we race with the bike,' and he say 'Ah, bo, really?' I say 'Yes, so is it possible we try a bike?' He said 'Yes,' so we started minibike racing in '92.

Maybe you should retire and become an actor, like Agostini did?
I think no! I like driving cars very much so maybe that will be the new fight. After bikes, rallying is my passion. But to say I'll do the world rally championship after bikes is unreal, because, fuck, you have people who've been racing rallies for 25 years, while I'll be starting from zero. I don't know if I can be fast enough. Yes, I'm quite good because my father has raced rallies for the last ten years and I sometimes go with him, so I understand it a little, and I'm quite fast with a WRC car like Subaru or Toyota. I did a Michelin championship in the Canary Islands at the end of 2000 and I fought with Panisi, who won a round of the WRC this season, but I lost five or six seconds to him in two minutes, so I'm not the best in the world, and it won't be very easy to change sports.

I guess your other choice is a very, very long retirement.
Yes, for now I have something to do here, though I don't know how long for. The problem is that I'll be finished by the time I'm 30. And that's too long a retirement, so it will be necessary to have something new to do.

CHAPTER 21

THE INSIDE STORY OF THE MOST EXOTIC GP BIKE IN HISTORY

June 2002

Four-strokes returned to GP racing in 2002, 21 years after the last four-stroke contested the premier 500 world championship. That bike was Honda's fabled oval-piston NR500, and this is its story

Four-strokes took over GP racing at the start of 2002, when new regulations allowed 990cc four-strokes to take on the 500 two-strokes that had dominated for so long. Cynics viewed this transformation as a final victory for Honda, the four-stroke fans who had been trying to make GPs a four-stroke deal for 25 years.

When Honda first contested the world championships in the 1960s, four-strokes were king, but as the strokers got up to speed, Honda quit and stayed out of GPs for a dozen years. When they returned in 1979, they did so with a four-stroke, even though two-strokes were all-dominant by then. The wondrously exotic oval-piston, 32-valve NR500 raced for four years, cost Honda billions of yen and never scored a single world championship point, though it did win a couple of low-key national events. Nevertheless Honda rated the project a success, because it taught them plenty about four-stroke technology, much of which will help them in the new four-stroke GP era.

This is the story of Honda's NR500 as told by five people close to the project – Youichi Oguma, Seiki Ishii, Gerald Davison, Mick Grant and Ron Haslam – and an outsider – GP journalist Mick Woollett.

Oguma was one of Honda's most charismatic warlords and the man who masterminded the NR's first win in a low-key Japanese race. He always said what he thought. Engineer Ishii started out working on the NR's ultra-complex carbs before becoming HRC team manager in the mid-1990s, looking after NSR250s and 500s.

Davison was team manager of the Honda International Racing Company and the man who oversaw much of the NR saga, liaising between Honda's engineers and their riders, like Grant, a TT expert and top GP rider of the time. Grant spent two fruitless years developing and racing the NR before youngsters Freddie Spencer and Haslam had a go. Haslam was on his way up the racing ladder when Honda gave him the NR; he later went on to race the factory's NS and NSR500 two-strokes.

Woollett was a doyen of 1960s and 1970s GP journalism, an old-school writer who could always see through the PR fog.

Gerald Davison 'Soichiro Honda used to hate two-strokes; if he saw a two-stroke engine in R&D, the engineers would tell him it was a lawnmower engine. Of course, Honda wanted to get back into GPs, we'd been out too long and we were losing commercial ground to Yamaha, but the NR was conceived right at the top of the company by people who weren't in touch. The passion within Honda was four-stroke but these people had no grasp of the gap between two-stroke and four-stroke technology, they simply believed that Honda could win by putting enough muscle into it. What we ended up doing was like trying to put a man on the moon.

'I was in Japan for the press launch of the CBX1000 six. I was pretty close to Kawashima (team manager of Honda's original TT team in 1959 and then president of Honda Motor) and he sent for me, asking me to write a speech for the press. We got well into it and then he said he wanted to announce that Honda would return to GP racing, with a four-stroke. I was shocked but he thought it was funny that he'd told me in this way. Then he told me I was going to organise the whole thing.'

Mick Grant 'When Gerald was trying to get me to sign a contract he told me they'd got some radical ideas which frightened me a little. Like they'd use liquid nitrogen to cool the motor so they wouldn't have radiators, and they'd use a lot of ceramics, which were almost unheard of at the time.'

Gerald Davison 'The management said "We're going back into racing and we don't want anyone old, this project will help young engineers cut their teeth". That was a miscalculation because there was no one within the NR group with any racing experience, it was all green. Silly mistakes were made but no matter how dark things got, no one ever asked for advice from people like Michihiko Aika (the engineer who masterminded Honda's 1960s GP successes).'

Mick Woollett 'I wrote at that time: "What are they doing?" They didn't seem to realise that things had moved. I didn't see how it could possibly succeed against the latest two-strokes but I never expected them to fail quite so totally or dramatically. The thing they built in '79 wasn't even as good as the '76 MV Agusta (the last four-stroke to win a GP, at a wet Nurburgring in '76), it was slower and it didn't handle half as well. That first year it had 16-inch wheels, a funny frame and weird forks. The next year all that was gone, it had a British-made Maxton frame, 18-inch wheels and ordinary forks. It was all just an engineering exercise.'

Mick Grant 'When I arrived at Honda R&D I went into the workshop and it all looked so convincing, I couldn't believe it wasn't going to work. But when I first rode it the engine wouldn't tick over at less than 7000rpm because there was no flywheel. The power started about 12,500 and though it'd run on to 21,000, it was all done by 17 five. And it felt slow, very much so. I was four seconds off the Suzuka record and I was riding as well as I'd ever done in my life. The engineers couldn't understand why it wasn't going quicker, they almost didn't want to grasp the reality.

'The handling wasn't a big problem, but with less than 100 horsepower it wasn't going to be. The main worry was the aluminium monocoque chassis, it kept cracking. I'd do three laps, come in and have it welded, then another four laps and the same again. It didn't make for happy motoring! The monocoque was a great idea, it would've worked well in carbon fibre. There were lots of good ideas but they jumped in too early; they should've kept it under wraps and kept testing.'

Mick Woollett 'We all just fell about laughing when the bike made its debut at the British GP. It was such an absolute total balls-up, the only reason they got on the grid was that someone pulled out. Then poor old Granty fell arse over head at the first bend and the bike burst into flames! A lot of people hated Honda because they always had the most money, though we were delighted they'd come back into racing. It was good to see them get beaten and the NR kept us amused for a few years.'

Mick Grant 'At Silverstone we went out for first practice with the 125s and 250s and there were TZ250s pulling away down the straights. The added problem was that Mr Honda was there, so the pressure on the engineers must've been huge.

'It wasn't so bad for me because I knew I was riding good. As a racer, you can win and be pissed off because you've not ridden your best, and you can come away from a race with a lower placing and be happy because you rode 100 per cent.

'We'd never have finished Silverstone because – and I don't know if I should say this – the bikes didn't have enough fuel in them because Honda didn't want to finish last. The NR was a bastard to start and when I leapt on, I was on the back of the thing and it wheelied, pumping oil on to the rear tyre, so when I laid it into the first corner, down I went. I was disappointed but it wasn't like I thought I was going to win. I never said "let the bastard burn!" As a racer you've got to believe in what you're riding – if you don't you can't give your best. My two years with the NR were great, it was such an experience. People called it the "Never Ready" but I never thought the bike was a joke.'

Gerald Davison 'At GPs we had two teams to look after the bikes, one that worked at the track during the day and another that worked away from the track, in secret, rebuilding engines. These Japanese engineers slept during the day and spent all night rebuilding the motors because we couldn't run them one day and rely on them the next. Build-time for each motor was something like eight to ten hours.

'We took some NR parts to a Buddhist temple for blessing, it was pretty spectacular, with dancing girls and music'

'By mid-1980 it was obvious we needed to do something drastic. In Japan I told Irimajiri (NR engineer) that the project was more like a school for engineers than a race team. Half joking, I said he should send the team to a temple and tell them to reflect on what they're trying to do. The very next day he did just that! A fleet of minibuses took us to a Buddhist temple and we took along some bike bits for blessing. We arrived at this beautiful place up a forest-clad mountain, with dancing girls and music. It was pretty spectacular. The Japanese are quite ambivalent about religion. If they're in a fix they go to a temple and say a prayer; you never know, it might work. I had this vision of a new dimension to racing – we'd turn up on the grid with a Buddhist monk, while some Italian team might have a papal representative. I suppose the temple visit might have made the people feel better, because the constant struggle was making some of the engineers closest to the project look ill.'

Youichi Oguma 'In 1981 I was working on Honda streetbike projects when suddenly my boss says you must help NR. I was concerned because the NR wasn't doing well for Honda. I made big voice to my bosses: "The NR idea is stupid, impossible!" But they put me in charge for a Suzuka national race, saying that if I made the bike win, I could go back to street projects. We made clever fuel-stop strategy for Suzuka and won the race but the bosses said I must stay with the race team.'

Mick Woollett 'The whole oval piston thing was so wrong, they should've thought about it for one minute and discarded the idea. It's a horrible concept: long pistons with two con rods each, all that friction and rocking motions too. All the bloody thing could do was scratch around with the also-rans on RG500s, then in 1981 they put the best rider in the world on it. Freddie Spencer rode his guts out at Silverstone, got up to fifth, then it blew!'

Seiki Ishii 'I came to Europe with the NR in 1980, working on carburettor settings and engine development. My best memory was doing a non-championship race at Laguna Seca in 1981. Freddie Spencer was racing the NR and Kenny Roberts his TZ750. They had a big fight in the heat race and Freddie won. They had clutch start for this race but in those days GPs were push starts, the NR was not easy to push start. My other good memory was sitting in the forest at Spa, watching Ron Haslam ride the NR in the 1982 Belgian GP. He got 11th, just one place outside the points.'

Ron Haslam 'Kork Ballington was in front of me at Spa and he cut the chicane. He should've had so many seconds added for that but we were too late with our official protest. We should've been tenth and that would've given the NR its first point. Honda were disappointed but not too much because they'd had higher hopes for the bike, they'd wanted it to win GPs. The bike weren't bad by then – it had more speed than the best privateer 500s but you still couldn't get near the factory bikes.'

Seiki Ishii 'I still believe the NR could've won GPs; by 1982 it was producing 130 horsepower. If we could have solved durability, we could've improved performance. The main problems were valves and piston rings. Nowadays that wouldn't be a problem because materials are better. Also, if GPs had been clutch starts, I think it would've been easier to win races. Of course, the results were not satisfying but Honda learned so much. The slipper clutch [used in most modern superbikes] came from the NR, plus we learned about V4 technology, gear cam train, carbon brakes and so on.'

Ron Haslam 'I really enjoyed the bike. Even so, when I first rode it we were getting a lot of blow-ups and that gave me a few panics because it threw oil on to the rear tyre. The motor would always chuck its oil out and then blow, so we cured that in the simplest way by putting the breather where I could see it, inside the screen. If I saw oil, I'd kill the motor, and we made a lot more progress that way because we didn't blow so many engines.'

Youichi Oguma 'I told my bosses again that the NR had no potential. We'd spent over three years of development budget and still couldn't beat the two-strokes. I began to look at Honda's two-stroke motocrossers. Honda was dominating motocross and I wanted that technology. Honda sent me to a GP and I confirmed what we needed, timing other bikes with stopwatch, taking photos and so on. My report said it was impossible to win with the NR, that if we continued, we'd have to do hara-kiri (Japanese ritual disembowelment). My report exploded at Honda like a terrorist bomb. Then the bosses ordered Miyakoshi (the engineer in charge of Honda's motocross programme) to help the roadrace department. We went to a drinking club together and drank sake, discussing what kind of two-stroke engine we needed. We both chose V3 because other types were too heavy or complex. We worked very fast so the two-stroke NS500 could replace the NR. This bike won Honda's first 500 title in '83 with Freddie Spencer.'

Gerald Davison 'After the NR project folded I was taking care of Honda's interests at the FIM, trying to get the FIM to agree to a four-stroke GP formula. All they'd agree to was turbocharging at half capacity, which wasn't the ideal solution for Honda but their engineers gave it a try anyway. In '85 they built an NR250 turbo twin which made something like 150 horsepower. They were determined to use an oval piston bike but the turbo was never raced. And yet with four-strokes coming back to GPs I'd say the oval piston idea still has tremendous potential.'

CHAPTER 22

QUIET STORM FROM
THE WEST

July 2002

**John Hopkins came from nowhere to race a Yamaha YZR500 in
the inaugural MotoGP championship in 2002. Even Yamaha had
never heard of the teenager from SoCal, but things didn't stay
that way for long**

Acclaiming future world champions is always a risky business. Fifteen
years ago, when I was editor of *Performance Bikes* magazine, we ran a
centre spread of up-and-coming Aussie talent Kevin Magee, the caption
proclaiming 'One day this man will be world champion'. The likeable
youngster had just won his first GP – beating Eddie Lawson, Wayne
Rainey and others in one of his first 500 rides – and it seemed he was
so gifted that it could only be a matter of time before he won a world
title. But racing isn't so simple, Magoo ran into a few issues that stopped
him getting it together.

But we never learn. Early in 2002 I named Daijiro Kato as the man most
feared by Valentino Rossi. I interviewed him a couple of weeks after he'd
harried Rossi at Jerez, but life went pear-shaped for the little Japanese at
the next few GPs, he started crashing his NSR500 rather too often. This
seemed like the usual 500 learning curve of a 250 genius – fast out of the
blocks, then faster, then crash, crash, crash. (In fact, deeper investigation
revealed that HRC had given Kato some wacky NSR engine spec that
proved impossible to tame.) Only time will tell if Kato can pick up the
pieces, get his confidence back and start rattling Rossi once again.

Which brings us, by a rather circuitous route, to John Hopkins. This
American teenager, born of British blood, has been stealthily working
his way towards the front of the MotoGP pack since scoring points first
time out at Suzuka in April 2002 (after two race crashes, no less). He's
been learning quietly, gaining confidence and getting quicker little by
little. This is the only way to do it in GP racing's big class – you walk

before you run or else you're taking giant, bone-crunching leaps through the air. By Donington in July, Hopper was quick enough to make the provisional front row and after eight races he was the only man apart from Rossi to have scored points each time out. For a 19-year-old riding 500s for the first time around tracks he's never seen before, that's seriously impressive stuff.

Hopkins had slipped into GPs at the start of 2002 almost unnoticed. While the racing world whipped itself into a froth about the new MotoGP four-strokes, Red Bull Yamaha WCM (for World Championship Motorsports) had signed this unknown kid who'd been thrashing GSX-R1000s around the States. Even Yamaha, who have to sanction Red Bull's signings, were wondering if WCM race director Peter Clifford had taken leave of his senses. Hopper had won the 2001 American Formula Xtreme crown, but so what?

Clifford, a former bike journalist, and one of the few GP team bosses prepared to take risks in nurturing new talent (most of the paddock thought Clifford was nuts when he signed Hopper's Red Bull team-mate Garry McCoy in 1999), had given the teenager a couple of runs on his YZR500s during 2000 and 2001, following a tip-off from American bike journalist John Ulrich, who'd spotted Hopkins before he'd even hit his teens. Ulrich, by the way, is the guy who recommended a certain Kevin Schwantz to Yoshimura Suzuki way back in 1984…

So who is John Hopkins? He sounds American but that SoCal drawl disguises 100 per cent Limey blood coursing through his veins, his parents hailing from Acton, a not particularly salubrious west London suburb. His dad, who died from lung cancer when Hopper was 12, was well into bikes and even raced the TT before heading west. The family emigrated to the States in the mid-1970s, settling down in Ramona, close to the Mexico border, and pretty soon dad was hooning around the desert on dirt bikes. Hopper joined him at the age of three. 'First time I ever rode a motorcycle was in the desert, my dad figured he'd put me on this little Honda 70 because I was already riding my bicycle pretty well, hittin' little ramps, jumpin' off kerbs and stuff. Every weekend we'd head out into the desert with a van full of bikes, camping, having barbecues, hanging out with family and friends.'

Pretty soon, of course, Hopper wanted to do more than just thrash through the dunes. 'We were watching one of my dad's buddies race motocross at Ascot and I saw some kids racing PW50s, so I asked my dad "Can I do that? Can I race?" We were out there the next Friday and my whole life has been motorcycles ever since.'

Hopkins started motocross, dreaming of becoming a Supercross pro, but got sidetracked during an Oklahoma national. 'They had this go-kart track where they were running YSR50 races and they were letting kids ride around on their PW50s. Being a roadracer, my dad thought it'd be good for me. It was kinda funny because everyone was riding their PWs on dirt-track tyres and I was on knobbies, I did four races and ended up pulling away and lapping up to second place every time; it just came natural to me. But until I was 11 tarmac was just my hobby, my real thing was motocross.'

His moment of awakening came at Willow Springs, when a family friend offered him a run on a Honda RS125 GP bike. 'That's what changed my whole perspective, it was the thrill of everything – the handling of the bike and doing the straightaway – that just made me focus on roadracing, and from then on I was looking at Schwantz and Rainey.'

But Hopkins was still too young for the real hard stuff. Until he was 14 he had to make do with YSR racing and a once-a-month track-day thrash aboard the RS125. He'd already graduated to 250s at the age of 15 when a rash of blow-ups persuaded him to return to motocross. 'I got frustrated, I said 'I'm done with this, this isn't getting me anywhere, I'm gonna concentrate on motocross'. That's when John Ulrich gave me a call and asked me if I wanted to try one of his GSX-R600s. The bike was strange, it was like riding a big boat after what I'd ridden.' So Ulrich got him a start in the Aprilia Cup for hotted-up RS250 streetbikes and Hopper won the '99 title at 16. 'The bonus was a ticket to Italy, to go test a GP 125, plus a few days vacation in Florence, Rome and Venice; that was definitely a mind-changing deal.'

'Next thing I know I'm shooting through the air, looking down at the ground thinking, "all right, why did this happen?"'

After that he raced GSX-R600s and 750s for Ulrich's outfit, winning the 2000 Supersport 750 title and shifting up to Formula Xtreme for 2001, riding a 185 horsepower GSX-R thou. 'From there the thrill just started gaining and gaining and we ended up getting the championship. The 1000 was a lot of fun, it definitely got me familiar with the speed but without the handling and acceleration of the 500.'

So how do you compare riding the 1000 and the 500?
With the 500 you've got to be a lot more focused, tons more focused, a lot more determined and a lot more physically fit. It was fun slidin' around on the 1000, backin' it into corners, comin' out and just lightin' it up. I had a couple of samples of the asphalt when I first started riding it, so you gotta learn your limits as fast as possible. It takes longer to learn the limit of the 500, in fact it's almost like they have no limits. On the 1000 you can have big slides, huge slides, but mostly you can recover, with the 500 you make a mistake and you're not gonna recover. If it steps out too far, it's gonna bite you, it's gonna get you hard.

The 1000 is more wobbly, so you get early warnings?
Yeah, I had a big one on the 500, testing at Valencia. I hadn't been sliding it, I was just startin' to learn to slide it. I'm getting on it out of a right-hander and the slide I had would've been just a minor tankslapper on the 1000, nothing big at all, so I kept it sliding, I didn't want to let off the gas, but then I found myself running all the way out to the kerb, so I thought I better back it off a little. The second I back it off, next thing I know I'm shooting through the air, looking down at the ground thinking 'all right, why did this happen? Okay this is gonna hurt'.

Has your team been telling you to take it easy?
That's always been my kinda approach, but Peter has definitely encouraged that. He says 'just take it easy, take it at you own pace, this is just a learning year, ride smooth, step it up little by little every weekend', and that's when the results come.

You've been consistent and running with some good guys; are you surprised?
Not surprised, just really happy with the way everything's been going. At the beginning of the year I was just thinking about finishes, I didn't want to push myself too hard. I don't want to try and take too big steps, you know, just a slight incline, just keep goin' up and up and up, make a couple of big steps here and there, a couple of times just little steps. I just want to keep improving until I get up to the top.

What are the big things you've learned this year?
Just riding ability and working with the team, getting to know them

good, plus the team is learning what I like done to the bike, my riding style and stuff.

Riding 500s is all in the set-up; how are you finding that?
To me, that's when you get lost. When I first started working with the team, I'd go out and ride, then we'd change it and I'd end up getting lost. If there's not a problem, to me there's no point in changing it, so now they've gotten to work with that, they come up with a base setting, then I go out and ride it, then if I do have a problem, I let them know. I tell them I'm pushing the front through some corner and they're pretty good at fixing that. I'd say I've gotten better the less changes we make to the bike.

So it's a case of getting used to the set-up, so you can predict what's going to happen?
Yeah, you're not gonna get the same feelin' out of the bike if you keep changing it, especially when you're havin' to learn the circuits, learn the tyres and everything about the bike.

What have you learned about riding?
I've had to adapt to a completely new style this year. I'm finding that one of my strong points compared to other riders is braking. I'm getting into the corners really good. I think that comes from motocross, I was always one of the best getting into the corners, I used quite a bit of front brake in motocross, though a lot more rear brake. It's kinda funny because I don't use any rear brake whatsoever on the 500, not in the wet either. The team finds that strange.

How do you get the bike settled into turns?
I guess I've got a good body set-up, a good body language to keep the rear kinda okay. I've had to work on my riding style to keep the bike settled because I'd rather not touch the rear brake.

What's the biggest buzz of the 500?
First, I'd have to say the competition, then the speed-to-weight ratio, just how fast it gets goin'. And when you're riding the thing fast it's like you're always on the edge, you're always right there. When you're riding a good lap it's a very fine line between keepin' it up and throwin'

it down. The thrill of that the whole time you're riding the thing is just really good – you've got it right there on the edge.

How do your lap times compare to last year's 500 times?
We'd have ended up bein' on pole at Barcelona last year, and my race time would've put me on the podium.

You were 18 on your GP debut, you must've thought you were about to wake up from a dream?
Suzuka was the biggest. I'm sittin' there thinking 'Oh man, I'm gonna be on the grid with these guys I've only seen on TV, I've never even met them in person'. It was a bit of a wakeup call, but once I started doing competitive times, within a couple of seconds of them, I started realising, you know, that they're just normal people, just like I am, maybe just a little more experienced. I had to go out and learn from them, use their experience to my advantage, learn from what they got.

Do you do a lot of following?
Yeah, quite a bit. I never wait out on the track, but I'm always trying to get behind someone and follow them and get around them, stuff like that.

So you're always having a go too?
Yeah, always havin' a go with them.

Do you ever wonder how it'd feel if you took out Rossi or Biaggi?
(Looks perplexed) It doesn't affect me, I mean they're racing on the same track as I am. They may be a little more well known but I'm out there racing, same as they are.

Are you surprised by how quick you got to GPs?
GPs are where I always wanted to be, ever since I started roadracing. Superbike was never a thing for me, I just had to get on a four-stroke back home to get where I am now. That was always my goal; I never even watched Superbikes on TV, always GPs.

So who was your hero, Schwantz or Rainey?
I was going for Schwantz, always rootin' for Schwantz. I didn't know too much about it, I just liked his riding style.

You remind us of Schwantz, you're excited by everything...
Oh yeah, I'm definitely excited about it, I'm not a quiet person. Schwantz was definitely my hero, then it was Doohan, just from watching his style and his ability to go out and win championship after championship. I found that pretty amazing.

Who's the best guy out there, who's amazed you most?
I mean, I definitely don't want to look up to any of them but I'd have to say Garry [McCoy], just for his riding style. I find that most impressive out of everything, it's just so different, it doesn't seem like top-level roadracing. Last winter when I first started testing properly with the team I followed him a lot at Sepang, but his lines are so much different from what I run. His slides take him all the way out to the edge of the track, where I like keeping it pretty much in line, drivin' it out. I hold it a little bit tighter, he kinda swings it out a lot wider with his sliding and then he kinda shoots back.

It looks like time wasting...
But it works out.

Are you looking forward to getting on four-stroke in 2003?
I've been really lucky to get one of the last rides on a 500, so I'm takin' advantage of that. That was my whole goal and I just made it on to one, so I'm really happy about that. But I think it's gonna be a really good thing to have a four-stroke next year, because I can combine my four-stroke experience from back home with my 500 experience and fill it all into the MotoGP bike. And with the knowledge of the tracks and the knowledge of the riders around me, I think it's gonna be really good. And, depending on what bike it is, I think it could be quite a bit easier to ride.

What's your best GP moment so far?
I'd have to say Assen, comin' into the last lap tryin' not to go too hard, but to judge it so I could stay ahead of Nakano. He ended up comin' by me on the brakes, I was really hard on them into the chicane and he just came right up inside of me. He kinda ran it wide, then we bumped a little into the chicane and then he went wide and came back across the front of me, then I shot up across the kerb and beat him to the

finish line, went through the roof. That was definitely the best moment, I was really goin' for top Yamaha two-stroke.

Nakano's a very smooth rider; is that you too?
That's one of my goals. I've heard it from the team, they're surprised how smooth I look and that's definitely a compliment because that's what I've always wanted to achieve, being a smooth rider.

But you've also ridden in some hardcase groups, with McWilliams, Laconi and so on...
I was with McWilliams and Gibernau at the beginning of the Assen race. They're were goin' back and forth, making some pretty dangerous passes, I'd say. I didn't want to get mixed up in that, so I stayed behind and, sure enough, McWilliams shot around the outside of Gibernau into the chicane, just went right in front of him and clipped his front wheel. Gibernau went down right then, so I was like, all right, that's one of them I don't have to pass, then I worked on McWilliams, caught up to him, then his bike broke.

So you're 19 and saying some 38-year-old is crazy!
Yeah, I guess it's strange!

Why've you always been so level headed?
I'd have to say I had a pretty quick childhood with my dad passing away as early as he did. I definitely had to take a lot in and learn a lot.

Tell us the story of the tattoo. [Hopper has a huge tatt on his back]
I wanted my name, then couldn't figure out what to get after that. The name was just the base of a back piece I wanted, just build it up from there. I wanted something to symbolise what my life is and what it's going to be, so I thought it'd be good getting a trophy girl. She's standing there, her hair's waving in the wind like the bike just went past, and she's holding the chequered flag and the American flag in her hands. Then there's the dress, that's because I couldn't figure out where to put the Union Jack part.

So she's not Geri Halliwell or Michaela Fogarty? [Both famous for wearing Union Jack dresses]
Neither of them, I never even knew.

Do you consider yourself American or British?
I've got an American passport, but I have the option because my family's still got European passports. I just consider myself both, I was born and raised in the United States, so I'm definitely American, but at the same time I consider myself British.

Where do you stay in Europe?
I've been living in Clermont-Ferrand [in France] but I just moved to Austria, where the team is based, because I'll get the chance to do a lot of motocross.

What else are you into?
I do a lot of snowboarding, and also surfing when I'm home, but always mainly motocross. I pretty much stay on motorcycles all the time.

What about music?
Fairly hard music [his girlfriend Desiree Crossman giggles]. Slipknot, that's one of them, Disturb is one of my favourites, then there's a punk rock band called Pennywise, I listen to them a bunch, and Bad Religion. Just all pretty hard and Garry likes that stuff too. We get on really well, I've been hangin' out with him at his place in Andorra.

And partying?
I'm keen on it every once in a while, it's good fun, you gotta let loose every once in a while, especially when the racing and the training is just boom, boom, boom, so every once in a while…

How often then, once a month?
[Desiree offers: 'We usually blow out every other week.'] Well, not blow out. I never drink unless it's Sunday night. I train every day, so I don't see any need to have just one beer. If I'm gonna drink…

Your favourite drink?
Depends what kind of night it is. If I'm just hanging out with some buddies, I don't mind Heineken. If you're gonna go out to a disco or whatever, throwing down a Red Bull and vodka is the way to go. I don't like dancing, I'd rather just go to a bar and hang out.

A lot of other top GP guys get well stressed these days, you don't seem to.
Yeah, I noticed that and it's kinda sad in a way. You've got to enjoy what you're doin'. You know, they've been in it a lot of years but if they're not having fun any more, what's the point of doing it? I think it's unbelievable to get to travel the world and race motorcycles.

And get paid good money…
But I'm not making half as much as a lot of the MotoGP field.

Epilogue: You've gotta love Hopper – he signed for Suzuki in 2003, took five seasons to score his first-ever MotoGP podium – then he signs with Kawasaki for a few mill. No doubt, the most expensive winless rider in MotoGP history.

MotoGP Mutterings: July 2002
Welcome to the smell of speed, the whiff of danger

Okay, so we've got our unobtainable MotoGP paddock passes around our necks and they're not just tatty bits of multicoloured card swinging from pieces of string, they're as shiny and neat and perfectly formed as your Visa card, just like the shiny and neat and perfectly formed world we're about to enter. The MotoGP paddock is someone's idealised vision of what the world should be, it's fake; of course, utterly fake, but maybe the real world's faker.

Welcome to the world of seriously wired weirdness and may I suggest that we begin by entering this hospitality suite fronted by an over-made-up beauty in a bikini, looking ever so awkward as she 'welcomes' us (by delivering one of them smiles that offers everything and yet nothing) into the 'glamorous' environs of her corporate dining awning – all leafy house plants, bangin' Italian house music, aluminium café chairs and plastic floor tiles. Behind the pits and well away from the speed and excitement, this is where we're gonna hang out, suck our corporate cappuccinos and relax. Except you can't relax. There's no place to hide in the MotoGP paddock, because the joint lives and breathes on racers' angst and mechanics' angst and team managers' angst and hostess girls' angst. We're not backstage at Glasto, for fuck's sake. There's no comfy floor cushions, horizontal hangers-on and clouds of weed smoke here, just the smell of speed, the whiff of danger.

We down our cappuccinos and head outside to discover the 'real' world of MotoGP, pacing alongside the perfectly regimented line of artics parked behind the pits, where the proper stuff goes on. There's 110 articulated lorries here and they all look like they've been parked by an obsessive compulsive with a GPS system. Which is exactly how it works. There's chalk marks on the tarmac to indicate each artic's exact parking position. If only God had been as meticulous when he made the world…

'Behind the staff is a bank of 12 TV screens, all broadcasting the same Japanese winter scene, calming Japanese folk music playing at low volume'

You want a look inside one of the trucks – okay, so we dive inside the Yamaha motorsport artic, parked alongside the two Marlboro Yamaha trucks. This is my favourite, it's one of those expandable artics, which grows six feet wider when parked, and inside it's just a little like being on the bridge of the *Starship Enterprise* – all computer monitors, coloured lights and earnest Japanese technicians poring over facts and figures, throwing you suspicious looks as you press the entry button and the sliding door schloooks open. Behind the staff is a bank of 12 TV screens, all broadcasting the same Japanese winter scene, snow gently falling to the ground, calming Japanese folk music playing at low volume. Very strange. This is Yamaha's holy of holies, no entry for no one, better leave and slide into the pits. More suspicious looks. A couple of mechanics give us the 'paddock nod', 'Awright, mate', 'Ciao!'; several more blank us because there's nice guys and not-so-nice guys here, just like the real world. There's a carpet on the floor and I challenge you to find one spot of dirt thereon, or one smear of grease on any of the bikes. The motorcycles are too much, too much to go into here, fabricated masses of one-off parts hand-machined from billets of unobtanium and worth more than people know, though only because no one dares to calculate their true value. Honda are rumoured to want £1.5 million to lease an RCV in 2003 and that certainly doesn't include development costs.

Back out of the pits, someone's shouting at us: 'Hey queer, come over here, I wanna word with you!' It's King Kenny Roberts and he's talking to us (he nicknamed me thus after I'd had my head shaved some years ago). The King is probably the greatest man in the paddock, so he gets to call you what he likes. He's also a bit of a psycho, like everyone else here, as you might already have noticed. No, he's more than a bit of a psycho, he's won dirt track crowns, 500 world titles and he's built his own motorcycle, and you need to be one hell of a psycho to achieve that much in your life. Which is why bike racing is cool, because it's an extreme world full of extreme people, within a world of mediocrity and normality. Okay, it is voluntary and it is only a sport, but it's still an extreme of human existence and about as close to being in a war as you can get without being shot at. Like we said – the real world is faker.

I have this theory that many years ago, some world government consipracy had the bright idea of creating this sport to encourage as many psychos as possible to spend their weekends in the same place, surrounded by ten-feet tall wire fences, to keep normal society safe from these crazies. So, forget the paddock, stay at home and watch the racing on TV, it's safer and much less hassle.

CHAPTER 23

PLANS FOR THE FUTURE? 'NOT REALLY, JUST TO BE IN MOTOGP'

July 2002

During his debut GP season in 2002 teenage star Casey Stoner was pretty laid back about his ambitions, but his talent and his determination were already there for all to see. And even as a 16-year-old he made a great interviewee...

Casey Stoner is the 16-year-old 250 GP rider with his eyes firmly set on the MotoGP big time. A multiple Aussie junior dirt track champ, Stoner contests his first world championship campaign in 2002 and he's already got factory bosses sniffing around him.

A bright and sparky kid, Stoner has the stamp of greatness upon him, no doubt whatsoever about that. He only started roadracing in 2000 and had never raced a 250 before the start of 2002. But second time out in South Africa he became the youngest rider in the 53-year history of the sport to qualify on the second row for a 250 GP. And at the Czech GP he scored a remarkable fifth-place finish, coming back from 15th on the first lap. But Stoner also jumped off a lot as he battled to get to grips with his 100 horsepower Aprilia RSV250.

Stoner's parents brought him to Europe to start his tarmac career in 2000, because he would've had to wait another two years to go roadracing if he'd stuck around Down Under. He was quick from the get-go, winning the 2000 British Aprilia RS125 Challenge and more importantly attracting the attention of GP talent spotter Alberto Puig, a former 500 star to whom GP rights holders Dorna had given the task of bringing non-Spanish and non-Italian blood into the southern Europe-dominated GP scene. Puig sorted him bikes for the super-competitive Spanish 125 series and also fixed him wild card rides for the 2001 British and Australian GPs. Stoner scored his first world points at Phillip Island but that ride cost him the British 125 championship, which he'd totally dominated in between trucking down to Spain every other weekend.

Even five-time 500 champ Mick Doohan, a hard man to please if ever there was one, is convinced of the kid's ability to go all the way. Micky D's not daft either, so he also jumped on the Stoner bandwagon, offering advice and opening doors wherever he can.

You've not been to school for a while?
I haven't been to school since I was 12. Even in Australia, when we did dirt track, we didn't have time for school, because we were always away racing. I did quite well at school but never liked it, I absolutely hated it.

When did you start riding?
Ever since I was born! When I was 18 months I was doing the throttle, sitting on the bike, with my cousin on the back, turning the throttle on a Pee Wee. My dad raced a bit, and my sister raced before I was born, so I grew up with her riding around the place. I started doing dirt track on a Pee Wee.

Dirt track has produced a lot of good riders, basically everybody who does roadracing in Australia did dirt track. If they made dirt track a world championship thing and it was big, I'd like to do that better than roadracing. It's just really enjoyable, I absolutely love doing it, it's just a fun thing. I did speedway for a bit but it's not the same. Dirt track's just really good, you get oil tracks, so it's like supermoto but slipperier, you've got to choose the right lines between the loose stuff and the shiny stuff, a lot of different things.

When did you start dirt track and then roadracing?
At four and I finished at 13 when we came to Europe. You can't roadrace till you're 16 in Australia, so I started at 14 in the UK. Alberto had heard of us doing quite well in the last couple of rounds of the 2000 British championship, so he asked us to do the last two rounds of the Spanish championship to see how we went.

We had a few problems but I didn't do too bad, so we got on his team and went testing at the start of 2001. I did really well on a standard bike, so Alberto was quite impressed and pushed Honda to get better parts. I was very grateful for that, plus I had the opportunity to do two GP wild-card rides, that all helped and gave me experience.

So you never roadraced before you came to Europe?

I once rode a Moriwaki 80 around a go-kart track but we had a few complications with the people who run the Moriwaki grand prix 80 series, they wouldn't let us race in the championship. It was a bit weird; I was old enough, I'd got the licence, I'd got the approval. There's a lot of jealousy in that kind of thing. The guy who runs the series didn't get along with us because we didn't go through him. All the other kids had bought their bikes off him, they'd done everything through him but we did it our own way. He didn't like us because of that, so he didn't let us race.

Do you get a lot of stuff like punch-ups in kids' racing?

There's a lot of punch-ups! Normally not between the kids, most of the kids get along pretty good. It's just the parents, very strange. I only had problems my last couple of years of dirt track. I'd been winning for quite a lot of my life, then all of a sudden they started saying I was a dirty rider and shit like that. I'd been going up the age groups, so I was racing against kids who I didn't normally race against and they weren't used to me. All the other kids I'd ridden with through the years didn't find me bad at all, we're just all good mates.

It was just when I went into the older age groups and I was racing and roughin' it in there with them and they didn't like it. But I've seen seniors race and when those guys get there they're gonna shit themselves. I always wanted to race seniors because I've always been quite aggressive. In roadracing I need to learn to be more aggressive, but in dirt track I knew exactly what I was doing with the bike.

Do you consider yourself more mature than other 16-year-olds?

When I went back to Australia after two years here I just had a different look on things, I guess because the only people I'd really had to talk to were adults.

Do you find life on the road hard?

Very hard. It'd be a little easier if I was driving, because it'd pass the time and I'd probably enjoy it.

Does it feel like an adventure or are you gagging to get to the next race?

I'm basically gagging to get to the next race and try the next track. I travelled from England to Spain a lot of times last year, so it's the same road every time: Yeah, seen that… Yeah, seen that…

Do a lot of kids race just because their dads want them to?
It happens a lot in dirt track, the parents have a lot of money, they have the best bikes and the kids come back in bawling their eyes out because they know they'll get a flog off their dads because they didn't win; it's just not right. But most of the good riders have always wanted to do it all their lives.

Do you feel pressure?
I put pressure on myself and all this crashing has put a bit of pressure on. I've tried to ease it off a bit but I still seem to be crashing.

'The data-logging said I was doing 191kmh when I crashed but it was the only crash in which I haven't hurt myself one bit'

You had a huge get-off during the South African GP, tell us about that one.
I felt it go, thought I'd got it back but then it went again. When I was flyin' through the air I was thinking 'this is gonna hurt', because I knew I was gonna land on the bitumen. The data-logging said I was doing 191kmh when I crashed but it was the only crash in which I haven't hurt myself one bit.

How is the 250?
I'm not positive enough with myself to make passing manoeuvres. I'm getting better but at the start of the year I was terrible; on the 125 I could pass anywhere, I'd just do it. It's just a matter of getting more confident on the 250. I know what I'm doing wrong, I've just got to get my head around it. The first few meetings I was really confident with sliding it and stuff and I wasn't crashing. I was really confident at Le Mans, except for the corner where I crashed [Stoner broke a wrist in that accident].

Tell us about your Mugello crashes a fortnight after Le Mans.
I should've been a bit more preserving, because I thought the wrist was gonna be all right. I had a lot of painkillers in it, so I didn't have any pain in my wrist and that was the problem, that's why I crashed on Friday morning at Mugello. After that crash I was very concussed, I

don't remember half of it, but because I didn't do too bad Friday afternoon, I thought I'd give it a try next day. Then I fell off again, exact same place, exact same crash, except the bike spun around and walloped me one in the head. That probably knocked some sense back into me because I felt better after that one. I just wanted to ride, I don't even remember making the decision.

What you do for fun?
Play my PlayStation quite a bit because I don't have any friends to hang around with, plus I've lately been very bored because I've had injuries, so I haven't been out on my motocross bike or mountain bike. Back home on the Gold Coast my parents have got a static caravan park. There's a big beach five minutes away, then 500 metres away there's flat water, for fishing, boats and stuff. I can't wait to get a car in Australia, so I can get around, do things and see mates, so I'm getting an English licence at the end of the year.

Do you drink?
No. I'm not goin' to drink either, only tiny little bits.

Were you a good boy or a bad boy at school?
Medium, I think. I wasn't bad but I wasn't good.

Do you have friends in the paddock?
Chaz [Davies] pretty much, he's the only British person who's got any time. Before the British GP I stayed at Chaz's house and met all his mates. I really enjoyed that.

What about girls?
Not at the moment.

How has Puig helped?
I definitely wouldn't be here if it wasn't for him, he pushed a lot for me to get this ride. He knew I could do something. He'd been great with me all through the Spanish championship. He lets us borrows his mother's car when we stay at his place in Barcelona, he lets us use his motocross bike, his supermotard bike, his trials bike, he just lets me use anything he's got, he's a real nice guy. He's been absolutely fantastic.

Does he coach you on riding or mental attitude?
Not so much on riding, just how to control my head, what to think about. He doesn't know what the bike's like, so he knows he shouldn't interfere with things he doesn't know about, but the stuff he does know about he helps me with. That's what it's all about here, how to control yourself – it's not how good you are, it's how good your head is. Most things on riding I'm learning for myself.

Did you want to race 125 or 250 this year?
I'd wanted to get on a bigger bike for a year or so. I had a go on a 250 last year and absolutely loved it, so I just wanted to get on something with a bit more power. It's definitely more fun, but also a lot harder. It's just how to keep your head when you crash because they're scary machines. With the 125 you could crash it and get straight back on. The 250 is so hard to get right, and when you crash you get a bit scared of it. I'm getting there though, I'm learning from my crashes.

Are you surprised how competitive you've been?
South Africa was the biggest surprise, my second meeting and I was eighth in qualifying. I was like 'you got to be joking,' I didn't believe I was that close. The field has been spreading out over the last few races, the Aprilia factory bikes have been upping their pace, leaving the rest behind but I'm still not too far off the rest of them. I've just got to learn more about set-up.

Who were your heroes as a kid?
Pretty much just Doohan, my whole life. I didn't even know what the 125 class was until '98 or '99, all I knew was 500s.

Did you watch GPs on TV?
Since I was three or four. Doohan was there from '89, so I've followed him my whole life. Mum and dad used to tape the races, but not any more. You get wrapped up in what you're doin' yourself. You go through so much stress and ups and downs during a GP weekend that you can't really be bothered to watch the other races.

Are you enjoying it?
Definitely, yes, but sometimes when I crash I can't figure out why. I go

through a lot of pressure trying to figure it out, trying to get the set-up right. I feel bad for the team, I'm tryin' to figure out what's goin' on, but I can only explain it to myself, I can't exactly explain in words what I'm feeling.

How's the team about the crashes?
They say don't worry, but you can always see it in their faces, which just makes you feel worse.

Plans for the future?
Not really, just eventually to be in MotoGP. I'd have liked it to have still been 500s, because I think they're great, but four-strokes is the class now. Alberto is my manager and he knows what he's doing, he'll get us in the right place, I think.

Epilogue: you know it – five years later Stoner kicked Rossi's arse to become MotoGP world champion.

MotoGP Mutterings: *August 2002*
You don't have to be mad to work here, but it helps. Here's some more weirdness going down within the GP paddock...

You may have heard of Dr Claudio Costa. He's the, erm, extraordinary Italian physician who stitches, bolts and plates top racers back together when they smack themselves up. Costa and his crew of surgeons and physios roll up at every GP with their own very special equipment – scalpels, Black & Deckers and one of the most impressive drugs cabinets known to man. Inside the Clinica Mobile – otherwise known as the House of Pain – they perform all manner of gruesome ops on pro riders who will endure seven shades of suffering to get themselves back on track tomorrow rather than the day after. 'And if the pain gets too much, Valentino, just pop a couple of these...'

Costa's methods are applauded by some, mostly riders and their managers, anxious to keep the money flowing, but not by more circumspect onlookers, who fear the long-term effects of the patch 'em up and send 'em out mentality. But, hey, no one forces these guys to do what they do, and anyway, imagine the quality of painkiller they'll have in 2040, when Rossi and his peers will be shuffling into their arthritis-racked dotage.

Whatever, Costa has just published his autobiography, which has to rate as one the most bizarre books to hit the shelves since The Holy Bible, or maybe *Trainspotting*. Entitled *Tears and triumph: my life in the Clinica Mobile*, the doctor's own brand of very weird religious-tinted philosophy gushes and oozes from every page. Here are a few rib-tickling highlights.

'As you lay on your bed of thorns, wounded by fate and as your tears glinted in the faint light of the hospital room'

First, Costa's paean to Mick Doohan, the man whose right leg he saved in 1992. Good doc or bad doc, Doohan might've been a one-legged non-world champ if Costa hadn't saved the limb from amputation, but be warned, you may need a hanky here. 'As you lay on your bed of thorns,' writes Costa. 'Wounded by fate and man's arrogance and as your tears glinted in the faint light of the hospital room, we thought those tears would never fill the abyss of your distress or soothe the suffering of your injury... and indeed they soon ceased to stream down your pain-struck cheeks and in an instant those feelings of hope and desire which sustain a human being as he shoulders life's burdens returned to the fore: the hope of going back to racing and the desire of going back to winning.

'And when you did go back to racing, your wounds still bleeding, we saw your spirit bloom, invading your being as if emerging from some half-sealed casket. But time, unrelenting, continued to yield only pain, suffering and disillusionment, and desire was unable even to find shelter in the sweetest of harbours...

'Then, suddenly, the casket of treasures which every human being carries inside himself opened completely and you, Michael, saw your entire self, from the depths of your soul to the heights of reason. You had become world champion for the fourth time. And in the joy of that instant, you felt that the theatre of pain had vanished, that it had ceased to exist, and you learned that time, which had cruelly defined your suffering, no longer was. You realised in happiness the human being becomes, in that precise instant, eternal, and you breathed immortality in the embrace of victory.' Stop it, doc, that's hurting me!

Doohan, of course, winces with embarrassment whenever you remind him of the doc's eulogy, probably more than he grimaced when the surgeons drilled that Ilazaroff gantry into his leg. Incidentally, all

Ilazaroff patients (should that be victims?) pop morphine daily to kill the pain. Mighty Mick took paracetamol.

Here's another Costa classic, referring to Carlos Checa's Czech GP comeback from the scary, life-threatening injuries he suffered at Donington 1998. 'As I approached the Spanish rider's pit area I had an odd feeling, as if I were about to enter an unusual, almost holy place. Its occupants were there as usual… yet something impossible to define, something peculiar was hovering in the air. Carlos finished the race… those present lined up like devout friars along the sides of an altar… Then, taken aback, I realised who had helped Carlos pick himself up. It was the same "Old Lady" who had befriended him in Sherwood Forest near the hospital of Nottingham and had become his friend. The lady that no one remembers or wishes to remember. The "Lady" St Francis referred to as Sister Death!' Jesus, Mary, Joseph…

Finally, Costa's thoughts on motorcycles. 'The motorbike is a symbol of energy. It is not, as most might think, technological, but natural. It is that animal part of the ancient centaur that safeguards our instincts and frees them to ride out and seek the answers to questions that torment us. Not even the fury of the wind can stop this quest for freedom, this attempt to seek answers different from those that society palms us off with daily.' You see, deep within the weirdness, now and again Costa does get it right. Kind of.

Epilogue: the Clinica Mobile celebrated its 30th anniversary of looking after GP riders at the 2007 San Marino GP. The invite read thus: 'Thirty years ago, Clinica Mobile, the little travelling hospital of the mythological world of motorcycling, was created. Throughout the years, our clinic has become a home for the heroes, an altar for riders to celebrate the magical ritual with which they resurrect from their injuries, from their fractures, from their illnesses, to climb the enchanted mountain of motorcycling, the mountain with only the stars in heaven above it.'

The invite included an illustration of a rider climbing a rocky mountain towards the starlit heavens while wearing leathers and helmet and with both arms and both legs heavily bandaged…

CHAPTER 24

SEX ON THE RACETRACK

September 2002

Cagiva's C594 500 GP bike and Aprilia's RS3 Cube MotoGP machine are two of the sexiest bikes ever to have graced a racetrack. The Cagiva was more than pretty, it won GPs. The Aprilia didn't, possibly because it was too far ahead of its time with pneumatic valves and ride-by-wire throttle

**Cagiva C594: Kocinski's 1994 bike had it all –
passion, romance, success**

The Cagiva C594 has its place in history as the last Italian machine to win a 500 GP. But this is not what makes the bike so seductive. The C594 was the culmination of almost two decades of extravagant though ultimately unproductive investment by the Castiglioni brothers, who owned much of Italy's motorcycle industry, from Cagiva to MV Agusta, from Ducati to Moto Guzzi.

Claudio and Giancarlo Castiglioni are industrialist empire builders, renowned for their hardnosed business dealings, and yet their grand prix adventure was marked by a singular lack of penny-pinching business nous. They went racing because they loved it, and in an age when accountants rule the corporate world, knowing the price of everything and the value of nothing, that's to be applauded. The Castiglionis had a passion for racing, with a capital P.

In this sense the brothers were the last in the line of Italy's romantic old-school motorsport patrons, men of means like Count Domenico Agusta and Enzo Ferrari, who ruled over their stables like 20th-century Machiavellians, enjoying the behind-the-scenes political machinations as much as they adored the wondrous machines they put on the racetrack. The Castiglionis poured tens of millions of pounds into their GP project, without ever building a range of road bikes that might profit from their investment. And just when they were on the cusp of wresting the 500 world championship from the Japanese, they quit.

In fact, the brothers didn't fall from GP racing, they were pushed, by a bunch of bankers. If they had managed to get away with their megabuck hobby for 16 years, they were finally told to stop playing in 1994 when a consortium of banks rescued the Castiglioni group from the financial difficulties that also threatened to engulf Ducati. The banks' accountants insisted on the curtailment of GP activities as a precondition of their rescue package. Ducati were allowed to stay in World Superbike because that series offered a direct commercial kickback.

During Cagiva's final years on the GP scene, when they were at their most competitive, the Castiglionis steadfastly refused generous offers of commercial sponsorship, for the simple reason that they wanted a blood-red motorcycle, just like the older Ferrari F1 cars that are still worshipped the world over. Perhaps it's just as well that Cagiva's GP dream ended when it did, before its purity got perverted by 21st-century racing mores – blanket corporate sponsorship and dodgy team orders.

It is also somewhat ironic that Cagiva only achieved success with two wholly un-Latin riders – American racing automatons Eddie Lawson and John Kocinski. Of course, both men have a huge passion for motorcycles and racing, but it took the strange brew of their cold-blooded brains and the Italians' warm-blooded hearts to win Cagiva's three GP victories, between 1992 and 1994.

The C594 was a development of the previous year's C593, which was created out of Lawson's invaluable input during 1991 and 1992, when he won the factory's first GP after a clever tyre gamble at a damp 1992 Hungarian GP. The machine was totally redesigned for '93, when Kocinski became the first Cagiva rider to beat the Japanese V4s in a head-to-head race on a dry track. The following year the weird one from Arkansas won again and led the world championship, slipping to a best-ever third overall at season's end, behind Mick Doohan's Honda NSR and Luca Cadalora's Yamaha YZR. During these years the Cagiva crew was headed by affable engineer Riccardo Rosa, who, along with several of his engine and chassis technicians, was later switched to the Castiglionis' latest baby, the MV F4 (né Cagiva).

Rosa brought a much-needed pragmatism to the reds' show. Before his arrival, Cagiva had always been keen to experiment where the more businesslike, less imaginative Japanese teams feared to tread. Cagiva were evaluating fuel injection in 1989 and built a gorgeous all-carbon-fibre chassis for rider Randy Mamola the following year, well before the Big Four were involved in similar ventures. But racing proves time and again that success is achieved by effective application of known technology, rather than by brave forays into the technological unknown, so Rosa focused his team's efforts on research and development that would bring immediate results.

The 593 and 594 were styled by Rosa, along with chassis designer Romano Albesiano and Claudio Castiglioni, who liked to involve himself at every level of the project. 'The bike's style came naturally during development,' says Rosa, who went on to work with Benelli's Tornado triple. 'I think that good style is very much linked to aerodynamic efficiency, as Enzo Ferrari once said: "If a car is beautiful, it will also be functional".' You see, the function equals beauty equation works both ways.

The C594 is an object lesson in clean, straightforward design, in which its creators have maintained their focus on functionality, letting the machine's mission define its appearance. And it's almost certainly no coincidence that Ducati's 916 style icon has more than a passing resemblance to the bike. Rosa gave 916 designer Massimo Tamburini a C594 for his design offices, and Tamburini had already borrowed heavily from an earlier Cagiva 500 for his design of the marque's Mito 125 streetbike.

Rosa presided over three years of great industry and success within Cagiva's race department that coincided with a period during which much of Italian commerce was starting to enjoy something of a renaissance, mating its age-old talent for design and manufacture to modern-day business practices. It was a far cry from Cagiva's earlier days on the GP trail, when the team staggered along Don Quixote-style, jousting ineffectually with the 'windmills' of the Far East. The first ten years at least were rarely any less than tragi-comic, riddled with rider walk-outs, mechanical meltdowns and tales of trickery. Legend has it, for example, that the first Cagiva 500 of 1979 was built around a set of Suzuki RG500 crankcases nicked from Suzuki's factory team HQ in Surrey the previous summer. That's the Cagiva GP story – wrapped more in romance than in sex.

Aprilia RS3 Cube: Frighteningly fast, good-looking and Italian

Can brutal be beautiful? Or sexy? In motorcycling, almost certainly yes. Aprilia's RS3 Cube looks beautiful in a brutal kind of a way. It looks like it might hurt you. Badly. And it sounds like it wants to hurt you. No, really.

The new breed of four-stroke MotoGP bikes are sexy like 500 two-strokes never could be. Five hundreds ruled the world for decades but always sounded like tricked-up scooters, whereas the earth moves every time the Cube rumbles past. Styling is a visual thing, of course, and yet the noise that tracks a motorcycle as it rocks on by is just as important. The Cube sounds wonderful, like a tumult of bellowing bassoons at the front of an ancient army, weaponry glinting in the sunlight as it rushes onward towards the gates of Hades. You see, we're already getting carried away here, but this is what Italian racing motorcycles are all about: Aprilias and Ducatis engage the emotions in a way that Hondas and Yamahas never will.

'The Cube sounds wonderful, like a tumult of bellowing bassoons at the front of an ancient army, weaponry glinting in the sunlight'

Aprilia knows this. Yet factory race chief Jan Witteveen insists that form follows function in the Noale race shop. The Cube's styling was born out of a desire to win races, not to flog streetbikes, but since function is beauty, these two intents usually deliver the same end result. 'No one at Aprilia tells us that we need a nice design for marketing reasons,' proclaims Witteveen, the main man behind the little Italian marque's Superbike, 250 and 125 successes. 'Our first target is always performance, though I also believe that the emotion of the fans, and of the people who work with the bike, is important.'

The Cube's shark-like look was created in the wind tunnel, or rather a virtual wind tunnel, to cope with the particular aerodynamic demands of MotoGP racing. Which doesn't mean top-speed slipperiness, even though the RS3 was the first MotoGP machine to crack the 200mph barrier at the 2002 Italian GP. Racetrack aerodynamicists, like Aprilia's Corrado Ficuccello, have realised that chasing the lowest-possible drag coefficient will gain 0.2 seconds at the end of a racetrack's longest straight, and lose a whole second through the twists and turns because less drag usually means more lift, which badly affects handling.

Aprilia's work in their virtual wind tunnel – that's a computer aerodynamics program to you and me – was complemented by real-world development at military airbases in northern Italy, where the Cube's onboard datalogging clocked 205mph. 'But that's not a real speed because it was measured at the rear wheel,' adds Witteveen. 'And you get a lot of tyre slip at that kind of speed.' That's double-ton wheelspin, very sexy.

The Cube was so powerful off the drawing board that rider Regis Laconi initially struggled to control the brute. He would invariably head the top-speed charts while his lap times languished somewhere outside the top ten. So Aprilia have steadily detuned the motor, replacing top-end horsepower with mid-range torque, and each time they do that, he gets quicker.

Nevertheless, whenever the Frenchman with the, erm, enthusiastic riding style climbs off the bike, he looks like he's just gone ten rounds with some mythical six-headed monster. Eyes bulging and sweat glistening, Laconi mimes the experience of riding the 220 horsepower Cube as a horseman might act out a wild-stallion ride towards the apocalypse: arms straining from their sockets as he's dragged towards the horizon at a terrifying rate, with seemingly little control over his destiny. So the former 500 and Superbike winner obviously adores the bike. 'It really kicks in every gear, more than my Yamaha 500 ever did,' he jabbers, still pumped after another practice run. 'It feels like a 500 but with more power and much more torque. The engine internals are very light, so it picks up revs really fast and accelerates like crazy.'

The Cube's Cosworth-designed inline triple is crammed with more radical technology than any of the Japanese MotoGP bikes, namely pneumatic valves and a super-small, super-light, F1-style AP Lockheed carbon clutch. Also sexy. 'We have more than enough power, so the pneumatic valves aren't necessary at this moment,' adds Witteveen. 'But if we need to increase performance in the long term, they will give us a useful margin.'

And this is where Witteveen contradicts his earlier declaration that Aprilia's racing department has no truck with the men from marketing. 'We chose a three cylinder because I was sure the Japanese wouldn't make a three; we wanted to be different. Of course, our computer simulations told us the three would be good on the track, and since it's more difficult to make horsepower with a three rather than a five, this helped us in deciding to use pneumatic valves. We liked the idea because we wanted some high technology in the engine.'

Least sexy of all, manufacturing costs also helped determine the Cube's configuration. 'An inline multi is cheaper to produce than a v-twin, a V3 or a V4, because you only need one cylinder head, one cam drive and so on.' Such are the humdrum considerations of the production line. But wait, this surely means there'll soon be a Cube road bike. 'Not this year, not next year, I don't know when,' insists Witteveen. And if there ever is a street Cube you can be certain it will be a dead ringer for the racer, because the link between track and street is particularly crucial to Aprilia. The company only started making motorcycles in the mid-1970s and would be nowhere in the global consciousness if Max Biaggi, Valentino Rossi, Laconi et al hadn't put its name up in lights.

Meanwhile, the Cube racer is expected to get quicker and quicker. The 2002 bike is well over its MotoGP-minimum weight limit and will stay that way for some months, while each prototype part is whittled down to size and recast or re-machined in unobtanium. Witteveen reckons his creation is currently losing a kilo every GP (it's the new MotoGP diet: lose a kilo a fortnight, only £45,000!), which suggests that the Cube will be pretty trim by Christmas and down to the 135-kilo limit by the start of the 2003 MotoGP season.

Quick, shapely and Italian, the Cube's sexiest attribute is probably its potential to beat Honda. 'We have a chance to beat them because, I hope, we have more fantasy, more creativity,' Witteveen says. 'If economic power was all that mattered in racing, Honda would win everything, but we've already demonstrated that's not always so.'

And he's not the only man who believes, as one rival Japanese factory engineer recently let slip: 'The Aprilia will soon be kicking our asses'.

The little guys defeating the big guys, now that is sexy.

Epilogue: Sadly, the Aprilia never did beat Honda. World Supers champ Colin Edwards rode the bike in 2003 and got his arse burnt when the bike caught fire in Germany. In 2004 Jeremy McWilliams did his best to tame the fiery beast. But the factory was already in dire financial trouble and so the Cube project was crushed, exactly a decade after the Cagiva went west. Shame.

CHAPTER 25

I'M A LOSER, BABY, SO WHY DON'T
YOU KILL ME?

November 2002

So sang the great Beck a few years back. But just how bad do bike racing's biggest losers feel? Grand Prix and World Superbike nearly men Randy Mamola, Aaron Slight and Ralf Waldmann reveal what it's like never quite to shake off the habit of finishing second

Racing is all about winning, but if anything, it's more about losing. There's only one victor in every race but many vanquished. And it's the winners you get to read about, while the losers barely rate a mention. Yet, just as the devil has all the best tunes, it's the losers who've got all the best tales.

In 500 GPs and World Superbikes, there's two king losers: Randy Mamola and Aaron Slight. Mamola won 13 GPs and finished second in four 500 world championships during the 1980s; Slight won 13 Supers rounds (that scary number again) and made the top three in the world championship six seasons running from '93. Both men were at the top of their game for years, as fast as anyone out there, but somehow they never quite won a world championship, so they're left to live out the rest of their lives wondering what might have been, the memories of those big days that didn't turn out right forever eating them up inside.

There are plenty of reasons why Mamola and Slight never struck gold. Racers get slagged for whingeing but, in all honesty, their excuses usually are reasons. No one ever had a perfect race, there's always something that might've panned out better. The potential for cock-up is immense. Riders are at the mercy of inanimate objects, thousands of components that might not work exactly right. Or the weather may go wrong, even a two-degree temperature change can confound a tyre choice. And then there's 30 other very animate riders out there, all quite prepared to ride into you at 140mph. Like war, the winner is generally the one who has the fewest fuck-ups, it's all ifs and buts.

Slight, whose bike career ended prematurely at the end of 2000, still hurts bad. The title of his autobiography *You Don't Know the Half of It* certainly suggests that there was a whole load of emotional investment and ifs and buts that he wanted off his back. 'Writing the book was a sort of therapy for me,' says the New Zealander, who switched to racing cars after he quit two wheels. 'I couldn't go through all the ifs and buts here, because there's so many of them, but the biggest one was the rules. I was the nearly man of Superbikes because I was riding a 750 four when everyone was winning on 1000 twins. Now everyone knows you've got to be on a twin, but I was screaming about that for ten years.'

Of course, Slight did eventually get to race a twin when Honda unleashed its SP-1 in 2000, but that's the year his head went pop, a 'cavernous malformation' in his brain causing the stroke that prematurely ended his career. Some people never get the luck. And there were other moments, like '94, when a blow-up at Hockenheim and a disqualification at Donington cost him the title. Or '96, when he led the championship into the penultimate round, only to suffer a bad attack of flu at Albacete. 'I got sick when Honda sent me to the Cologne show to do publicity stuff, I'd argued for hours to try and get out of it.' Or '98, when he was up for the title but his team never instigated team orders to help him out. That contest went to the wire with Ducati's Carl Fogarty at Sugo, where Slight had tyre problems. 'That year I won five races, Carl won three and still took the championship.'

So does Slight's ultimate failure to win a world title still keep him awake at night? 'I really have to make sure it doesn't have that effect or I'd stay awake forever. I started racing cars because that's the only way I could take my mind off it; it had a huge effect on me.'

Mamola, a decade into his retirement from GP racing, is a little more distant from his failures and therefore more sanguine. Like Slight he had his disasters, like when he led the 1980 championship into the final round at the daunting Nürburgring. First time out at the lethal 14-mile circuit, the 20-year-old needed a win to take the title from King Kenny Roberts. He was leading when his RG500 popped an oil seal. The following year he signed with Nava helmets, whose visors fogged up so badly that he couldn't see where he was going in wet races. 'Trying to hold your breath at 170mph with your heart doing 150bpm, I was furious.' Or '84, when he only secured a ride three races into the championship. Or '86, when he was fighting Eddie Lawson for the title and crashed during practice at Silverstone, cracking his right shoulder. He raced anyway: 'I remember sitting on the grid, I couldn't lift my arm, so I had to crawl my hand across the gas tank to get it to the throttle'.

For sure, luck plays a part in racing, just as it does in life, though sometimes you make your own luck. As someone once put it: 'the more I practise, the luckier I get', and in racing you've got to do everything to stack the odds in your favour, whether that's signing for the right team or playing in-team politics to mess with your team-mate's head. Slight did neither of those things. When the chance came to sign for Ducati in '95, he stuck with Honda. Wrong decision. 'I never trusted what was going on at Ducati. You work with Japanese and you get paid every month, work with Italians and you get paid when they want.'

'I kick myself in the ass but at the same time I'm patting myself on the back'

Slight was also unlucky with his team-mates, lining up alongside a succession of hard nuts, men who would stamp on anyone to get what they wanted. It's probably no coincidence that his erstwhile team-mates Fogarty, Scott Russell and John Kocinski all won the title. 'During my Honda years it felt like Honda were testing me, like they didn't believe in me. It was like "we'll put another world champ next to you and see how you fare".' It seems Slight didn't have the psycho psyche to deal with these situations.

Mamola is also accused of being too much the nice guy, too much the fun guy to be world champion. 'Yeah, maybe that's true,' he says. 'I can look at it and think I should've pushed myself harder, but I went into every race trying to win. Do I still kick myself in the ass? Yeah, I kick myself in the ass but at the same time I'm patting myself on the back. Sure, I made mistakes, I lost championships because I crashed or because my bike broke, so who do I blame? I don't blame anything, it's just what happens.'

Slight worked hard to bring out the devil from inside; that's what those Mohican hairdos were all about. 'When I first left New Zealand I took out my earrings because I wanted a ride, but eventually it was like, fuck that, I've got to rebel, do what I want to do.' But however hard he tried, he couldn't be the bad guy. 'One of my worst points as a racer is that I like people to like me,' he says. 'I think that's a good trait in life, but as a racer it's a bad trait. At the end of every season I'd go home and write down the positives and minuses of the year, and I'd fix everything I could. Every year I wrote "Don't be such a nice guy, think of yourself," but you are what you are, I was just too soft.'

In fact, Slighty has had his moments of badness, including feuds with both Foggy and Hodgson. 'There was a bit of drama at Sugo '98, when I had that run-in with Neil. On the grid for race one I walked up to Carl and said "I guess it's between you and me", shook his hand and walked off. On the way back, I don't know what possessed me, but I saw Neil and said to him: "If I poke a wheel up, will you give us some room?" That was like a red rag to the bull, every chance he got, he carved me up, I think we came together about six times, so after the race I rode up behind him and smacked him in the kidneys. He stopped, I parked my bike against the barrier, went over, grabbed him by the chin piece and dragged him off the bike. Yeah, I saw red, but it wasn't about him that day, it was the championship slipping away.' Ironically, that incident highlights Slighty's gentler side, not his ruthlessness. Few other racers would even dream about shaking hands with a rival on the grid at such a moment, and few would dare ask a fellow rider for any quarter.

Not surprisingly, he cites that day's second race as the gloomiest moment of his career. 'I made the best start of my life, from tenth on the grid to fourth at the first corner, and when I turned on to the back straight I saw Carl pulling away, I could feel the championship slipping through my fingers.'

Mamola's darkest moment came at the end of '87, just after he'd finished second overall for the fourth time. Roberts, boss of his Lucky Strike Yamaha team, sacked him and brought in Wayne Rainey.

Both Slight and Mamola console themselves with the fact that they didn't do so bad; second place may be the first loser, but it's heaps better than 28th. 'When you look in the record books and your name's not listed as world champion, that kinda hurts,' adds Mamola, now married with kids and living in Barcelona. 'The thing that keeps my head above water is that I stood on the podium in three different decades – the 1970s, the 1980s and the 1990s – and that I got to ride with some great guys like Kenny, Sheene, Spencer and Lawson, Rainey, Doohan and Schwantz. I've beaten people who were world champions and I outlasted them. And those guys all look at me and go: "Man, you should've won one". Okay, that makes me feel good because I'm accepted as one anyway.'

Eventually the only way to cope with any kind of failure, to stop yourself becoming a bitter old man, is to put things into perspective. 'When you're racing it's everything, you're so focused, that's all there is,' says Mamola, who's heavily involved in charity work between working for Eurosport at GPs. 'Man, since I stopped, the world is huge and racing is so tiny, and the Riders for Health thing is beyond standing on the podium, because it's something for the world.'

Slight has managed to transform the negative of his life-threatening medical condition into a positive, and he's convinced himself that being the good guy isn't so bad after all. 'I'm lucky I've had a life-altering experience,' he says. 'When I look back now I think I didn't do such a bad job, and how many top guys have stopped because of racing injuries? I think how lucky I am to get out of there still walking. And if I get in that "what if?" mode, I just tell myself that I could still be working on farm bikes in a bike shop in New Zealand; I've seen the world and the last five years of my career I earned good money. Motorcycling was such a huge part of my life but it's such a small part of your whole life, I've still got 60 years to live and I'm just glad I'm living that as Aaron Slight and not as Fogarty or Kocinski.'

Tears before bedtime with Waldi – another loser who never lacked emotional investment

Ralf Waldmann is the most successful GP rider in history never to have won a world championship, though he mostly contested the lesser 125 and 250 classes. He's also a very funny man, with a Teutonic knack of loudly hitting the nail on the head. At the 2000 British GP, when he heroically came from 90 seconds down to win the 250 GP after an apparently idiotic choice of rain tyres came good when the heavens opened, he opined: 'The difference between idiot and hero is very small'. Few truer words have ever been spoken in motorcycle racing.

Waldi won 20 races in a GP career spanning 15 years, twice finishing second to Max Biaggi in the 250 world championship (by just two points in '97) and twice third in the 125 world championship (in '92 he squandered a 30-point mid-season lead, eventually losing out to Alessandro Gramigni).

Sadly, Waldi is likely to hang on to the 'Most successful rider in history never to win a world title' label for some time. I wonder if these words lull him to sleep every night like some kind of Satan's lullaby.

'No, no, this is all behind me!' he says brightly. We're talking in the back of his team's truck, not in a palatial motorhome, during his brief GP comeback during 2002. I'm sat on a drum of gas, he's on a pile of tyres, and he thinks this is hilarious. It seems that Waldi really is happy with what fate has bestowed on him. We distil the reasons for his two closest world-title failures to two moments. In '92 his Honda 125 team had a mid-season meltdown, a bitter feud between his two chief mechanics erupting into a pit-lane brawl. In '97 he chose a wrong-compound tyre for the penultimate Indonesian GP. He finished that race seventh when fourth place would've given him the title. Just ten seconds separated fourth from seventh.

'If you look for reasons, you find them,' he says, a little more glum, the memories seeping up to haunt him. 'Before '97 it was brilliant with the money, with the stuff we get, but then we lose our sponsor and it was really shitty, because we don't have enough money. We have minimum of budget and only one bike; Max has two bikes.' I notice a slight tremble in Waldi's voice, and, yup, he's welling up. Jeez, I've opened a real can of worms here. So it does still affect you, then? 'Little bit, yes,' he trembles, rubbing swollen, watery eyes. 'Doesn't matter, it's true, so no problem, I live with that or I don't live with that.'

This is getting heavy, I almost feel like giving him a hug but feebly proffer some kinder words. But you had a good career... 'Ja, ja, ja.' And you were really popular... 'Ja, ja, ja, and I have so much fun when I make races.' My next attempt at cheering him up is even more cheesy, but knowing what many world champions are like, I kind of mean it. So Ralf, if you had the choice of being a nice guy without a world championship, or an asshole with a world championship, which would you be? By now Waldi's on an emotional rollercoaster and suddenly he's in hysterics. 'Ha, ha ha! Ja, ja, ja, it's better nice guy and not world champion.' A big grin and another rub of those puffy eyes.

'I don't know, maybe I was not lucky enough to get a title, or maybe I'm not fighting enough, or maybe a funny guy like I am, maybe I'm not strong enough. World titles is what every racer looks for, but I had so many nice races and I win 20 times, so I must keep this in my memory, not one title. For sure one title would be nice but the wins are also very important, I think.'

CHAPTER 26

THOSE WERE THE

HAZE

November 2002

Smoky ol' two-stroke 500s and disco conquered the world in the 1970s. Barry Sheene and friends trace their years at the top of the GP power curve

Back in the 1970s, GP racing didn't just look great and sound great, it smelt great too, although that had nothing to do with the great smell of Brut, the pervading whiff in Barry Sheene's caravan. It was sweeter than that. Back then, racetracks were a fog of Castrol R fumes exuded by the 500 two-strokes that were starting to kick ass, the warm grey taste filling your nostrils with mineral-based sweetness each time a national flag was dropped to start a grand prix.

Castrol R was the smell of a generation – the wide-lapelled jetsetters who battled those medieval 'stinkwheels' to world domination, apparently consigning four-strokes to the dustbin of racing history. Like smoke machines in nightclubs, the two-stroke haze added a layer of mystery – and therefore romance and glamour – to proceedings. Like maybe, just maybe, you might catch a glimpse of Sheeney's bird Stephanie Maclean through the sweet, sickly greyness.

It wasn't all glamour, of course. Those early 500 two-strokes were nasty pieces of work – their engines likely to lock solid at the most inappropriate moment, skewing the machine sideways and jettisoning the rider skyward, seriously dangerous when tracks were adjoined by brick walls and telegraph poles, not cosy expanses of gravel trap. The bikes were agonisingly noisy too, for it wasn't until the late 1970s that anyone even thought about silencers, by which time many an eardrum had been shredded (presumably they couldn't think for the racket).

Tommy Robb, whose GP career straddled the four-stroke and two-stroke eras, was one of many who suffered. 'Seizures were always a worry,' says the Ulsterman who rode factory Honda four-strokes to several GP wins in the 1960s, later contesting world championship events on Yamaha strokers, the forerunners of the RD streetbikes. 'And when an engine locked up, it locked up very quickly, which is why I wear two hearing aids today. If you wanted to catch a seizure early you needed to notice that slight pinking noise just prior to a seizure, so I never wore cotton wool in my ears. The two-strokes shattered my inner ears.' 1970s racers like Robb had a phrase for that misleading moment of serenity that heralded a seizure: 'whispering death'.

> 'I miss the two-stroke sound very much, even though it shattered my inner ears, and the smell was wonderful'

And yet Robb has no regrets. 'I miss the sound very much, it's done me damage but I wish it was still the way it was. I feel sorry for people who never heard racing in the 1960s and 1970s. And the smell was wonderful, when we got around a table we used to joke that we should get a little tray of Castrol R and set it alight, just to get the atmosphere for the chat. It was lovely.'

Robb finished third in the 1971 Ulster 500 GP aboard an ageing Norton single. More than half a lap ahead, Australian Jack Findlay was making history, riding a Suzuki TR500 to victory, the first-ever two-stroke premier-class win. Findlay's air-cooled twin, a somewhat basic development of the T500 streetbike, had a powerband, oooh, 900rpm wide, but it was the start of something big.

Two years later Sheene was developing Suzuki's seminal RG500 square four, with which he won the '76 and '77 500 titles. 'The two-strokes were lighter than the four-strokes and they had more horsepower but they were far less tractable,' he recalls. 'The first RG I rode at the end of '73 started at nine grand, below that there was nothing, and when I say nothing, I mean nothing. To get it out of the paddock you had to scream it at 10,000rpm or it wouldn't even clear, and it stopped at ten-five, so once you'd got it clear at nine-five, you had 1000rpm to play with. I told them it was a waste of time unless they spread the powerband, but they were going "But Barry-san, it's got 105 horsepower!"'

By then the two-strokes were winning now and again, mostly when Latin heartthrob Giacomo Agostini and his mighty MV Agusta four-stroke had already wrapped up the title, Ago indulging himself on some Caribbean beach while the also-rans completed the championship. And yet Agostini could see the writing on the wall. In '74 he terminated his nine-year relationship with Count Domenico Agusta and signed for Yamaha. The two-strokes were getting faster and more refined with every race – the four-cylinder OW26 which the Italian stallion rode to the following year's 500 title had a powerband almost 2000rpm wide – while the four-strokes were going nowhere. But guys like Sheene – accustomed to spending their winters partying hard – paid a high price for the strokers' improving usability. 'Foolishly enough I told Suzuki I'd come to Japan at the end of '74 and stay there until the engine was right,' he says. 'I was there for five weeks, the biggest jail sentence I've ever served in my life, a nightmare, but the bike came good.'

The only riposte that the four-stroke faithful had had to the stinkwheels' two-power-strokes-for-the-price-of-one technology was multiplying cylinders and gears, as Honda had done with their five-cylinder/eight-speed 125 and six-cylinder/seven-speed 250. But new technical regulations, intended to reduce costs, limited the number of cylinders and gears, outlawing Honda's most exotic creations, including a 250 V8 and 500 six that were rumoured to be on the drawing board. The new rules swung the advantage irrevocably towards the two-strokes. Only by rewriting the regs for 2002, when four-strokes were given a near 100 per cent capacity advantage in MotoGP, was the reign of the two-strokes ended.

As the 1970s accelerated to their disco-pumping peak, Sheene's hair grew longer and the two-stroke's powerband grew wider. 'By the end of '76 people knew the four-stroke was finished,' he adds. 'In '79 the RG would start at seven five and go through to 11,000; it was just the extra knowledge they had about porting, expansion chambers, ignition timing, everything.'

And they just kept getting better. Improved metallurgy, lubrication (the fog of Castrol R finally cleared around then) and all-round know-how increased reliability, performance and ridability quite dramatically. But you never get rid of all your problems in racing – back then Sheene's just changed from dodgy two-strokes to pesky Americans.

Kenny Roberts had arrived in Europe in '78 and swiped the title from Sheene at his first attempt. By the time the King quit at the end of '83, when he lost out to Freddie Spencer and Honda, Americans pretty much ruled the scene. And new-fangled technology was broadening powerbands still further. Sheene again: 'By '86 or '87 you could ride a

*'I told them it was a
waste of time unless
they spread the
powerband, but they
were going "But
Barry-san, it's got
105 horsepower!"*

500 around town if you fitted low enough gearing;
they were increasingly a lot easier to ride.'

Well, maybe easier to ride out of pit lane, but not so
easy at the ring-dinging limit. Fuelled by a global
economic boom that fattened budgets and hastened
development, two-stroke technology really came
together in the mid-1980s. Horsepower outputs
exploded, and suddenly things started to get serious.

There'd been cash in the 1970s, but the lucre was
spent with Dancing Queen-tinged innocence and
abandon – frittered away chasing chicks at Tramp, tooting coke in Ibiza
and filling the garage with Rollers. The party stopped as the 1980s
kicked into gear – the boom pumping serious money into sport for the
first time. Evermore-bloated budgets raised the stakes for the riders
and the people making the bikes, so engines got quicker, tyres got fatter
and chassis stiffer. All of sudden, riders needed to be more than half fit
to ride the things, so the flared-up, Gitane-puffing playboys caved in to
the cool-headed, cold-hearted professional automatons, pumping iron
and riding sideways.

This was also the age of the computer, when data acquisition allowed
engineers to fully understand the inner mysteries of the life of the two-
stroke, so they could hone efficiency to dizzy new heights, not only in
peak power, but also in power delivery. Reed-valve induction, power
valves and digital ignition mapping calmed engine character, though
Roberts missed out on the luxury of reeds by just one year. 'It was only
after Yamaha copied Honda and went to crankcase reeds in '84 that the
Yamaha got pretty ridable,' says Roberts, who spent his GP years
heroically wrestling with much less friendly piston port and disc valve
induction. 'The reeds just broadened out the whole powerband, so you
could spin the tyre and know where you were with it.'

Up to a point, anyway. The OW70 V4 that Roberts raced in '83 had
135 horsepower, by the early 1990s Honda's NSR500 V4 was screaming
out 170, and riders were once more running out of traction, the endless
cycle of engine and chassis development spiralling upward. Once again
it was Honda that divined the way forward, creating the 'big bang'
engine for Mick Doohan in '92. This firing order bunched the V4's
power pulses together, giving the rear tyre time to regain traction
between each salvo. Roberts again: 'The big bang was the one, it just

smoothed everything out, so the rider wasn't always playing catch- up with the throttle, but Yamaha's "big bang" was just a Band Aid for a shitty powerband. Honda were the only ones who ever got their powerband truly linear, so the rider had the throttle response to really control the bike when the rear tyre was spinning. Honda always has more money, so they got all the stuff right – cylinders, pipes, carburettors and, most of all, the electronics.'

Suzuki never got it quite right either, as '93 World Supers champ Scott Russell discovered when he raced RGV500 V4s in '96. 'You better take your time with this thing,' he said. 'Or else you'll be pulling straw out o' your ass and having Dr Costa shoot Novocaine in your feet.'

Honda got it so right that Doohan was soon calling for sharper power delivery, surely the first time anyone had asked for such a thing from a two-stroke. Mighty Mick reckoned he could handle something a bit more fiery, and he was right. Honda gave him a 90 degree motor for '97, when he won 12 of 14 races. The last time HRC ran an even-spaced firing order was in 1990, when Doohan & Co were regularly jettisoned over the highside by the screamer's lairy power curve. Soothed by a black box-load of hi-tech electronics, the new-age screamer demonstrated just how far two-stroke technology had come.

Despite Doohan's towering talent, the 500s were running into a brick wall with lap times by the late 1990s; once again they'd got too powerful for existing chassis and tyre technology. King Kenny had a clever idea – to build his own 500, a less powerful but more nimble three-cylinder, rather like Spencer's NS500 triple that had beaten his lardy V4 in '83. The KR3 might've matched the NS if tyre technology hadn't leaped forward, once more allowing the V4s to take advantage of their 190 horsepower engines before they were legislated into extinction in 2002.

CHAPTER 27

ONE GIANT LEAP

FOR BIKING

November 2002

Honda's all-conquering RC211V took over from the NSR500 as the fastest race bike in the world but what made the bike so devastatingly good? Only one way to find out – ride Valentino Rossi's RCV

At the end of 2001, Honda's NSR500 ruled the world, the greatest race bike ever, the most wanted race bike on earth. Now the NSR is obsolete and unwanted, its reputation swept away by its four-stroke successor, the RC211V. And now I know why. Testing the RCV and NSR back to back at Valencia the day after the 2002 season-ending Valencia GP, the RCV takes your breath away, helps you do things you never thought you'd do on a motorcycle. Then you ride the NSR and it's a bag of nails – it doesn't stop, turn or go, it's vicious, awkward and too damned demanding.

I feel weird slagging the once all-powerful NSR but I'm not alone. Alex Barros, who'd beaten fellow RCV rider Valentino Rossi in the previous day's race, turned up during the test to ride the NSR he'd ridden during most of 2002, just for old time's sake. He rode a handful of laps on the machine, returned to the pits and handed it to his mechanics, announcing: 'This bike is sheeeet!'

How can this be? How can Barros heap scorn upon a motorcycle that had taken him to three 500 GP wins during the previous two seasons? Maybe because its successor took him to two MotoGP wins during just four races at the end of 2002. But more so because the RCV is a quantum leap forward in all-round engine and chassis performance. It's both faster and easier to ride than an NSR500, and you can't say anything better than that about a race bike.

Riding the RCV leaves you dizzy, struggling to translate its other-world performance into words and wary of getting carried away on a wave of gushing hyperbole. But what the hell, this is like no other motorcycle I've ever ridden. It consigns every turbocharged, nitrous-boosted, avgas-crammed psycho bike I've ridden – including 500 GP bikes and World Superbike winners – to limpid greyness, though maybe not for the reasons you'd expect.

You'd think that the RCV would blow you away with its speed and power – surely any motorcycle that can accelerate past an NSR500 like it's stood still must be a brain-frazzling terror. But the V5 isn't like that at all. The bike's most remarkable characteristic is its user friendliness, not its insane power-to-weight ratio (1.5 horsepower per kilo compared to an NSR's 1.45bhp/kg or a GSX-R1000's 0.82bhp/kg) that delivers a hilarious frenzy of acceleration, kicking up the front wheel in second, third, fourth, whenever.

'The RCV consigns every turbocharged, nitrous-boosted, avgas-crammed psycho bike I've ridden to limpid greyness'

You shift gears at 14,750rpm, though HRC say the motor will go to 16,000, and there's no apparent powerband. The RCV is never scary, which is some achievement for a 220 horsepower motorcycle; it's like a 500 that wants to be your mate. Five hundreds aren't friendly – they're nasty, evil pieces of equipment that'll mug you given half the chance.

Most of all, and I don't quite know how to say this without sounding ridiculous, the RCV feels like a toy, so manageable that you can play around with the thing and it'll do whatever you want it to do, go wherever you want it to go. And this is what HRC were aiming at when they created their first four-stroke GP racer in more than two decades. RCV project leader Hejiro Yoshimura wanted the bike to be 'easy to manage, like a motocross or trials bike', and that's pretty much what it feels like – a 220bhp trials tool, very cool.

HRC achieved this goal largely through a radical centralisation of mass, starting with the 75.5 degree vee engine, which is significantly more compact than any other big-capacity four-stroke, including Honda's SP-2 World Supers motor. The V5's mass is highly concentrated, with an almost spherical shape, allowing ideal location of centre of gravity and centralisation of mass, which play a vital role in the bike's remarkable steering and handling. This concept is consolidated by the super-compact semi-dry sump lubrication system and the low-slung gas tank, allowed by the Unit Pro-Link rear-suspension system which eliminates the need for an upper chassis shock mount.

When you ride the RCV, it feels like its entire mass has been tucked into the size of a football just beneath your stomach, offering amazing control. The bike seems two feet long, so you don't ride around corners so much as dive in and out, and yet it has none of the nervousness associated with a short wheelbase.

Racing at the limit is all about confidence, and the RCV delivers shed-loads of the stuff because engine/chassis/suspension integration allows a remarkably balanced machine. The RCV's neutral behaviour also reduces the need to rework set-up at every track, so the rider can use the same settings week after week, which allows him to intimately understand the bike's behaviour, so he knows what it's going to do almost before it does it, which gives him yet more confidence, so he can ride even harder.

The RCV is so good at cornering that it makes an NSR feel like hard work. Four-strokes are easier to ride around corners than two-strokes because they've a constant connection between throttle, tyre and tarmac, which is why Superbikes run so close to 500 lap times. Shut the throttle on the RCV and the engine helps you turn the corner, shut the throttle on the NSR and there's no rear-end connection, the bike wants to go straight, so you have to do all the steering through the handlebars.

The RCV seems committed to helping the rider in every way possible, very unlike 500s, which only yield their real potential to the most accomplished riders. You notice this at every point of the racetrack – the RCV happily rides through fast sweepers on a trailing throttle while the two-stroke surges and snatches. And if you misjudge your braking aboard the RCV, the engine helps slow you down. Get your braking wrong on the 500 and it's panic stations, because there's zero engine braking!

The four-stroke's character doesn't only help you ride into corners more easily than the two-stroke's, it also helps you coming out of the turns. The RCV has so much power and torque that it's almost impossible to find yourself in the wrong gear when it's time to crack open the throttle. Not so with the NSR – run into a corner in too high a gear, with say 8500rpm on the tacho, and the motor's barely interested in getting you down the next straight.

HRC also designed lateral flex into the RCV's chassis to improve feel through corners and to offer less snappy slides. Inbuilt chassis flex is an increasingly important consideration in racing design, because as lean angles increase, suspension efficiency decreases, so engineers have to find another way of absorbing forces driven into the chassis. A too-rigid chassis also delivers too much torque reaction to the rear tyre, causing difficult-to-control wheelspin.

For many years racing purists have considered four-strokes to be second-rate race bikes, but only because pretty much every four-stroke racer of the previous three decades used a turgid street engine. The RCV and its rivals are the first prototype four-strokes since Honda's and MV Agusta's GP bikes of the 1960s and 1970s. The RCV feels like no other four-stroke you've ridden, with a real crack to the throttle. It's like a two-stroke without the hassle. Believe – prototype four-strokes rock!

CHAPTER 28

There's more than one way
around a racetrack

December 2002

**World Supers rivals Colin Edwards and Troy Bayliss use hugely
different riding techniques – Edwards silky smooth, Bayliss
apparently out of control, so how come both work so well**

The duel for the 2002 World Superbike crown was probably the most
climactic Supers championship ever. And, somewhat strangely, the
contest reached its climax at Imola and panned out just like the best-ever
500 world championship battle. Back in 1983, King Kenny Roberts and
Freddie Spencer were neck and neck going into the final 500 GP at Imola,
Roberts needing help from Yamaha team-mate Eddie Lawson if he were
to sneak the title from his Honda arch-rival, just like Troy Bayliss needed
help from Ducati team-mate Ruben Xaus to overhaul Honda's Colin
Edwards at Imola 2002. But Xaus wasn't up to it, just as rookie Lawson
hadn't been in '83. Enough of the history lesson, though...

Bayliss and Edwards couldn't have ended up running closer to each
other – both on the track and in the points chase – and yet you'd be pushed
to think of two motorcycle racers who look so different when they're on
their bikes. Bayliss looks like a maniac – all wobbles and tankslappers –
while Edwards looks like he's out for a Sunday afternoon cruise.

So how did these two riders develop such contrasting styles? And what's
it like to duke it out with someone whose technique is so different from
your own? Does Edwards get scared witless by his opponent's apparently
out-of-control shenanigans? And what exactly did Bayliss teach Edwards
that crucially helped change the course of their title battle?

Colin Edwards
How come you're so smooth on a bike?
I'll be honest with you, it started from my kid motocross days and it
just carried over. When I was motocrossing, David Bailey was god to

me, he was my childhood hero and is still one of my heroes to this day. He was obviously the smoothest guy out there, and like any tennis player or golf player or whatever, when you're comin' up, you want to emulate their style or their swing, and that's basically what happened. I saw what Bailey was doin' and just tried to emulate him, he was super smooth and that's what I aimed for. I knew that being smooth, the less out of control you were, the more you kept it off the ground and so the faster you could go. I learned it from a young age, to keep everything under control, and that kinda carried over to roadracing.

Do you ever get ragged?
You know, ragged to me would just be a small moment for Troy! What I consider ragged, you probably wouldn't even be able to see on TV. Although I'd feel it, I'd correct it before anybody even knew what happened. That's the way I've learned the game.

Troy reckons you really hang over the front
That wasn't something that was built into me. When I was at Yamaha I had what I'd say was a neutral riding style, that's the way it looks when I watch tapes from yesteryear. Whereas as soon as I got with Honda, the only way I could turn the sonofabitch was to put everything I had on the front of the thing, you know. That's been a Honda character forever, if you look at the way Mick [Doohan] used to plough the front, it's just Honda understeer.

What's it like following Troy?
You know, when I follow Troy there's so much shit goin' on, that's the only thing I can say! And half of it is his sparky toe scrapers. I thought sparky things were illegal, I don't know, but that obviously bugs the shit out of me, you just think he's gonna crash every other corner when he's got sparks coming off. The knee pucks that I use are leather and every time I touch them down it's a little puff of smoke, so people think my bikes blowin' up or some shit. It smells like ass when you're following me because it's burnin' leather!

Whenever I follow Troy it's entertaining, that's for sure, though it's not as entertaining as following Haga! Troy stays on his lines but he always asks a lot from the bike, he's constantly asking for that next little inch and the thing's gettin' sideways and jumpin' and wrigglin'. I think a lot of that's the difference between Ducati and Honda. Whereas I know where the edge is with the Honda, I think the Ducati is maybe more grey in that area. Just from watching him, it looks like the Ducati is either hooked in or it's not; everything feels right, you go to hit it and next thing it might snap itself a little sideways. Whereas with the Honda, it'll step out an inch but before it even snaps real sideways you can control it.

> 'Following Troy is entertaining, he's constantly asking for that next little inch and the thing's gettin' sideways and jumpin' and wrigglin'

Troy is ragged, but are his lines consistent?
You don't win all those races without being consistent! He's definitely consistent when I follow him, you know, hitting the same spot, the same couple of inches every lap, he just goes about it differently. Sometime he might out-brake himself or he might brake a little bit early but he always manages to hit around the same area into the turn. It's just something you ride with, you just follow and watch what's happening.

Do you ever get wary of him?
At times, though not necessarily when he's alone, just when I've gotten behind him when him and Haga have been touchin' and bumpin' and kickin' the shit out of each other, that's when you get a little bit wary of being really close because one of them might go down or whatever. But when he's on his own, no, nothing really throws you out to chop the throttle or anything.

Are there advantages and disadvantages to your different styles?
Earlier in the year, with Troy's style, he was in the corner and out of it before I'd even got my thing tipped in. I think he's really aggressive on digging the front and getting the thing fully flexed and turned, then stood upright out of the turn, while I'm running wide on the corner. Whereas when I got more horsepower after the Eight Hours in July I didn't have to carry the absolute limit of corner speed and run wide, so I could afford to get in a little bit like him – dig it in and go.

He steers his thing hard…
Hell, you can see him, sometimes his position on the bike is so funny

that you know he's just wrenching the shit out of the 'bars to get the thing over, that's just Troy's style. I'd almost say it's a bit like Fogarty's – rough on the bike and wrestling it. I mean you really see it, you know, whereas whenever I see myself on TV I just look like a slow fucker. It's like 'man, couldn't I work just a little bit?', but that's when I go my fastest.

So do you think it's the Ducati that dictates his style?
Yeah, you could say maybe it's the Ducati that made Fogarty and Bayliss ride like that, but then you look at [Troy] Corser, he obviously made the thing ride good. I would say if there's anybody out there with a similar style to mine it's Corser – never really out of shape, keeps the thing in line, and goes white line to white line. It's just different techniques and obviously he made the Ducati work really well. I mean, it might be a characteristic of the bike, but I think a lot of it is in Troy's ridin'.

What did you learn from Troy this year?
The thing I learned with Troy is that you never ever give in. It doesn't matter if you've got five, six or seven seconds on him, the guy just does not stop. I know a lot of riders out there, and I'll agree I was one of them, who when somebody pulled out five or six seconds on me, well shit, I've only got six laps left, I'm not going to make up a second a lap, so you settle for the position you've got and you take it home. Whereas Troy…. [Edwards adopts slow-paced, deep-toned voice like a trailer for a horror movie] doesn't… believe… in that… he's just flat-out from go to stop. At times when you think it might be an easy win you still gotta ride your ass off just to keep the gap. With Troy you can't even allow the gap to come down two or three tenths a lap, instead of almost cruisin' to the finish.

I'll be honest with you, I've never raced against anyone like him. I mean he's awesome – as a rider he's awesome and his mental determination is awesome. He wants to win, sure we all do, but the thing I learned from him is that when I get out front I'm going, I keep the lap times going, until I know it's two laps from the end and I've got five or six seconds, so I can afford to catch my breath and go on to win the thing. It used to be the last five or six laps, whoever was a few seconds back would ease off a little bit or whatever, but not with Troy.

Troy Bayliss

Why do you ride the way you do?
A lot of guys ride quite similar and then there's guys that stand out and have got their own styles, there's plenty of them about. When you first start roadracing you hop on the bike and whatever makes it go where and when and how you want it to go is what works. You come up with your own little ideas, and it just happens like it happens.

Have you always ridden aggressively?
Yep, I've always had the same sort of style. For sure I used to be more ragged [laughs]. I look quite a bit smoother than I used to, though even now I look like I put a lot of physical effort into it and I actually do.

So when did you change from super ragged to smooth ragged?
I think 2001 was the only time it settled down a bit. When I was racing in England a few years back I started to get a little bit more smooth, but when I first came on board of Ducati to have a go in World Superbike I was pretty... I don't know about ragged... but very physical on the bike. In 2000 I was trying to get the Ducati job for 2001 and I didn't know the bike or anything very well; I was riding Michelin for the first time, everything was new, and I had to try and get myself a job. But I think I've settled down a little bit since.

Were you aggressive as a club racer?
For sure, they used to call me 'the can opener'! When I did club races before I got into national events we used to do, like 10 or 12 races a day, so it was always the same guys in the same races, and the first and second corners were always absolutely crazy. I used to ride a KR-1 and we were riding in Formula Two, up against 600 Supersports and stuff, all sorts of different bikes, so it was quite funny. It's a good place to start, that's for sure.

Is aggression what it's all about?
The bikes are getting so fast and so powerful that to get the last bit out of them you've got to put a lot of physical input into them. Like when you do loads and loads of laps on a test day you really feel it. Over the last years Superbikes have become much more fast, but they're already

very close to the 500 and MotoGP times, so I can't see them getting too much faster. I think physical fitness really does play a part – it definitely does for me. If I wasn't fit and feeling good I wouldn't be able to ride like I do, I have to be able to really muscle the bike around.

I have the bike quite flat, the geometry's not like very steep. Ruben's and Ben's [Xaus and Bostrom, Bayliss' factory Ducati team-mates] bikes are set up so steep that I can't ride them, but them guys are bigger and stronger than me, anyway. I ride the bike like a chopper, type of thing, that's just how I like to ride it, so yeah, I have to work it over! I don't feel comfortable with a steep set-up, it's just how you're brought into it, people want their bikes certain ways.

Learning your way on proddie bikes must've influenced your style.
After the KR1 I did 600 Supersports. I can see that guys who started in 250 production and then went to 250 GP bikes went in a different direction, so for sure they'll ride different. I'm used to sponges, that's just how it is.

Does your style ever cost you time?
There's some places where I suffer a bit for it, but I don't like to change the bike too much, because it's hard to get comfortable again. Once you're to the limit of a motorcycle, it's hard to change it, then find the limit with a completely different set-up, so I don't steer too far away from what I've got.

At which tracks do you suffer?
Assen was a bit difficult for me – there's a lot of changes of direction when you're hard on the throttle.

Is there also an element of joy in your riding style?
Yeah, for sure, when things are working good, I love riding the bike. It's not fun all the time, sometimes it's a drag when you're struggling, but when you get to thrash something around that's the best you can get and it's not yours, it's quite nice, it's a ball!

Does your style help with intimidating other riders?
I've never had anybody come up and tell me they've got a problem with my riding. But maybe you could run into a hairpin corner by

someone, pull the clutch in and just hold it on the stop, that'd scare them more! [laughs]

Have you ever tried smoothing out your riding?
There's some places you do have to change your style. The biggest place I've had to do that is Daytona. You've really got to get off the bike and keep it a bit upright because you've got a very hard rear tyre and you've got to do a lot of laps on it. There's no grip there, so you've got to try and get the bike up, so I did change my style a little bit there.

   Also, every now and then I hang off the inside of the bike a bit more, to try and pick it up a bit, because when once you're hanging over the bike and you're at full lean there's very little grip there when you try to open the throttle. Mick Doohan used to hunch right over too, though I never tried to copy him, it's just the way I was.

Do you think the fans prefer your style?
I guess if you're very smooth it can look a little bit dull, whereas I'm fighting with the bike and I'm very active on the bike, so I guess it makes good watching. Some people get really excited about it and some people who know me, they know I'm a pretty tame sort of a guy, then they seem me riding the bike and they can't watch me [more laughter] because they think I'm going to crash. That's quite strange, so yeah, I get funny reactions.

Do you let out an explosion of aggression when you jump on the bike?
I'm pretty laid back off the bike but I've always been aggressive on the bike. When I hop on the bike it's like another me, well, not another me... I don't feel like I'm riding crazy, I don't even feel like I'm so active on the bike, I feel totally in control and I actually feel smooth at the moment, smoother than I've ever done. So I must've been pretty ragged a few years ago!

What do you do for the wet?
I just slow down quite a lot, that's about it! But the tyres are comin' a lot better than they used to be and some of the tracks are pretty grippy now. I learned my wet-weather riding when I was racing in England. I wasn't fast in the rain when I moved there but I done quite a lot of wet riding in BSB [British Superbike], plus Michelin have got really good

wet weather tyres now. Eventually it clicks with riding in the rain, so now I don't mind riding in the wet at all.

Who rides like you in MotoGP?
Maybe Capirossi, he really gives it a hard go. And Rossi does as well, he gets on it, he's always got it backin' in and jumpin' around.

How do you compare your style to Edwards?
Yeah, we're quite a lot different aren't we [laughs]! I like watching Colin on the bike, he can slide it out. He definitely looks more smooth than me but I like his style. It's a good style, he hangs right over the front doesn't he? I still learn stuff but I think Colin learned a bit from me this year, he learned not to give up so much, so he was really hookin' into it those last races.

MotoGP Mutterings: December 2002
Less is more, they say, so does more technology mean less exciting racing? And if so, should upcoming MotoGP technology be banned?

The first season of MotoGP wasn't so bad. Okay, so Rossi won a few too many races, but the action got tighter as things went on, not the other way around, which bodes well for next season when the grid will be rammed with four-strokes – Ducati and Proton joining Aprilia, Honda, Yamaha, Suzuki and Kawasaki.

What makes the four-strokes fun to watch is the sideways corner-entry chaos, with the hottest guys cheerfully backing into turns like they're riding single-pot trail bikes on the dirt, not slick-shod 220 horsepower racers on asphalt. The quickest MotoGP bikes are pretty wild out of turns too, those big 990cc motors burning more rubber than the 500s ever did. Which is all good – we want to see riders wrestling to stay in control, it's what racing's all about. But for how long will this kind of madness go on? Not much longer if progress has anything to do with it.

GP racing is now entering an era of space-age racetrack technology, fuelled by mega-money factory MotoGP budgets, in which computer software rules. In fact, the thin edge of the hi-tech wedge is already visible, or in this case, invisible. How often have you seen Carlos Checa getting all crossed-up into turns on his Yamaha M1? Never, because the M1 uses a computer-controlled engine-braking system which keeps everything nicely under control on the way into corners. And Honda and the rest have got to be working on their own versions of the M1 system, so pretty soon everyone will be cruising into turns all neat 'n' tidy. And, as traction control gets better, they'll all be cruising out of turns all neat 'n' pretty too – none of that oh-so-scary sideways action.

Okay, so maybe the future holds less highsidin', tankslappin' TV fun, but at least racing should get closer, just because all the bikes are so good. In fact the opposite tends to happen – witness the 'racing' joke that is F1 cars, where the pit-lane computer geek has long been king, and technology overkill long ago replaced the concept of actual racing as entertainment. The problem is that overtaking gets too difficult once there are no bad bikes out there. Ever-improving braking systems have the same effect, because the shorter the braking zone, the less room for passing.

> *'Nowadays everyone brakes about the same damn place, leans into the corner the same place and goes around the corner at the same speed'*

Things were different when bikes were less advanced and machine set-up was more of a hit-and-miss affair; weird shit happened in races because riders could make the difference, overcoming a settings cock-up or an equipment deficiency with some inspired heroics. And when tracks were more dangerous, a brave rider (or a fool, you decide) could make a winning difference through a lethal corner, through which his more sensible rivals might crucially back off. There's not so much call for that any more – all GP tracks are pretty much as safe as they can get, no one backs off anywhere, everyone rides the ragged edge through each and every corner. You only need check GP qualifying times – these days it's rare for the top ten to be separated by more than a second – to see the scale of equality.

'Nowadays everyone brakes about the same damn place, leans into the corner the same place and goes around the corner at the same speed; some guys just do it a little bit better than others,' says former 500 champ King Kenny Roberts.

Perhaps the only way out of this loop is to restrict technology and (I don't really mean this) host GPs at faster, more dangerous racetracks.

But how would you keep the bikes nice and out of control? You can't really specify stuff like chassis with hinges in the middle; well, you could… No, the bad stuff is electronics, so bad that even the riders don't want their bikes running fly-by-wire. 'Already in F1 the driver doesn't even shift gear,' adds Rossi. 'So the driver becomes very much less important. I'm a rider, so I don't want this.'

Roberts, however, believes that the Japanese factories, who effectively run world-level racing though the MSMA (Motorcycle Sports Manufacturers' Association), won't do anything about keeping technology under control. 'No one's thinking about this kind of stuff and I'd imagine that in three years' time people will be saying the racing's boring,' he adds.

Gloomy stuff for armchair race fans. But perhaps I'm missing the whole point – future technology will make sportsbikes so user-friendly – with ABS, traction control and computerised engine braking – that you'll even be able to ride pissed. The future is indeed bright.

Epilogue: I hate to say I told you so, but…

CHAPTER 29

THE TALE OF

SLIDE

March 2003

It's the flashest trick in the book and the riders who are best at it are the riders that win races. This is the history of rear-wheel steering and the masters of slide, before traction control came along and spoiled everything

In the good old days, when men were men and a fast 500 GP bike rattled out, ooh, at least 50 horsepower, the fastest way around a racetrack was knees tucked in, wheels in line, chin rattling on the gas tank. But time moves on. With more than two hundred horses kicking through the rear tyre, wheelspin is something you've got to live with, so you'd better use it to your advantage.

The number-one reason that racers spin the rear is to steer out of turns. Getting sideways points the front end back towards the corner's inside, tightening the rider's line, giving him more room to get on the gas, which means more speed down the next straight. It's like using the handbrake in a car, except you're breaking traction with throttle, not brake, and you're doing it to go faster, not slower.

Rear-wheel steering came from US dirt track. American racers used to start their careers riding ovals and then roadrace, and having grown up sideways it was only natural they'd be the same on tarmac. King Kenny Roberts was the first serious back-end boy and his success encouraged a whole generation of bad-ass American and Aussie dirt trackers to go GP racing. Also, it just so happened that 1980s 500s were kicking out way more power than their tyres and chassis could handle, so there was only one way to subdue them: kick 'em sideways with big fistfuls of throttle and slingshot out of the turn.

Roberts, Spencer, Lawson, Gardner, Rainey, Schwantz and Doohan all ruled GPs after starting out on the dirt. But during Doohan's mid-1990s reign, chassis and tyre technology improved so that tarmac-fixated Europeans could ride 500s like 250s, using corner speed rather than sideways exits. Guys like Valentino Rossi went dirt-track training anyway, gaining themselves a crucial edge. And then along came ex-speedway nutter Garry McCoy, ushering in a new age of slide during 1999 and 2000.

King Kenny Roberts: first man sideways

Kenny Roberts never felt right on a roadracer until he started sliding. Like other dirt trackers, sideways was what he knew best, things felt safer and more comfortable that way.

'It was Ontario Motor Speedway in '72, I think,' recalls King Kenny, 500 champ in 1978, '79 and '80. 'I'd just started dragging my knee, and that helped me feel the bike slide. Then I started setting it up through the turns for the slide, that's when everyone went "you're crazy, you're nuts", that's when it all started. If I hadn't been a dirt tracker, I wouldn't have done it, wouldn't have had the feel, wouldn't have known what I was looking for.

'I started setting it up through the turns for the slide, that's when everyone went "you're crazy, you're nuts", that's when it all started'

'I went to Imola that year and I put it on Giacomo Agostini pretty bad, even though he was 13 time world champion and I'd never seen the place before. I could find the limit, while Ago was a line racer, so it was much harder for him to define the limit. If you gave him eight days of practice he could ease up on it but otherwise I'd smoke him.'

Roberts believes that spinning the rear is an essential weapon, not only for steering but also because it allows more feel.

'You do it so you don't need to ride the line. You can start sliding it and that points you in the right direction, plus, when it starts to slide, you know exactly how much traction you have and where your traction limit is. That's Biaggi's problem; he rides 500s like they're 250s, so he feels the limit with the front tyre, and when you find the limit with the front, it's another thing to save it. Sliding takes the front out of the equation.'

There's corners on every racetrack where the ability to slide is totally crucial. Roberts cites Daytona, where riders come on to the banking, giving full gas for the all-important 190mph blast to the finish line and trying to miss the wall. 'You'd be pointing the bike up the banking, goin' like hell and goin' too fast to make it, just by using lean. So you'd aim at the wall, then lean it over at the last moment to break traction, the bike would kick sideways and away you went. If you didn't you'd have to nick it back on the throttle and that lap was gone.'

Although the aim is always the same, other racers have their own way of getting sideways and Roberts knows the differences better than anyone, having watched trackside since the mid-1980s.

'It depends on the rider and the bike. If you've not got the power, you can do it with lean angle – lay the thing over so it breaks traction. Doohan did it like that – he'd exit the corner a little too fast, lean a little more, then give it more gas so the tyre would light up and fix his line. McCoy is a little different from Mick, he sets it up with a lot more rpm, he's slower mid-corner, sets it up a little earlier, then gases the hell out of it.'

Despite tyre and chassis improvements, Roberts insists dirt track is essential training for anyone aiming at a premier-class crown. 'Alex Crivillé wouldn't have been champ in 1999 if he hadn't gone to my dirt-track school' – Alex said so himself. Guys like McCoy obviously know how to do it and Rossi messed around doing dirt track when he was a kid. He still does some on his XR650, he knows how to do it.'

Wayne Rainey: sideways is as normal as going straight

Like all the greatest rear-wheel steerers Wayne Rainey learned his racing craft as a child. Sliding and throttle control were nurtured into him from the earliest of ages.

'As a kid, being sideways was as normal as riding in a straight line,' says Rainey, who emulated mentor Kenny Roberts with a 500 title hat trick in 1990, '91 and '92. 'When I started roadracing in the early 1980s, I didn't know if it was right or wrong but it was what I felt comfortable with. If the tyre wasn't spinning and the bike turning, I didn't feel right. I liked it spinning because it gives you a safety buffer, you kinda know where you can go with it.

'In fact, sliding is the easy part, the difficult part is front-tyre feel. The key to my riding style was getting through that area really quick, getting the front tyre out of the way so I could get on the throttle. When you brake and flick, it's all front tyre, which is kinda risky.

'The advantage rear-wheel steering gave me was huge. And it's just the same now – watch Rossi, he's getting a bit sideways now. It's great when you've a lot of grip because you can use more throttle than the other guys, and when the grip starts to fade, you know where the traction is.

'To me the throttle was everything. But when you're doing this you're talking very small changes in throttle opening because you're at the limit of everything – throttle position, chassis flex, tyre flex, you're feeling all that stuff. Spinning the rear relieves pressure on the tyre, relieves pressure on the suspension and that widens the safety area. But you're only spinning to keep the bike turning, just to keep it on track. There's no performance advantage in spinning like speedway. I think McCoy will get better at it, he'll know where to spin and where not to spin, whereas now he spins too much. Most of the time you don't want the tyre to spin much at all, you want it to drive maximum, you're always focused on drive.'

But there are times when getting truly, madly, deeply sideways does have its uses. 'I used to do it just to piss off the guys behind me because they couldn't do it. It was just intimidation.'

Rainey reckons that rear-wheel steering will always be around because traction control won't work in bikes (but time has proved him wrong). 'The tyre contact patch is so small in bikes and that's what you rely on. You need to control that contact patch, you don't want a computer controlling what the tyres are going to do because they're so much less forgiving than in a car, and on a bike you're always changing lean angle and so on. Plus, in a car you spin, but a bike throws ya.'

Mick Doohan: oversteer, understeer, wobbling free

Many fans will always remember Mick Doohan for his artful, crossed-up corner exits, etching arcs of molten rubber on racetracks around the world. But The Mighty One insists he wasn't a total rear-wheel steerer. In fact it was his input during the 1990s that brought emphasis back to the front tyre, and the Aussie's deadliest weapon was always high corner speed.

'My first roadrace stuff was production racing and when the bike started to break traction, I found it was quicker to keep it sliding rather than not keep it sliding. After dirt track, I'd tip the bike into a turn and expect it to go sideways, so it wasn't a problem when it did.

'Then when I first started 500s, the Honda's engine was pretty wild, so the fastest way out of a turn was a bit sideways, rather than running out of racetrack. But once the tyres got better, the quickest way was to keep the bike in line. You'd only start sliding and spinning it up if the tyres were going away. When it comes down to it, the reality is that sideways isn't quickest, and I wanted to win races, not look good, so I only used it when I had to.

'Sure, a little bit of oversteer helps the bike steer and it's also good if you're running out of racetrack, though I always found rear brake to be a better tool to stop understeer. Also, having the rear spinning feels safer, rather than having the tyre on an edge where you don't know when it's going to break loose.'

The five-time champ reckons he was more of a drifter than a serious sideways merchant. 'I was more into the drifting slides, rather than the actual "get in, turn it and wheelspin it out" stuff. I was always into corner speed, so a lot of my slides came from that – the bike would start to drift and I'd just keep it drifting, laying black lines from lean angle.

'If you've got great grip, there's no need to slide around and get the bike unsettled. But once the tyres start losing grip, the momentum you're carrying through a turn makes them drift, and other than slowing your corner speed by shutting the throttle, which will slow your lap times, you start slowly feeding in the power to take some weight off the front, which keeps the rear sliding and also introduces some wheelspin. So you keep that going, but not to a degree where you're completely sideways, sitting there spinning and burning rubber, looking fantastic but not going forward.'

Despite his insistence that McCoy's fully sideways antics aren't the way forward, Doohan agrees with Roberts that mastery of the rear is vital. 'If you're confident enough to slide when the bike or the tyres aren't working at their optimum, then you've got an advantage. A lot of guys can slide the rear when they've got good grip but when the tyre loses its edge they don't know the limit. You've got to have the feel to ride the tyre and use throttle control to spin it up just enough, so you're going forward, not just smokin' rubber.'

Garry McCoy: there's sideways, and then there's sideways
Serious sideways antics seemed to have disappeared from 500 racing until Garry McCoy came along in late 1999. The ex-speedway rider found that the only way he could ride his YZR500 was oval-style, oversteering like crazy, smokin' the rear like a bastard. So much so McCoy has choked rivals on the fumes.

'We went testing at Estoril and Noriyuki Haga hadn't been there before so I said he could tuck in behind me,' recalls McCoy with a mischievous chuckle. 'I gave him a little wave to say "come on, let's go", then did two or three laps, looked back and he wasn't there. Back in the pits I asked him if he'd followed me. "No," he said. "I need gas mask – too much rubber smoke!"'

McCoy's rear-end slides aren't subtle like Micky D's, they're wild and glorious and they seem to work. 'With speedway, you're sideways all the way in, just washing off speed, you don't even touch the throttle until halfway though a turn. You start off at half throttle and just play with it from there, it's a feel and experience thing. In roadracing it's different at every track, at every corner and sometimes from one lap to the next. It depends on the type of turn, whether you're alone or with other riders, all that kind of stuff.'

Despite the extremity of McCoy's slides, he initiates them like Doohan, with corner speed rather than throttle. 'It starts when you're carrying a lot of corner speed and the rear starts washing out. The real buzz is getting the rear loose as I back it into the turn, keeping it sideways all the way through and all the way out. But I never – and I know I shouldn't say this – feel out of control with the rear. If I'm going to crash I always feel like I'm gonna crash with the front.'

McCoy's antics do indeed look crazy – especially in 2003 when he was racing Kawasaki's MotoGP bike on Dunlops – but there's a method in his madness. 'Once the rear is loose I spin it up to help get the bike turned and then I can also adjust my corner exit line with the throttle. If I'm going to run wide, I give it more throttle, if I want to go wider, I use less throttle. I use it on some turns more than others. If it's a corner followed by a long straight, I'll want to get more drive so I don't use it so much.'

McCoy has found that perfecting the sideways art isn't just a matter of riding style – bike set-up and tyre choice are also crucial. 'When I started riding the 500 it would spin up but we didn't have the set-up to make it work with spin. The rear will spin easier with a hard spring but you don't get drive, so we've just kept going progressively softer ever since.' McCoy also uses different ignition mapping compared to fellow Yamaha 500 riders like Max Biaggi, because he likes a sharper power delivery to keep the rear nice and loose.

Intriguingly, McCoy's style makes his rear tyre run cooler than his rivals', which means he can run much softer compounds, but how can this be when he appears to be giving his rear so much grief? It's because the tyre is spinning rather than digging in, so while surface temperature is higher than normal, there's not so much heat driven into the all-important core of the tyre.

CHAPTER 30

How Ducati humbled Hamamatsu

March 2003

This is where Ducati's MotoGP legend began – during the winter of 2002/2003. Even back then it was obvious that the Bolognese had what it takes to beat the Japanese

Jerez IRTA tests, late February 2003: Suzuki MotoGP star Kenny Roberts Junior is standing outside the Ducati Marlboro Team pit, jealously eyeing Troy Bayliss' Desmosedici V4. 'Looking at that thing, you wouldn't think it'd go around a racetrack, but…' his voice trails off and he shakes his head in disbelief. A few feet away Suzuki team-mate John Hopkins' body language speaks of similar envy, the young American recounting how Bayliss had earlier rocketed past him on the main straight, like 'they've got a Ferrari engine in there,' and how the Italian V4 had drive, traction and bullet-like acceleration where Hopper's Japanese V4 was all over the shop.

Even if Roberts isn't moved by the Duke's swoopy, retro styling and its ancient-looking steel chassis, everyone is impressed by the Desmosedici's speed, and with good reason. Consider what this tiny Italian factory has done – they've built their first proper race bike in 30-odd years and are bang on the pace, pretty much right out of the box. With no changes to engine architecture and no major chassis transformations they topped official pre-season testing, posting the fastest-ever top speed recorded by a racing motorcycle – 203.9mph at Catalunya, Spain. Compare this feat to some of their Japanese rivals: Suzuki, who have built a brand-new bike from the lessons learned from a full season in MotoGP, but are still struggling to find front-running pace; or Kawasaki, who have been racing their ZX-RR in various guises for a full year, but are even further behind; or even Yamaha, who went through a myriad of important engine and chassis alterations before they got their M1 up to speed. Honda, it seems, are the only other people who know how to get their concepts spot on from the drawing board up.

So why are Ducati so good at getting motorcycles to go around racetracks so fast, so quickly? Just how are they making some of their MotoGP rivals look just a little second rate?

The marque's amazing run of success in World Superbike – nine riders' titles and 11 manufacturers' crowns in a dozen years – suggests that the men from Bologna know what they're doing. But it was always easy to attribute much of their Supers' success to the WSB rule book, which gave 1000cc v-twins fundamental superiority over 750cc fours. And anyway, some people would argue that the Japanese have never taken Superbikes that seriously, because, however futuristic Japan might appear, it's also a temple to tradition, so the 55-year-old GP series always takes precedence over the Johnny-come-lately Superbike series.

The Desmosedici V4 is fulsome proof that Ducati haven't just been enjoying the easy life in World Supers, it proves that they really do know what they're doing, better than just about anybody, whether they're building a street-based racer or a full-on GP prototype. 'Ducati have had the best Superbike for many years, even though Honda were trying very hard,' says one paddock insider, a technical partner to Ducati and several Japanese factories. 'In 2002 I think the 998 was a better bike than the Honda, the only thing that lost them the title was Troy's Assen crash.'

Ducati Corse boss Claudio Domenicali refutes any suggestion that Honda gave them an easy run in Supers. 'Some of the Japanese factories developed very exotic Superbikes. Also, we share some technical suppliers with the Japanese, and they told us that Honda were spending more money in Superbike than in GPs during the years of the RC45 project.'

Money, of course, is one of the biggest factors in achieving racetrack success. But while Ducati are a much smaller concern than their Japanese rivals, they don't necessarily suffer financially. Ducati Corse is a tight-knit independent company, which quite probably utilises its budget more effectively than some sprawling, many-headed corporations. 'Our MotoGP project is well funded,' adds Domenicali, who won't reveal the MotoGP/Superbike split in Ducati's £20 million annual race budget. 'Thanks to the commitment of our company and of our sponsorship partners, we've been able to find a good budget. Five years ago we couldn't have done this, because our company was smaller, we were just in the early stages of our turnaround, and from an engineering point of view we didn't have enough experience to tackle the MotoGP challenge.'

So, if booming sales of the 916 and its successors resolved what should be Ducati's one major disadvantage against their Goliath-like rivals, what might be the advantages of being small? In fact, smallness in itself is the major bonus of being small. It means a tight-knit team of engineers, short lines of communications and quick decision making. And since speed off the track is vital for speed on the track, Ducati Corse have a very crucial advantage over the corporate giants.

'If we have a problem with something that we don't understand, we phone Loris (Capirossi) and he's at the factory half an hour later, and the next day we start designing a new part,' explains Ducati's chief MotoGP engineer Corrado Cecchinelli. 'I think the only other difference between us and the Japanese is that we design the bike and race the bike, while it looks to me that with them, maybe someone designs the bike and someone else races it.' Domenicali adds: 'With Ducati, the same people who are at the race on Sunday are back in the office on Monday, so we are more like an F1 car team than a bike race team, which means we can be very quick in making improvements.'

'Ducati's racing philosophy: simplicity, not daring too much, and doing what's in our tradition because we know what we're good at'

This is the kind of thing that can have a huge effect on a rider's state of mind and his results. Colin Edwards has noticed a big difference since joining Italian factory Aprilia at the end of 2002, after years as a factory Honda and Yamaha Superbike rider. 'With Aprilia, you ask for something and you've got it. With HRC, you give them lots of ideas, but they've got plenty of their own. It takes time to filter in your own stuff, so it might be three or four months before you get something. With the Japanese, everything seems to take time, like, the Honda I had at the end of 2002 was the bike we wanted at the start of 2001. With the Italians it's more of a free for all.'

Of course, there's more to Ducati than its humble dimensions. Cecchinelli describes the factory's basic racing philosophy thus: 'simplicity, not daring too much, and doing what's in our tradition because we know what we're good at and we know it works.' In other words, it's the old KISS principle – 'Keep It Simple, Stupid!', beloved of Jeremy Burgess, the man who guided Valentino Rossi, Mick Doohan and Wayne Gardner to premier-title glory. It's all about assembling a good crew of young and open-minded engineers who can work together, then letting them get on with it, rather than making the mistake that many enterprises make these days – trying too hard and out-thinking themselves, because they've failed to understand the basics of what's required to achieve their goal.

Which explains why Ducati are steadfastly sticking to what they know best. True, they had to ditch plans to build an oval-pistoned v-twin MotoGP bike, because even a super-trick twin wouldn't make enough power, but they're still flying in the face of conventional MotoGP wisdom with a desmodromic 90-degree V4 housed in a tubular-steel frame. This is significant because no one has ever made a success of doing things differently to the Japanese in the premier class. The last non-Japanese factory to win in 500s was Cagiva, who achieved success by building a Yamaha YZR clone. And yet Aprilia have proved that you don't need to slavishly copy the Japanese to beat them – the little Noale factory dominates the 250 world championship, using their unique disc-valve 250 to defeat Honda's and Yamaha's reed-valve bikes.

In MotoGP, Honda, Suzuki and Proton have all gone for much narrower Vs than Ducati – 60 to 75 degrees – citing compactness as their motivation. And yet the 90-degree Desmosedici motor looks tiny, maybe even smaller than the 998/999 v-twin (though no one has so far managed to infiltrate their MotoGP pit with a tape measure). Ducati were determined to stick with their right-angled configuration because it keeps their MotoGP tool within the Ducati tradition, which is why they sometimes cheekily refer to the motor as their 'super twin'. Anyway, the 90-degree layout offers intrinsic engine balance, which means minimal vibration and good mechanical efficiency, crucial factors in a motor that revs to over 16,000rpm.

Ducati's unique desmodromic system – created by fabled engineer Fabio Taglioni way back in the 1950s – is another element of their heritage that absolutely had to be a part of the MotoGP bike. The system uses rockers to close as well as open the valves for super-accurate valve operation, whatever the rpm, and minimum power loss. Strange that the Japanese have never built their own desmo motors, most probably because it would be too much of a rip-off.

But it is in the chassis department that Ducati have really gone their own way. While rivals stay faithful to the ubiquitous aluminium beam frame pioneered in the early 1980s by Yamaha's 500 GP bikes, Ducati prefer to stick with an apparently archaic concept – welding together a few lengths of tubular steel. Once again, it's a tradition thing. 'We are confident with this kind of frame, it's our tradition,' says Cecchinelli. 'Plus it's light enough and it's stiff enough, so why go with something else? I'm sure we're better staying with what we know.'

Although Ducati's ultra-minimal steel frame looks old fashioned, there's plenty of evidence to suggest that it might actually be superior to a chunky beam chassis. Stiffness is not everything in bike racing – engineers want their frames to flex in certain situations, most crucially mid-corner, where ultra-high lean angles prevent the suspension from working effectively, contributing to chatter, and on corner exits, where the right amount of flex can smooth out a rear-tyre slide.

You only need to examine the wacky twin-shock Yamaha M1 from 2002, complete with 'anti-chatter' dampers, to realise that the Japanese are heading up some weird alleys in their efforts to sort chatter and flex problems. There seems to be a fundamental contrast in philosophy here: while Ducati keep it dead simple, maybe Yamaha are thinking too hard.

It would be easy to slump into national stereotypes here, suggesting that the Italians are more intuitive in their approach to racing, while the Japanese are deeply scientific, maybe too scientific. But that would be nonsense – Ducati are every bit as scientific as their Japanese rivals. And yet maybe their engineers are more pragmatic or more down to earth than some Japanese engineers, whose obsession with pushing things forward can sometimes lead them up development cul-de-sacs. Pragmatism might not be considered a typical Latin characteristic, but Ducati have definitely got it, and they've blended it well with their Italian passion and love of heritage.

Of course, we are talking slightly out of turn here, because the Desmosedici has yet to turn a wheel in anger. Testing isn't racing, however many lap records you break, and Ducati are very aware of being over-confident at this stage. As Cecchinelli says: 'Always remember, you only get points at races! I think we've done well to be doing such good lap times so soon, but I'm not surprised because our aim was to be competitive as soon as possible. We want to fight for podium results but this season won't be easy – there are so many factory bikes and so many great riders that you can be just a few tenths slower than the fastest guys and you're 12th.'

Domenicali predicts a rollercoaster ride for the reds: 'We will have some ups and some downs over the next few months because we don't know many of the GP circuits, so sometimes we'll find the optimum balance and sometimes we'll miss that. Racing is all about how everything fits together, it's about work, dedication and a little luck.'

Duke of balance: How Ducati adapted from WSB to MotoGP

The Desmosedici is Ducati's first full-on, big-bore racing bike in three decades. Ever since the 1970s the Bolognese have made their name with street-based racers, from the GT750-based Imola winner of 1972 to the World Superbike-conquering 916. Racing MotoGP prototypes should be a very different deal but MotoGP engineer Corrado Cecchinelli doesn't believe there's such a great difference between Superbikes and MotoGP machines.

'I wouldn't say, for example, that the MotoGP bike brakes harder,' says Cecchinelli. 'Because braking is down to geometry, even many streetbikes have enough braking power to lift the rear wheel, so it's a case of how low you can get the bike. The only real difference between MotoGP carbon brakes and Superbike steel brakes is that the carbons are lighter.

'The difference is that MotoGP bikes are lighter and much more powerful, so the game is to exploit all the advantages from having such a big amount of horsepower. You can do everything with chassis set-up in search of more acceleration, but then maybe the bike won't handle any more, so that's the compromise you have to make.'

In fact Ducati don't believe in incorporating too much adjustability into their race chassis, rather like Honda. They reckon that large changes to a bike's set-up only makes its handling unfamiliar to the rider, which means he won't know what to expect, which means he won't have the confidence to push to the very edge.

'It's better to think deeply about what you are doing, find a good compromise, and leave it like that all season,' affirms Cecchinelli. 'The general conclusion, going from the success of Honda and ourselves, is that this is the right way.'

Cecchinelli considers the current Desmosedici to be extremely conventional – a strong point at this stage – but it won't stay like that forever. 'We are certain that we haven't yet fully exploited the traditional areas, so we want to be 100 per cent with that before we start work on electronics and space-age materials. I think electronics will become more and more involved, everyone's already talking about Aprilia's ride-by-wire throttle, and maybe Yamaha using electronic suspension control.

'So far we aren't working on traction control or an active slipper clutch – our clutch system is exactly the same as our Superbike, only the dimensions are different. But traction control will become important, because in MotoGP you have too much engine, so you have to use as much of it as possible. But we are far from having any such device, for now we just pay good riders to do that!'

He's not wrong – the awesome-sounding Duke is so loud that you can easily hear Bayliss and Capirossi battling wheelspin from trackside, pretty much out of every corner; Capirossi more so because he likes a front-end-loaded bike which costs him rear-end grip. 'Loris likes the bike more loaded on the front, while Troy likes it lighter. Troy can ride with a bike that moves around more, which gives him more traction, while Loris wants the front right there, he likes a stiffer bike.' Their different demands almost certainly stem from where they started their race careers – Bayliss on soft and wobbly proddie bikes, Capirossi on super-taut 125 GP machines.

Ducati's racing history
Ducati announced its decision to contest the new four-stroke-based MotoGP World Championship at the Spanish GP in May 2001. Already the dominant performer in World Superbike, Ducati was attracted to the new championship because, unlike the streetbike-based Superbike series, MotoGP demands prototype machines, allowing engineers to experiment with avant-garde technology that will help Ducati maintain its edge as a hugely successful manufacturer of high-performance streetbikes.

Since the 1970s Ducati has been renowned for its range of v-twin (with L-shaped configuration) desmo sports machines that have won fans all over the world. Created by celebrated engineer Fabio Taglioni, Ducati's early 750GT and 900SS v-twins scored unforgettable successes in the Imola 200 and the Isle of Man TT. In the late 1980s the air-cooled, two-valve v-twins were replaced by a liquid-cooled, four-valve v-twin, designed by Massimo Bordi, which scored victories at Daytona and in the inaugural World Superbike event.

The latest incarnations of this lineage – the 916, 996 and 998 Testastretta – have been the dominant force in World Superbike during much of the last few years, their user-friendly power and easy handling making them difficult machines to beat. Following the decision to extend its racing activities into MotoGP, Ducati initially considered creating an all-new v-twin prototype for the class, but engineers eventually opted for a V4, maintaining the marque's trademark 90-degree cylinder configuration and desmodromic valve actuation system.

The all-new Desmosedici V4 made its track debut in August 2002 at Mugello, Italy, ridden by Vittoriano Guareschi. Full-time MotoGP riders Troy Bayliss and Loris Capirossi joined the Desmosedici testing programme in November, the bike breaking its first lap record at Jerez, Spain, in December 2002.

Epilogue: Ducati's racing philosophy has done them well. Four and a half years after I wrote this story they were MotoGP world championships for the first time, winning both the constructors' championship and the riders' title with Casey Stoner.

CHAPTER 31

ZEN AND THE HEART OF MOTORCYCLE RACING

June 2003

It's more important than a ten horsepower engine boost, more important than a super-sticky rear slick, and it's all in your head... It is the Zen-like psychological state of grace that every racer craves

When you peel away the layers that make up the sport of motorcycle racing, you go through a lot of flesh and metal – engine power, suspension set-up, tyre choice, riding technique, physical fitness and bravery, all of them quantifiable to some extent. Then, if you look deep enough, you'll sometimes find something else, something much hazier, less easy to define, let alone quantify. Some people call it mystical or Zen-like, some top riders believe it to be spiritual.

It is the innermost core of the rider's being, the very centre of the mental force that Mick Doohan reckons is 90 per cent of what racing is all about. You might almost suggest that it is the rider's soul at work. What we're talking about is the psychological condition called 'flow', or 'in the zone' as some Americans prefer to call it. Flow is an almost transcendental state of mind experienced by many sportsmen on all too rare occasions, during which the individual's normal capabilities are effortlessly surpassed – everything seems to go right, you're riding faster than ever and if you make a mistake you seem to have corrected it before you even made it. The world around you seems to slow down, go quiet, and you're operating in an altered state of consciousness, the thinking part of your brain shutting down while the intuitive part fires up. It's pretty weird, believe me.

Not surprisingly, this is the state of mind that professional sportsmen attempt to enter each time they compete. But flow isn't like that – it comes of its own accord, when various factors mysteriously gel together. Plenty of serious research has been done into the subject over recent decades but it's still nebulous in the extreme. There are certain procedures you go can through in an effort to encourage flow – most notably meditation and visualisation – but they're far from guaranteed, for normal mortals at least. As sports psychologists say of the zone: 'It is indeed a place, but a map won't get you there'.

I experienced flow maybe three times during my ten-year racing career, and each of those episodes is still vividly clear in my mind. They occurred at Brands Hatch, Spa Francorchamps and the Island, and each time I was riding effortlessly beyond my normal limits. British Superbike champion Steve Hislop reckons he may feel the flow three times a season, while five-time 500 king Doohan reckons he had it pretty much every time he raced. So was it the Aussie's ability to feel the flow that made him arguably the greatest racer of all time? Perhaps.

Hislop describes his flow experiences thus: 'You have those moments when you think "Fuckin' hell, I'm on it here", but it's cool, it's dead relaxing and peaceful. You're just spot on, faster than ever and you're not even breaking into a sweat. It's a nice feeling when you get it, if they could only bottle the stuff so you could guzzle it...'

Doohan's great rival Wayne Rainey also enjoyed some flow moments. In fact Mike Sinclair, the engineer who fettled Rainey's Marlboro Yamahas, reckoned that Doohan and Rainey were the only ones who could 'get in that headspace where they are 100 per cent fast. Some guys don't have a problem getting there every time they ride, guys like Wayne and Mick, others find it harder.' Sinclair wasn't aware of flow at the time, but he knew something spooky was going on inside these guys' heads.

Rainey still has memories of flow, bright as a button in his mind, one of which manifested itself as an out-of-body experience. This is nothing unique – F1 legend Ayrton Senna reported a similar experience at Monaco in '88. 'I won over 20 GPs and there's only a few that stand out,' says Rainey, 500 champ in 1990, '91 and '92. 'Some were really strange, some were a lot of fun and some were a lot of work. But the ones that really stand out were the ones that were just odd. At Suzuka in '93 I had, like, an out-of-body experience. It was like I was looking down at myself going into the fast right before the hairpin and laughing, smiling and giggling. It was so odd, I remember thinking in the post-race press conference: "there's no way I can say something about that or they won't let me do the next race".

'That moment is so clear to this day. I don't know how or why it happened, but I know it did happen. That race was awesome, the best I'd ever done, I think I was having so much fun on the bike, really enjoying what I was doing, probably more than ever in my career.

'I'd gotten a bad start, Schwantz was riding good and was leading. I was thinking: "Man, he's gonna take off!", then I caught him, passed him and pulled out a bit. I was the only guy on Dunlops and my tyres went off a little, so I was able to slow down some, cool the tyres off, drop back to fourth, then make another charge towards the end. Normally you can't do things like that in a race, you're normally flat out all the way, but I was able to exploit the advantage I had with the tyres, and that's what won me the race. I knew I had a performance advantage with the tyres, just from the way I could manoeuvre the bike, put it in different areas of the corner and kinda intimidate everybody and enjoy that. It was like turning around and sticking your tongue out at them, that's the way I felt. When you can think that way and you're in a world championship race, when there's so much on the line, I was just feeling like a kid. I was thinking: "This is not meant to be this much fun!"'

Rainey's Suzuka experience tallies with research by psychologist Mihaly Csikszentmihalyi, the man who first investigated flow in the early 1970s. He surmised from thousands of interviews that flow is 'a common subjective experience of pleasure, interest and even ecstasy, derived from activities that perfectly match one's skills with the demands for performance'. Rainey's talents were obviously entirely matched to what he was required to do.

Dean Miller, Rainey's trainer during his GP years, recalls another moment of Rainey flow. This was at the '93 Czech GP, the race which preceded the crash that ended his career. 'Very inexplicably Wayne took off, passed everybody and won by six or seven seconds,' says Miller. 'Afterwards he couldn't remember anything that had happened during the race, he talked about music and tunes going through his head, all these strange processes going on, and the race came so easy. It was a very strange race to him, but very successful, very satisfying and very ethereal, in a kinda "out there" way. That's the so-called Zen-like feeling you get in the zone. Flow can also happen in training, I call them "golden days", when you can run forever and you don't get tired.'

So extreme is the sensation of flow that Rainey found it slightly disconcerting recalling these moments for this story. 'Thinking about this is going to screw up my whole day,' he said. 'I could get a lot more deep and spiritual, but it doesn't mean that much to me no more.'

Of course, flow doesn't feel spiritual to everyone. Doohan has experienced flow, even an out-of-body moment, but he's more prosaic about it in his archly down-to-earth Aussie way. 'People talk about Rainey and Senna having those out-of-body moments, and it's exactly what you feel, you definitely visualise yourself from the outside,' Doohan says, going on to explain his theory behind the saved-the-slide-before-you-even-had-it feeling. 'I think it's because you've basically gone through the turn before you've actually gone through it, so you've imagined what could happen before you come across it, so you're well prepared for, say, the front to push. You think the front's going to push because of how much speed you're carrying going in there, or you think the back's going to break away mid-turn because you're carrying a bit too much momentum in the middle of the corner. So you catch the slide as it's happening, because you're well prepared for it, you basically know it's going to happen. You're that far ahead of the game that everything is in slow motion, but it's not even in slow motion, your thought processes have just gone through what's going to happen or what could happen.'

Now you know why Doohan was so astonishingly good – he had everything worked out in advance. 'Putting a lap together is all about being prepared for the next corner before you approach it. It's not so much visualisation, you just know what's coming up, you know what needs to be done. Flow happened most of the time to me. Whenever I was on top of it, things would seem to slow down, but that's just because I was in the rhythm and riding all the time, so it seemed slow. If I were to hop on a motorcycle now, everything would happen about five times quicker!'

But while Doohan tends to dismiss any otherworldly explanations of these strange forces, he worked hard during his career to utilise them to his advantage. During GP weekends he was known to be distant and uncommunicative, almost to the point of rudeness. This was simply him doing what most pro-sportsmen do to get in the zone – concentrating on his own little world within which he was relaxed, calm, self-confident and focusing on bike and track. Any other outside distractions – journalists, fans, pretty much anyone – were unwelcome.

'From the time I arrived at the circuit it was all about the race, just getting your head together for that moment,' he adds. 'Most of the time I'd arrive on Thursday afternoon; some riders seem to love getting there earlier but it's just too hard to remain so focused for that long.'

Rainey also spent entire GP weekends focusing on Sundays, working to get his brain into that state from which the flow might just spill forth. He remembers his pre-race preparations – designed to encourage flow – taking on a scary intensity. 'As my career went on I was just waiting for Sunday,' he recalls. 'Friday and Saturday were a waste of time, I was always building to Sunday. I had a little ritual before the race, if you want to call it that, or a routine, that would get me into the right state of mind. I'd get myself into this once a weekend, I'd be dancing around my motorhome, kicking my leathers, or I'd sit there, focusing on the feeling of being excited and wanting to spit nails and rip the handlebars off the bike. It was like going out to fight. The music depended on the mood I was in, maybe a bit of country, or it could've been pop or rock 'n' roll. It was never the same, but when I left the motorhome I was always ready.

'I'd sit there, focusing on the feeling of wanting to spit nails and rip the handlebars off the bike. It was like going out to fight'

'If people had come into the motorhome they'd have thought I was nuts, they'd have said: "Man, you better take a break!" I always looked forward to the preparation; it was one reason I raced. Basically I'd think about the race completely, so when I got on the bike I was pretty relaxed. It was much more intense getting ready. I enjoyed that part of my career – those one or two hours before the race by myself. It was very intense and very exciting. But it was also a lot of work, a lot of commitment, a lot of dedication and desire. You give up a whole lot for that.'

Rainey isn't the only rider to have psyched himself up on his motorhome hi-fi. This is Hislop: 'You've got to get away from people prior to racing. I use dancey-type music, really get myself buzzing. It's quite funny, if you go along the line of motorhomes before a British Superbike race, you'll hear music blaring out of most of them as everyone tries to pump themselves up.'

All good racers have their own pre-race rituals, none more conspicuous than Valentino Rossi's. Like many riders' systems of preparation, the world champ's routine allows him to slip into an almost dream-like state, so he can maintain his focus and maybe enter the zone, because he doesn't need his consciousness to do anything. Perhaps this dream-like state also calms nerves and blocks out those little distractions that might jog him out of that peaceful frame of mind. In racing, the tiniest diversion can disrupt your whole mental state – like losing a glove and panicking for 30 seconds while you look for it – which is why Rossi always keeps his leathers, helmet and gloves in the same place, and why he keeps the same breakfast, lunch and dinner schedule. It's all about the routine. 'If I know exactly where my things are it gives me a feeling of calm and security, so I can think only about the bike,' says Rossi, whose crew chief Jerry Burgess has seen it all before. 'Valentino's method of operation is the same all the time, just like any professional sportsman's should be,' says JB. 'Mick used to do it, he used to spend minutes and minutes putting his gloves on, it was a concentration thing, leaving one world behind and preparing to enter another.'

Miller adds: 'Valentino's record is superb, because he's never changed anything. He still stays up late, still turns up for morning practice with his hair all matted and sideways, just like Schwantz used to, but he's consistent, he keeps the same pattern of behaviour.'

Miller believes that no one has ever been better at pre-race visualisation than three-time 500 champ King Kenny Roberts. And he should know – he's worked with some of the greatest riders of the past two decades, from multiple 500 champs Roberts Senior, Rainey and Eddie Lawson to 250 and Supers champ John Kocinski and one-time 500 champ Roberts Junior. King Kenny was a genius at the visualisation process – riding the track in his mind, so he'd already done it all before he even got there. Miller recalls one episode particularly clearly – when Yamaha brought Roberts out of retirement to contest the 1985 Suzuka Eight Hour race aboard the brand-new FZR750 Genesis. It was Roberts' first four-stroke roadrace. 'We were struggling about a second and a half off pole,' recounts Miller. 'So one lunchtime Kenny says: "let's go back to the hotel". He told me not to let anyone knock on the door, he didn't want anyone bothering him. So he's laying flat on the bed, doing lap after lap after lap for about 50 minutes, then he gets up and says "I've found it, I've found half a second here and a second there". We go back over to the track and he qualifies on pole, just like that. Kenny could visualise better than anyone.'

Visualisation is a kind of meditation; it's like practising in your mind, as Miller explains: 'If you think about something long enough, it's going to happen'. Maybe most pro racers don't prepare for races in the lotus position but they all have their own meditation rituals – Rainey dancing around his motorhome, Doohan fiddling with his gloves, Rossi fingering his earring.

'Everyone has their own way,' Miller continues. 'Some guys put the left glove on first and their helmet goes on in a certain way. Or you watch basketball players and some of them have to drink a special kind of water from a special kind of bottle. You get these crazy situations where guys are trying to put themselves in that zone. Rossi's process obviously works for him, it's repetitive and it's in his best interests not to change it.

'Racers have a whole lot of anxiety and pressure to deal with, especially sitting on the grid. Everybody attacks that anxiety differently. If you look at Kenny Junior he sits on the line with his arms folded, sunglasses on, earplugs in, head down – he's in a focus zone, visualising something in his mind, which may include the first lap. Whatever he does works for him, because he always gets a good start based on that visualisation.

'Wayne listened to rock 'n' roll to engage himself and gear himself up. Eddie Lawson was a little different, he'd sit in his darkened motorhome and prepare his helmets; anybody who went in there would think he was a caveman sitting in the dark, but that was just his visualisation process. Then there was John. People used to think he was a little crazy, which he was with his obsessive compulsive behaviour, but all that cleaning was the way he alleviated his anxiety to do his job. It's all about having a specific routine before you do whatever you've got to do, some sort of an ambience going on.'

Of course, it's not quite as simple as that. The process of preparation takes much, much longer than an hour or two before the race. 'It's also your background,' continues Miller. 'Your entire life goes into that process to get where you're at. And it all comes together in one moment – that's a lot of laps, a lot of practice, a lot of braking, a lot of cornering. And if it works, it just flows. It's an ethereal situation of everything coming together from everything you've ever accomplished and everything you've ever worked for.'

In other words, you only get there through absolute commitment to the cause, withering self-discipline and total concentration. There's no fast track, easy route to the realms of flow, it takes a lifetime of honing your skills. Doohan, however, warns of trying too hard, because flow is all about that perfect match of talent and task: simply forcing yourself to try harder won't work. 'I've done it myself,' he says. 'When you're under pressure you try to do too much, instead of trying to do what you're capable of doing. I think that's the biggest thing, convincing yourself that you're not going to go too far, but at the same time you have to go to a point where you feel no one can do any better.' Doohan was always a master of that kind of psychology – convincing yourself to do the impossible without allowing your brain to think it's impossible.

But if flow is so crucial to accessing a higher state of consciousness that can help riders go faster than ever before, why don't riders do even more to get themselves into the zone? Why, when sports psychologists are so much in demand from top golfers and tennis players, isn't the MotoGP paddock crawling with go-faster shrinks?

Miller believes he has the answer. 'Guys like Rossi, Doohan and Kenny Junior have grown through a system, they've developed a system that's successful for them. I don't think a sports psychologist could make any difference to these guys because they're already at such a level, so I don't think there's one person in our paddock who needs a sports psychologist, and that includes John Kocinski. Back in 1990 Kenny (Roberts, who successfully guided Kocinski to that year's 250 world title) brought in a psychologist to work with John because he thought the kid had a problem with obsessive compulsive behaviour. This guy also said he thought John had a problem and I said: "Well I'm under the impression that John's here to race motorcycles and he's winning everything and now you've alerted the guy to the fact that he's got a problem". So I fired him. Kenny wanted to know what was going on, so I told him: "I know you think John's strange but did you ever see yourself lay down in a motorhome and do the things you did to prepare for a race? People would've thought you were crazy, just like people would've thought Wayne was crazy if they'd seen him jumpin' around listening to music, just the same if they'd seen the way Eddie cleaned and prepared his helmets in the dark." Basically I think all these guys are crazy – because they all ride motorcycles real fast!'

Maybe it's the innate danger of motorcycle racing that really keeps the sports psychologists out of bike paddocks. Employing well-used mental-preparation models to help golfers to putt better or tennis players to serve harder is one thing, but getting into the darkest recesses of a racer's brain, where the rider has to confront the never-ending dangers of riding on the giddy limit is something else altogether. And trying to mess around in there might only destroy the magic. Which is why the sport of motorcycle racing sometimes feels like much more than that...

MotoGP Mutterings: *July 2003*

Motorcycle racers aren't the only guys who feel the need, the need for speed. Which could mean some big-buck sponsorship opportunities for MotoGP...

So, coalition fighter pilots are popping speed pills to help them stay awake during military operations in the Middle East. Pretty mad, eh? Some guy, buzzing off his nut, scything across the sky at mach two and carrying enough munitions to flatten a small town. Gives a whole new meaning to the phrase 'war on drugs'.

But there's no cause for concern. Just so long as these knights of the sky are administered the correct dose of amphetamines, it's perfectly safe, say the USAF. In no way whatsoever are these jet jockeys compromising their ability to carry out their duty, though this whole story arises from an Afghan campaign friendly-fire incident in which four Canadian soldiers were killed by a laser-guided bomb unleashed by an F16 pilot who was on USAF-administered amphetamines. The fact that it's illegal to imbibe this drug at, say, a Saturday night house party, is irrelevant. As is the fact that dextro-amphetamine, the USAF's usual stimulant of choice, 'may impair the ability of the patient to perform potentially hazardous activities such as operating machinery'. And, you'll also be happy to hear that speed is only administered to relieve pilots' tiredness; the drug is absolutely not intended to raise their aggression levels, although dextro-amphetamine's known side effects do include agitation, irritability and moodiness.

Anyway, this has got me thinking (always a risky business). If amphetamines make fighter pilots perform better, surely this gear has got to be good for motorcycle racing. Currently, performance-enhancing drugs are banned from most sports, but in the light of USAF evidence aren't we perhaps being a little old-fashioned? A few years back Fat Boy Slim proclaimed better living through chemistry, now we have (apparently) better bombing through chemistry, so why not better racing?

I feel there's every reason that MotoGP racing should take the lead here, since GP bikes have so much in common with jets, as Warren Willing, engineer to 500 world champ Kenny Roberts Junior once said: 'Dynamically, a bike is more like a fighter plane than a car'. And doesn't every bike racer or R1 rider half think he's a jet-fighter pilot? And wasn't the first-ever 500 world champ – Les Graham – a World War II pilot?

The parallels are undeniable, but here's the real clincher: pharmaceutical companies are some of the world's richest organisations (the world's top five drug companies have twice the GDP of all sub-Saharan Africa), and MotoGP racing will soon need a serious cash injection, because tobacco sponsorship is about to get the chop throughout Europe. The sponsorship opportunities with the pharmaceutical industry are dizzying; indeed I've already lined up meetings with the people from SmithKline Beecham (manufacturers of Dexedrine), Bayer and Pfizer because they've got shitloads more cash than the tobacco industry. I see SmithKline Beecham Honda, Bayer Yamaha and Pfizer Aprilia, all the teams vying with each other to develop the ultimate pre-race stimulant – a whole new dimension to racing technology.

'Pharmaceutical companies are some of the world's richest organisations and MotoGP needs a serious cash injection'

Then next month I'm heading to South America for a fact-finding tour, investigating further sponsorship possibilities, should MotoGP's governors consider further deregulation. I'll be spending a fair amount of time in Colombia, Peru and Bolivia, working on future deals for teams and various MotoGP events. I foresee lavish hospitality opportunities with, say, Team Medellin Honda – champagne, lap dancers and wraps of the finest Bolivian marching powder available to all VIPs and members of the media in the team's paddock hospitality area. And I see terrific marketing opportunities for trackside white lines, which I feel have been foolishly overlooked up until now.

And once I'm done down there, I'm heading to eastern Europe to pursue yet more marketing opportunities for MotoGP's twinkly bright future. Much of the world's Ecstasy originates from factories behind the former Iron Curtain, and I'm keen to discuss brand-promotion deals with these guys too. I can see it now: the White Dove German GP, or maybe the Mitsubishi British GP (that's Mitsubishi as in the pill, not the motor, dumbo).

I'd like some input from you the readers on this project, because I want it to work for everyone involved – riders, teams, sponsors and you, the paying public. For example: do you reckon that individual riders should stick to their own team's pharmaceuticals, or should the entire grid be treated with the same product, perhaps that of the event sponsors? Not as easy a question as you might think – because if we popped a Mitsubishi tab down each rider's neck before the British GP, the action might be somewhat limited. I suspect it would mostly involve riders lying down on the grass by the grid, almost certainly with grid girls, and making gentle rhythmic movements. But it could be worth a try.

Finally, I have an abiding vision etched in my mind apropos this jets/amphetamines business which I really want to share with you. It involves an F16 pilot of the future, his flying mask cleverly adapted, leaning forward over the dash (do F16s have dashboards?) and snorting a big, fat line as he pushes the joystick forward, anxiously fingering the rocket release button and shouting: 'Yeeehaaaaa! Die you motherfuckers!'

Peace, dudes!

CHAPTER 32

HAYDEN: HOW HE LEARNED TO WIN THE MOTOGP CROWN

September 2003

Nicky Hayden made the kind of steady forward progress during his debut 2003 MotoGP season that suggested he just might be the new Steady Eddie Lawson. Okay, so he may never win four world titles like Lawson but at least he went on to wear the crown once

Nicky Hayden is GP racing's new paddock pin-up. Swooning PR girls secrete photos of him on their laptops, captioned 'truelove', female Dorna employees collapse into fits of girlish giggles whenever the Kentucky Kid wanders into view and a red-faced Spanish journalist misuses a Repsol Honda press conference to ask the 22-year-old US Superbike champ if he'd accept his daughter's offer of a date. Hayden definitely got a lot of attention from the ladies in his debut world championship campaign, but, like most things in life, the kid from Kentucky seems to take it all in his shambling, loose-limbed stride.

Not that his attractiveness to the opposite sex matters to anyone but him, but what does matter is that Hayden is more than GP racing's new pin-up, he might just be GP racing's new Eddie Lawson. Obviously it's way too early to compare Hayden with Steady Eddie, the most successful premier-class racer of the 1980s, but there are promising similarities. Like Lawson, Hayden is American, like Lawson he started out in dirt track and like Lawson he came to GPs wearing the US Superbike crown. But the crucial likeness is Hayden's steady approach to racing that sets him apart from most thrusting youngsters.

Despite the pressure of riding for GP racing's best team, aboard the best bike and with Valentino Rossi for a team-mate at Repsol Honda, Hayden was prepared to take his time in 2003, never trying to run before he could walk. Sounds easy enough but all the evidence suggests that it's not easy for talented young racers who have a depressing habit of trying too hard too soon, crashing their brains out and thus losing the confidence they need to exploit their talent. By the very nature of their profession, racers have little or no patience, they want to get wherever they're going – whether it's to the next corner or to their first world championship – as fast as they can, and damn the consequences of getting it wrong.

Hayden sensibly used his 2003 MotoGP apprenticeship to gain confidence one step at a time: build some confidence, go a bit quicker, build some more confidence, go a bit quicker and so on. It's the same strategy that Lawson used when he came to GPs in the early 1980s, and though it doesn't grab overnight headlines, it has created a solid foundation on which Hayden should be able to build in subsequent seasons when he know the tracks, the bikes and the tyres. True, Hayden's 2003 results aboard the RC211V weren't as strong as Lawson's debut season aboard Yamaha YZR500 in 1983, but GP racing is different these days. Back in Lawson's day there was just a handful of factory bikes, now they're all factory bikes, with the top ten separated by less than a second. That's why Hayden didn't set MotoGP on fire, but those in the know were impressed by his slow-burn campaign, because they looked deeper than mere results, noting that his race pace was often within half a second of Rossi's during the closing stages of the season. At Motegi, where he scored his first top-three finish, he finished just five seconds behind winner Max Biaggi.

And unlike most quick kids, he doesn't crash. Hayden fell just four times in 2003, despite having to learn his way around a new bike, new tracks and new tyres. Compare that record to Nori Haga (15 crashes), Jeremy McWilliams (11), Alex Barros (10) and Marco Melandri and Troy Bayliss (9). As Rossi's crew chief Jeremy Burgess says: 'Hayden is the stand-out guy this year. He's not shown me anything that suggests he won't make it all the way to the top. He's a little bit not right on his corner entries but he's got good machine control. He's impressive.'

Off-track, Hayden's and Lawson's parallel lines peter out. Whereas Lawson never appeared to enjoy his racing, from the outside at least, and resented the media big-time, Hayden had the time of his life during the summer of 2003 and doesn't mind talking about it. His is a new attitude that pervades the GP paddock; the latest generation of pro-GP racers like Hayden, Rossi, Bayliss, Edwards, Gibernau and Co take their racing just as seriously as men like Lawson, but they're having a lot more fun. They seem to have got their professionalism in perspective with the rest of their lives, which some 1980s heroes never managed to do.

Nicky, you come from a real racing family, right?
Yup, my elder brother Tommy (24) races 600s for Kawasaki in the States, my little brother Roger Lee (20) races for Erion Honda and my dad was a pro dirt tracker. Even my mom raced in local 'powder puff' races, that's like chicks' racing, and my elder sister too. My little sister is the only one who's never raced.

'Even my mom raced in local 'powder puff' races, that's like chicks' racing, and my elder sister too'

You started out in dirt track, how come you switched to roadracing?
I quit doing dirt track full-time when I was 13, but I've still been doing it some all the way up until right now; this is the first year that I don't do it any more. I love dirt track and I think it helps make me a better rider, but once I started roadracing I just liked it better, plus there's a lot more of a future in roadracing – unfortunately dirt track is pretty lame in America right now, it ain't goin' anywhere.

Tell us about the time you and your brothers monopolised the podium at a Grand National dirt meet…
Yeah, we got first, second and third in a Grand National in Springfield, Tennessee, last fall against (Jay) Springsteen, (Chris) Carr and all the top American dirt trackers. It was such a shocker!

You've had a slow-burn rookie GP season, while many youngsters are in so much of a hurry…
It'd be nice to have just dropped in at the front but that's not what happened. Even when I first started AMA roadracing I didn't just kill it. Honda pretty well told me they wanted me to learn, they didn't want me tearing up a lot of equipment and they wanted me to stay healthy. But now it's starting to feel right and hopefully when it clicks I'll be there. They've not put any pressure on me, the only pressure comes from myself.

When did it start to feel right?
At Assen. I really liked Assen because it's got banked corners that gave me a lot of feel from the front. I felt sooooo good that weekend and I

just kept building from there. Everyone said Assen is so hard to learn but I got up to speed quick and got a real good feeling. There'd been a few races I hadn't done a lot, so I had a little talk with myself and I've definitely picked it up since then. I'm excited about the last few races; hopefully I'll start stringing them together.

Have there been moments when you've thought: I'm in too deep here?
Not to that point. Sure there's been a couple of times where I've thought 'man, I've got to get it together', like when I qualified 18th at Mugello, but I've never been to the point where I wished I was back home. I've had to prove I'm serious, that I'm not going to lay down just because a couple things didn't go my way. I just kinda regrouped, I decided I've got to have more fun riding and not be so hard with myself – just go out and do the best I can. That was on Friday night at Barcelona. I lay in bed and thought it all over, and from there each race has been better and better.

At the beginning of the year I was really lucky to have so many people helping me but maybe it caused me to think too much. Tady (Okada) and Mick (Doohan) were helping me, and I was just thinking about it too much, instead of going out and doing what I do and just ride. That's what I do now – I'm still serious, I'm still focused, but sometimes you've just got to do what comes natural and let it rule.

How have Tady and Mick helped?
When I was struggling those guys were really cool about not being too hard on me, just being honest. Also, they've helped at some of the tracks I'd never been to, just telling me what to expect, what to watch for. Like at Assen, it started raining on race day and I only got one lap in the wet before the race. They were like 'Hey, this track's good in the wet, you can push, but it does puddle here or there'. So they've helped with that kinda thing.

Do you have access to Valentino's set-up?
A little bit. I'm sure if it came to it I could maybe get everything but that's not how my team works. Sometimes if I'm not sure what tyre I'm gonna race on; I'll be like 'What's happening here?' to JB (Jeremy Burgess, Rossi's crew chief), 'What does Valentino think about this or that tyre?' but I've hardly done that any. The team's got a good chemistry, everyone gets along good, works hard, there's a good morale.

What do you make of the other riders?
About what I expected. I raced World Superbike at Laguna last year, so I got a good idea where those guys are at and I knew MotoGP was going to be even more, with even more guys. I knew that racing at world level wasn't going to be easy, just seeing how hard these guys push for the whole race, and it's been even more than I expected. I'd be disappointed if it wasn't like that. These guys are the world's best, I've a lot of respect for them. In America the pace starts out really good but then guys drop off – but look at Brno, Rossi's fastest lap was the last lap. They're just really good and steady.

Has anyone amazed you?
Maybe I've thought that but I wouldn't say it to myself, it's not going to do me any good to sit in the motorhome and think these guys are unreal! Sure I've seen some stuff, I mean Biaggi is so smooth, even on his fastest laps he's just glass. There's a lot of guys, but one guy who's really impressed me is Bayliss. No matter where he qualifies he goes to the front quick and just stays there, he's impressive.

Have you learned anything, riding-wise?
Yeah, I'm a lot different now. At the beginning of the year I was still riding it like a Superbike, keeping high corner speed. Now I've learned to get the bike stopped and turned, so I can then really use 200-plus horsepower. On the SP-2 your line just follows the corner, on the RC211 you go deeper and square it off. I've learned other stuff too. In America I ran Dunlops and we'd have two or three tyre choices, while now I have to test more tyres, so I'm getting better at picking stuff up quicker.

Why don't you use high corner speed on the RCV?
The Superbike doesn't have the power, so you can carry that high corner speed and still open the throttle coming out of the corner with the thing on its side, whereas with this thing you gotta have it picked up so you're on the fatter part of the tyre. I'm still working on that. Also, in America the tracks are narrow, so when I got to some of the wide GP tracks I wasn't using all the track I could. And in America you gotta stay off the paint, if you hit the paint it's not going to be pretty, but here you've got to have the confidence to run out onto the paint.

Are you surprised by how badly some of the other factories are struggling?
I don't know, I've not thought too much about it, I just ride the bike.
People struggle, you know.

You must be happy you didn't end up riding for Yamaha.
You said it, not me!

What was it like getting back on a Superbike at the Suzuka Eight Hours?
It was enjoyable, but not nearly as fast and not as much feel. I enjoy the
211 because it's more fun to ride.

You seem very happy-go-lucky.
That's my style, the way I've always been. I'm the kind of kid that likes
to have fun. And to be here is awesome! The two-week break before
this race (Estoril) was too long for me, I just wanted to start racing
again. But that's just me in general – I like to kick it and have fun,
that's when I ride my best.

What kind of race face do you put on?
I'm not the kinda guy who's got to get himself motivated before the
race. I'm already too excited, so I'm trying to relax, just chilling out and
not getting nervous, I'm on the grid laughing because, hey, it's the best
part of the weekend. Qualifying has been my weak point, practice is
cool but I can't wait for the race, that's when you get to go for it.

Would you call yourself aggressive?
Um, I don't really know, I don't think about it. I've never really felt
what I would call myself. Maybe there've been some riders who've felt
that, but not in a bad way.

What about your qualifying, how have you stepped it up?
It's always been one area where I've been weak. I grew up in dirt track
where you don't qualify, you just have scratch heats, so even when I
started roadracing in AMA I was never a great qualifier. Sometimes
when I put on a soft tyre I don't really go any faster, while a soft tyre
really helps some riders. More than anything I think it's knowing the
limit – the Michelins I'm using are really good, especially the front, but
when I want to go that little bit quicker, I don't know how hard I can

really push. I just haven't done good in qualifying and I don't have any excuses, but I've worked at it and my last race (Brno, where he made the second row for the first time) was my best qualifying. It may sound silly but during the summer break I took my lap timer home so when I was riding my motocross bike or my flat-track bike, instead of doing motos and stuff with my brothers, we had our own qualifying sessions, just going for one hot lap, and I think that helped.

What are your strengths as a rider?
I think I'm better in a race. When the race comes I always seem to find a little bit of speed. This year I've been getting really good starts which has helped me a lot. But I don't think I excel in one area, like on the brakes or whatever, I just try to learn a bit of everything.

What do you make of Europe?
I didn't know what to expect, so I didn't really draw any pictures in my mind that'd tell me it'll be this or that. I just came here with an open mind to see how it goes. It's been cool, the first two races in Japan and South Africa were pretty good but when we came to Europe everyone stepped it up even more, so I had to gas it up and try to raise the pace to their level. You know, these guys don't play, plus I've had a lot to learn – bikes, tracks and that. I've just had to find some speed and get faster.

What do you get up to between races?
I stay back in Belgium where the race shop is. I always find something to do – go motocrossing, do some training, go to the gym, go running in the parks. I just kinda kick it, just try and have fun. One week I stayed in England with one of my English mechanics, another time we went to a world motocross round, but pretty much I'm just waiting for the next race.

Done any sightseeing?
I've been travelling my whole life so I guess I take it for granted, but sometimes I make myself see stuff. Like I drove from Belgium to Le Mans with a buddy, so we weren't going to drive past Paris without seeing the Eiffel tower, so we went there and had dinner. Back home chicks ask me: 'Did you see this or did you go there?', so I do a little but not a lot. It may sound boring but I do a lot of the things I do just

because I know that one day I'll be sitting on a rocking chair thinking 'Why didn't I take advantage of being over there?'

Have you made friends in the GP paddock?
It's different to what I'm used to in America, because I've known a lot of the people there since I was a kid and my brothers are there. In GPs I don't really know a lot of people other than my team, so I pretty much hang out with my team and the guys at the Repsol Honda hospitality, just getting away from the racing. But as far as the riders go, not really. I mean they're friendly, when I see 'em it's 'Hey what's up? What's happening? And what about this and what about that?', but as far as going to play golf or hanging out, no.

And with Valentino?
We get along good, I have a lot of respect for him, but as far as hanging out, I don't really hang out with him.

You've had a couple of close shaves with Max on track…
A couple of times on Friday morning he came past way closer than he needed to be, when I didn't even know where the track goes. But it's all good, I like that part of it really, I think it's fun.

You mean it gives you something to go for?
Yeah!

Your family has been over for a lot of races; did you ask them to come over?
My mum and sister came over for the back-to-backs, while my dad's come to quite a few, just because he wanted to. They've never been to Europe, so they wanted to come and check it out.

Does it help to have them around when you're so far from home?
It doesn't hurt, it makes it nice. Plus my parents gave up a lot to help me race – they could've spent money on themselves instead of buying me tyres, so I wanted them to come.

So you get homesick?
Not really. When the European races started in May I did struggle a lot. My results weren't going that good, and you're not going to be having

fun when your results are bad. I've been home a couple of times in the breaks. I live on the east coast, it's not like coming from California, it's a smaller time difference and four or five hours less flying time.

You said a while back that you reckon all the paddock VIP hospitality is a bit OTT…
Yeah, when I first came here I was more impressed by the run-off on the tracks. Some of the tracks in America are a bit scary. They're really on it here, it's so much more organised, you don't see bikes laying in the gravel traps for a whole session like back home. That's impressed me more than how good the food is.

Have you been surprised by how little partying there is?
I didn't really come in with any expectation of that but it's pretty laid back. In America they get a little wild on Sunday night, some races you better look out because some people get pretty crazy! Racing paddocks are serious places but that's the way it is and I like to see people focused. But here everyone seems to know how to relax in the evenings, it's pretty mellow, Sunday night everyone goes their own way but that's cool. I'm not really a partier, I don't really drink.

We heard a story about you and your brothers getting so rowdy on a plane that they had to land the thing…
It was landing anyway, the story got out of hand just like they do, it wasn't near as big a deal as it got made out. There was a bunch of racers on the plane, and it was just racers the way they are sometimes, I guess, you've met enough, any of the fast ones have a little bit of an edge to them. It was really rough as we were coming into land, so my little brother put his helmet on and the steward didn't think that was funny. But my mom was on the plane and she wouldn't let us do anything out of hand.

What about the girls over here?
I don't have a girlfriend, I'm pretty much single, but there's a lot of hot chicks in Europe, there was definitely a lot of talent in the Italian paddock, and in Czecho.

It doesn't distract you?
No, I wouldn't say it distracts me.

So they've not been throwing themselves at you?
[After much laughter] Well, I mean I'm just a 22-year-old guy, what do you think?

Who were your heroes as a kid?
My main guy was Bubba Shobert [the three-time AMA Grand National champ whose career ended in his debut GP season after a freak accident at Laguna Seca]. He was the guy who did dirt track then roadracing, he had a big future till he got hurt. When I was a kid I went to a pro race, I was in the pits and he took extra time with me and my brothers, even though he didn't know who I was, so from there on out he was my guy. I try to remember that when I see kids and fans, I always try to be nice.

Do you have a grand plan?
Yeah, my plan is to be world champion, and more than once, pretty simple really. I'm trying to put the pieces together, to understand the life, to understand the circuits and the bike, and I know it's not going to be easy.

Epilogue: you know the story. Hayden did get it together and did become world champ.

MotoGP Mutterings: September 2003
There's more money than ever in MotoGP right now but not everyone has turned into arses. Hard to believe, I know...

Breathe in and relaaaaaaaaaaax... Time to head back into the primal-screaming MotoGP paddock, where Machiavelli would find the going tough and where trophy girlfriends paddle ankle-deep in testosterone as they prowl from pit lane to VIP hospitality suite. But we're giving all that a wide berth today; instead we're wandering along the millionaire's row of motorhomes, looking for some nice people to hang with.

They do exist in MotoGP, believe me, and the good guy count has blown up this year, thanks to the arrival of three new riders: Troy Bayliss, Colin Edwards and Nicky Hayden. These three former Supers stars are the total opposite of the biggest 'stronzo' (Italian for something we can't mention here) on the MotoGP grid, who I won't name. Oh, okay, I'll give you a clue, he wears a goatee. I mean, Bayliss, Edwards and Hayden actually treat people like me as fellow human beings, rather than some kind of untouchable. One senior figure in MotoGP calls us journalists 'The Scum', although I can't imagine why.

Anyway, let's kick things off by knocking on the door of the Bayliss wagon. Inside it's kiddie chaos – kids Mitchell and Abbey are larking around with McWilliams' boys and some other random paddock urchins. 'Hey Mitchell, it's a disaster in here, can you tidy up some of those Gameboy things,' pleads Bayliss reasonably, though this is just minutes after he's dumped his Duke out of sixth place in the Italian GP.

Bayliss is super cool. He's got fewer airs and graces than the pit-lane toilet attendant – a genuinely normal bloke with a very abnormal talent for thrashing a motorcycle half to death. But boy, can he be intense, with big burning eyes just like Mick Doohan's. In fact that's Bayliss – he's Micky D with a big cheesy grin. At the 2003 German GP he went skinhead purely to cheer up a pissed-off Ducati cook who'd had his head shaved, against his will, by fellow team members. His rock-solid attitude may have something to do with the fact that he understands the realities of life – he spray-painted motors for a living until his late 20s. Of course, he's got his quirks, like he gets a bit dark when things aren't going right and he's one of those riders who hates talking about bike set-up, because he's paranoid about his rivals discovering his secrets. Tech chats with Bayliss tend to go like this: 'Troy, what've you been working on?' 'The bike, mate.' 'What areas exactly?' 'All of it.' 'Front or rear?' 'Ah Jeez, the front.' 'Suspension, tyres, what?' 'Ah, just the whole front, mate.'

'You take a bull, you cut off its balls, you dangle them in front of its face, then you climb on its back'

When it comes to talking about his motorcycle, Edwards is the opposite; he's happy to get involved in deep technical chat while wife Alyssia changes baby Gracie's nappies on the next couch in their motorhome. And no one knows how to get their point across better; this is how he describes what it's like to ride his Aprilia MotoGP bike: 'You take a bull, you cut off its balls, you dangle them in front of its face, then you climb on its back'. Just like his old World Supers rival, Edwards is for real, he's far too much of a reasonable human being to let himself become a MotoGP arse. Most importantly, he does like a beer or five when he's not riding. At the 2002 Valencia GP (some time after he had wrapped up his second Supers title) he spent most of his time in Rossi's Nastro Azzurro hospitality unit, taking full advantage of the sponsor's product and talking with anyone who happened by. Again, that ain't normal practice in GP racing. Bayliss likes a drink too – he'll even sink a couple of glasses of wine the night before practice: 'Just to help me sleep, mate'.

I don't really know Hayden that well but he's having fun, which is the main thing. He greets people with a hip hop handshake and a 'How you doin', dude?', says 'Dang!' a lot and reckons everyone in the paddock is cool, with one exception. 'I haven't had a problem with anyone, other than Biaggi,' says Hayden. In fact, Hayden has had a problem with someone else in the paddock. Me. I gave the guy a bit of a scare a few weeks back; not my fault really, more the fact that I used to go out with a girl called Nicky. You see, she was on a group email I'd sent, at least I thought I'd sent it to her, but I must've been half asleep when I hit the 'send' button, because the message went to Nicky Hayden, not Nicky Walters. Oh, the dangers of modern technology, like a USAF 'smart' bomb gone awry. So what was in the email? Hmmm, it was an invite to a music festival, which a gang of us were planning to attend. The email went something like this: 'Hey Nicky, fancy getting fucked up in a field in Wales in August?' I explained the ghastly error to Nicky the next time I saw him. He laughed. Nervously.

CHAPTER 33

DIRTY TRICKS OF THE RACETRACK

September 2003

Racing is all about going fast but sometimes there's a rider in your way. So what do you do then? Get dirty. Mick Doohan, Niall Mackenzie and King Kenny Roberts discuss the dirty tricks employed by desperate racers

'Motorcycle racing,' as Max Biaggi once famously said after a rival accused him of dodgy riding, 'isn't ballroom dancing.' Pretty obvious, really, but bike racing is much nastier than that, and probably more bitchy too. It's more like high-speed rollerball, though more subtle. There's not a half-successful racer in the world who doesn't get up to some kind of mischief in his quest for glory (though in researching this story I quickly realised that it's only retired riders who'll talk about this kind of stuff), while the more evil riders commit truly heinous crimes that risk rivals' lives.

There's the standard dirty tricks that everyone does – like gently moving a rival off line when braking into a corner, or easing an opponent away from the grippy line mid-turn. Then there's the nastier tactics – like shutting the throttle halfway through a corner to force someone into taking drastic avoiding action, thus losing them vital time. And then there's the seriously dangerous stuff – like running a rival onto the grass at high speed, or deliberately colliding with them, or hitting their kill switch, or shutting their throttle, or punching or kicking them.

Even legends like King Kenny Roberts and Mick Doohan happily admit to getting dirty. It's just what goes on, it's a war out there. Like it or not, bike racing is a ferocious game of testosterone-charged heavyweight boxing with high-powered engines attached. Maybe it'd be cool if it was all nice and gentlemanly but that's not how it works. Even back in the so-called chivalrous days of the 1950s and 1960s there are tales of be-goggled racers gobbing at each other mid-race! And if these revelations make you watch bike racing with a more cynical eye, so be it. If you want peace and love, there's always *Songs of Praise*.

Roberts wasn't one of the really bad guys. He insists that he never knocked anyone off when he was doing GPs, but the hard-knocks dirt-track scene in the States was different. 'One time going through this turn I felt this guy's clutch lever on my right foot, so I just gassed it and flipped him off,' says the King who won a heap of dirt-track crowns before taking back-to-back 500 titles in 1978, '79 and '80. 'He came over after and wanted to know why I'd knocked him down and I said, "Well, the reason I knocked you down is that you put your clutch lever on my foot", so he started shouting that I'd knocked him down and I said, "Yeah, and next time you do that I'll knock you down again". You know, it's just one of the things, if anyone does something like that to you, well, sorry… But normally it's the guys who aren't so quick who have all the tricks, the quick guys don't need them so much. Like me and (Barry) Sheene were real clean, we never did anything and we never had to. I never even thought about it, other than that time Freddie aced me off the track in Sweden (an infamous move that won Spencer the 1983 500 title). I thought about doin' something the next race but I still couldn't allow myself. Every guy has his style, every guy has his bag of tricks, and when you race them enough you start to learn who does what.'

Five-time 500 champ Doohan, who ruled the mid-1990s GP scene with a pitiless talent, was renowned as much for his ruthless aggression as for his awesome skill. 'I wouldn't say I've knocked people off the track but I've maybe "lifted" them off the track,' he says. 'Like when someone thinks they can go around the outside, you just pick up and modify your line. They're already committed, so there's only one place left to go, and that's normally off the track. I guess it's a good way to bring cocky people back to earth, just to let them know that it's not like this is your first race.'

Doohan had a couple of famous run-ins with a young Anthony Gobert in '97. Goey had made the mistake of goading Mighty Mick in the press and he paid the price on track. 'As much as everyone thought Goey was so great, he just had no racecraft back then,' Doohan recalls. 'You'd do quite a clean move on him, then he'd come at you from a different angle, so it was like, "Hello stupid, try this!", and the next minute he'd be off the racetrack. Then he'd come in complaining about dirty riding, but I wouldn't try to intimidate somebody when I'm not up to their speed and have nowhere near as much racecraft.'

Even former British champ, GP nearly man and all-round nice guy Niall Mackenzie had his moments of malevolence, like Snetterton BSB '98, when he rammed team-mate Steve Hislop off the track. 'Steve had some kind of effect on me, maybe because he'd done something to me earlier in my career, so I had no problem running into him and compromising everyone's safety,' he says, laughing at the madness of it all, as racers do. 'It was the last lap and I'd considered doing it at the Bomb Hole but I wasn't close enough, so I did it at the chicane. I just ran into the side of him, we both ran off the track and it cost us first and second, which Rob (McElnea, their team manager) wasn't too impressed about! I frightened myself thinking about it driving home that night, because if I'd done it at the Bomb Hole we'd both have been in hospital.'

Earlier in his career, Mackenzie remembers competing in the European final of the infamously crazed Yamaha 350LC Pro-Am series at Hockenheim and dealing with a much-feared French rival in homicidal style. 'The Brits ganged up on this guy,' he remembers. 'Me, Ray Swann, Graham Cannell and Kenny Irons decided he was a bit hot, and he was little, so we knew he'd be really fast down the long straights, so we bullied him. We took turns during practice – you get in a big slipstream thing there, you get to the front of the queue, then you get slipstreamed, so every time it was his turn we'd just run him off the track.' The Frenchman returned to the pits in tears and didn't cause any problems on race day.

I remember similar stuff going on at the Isle of Man TT – the last place you'd expect riders to threaten each other's lives. Perhaps thinking he was still riding Pro-Am on a relatively safe short circuit, Cannell drafted by me and cut across my front, the rear end of his bike just missing my front wheel. The idea of this trick isn't necessarily to knock a rival down, just to cost him some time and scare him witless. I'll leave Mackenzie to explain how the front-end chop works: 'That goes on a lot, still does. The guy behind has to back off because the rear of the bike is so solid, so when you get a collision, it's going to be the guy behind who goes down.' And in endurance racing, the funny guys at the Bol d'Or would hit your kill switch as they drafted past you down Circuit Paul Ricard's long Mistral straight. All very amusing, unless there's another rider just behind.

Everyone always used to say that Mackenzie was too nice to be world champion. But what about someone like Loris Capirossi, who won the '98 250 world title by ramming Aprilia team-mate Tetsuya Harada off the track at the last but one corner of the last race? Capirossi is just like Mackenzie – sweet as pie off a bike, transmogrified on track. That's racers for you – it's a Jekyll & Hyde deal. 'Unless you've been a rider you don't understand the red mist thing,' explains Mackenzie, who reckons the Capirossi collision wasn't premeditated. 'He could see the championship going, so he took a chance, sometimes there's no time to calculate the consequences. At worst he probably thought they'd collide, run wide and it'd be a scramble to the finish line but the red mist confused his judgement. I don't think it was a desperate attempt to take out Harada.'

Doohan reckons he was more victim than villain during his career. 'I've been done by guys who put you off the track even in a straight line,' he says. 'They draft you and when they're beside you they lean into you, put you on the white line, so you've got to shut down, or go on the grass. (Wayne) Gardner did that to me down the front straight at Phillip Island in 1990, at around 290kays. He drafted past and started pushing me over. I had to throw my foot off the inside 'peg, it was the only way to shift some weight to stop me going off the track. That was pretty blatant. And (Luca) Cadalora ran me onto the grass coming out of a six-gear right-hander at Shah Alam once, just ran up beside me and actually pushed me off the track. I'd never go that far. I'd say Gardner, Cadalora and Biaggi were the three worst guys I raced with. Biaggi even tries to intimidate people on slowdown laps.'

Gardner angrily refutes Doohan's version of events at Phillip Island: 'To suggest that I was a dangerous rider is a complete insult. I didn't come anywhere near him, I passed him fair and square, but that's when I had the broken fairing, which was dragging on the road, and I had a broken wrist, too. I remember quite clearly the bike wanting to steer to the left down the hill. Maybe the draft was bigger than normal because the fairing was half off, in fact I think they were thinking of black-flagging me at the time.'

Intimidation is the real deal. These mad stabs aren't just about winning a position there and then, they're about establishing a reputation with other riders. If everyone knows you're a nutter, they're more likely to get out of your way, so next time you're on track together, you're going to have an easier time overtaking them, and they're going to be more wary of overtaking you. 'Intimidation is what it's all about,' agrees Doohan. 'If you do that kind of stuff enough, it gets to the point where people know as soon as they see you: 'I may as well shut down now because it's not like he's going to do me any favours'. Sure, there's plenty of times I scared the hell out of people, and if they ran off the racetrack that was their problem, but I've never intentionally put anyone off the racetrack. It's just a matter of keeping your position on the track, and perhaps modifying your position from where you'd be if there was no one else there, for no other reason than to intimidate other guys and mess with their heads. Luca established his reputation with me by pushing me onto the grass at Shah Alam, so I knew that if I came up on him again, I'd have to pass him fairly swiftly or he might put me in a position I didn't want to be in.'

Mackenzie again: 'You need to establish your reputation from day one. You've got to stamp your authority and make everyone believe that you're not going to back off, because if you do back off, next time they're not going to let you in. If someone like Troy Bayliss shows you a wheel, you know he's coming through. And in car racing, Michael Schumacher has definitely got that respect, and he knows that they know he's there.'

'I scared the hell out of people, and if they ran off the track that was their problem, but I've never intentionally put anyone off the track'

Of course, racers live by the sword and die by the sword; you try and intimidate the other guy, but if he's bigger and badder than you are, maybe you'll regret having had a go next time you come across each other. 'You definitely remember who did what to you,' says Roberts. 'It's a highly dangerous sport but you have a zone you're comfortable with, then you have aggression and then you have anger. So it's like: "I'm not goin' to give that asshole an inch because he didn't give me an inch last time".'

Schumacher has been disciplined by F1 bosses for overdoing his king of the track act, but official retribution is rare in bike racing, maybe because squeezing rivals is so routine. Occasionally riders do get nailed, like 125 hard-nut Manuel Poggiali, who was disqualified from May's Spanish GP for brazenly knocking down fellow teenage headbanger Alex de Angelis. Or perhaps they cop an official reprimand, like when Biaggi ran Valentino Rossi onto the dirt as they swept onto the start-

finish straight at Suzuka in 2001. In fact both riders were censured for
that incident, because Rossi shouldn't have been so naïve as to believe
that Biaggi would give him the space to run past on the outside. In
other words, this is motorcycle racing – you should know you're not the
only maniac on the track. Following that clash, FIM president Francesco
Zerbi wrote an open letter to the pair: 'to reproach you both, in order to
invite you to more attentively and correctly control your actions and
reactions, without taking anything away from your fighting instinct,
your desire for victory, your skill, your courage and the sporting qualities
that a true champion shows to all the world.' Yeah, right. Ten
weeks later Rossi and Biaggi were boxing each other's lights out at the
Catalan GP...

Invariably riders get let off the hook because most of the crimes
committed on track are so subtle, and because they're very much a part
of bike racing. After all, it's the ducking and diving, the feints and the
parries and the scary moments that make the sport so exciting to watch.
For example, what Biaggi did to Rossi at Suzuka is an everyday ploy in
tight situations. 'Sometimes you don't get a good drive out of a corner
but you casually use all the track even if you don't need it,' explains
Mackenzie. 'You know the guy behind may get a good drive and try to
go round your outside, so you use all the track and the kerb, because
there's no way they're going to want to use the grass.'

Riders use a similar tactic on the way into corners. Mackenzie again:
'You brake a little longer than normal, so the guy behind can't turn in
where he wants to, because you're still there braking. You just slow it
all down, hit the apex as normal, and the other guy has to file in behind
or run off the track.'

Some riders do the same kind of thing mid-corner – just ease off the
throttle, so whoever's following has to back off, run off line and, er,
maybe crash. 'I was never really guilty of that,' says Mackenzie. ' But I
know a lot of people who did do it. Gardner definitely did, and I know
(Eddie) Lawson gave him a few warnings, told him the next time he
tried it he was going to be in big trouble. I remember Gardner doing it
at the last turn at Laguna Seca because it's so slow. You just get off the
throttle and then get back on it, the bike pretty much stops and the
other guy has to pick up. It's not hugely dangerous but it can cost
whoever a lot of time because they get off line and then they're probably
in too tall a gear. It's a dirtier tactic, I didn't use it because I felt like it

could cost me time, and it's definitely risky because the guy could run into you and you'll both be down. But it's very effective if it works.'

Shifting rivals off line is even more effective nowadays, because roadracing has become like dirt track, with a narrow grippy line, beyond which there's little traction. 'The thing is that bikes have got a lot more grip now, so you don't get the variation in lines that you used to,' explains Roberts. 'You used to be able to watch at a chicane and say, "That guy's got the right line and that guy hasn't", but now everyone's got the same line because they've all got so much corner speed. So there's only one part of the track being used – maybe a metre or a metre and a half – and the rest of the track isn't so grippy. So it's like dirt track, where you've got the grippy notch. You see a guy coming and you just move out to the edge of the notch, and that leaves them nothing.'

And if that doesn't work you can let a rival come alongside on the straight and just shut his throttle. Sounds crazy, but the late Kenny Irons (who died in a freak accident at Cadwell in '88) once did just that to 250 rival Pete Hubbard at Brands. Hubbard's bike was quicker, so Irons took his left hand off the handlebar as they approached the finish line and grabbed Hubbard's right hand, easing the throttle shut. Mackenzie and Irons were big mates and the Scot remembers the Luton rider's tactics with great affection. 'He did some scary stuff to me but he always did it with a smile on his face, just for a laugh.' Racers are strange people, with a strange sense of humour...

Insane in the brain, insane in the membrane
You wouldn't believe the off-track psychological torture that goes on...

Most racers don't even wait to get on the racetrack before getting up to their tricks. Psychological warfare is a major part of motorcycle racing and it takes all forms. When John Kocinski led the early stages of the '94 500 world championship, arch-enemy Kevin Schwantz put up a $10,000 bounty for anyone who'd sleep with Kocinski's girlfriend. Maybe Schwantz didn't expect anyone to go for it, but he knew word would get around the paddock and destabilise his rival. 'Kevin was quite good at that kind of thing,' remembers Mackenzie. 'He'd also say subtle stuff, knowing that Kocinski would read it. He didn't do it maliciously, but with a sort of air of intelligence.'

Subtlety is everything in the off-track psych-out. Riders who tell the world that they're going to kick ass on race day only inspire their rivals to try harder, which is why you don't often hear that kind of talk. Doohan was a master of keeping a low profile off track: 'People who say shit only drive people to beat them even more. I always found it best to be emotionless, then no one's got any more desire to beat you. I guess I was fairly radical about the way I went racing. I was there to do a job, I wasn't really interested in any of the other garbage going on, because there's a lot of that going on in the paddock. I probably came across as fairly cold and emotionless and I never used to say a lot, which kept people guessing as to what I was thinking. With some other guys there's not a lot of guesswork, but I wanted it so that people never really knew where I was at. I was just a bit of an oddball really...'

Mackenzie was probably Doohan's closest mate when they were doing GPs together. 'Mick was really aware of how Gardner would come out with whatever he thought, which would fire Mick up even more. He knew what motivated him, people winding him up made him dig in even more, so he was really conscious of not doing it to anyone else.'

Mackenzie's own brand of race psychology required him to be nice to everyone, whether he was racing GPs or BSB. 'There's two ways of dealing with rivals – you either don't speak to them or you're mates. Someone like John Reynolds wouldn't be rude but he wouldn't communicate, he'd just go away and get in his little shell. Now I'm not racing he's my mate but he told me recently that when we were racing each other he couldn't befriend me. I was the opposite, I'd be everyone's mate so they didn't hate me, a bit like Mick. Maybe Mick wouldn't make an effort to be friends with anyone but I was quite happy to be friends with everyone. [James] Whitham told me that when we were team-mates in '96, he used to try and dig deep to hate me, but he couldn't hate me enough to get more motivated. I was aware of that – if people were my mates they wouldn't be so desperate to beat me.'

That's your motorcycle racers for you – a lovely bunch of two-faced vicious bastards. Which is why we love 'em.

CHAPTER 34

THE COOLEST RACERS IN THE WORLD, EVER

September 2003

Ten racing icons with more than pure speed going for them

How to define cool? In a motorcycle racer? First things first – the guy's got to be seriously fast, obviously. Beyond that he's got to have an aura, an attitude, which is more difficult to define than mere speed. It's all about the way he carries himself, the way he looks, the way he acts, the company he keeps, how much fun he can handle. It doesn't necessarily matter what clothes he wears or which ladies he hangs out with, but the right gear and the right girl can make all the difference. Basically, he's got to be the kind of guy you'd want to spend a night out with, the kind of person who spreads a little fun around the place.

He needs charisma, he's got to be bright and funny, he's got to have balls and he's got to do things his own way – simpering, sponsor-friendly rentamouths don't get a look-in here. He'll require a love of the good things in life – partying, ladies, that kind of thing – and he'll need to be passionate about what he does, not robotic. Finally, he needs a certain I-don't-give-a-fuck air about him, and a few bad habits will help as well, but that doesn't mean he's got to be an asshole. So there's no specific template, some of these riders are cool because they're bad, other because they're good, others because they're nuts, others because they're funny and a few because they're a bit of everything.

1 – Barry Sheene

Barry Sheene wasn't merely a world-title-winning bike racer, he was a 1970s icon along with fellow sportsmen Pele, Muhammad Ali, George Best and James Hunt. Like them he was a sign of the times – brash and brave, cheeky and captivating.

He was the London boy made good, who raced like a demon, partied like hell and ran off with the wife of a top fashion photographer. You

'Sheene had it all down: the attitude, the mouth, the girl and the motor – he shunned boy-racer stuff like Ferraris in favour of Rollers. Proper geezer'

couldn't have made it up. Even his name sounded unreal, like bike racing's own David Bowie.

Sheene had it all down: the attitude, the mouth, the girl, the gear and the motor – he shunned boy-racer stuff like Ferraris in favour of Rollers. Proper geezer. And he definitely had a bit of the bad boy about him. Sheene's reputation as a hard-partying gossip-column regular did sometimes distract from his talent for racing motorcycles at a time when they were recalcitrant beasts, and when death really did stare riders in the face. Sheene will almost certainly forever have his place in history as the winner of the fastest-ever GP, which is pretty damned cool. He won the 1977 Belgian 500 GP at an average speed of 135mph, and this was around the terrifying Spa Francorchamps street circuit, threading his way between trees, hedges and rusting Armco on a fickle two-stroke that might lock solid at any moment.

Sheene's career peaked at a moment when sport and serious money collided for the first time, and, like many wealthy young sportsmen or pop stars of his generation, he was an engine for social change – breaking down barriers of English snobbery by walking into posh hotels wearing little more than a pair of cut-off denim shorts, refusing pleas that he dress suitably. He was a captivating character like Best, Ali, Pele and Hunt. These men played hard by day and even harder by night – their like will not be seen again.

Years in top level racing: (1971–1984)
Bikes ridden: Suzuki 50, Suzuki 125, Derbi and Yamaha 250s, Suzuki and Yamaha 500s
Greatest achievements: 1976/1977 500 world champ
Where is he now: died from cancer March 2003

2 – Gary Nixon

Gary Nixon was always in the running for the top ten, just because we'd heard a lot of hilarious stories about the guy. And then we met him. After five minutes he was definitely in. After a couple more drinks we were serious considering sticking him in the top five. We've never met another racer who's so funny, not even Kenny Roberts.

Nixon raced and partied with the best of them in the 1970s, and he straddled that era when four-strokes were getting overtaken by the strokers. In fact he represented that age of change more than any other rider, because one moment he was racing British-made Triumph four-strokes, the next Japanese-built Kawasaki two-strokes.

Nixon used to hang out plenty with Sheene, who used to call him 'Nickers'. He was a hugely fast racer, and would've won the '76 Formula 750 world title if there hadn't been a major FIM cock-up. But it seemed like the prime motive throughout his career was less racetrack success and more off-track fun. By all accounts, the American was pretty successful on both counts, but more so the second. He also broke masses of bones – several of his crunching crashes suffered at the handlebars of dodgy two-strokes that locked solid at 150-ish and pitched him into trackside trees. Like many of his peers he developed a certain fondness for medication during lengthy hospital spells – he once racked up a 60-hour phone bill while lying in hospital in the UK, phoning his American girlfriend on morphine. And how did he look? Like Krusty the Clown but effortlessly cool at the same time. Big respect, Mr Nixon.

Years in top level racing: 1963–1979
Bikes ridden: Harley dirt trackers, Triumph dirt trackers and 1000 triples, Kawasaki, Suzuki and Yamaha 750s
Greatest achievements: 1967 Daytona 200 winner, 2nd 1976 Formula 750 world championship
Where is he now: occasional classic racer/MotoGP gofer

3 – Kenny Roberts

Kenny Roberts is a bit of a redneck, and rednecks ain't cool, so how come the King gets into this list? Cheeky of you to ask, but Mr Roberts is the world's most open-minded redneck, someone who's managed to leave the prejudices of that cowboy world way behind him and come to terms with life in the real world. Of course he's done much more than come to terms with the world, he's ruled it. Roberts was the don of the Hicksville world of US dirt track, before he travelled to Europe relatively late in his career to lift the 500 world championship at his first attempt in '78, nicking the crown from Sheeney. He went on to win three back-to-back 500 titles, then moved into team management, winning several world championships before tiring of working with the Japanese and branching out to build his own motorcycle. In fact he's now built two. The breadth of these achievements surely makes him the greatest motorcyclist in history, which in itself is totally cool.

The King doesn't rack up coolness points for his style (except when he steps out in his English country gent garb), his cool comes from something deeper than that – his total commitment to the world of motorcycling, especially racing. The man should've packed his boots and headed for a rocking chair years back, but he didn't, he's still living in Banbury, England (The King lives in English suburbia!), making his life a kind of living hell while giving his undyingly faithful Team Roberts crew a great reason to live. No other racer has ever done what he's done. (Sure, Fogarty has built a bike but Roberts is the very core of the Proton project, while Foggy had his deal handed to him on a plate.) And Roberts is one of the few people in the modern-day GP paddock who's brave enough to get properly drunk and say stuff he shouldn't, even if he's plenty more polite than he used to be.

Years in top level racing: 1975–1983
Bikes ridden: Harley dirt trackers, Yamaha 250, 500, 750 (road and dirt), FZR750
Greatest achievements: 1978/1979/1980 500 world champ
Where is he now: Staying up all night doing KR5 dyno runs

4 – Valentino Rossi

Valentino Rossi is the shining light of 21st-century motorcycle racing. He's turned more people onto bikes than anyone since Sheene, though that doesn't necessarily make him cool. What does make Rossi cool is his sublime riding talent and the effortlessness in everything he does, both on and off the racetrack.

Rossi derives a huge amount of enjoyment from racing, and his infectious child-like enthusiasm is still there, even if the weight of his fame has dulled that famous smile. The truth is that Rossi is a bit of a hippy, just like his dad, so he likes having fun, which explains the sometimes daft victory celebrations that endeared him to millions early in his career. Back then he could never have guessed that fame would engulf him as it has done, which is why he often looks a little shell-shocked these days. Like any globally famous celebrity, Rossi has sold a portion of his soul to the devil, even if he did so inadvertently.

Of course he works hard at his racing, but he's one of those people who works in an effortless way – you never see him looking pained in the pits or giving shit to his crew. And once the racing is over, he likes a party. Anyone who has seen him in action at various season-ending piss-ups at Valencia realises that Rossi knows how to cut loose. These days pro-racers don't get to party like they used to – for all kinds of reasons – but we've no doubt that if Rossi had been around in the 1970s, he'd have been partying like it was 1979.

Years in top level racing: 1996–now
Bikes ridden: Aprilia 125, Aprilia 250, Honda 500, RCV and SP-1, Yamaha YZR-M1
Greatest achievements: 1997 125 world champ, 1999 250 world champ, 2001 500 world champ, 2002/2003/2004/2005 MotoGP world champ
Where is he now: On your telly

5 – Jarno Saarinen

Like most of the other riders in this top ten, Jarno Saarinen had something effortlessly cool about him – you only need to see photos of him fixing his Yamaha TD250's clutch to realise that he had a touch of Steve McQueen, a touch of James Dean about him. Saarinen was super fast, very bright and always funny in an age when motorcycling took no prisoners. He was killed in a multiple pile-up at Monza in 1973. Just like James Dean, his burgeoning talent was snuffed out in what might be called glamorous circumstances.

Saarinen was a wonderful motorcycle racer. He started out doing ice speedway in Finland, bringing a new style of riding to the world of roadracing – he was super smooth but he slid his tyres and was probably the first man to get his knee down without crashing. His riding technique inspired Kenny Roberts. He was a good mechanic as well, always happy to get his fingers dirty even after he'd become the star of the Yamaha factory team. And he knew what he was doing, so he was quite capable of taking a grinder to a cylinder in the search for more horsepower. He knew his bikes inside and out. He had also an innate sense of style and a great eye for detail, so his clothes and his leathers, his helmets and his motorcycles always looked very, very right.

He lost his life in a 250 GP while he was running away with the 500 world championship. If he'd won that year's 500 crown he would've become the first man to win the premier title on a Japanese-built bike. There's not many bike racers who died so long ago who are still deeply missed by the sport, and that probably tells you all you need to know.

Years in top level racing: 1970–1973
Bikes ridden: Yamaha 250, 350 and 500
Greatest achievements: 1972 world champ, winner of two 500 GPs
Where is he now: killed during 1973 Italian 250 GP

6 – Anthony Gobert

Okay, so most race bosses hiss with disdain at the mere mention of Anthony Gobert's name – which on its own is just about enough to get him in this list. Goey's everything a racer shouldn't be – a proper loose unit – invariably unreliable, sometimes rude and he likes to party way too much. But hey, bike racing's wildest child is super-bloody fast when he can be bothered. A few years back Goey used to derive immense pleasure from disappearing on benders between US Superbike rounds, reappearing with an impressive beer gut to grab pole position at the next race, baffling his rivals who'd been sweating down the gym for five hours, every day. Okay, so the gut would do for him in the race, but by then he'd already made his point. Kind of.

Gobert has won fans and made enemies wherever he's raced – in World Supers, US Supers, 500 GPs and British Superbikes. He's been sacked by more teams for a greater range of misdemeanours than most riders have had deals. And maybe he'll never quite harness his talent effectively enough to prove just how good a rider he really is. Which will be a real shame. But anyone who erects a 10-foot square swimming pool outside his motorhome in the GP paddock and parties well into Sunday night, long after his rivals have been chauffeured home to their Monaco residences, has done enough to get into our top ten. Which is much more important than any lousy world title. Honest.

Years in top level racing: 1994–2001
Bikes ridden: Suzuki 500, Honda and Kawasaki 750s, Ducati 998, Bimota 1000, CBR900
Greatest achievements: his problems stopped him fulfilling his potential
Where is he now: God only knows

7 – Mike Hailwood

Most people in the know believe that Mike Hailwood was the greatest motorcycle racer the world has ever seen. He had a magical natural talent that allowed him to achieve the impossible, but he carried his talent lightly, never taking himself too seriously, always up for a laugh. In fact it seems that he barely recognised how gifted he was; maybe it all came too naturally to him, so he couldn't begin to imagine why he was any different from anyone else. How cool is that?

Hailwood wasn't even desperately ambitious, it was his millionaire father that pushed him into the big time, and he certainly knew nothing about motorcycles – he'd just climb aboard and give it heaps. He was proudly technophobic, with zero interest in the complexities of set-up. Once asked by one of his engineers: 'What gear are you in through turn four?', Hailwood replied: "I don't know, how many gears has it got?' An apocryphal tale perhaps, but certainly indicative of the man's attitude.

Although he was polite and good-natured, Hailwood was afraid of no one. When he signed to Honda in '66, he flew to Japan to test the factory's evil-handling 500 four. Appalled by the bike's wayward behaviour and unable to properly explain his feelings to the engineers, he grabbed the bike's rear shocks and lobbed them into the lake behind the Suzuka pits.

In his later years Mike the Bike had a dash of loucheness about him, like the rich man's son gone partying, which brought with it a spectacular fashion sense. But while he liked a party he wasn't your typical alpha-male roadracer. Hailwood was a genuinely nice guy in a vicious sport.

Years in top level racing: 1959–1967 (comeback 1978/1979)

Bikes ridden: Ducati and EMC 125s, Mondial, NSU and Ducati, Honda 250s, Honda 350, Honda, MV Agusta, Yamaha and Suzuki 500s, BSA, Yamaha 750, Ducati 900

Greatest achievements: 250 world champ 1961/1966/1967, 350 world champ 1966/1967, 500 world champ 1962/1963/1964/1965

Where is he now: died in a road car crash in March 1981

8 – Giacomo Agostini

Giacomo Agostini's cool flows from a very different kind of blood than fills the veins of most motorcycle racers. Ago came from wealthy north

Italian stock (more classy than Hailwood's upmarket-spiv dad), but his family didn't bankroll his bike-racing ambitions. In fact, like many parents of motorcycling kids, they did the opposite: they tried to bribe him to give it all up with the offer of a brand-new sports car. Rich kid or not, Ago was determined to get his two-wheel kicks, so he turned down his parents' offer and used to sneak out of the house to compete in local hill climbs. In other words, he had the coolness deep within him.

A few years later he was signed by Count Domenico Agusta to ride for the renowned MV Agusta marque. Ago and the Count were the epitome of pre-summer-of-love 1960s cool – a talented, smart-dressing youngster funded by a mega-rich aristocrat. And, of course, Ago was desperately handsome, the ladies swooning at his feet from Milan to the Isle of Man. His good looks and bravery won him massive fame in Italy, so it was only a matter of time before some Italian director asked him to play the heartthrob in a couple of movies. Ago never made it to Hollywood, but then again, he didn't need to.

There will probably never be a more successful racer than Agostini. He lorded it over his rivals for years, riding his beloved MVs to 14 world championships. And when everyone said he couldn't win without MV, he went and won the 1975 500 world title on a Yamaha, becoming the first man to win biking's biggest prize on a two-stroke.

Years in top level racing:	1964–1977
Bikes ridden:	Morini 250, MV Agusta 350, MV Agusta, Yamaha and Suzuki 500s
Greatest achievements:	350 world champ 1968/1969/1970/1971/1972/1973/1974, 500 world champ 1966/1967/1968/1969/1970/1971/1972/1975
Where is he now:	retired from team management and living in Italian splendour

9 – Graziano Rossi

It would be wrong to stick Valentino Rossi in the top ten without including the racer who begat him. Even people who've decided that it's time to start hating racing's current golden boy find it difficult to really loathe the kid, and the reason they can't summon up the odium is that Valentino is the son of his father. In other words, he's a likeable human being and thus difficult to hate, which is cool.

Graziano was what most racers aren't – an educated intellect with a hippy's attitude to life. Dad Rossi cheerfully admits that he was never world champ because he was too soft. He was the archetypal too-nice-to-be-world-champion racer, always tempted to stop and offer assistance when someone crashed in front of him. Not that he was soft when he was racing, Jeez, he was so crazy he even scared Kenny Roberts.

Like several other riders in this list, Graziano is one of those people who cuts a dash wherever he goes, not because he attracts attention but because he's got that sweet-natured glow about him. He's one of those people who spreads brightness, which is why Valentino is the well-adjusted human being, while his biggest rival (Max Biaggi) is the desperate try-hard.

Graziano still comes to a lot of GPs, but he's quiet and in the background; he doesn't get off on his kid's success, so he doesn't stay in flash hotels, in fact he doesn't stay in hotels at all. He drives an old BMW estate to races and sleeps in the back. And it doesn't get cooler than that.

Years in top level racing: 1978–1982
Bikes ridden: factory Morbidelli 250, Morbidelli, Yamaha and Suzuki 500s
Greatest achievements: winner of three 250 GPs in 1979
Where is he now: hanging out behind Rossi's pit

10 – Johnny Cecotto

Johnny Cecotto's star shined bright and briefly in motorcycle racing. At the age of just 19 the Venezuelan emerged from nowhere to win the 1975 350 title, making him the youngest world champ until Loris Capirossi lifted the 1990 125 crown, aged 17. Cecotto was young and had the whole world at his feet, but he messed the whole thing up. He took three 500 GP victories over the next few years and then left the scene as quickly as he had arrived, which is pretty cool.

During his six seasons on the world championship stage, Cecotto exhibited the kind of natural talent and flair you'd expect from a Latin-American racer, while also appearing somewhat unbothered about using that skill to full effect. He gains big points for this – possessing excessive talent plus a lack of desperation to prove that talent is very cool, unlike having little talent and trying too hard to impress, which is very uncool.

Aside from the racing, Cecotto had the cool thing nailed down. Like his mate Sheene he was motorcycling's own little bit of the 1970s jet set, possessing all the accoutrements that went with that world. But here's the clincher – Cecotto is possibly the only afro in history to have won a GP. Okay, so it wasn't a real afro, but at one point of his career it pretty much looked like one, and it certainly wasn't a bad effort for a honky. Only one black mark against the guy, he moved into car racing. Not so cool.

Years in top level racing: 1975–1980
Bikes ridden: Yamaha 250, 350, 500 and 650s
Greatest achievements: 1975 350 world champion, winner of three
                               500 GPs
Where is he now: retired

The nearly super cool: Wayne Rainey, Loris Capirossi, Angel Nieto, Carlos Lavado, Marco Lucchinelli, Scott Russell, Niall Mackenzie and Tom Herron.

CHAPTER 35

IF YOU'RE NOT CRASHING, YOU'RE NOT GOING FAST ENOUGH

November 2003

The only things certain in life are income tax and nurses, they say, but not if you're a racer – better add crashing to that list

The race is into its closing stages, just a few laps of Donington remain to catch that guy in front who's been bugging you for the last few minutes of your life. It's the difference between a gong (or a MotoGP podium slot, if you fancy some proper dreaming) or no gong.

You've been having a bit of a bungee race with the bloke: catch him one lap, lose a couple tenths the next, win a few yards, lose a few, and the laps are running out. But your rear tyre is shot, so you can't work any harder getting out of the bends, so you're going to have to push a little harder on the front – brake a little later, risk an extra wisp of speed into the few corners where you think you might just get away with it. But, as luck would have it, it's the rear that lets go first – must've been more shagged than you thought. It smears sideways on the exit of Coppice, then flicks back as you shut the throttle in panicked reflex. From here it's like you've hit the button in one of those hyper-speed skyscraper elevators – sixth floor: haberdashery, household and men's underwear. Your outstretched right hand is the first to return to earth. 'Fuck!' Then your right shoulder. 'Agghh, fuck!' Lower back. 'Fuck, ouch!' Both ankles. 'Fuck, fuck, fuck!'

Now your head is jerking this way and that as you attempt to determine whether your once very trick motorcycle, now exploding somewhere out of your immediate sight, is heading your way. And then you're stationary, well almost motionless. The bomb-like racket subsides until all you can hear is the wail of bikes hurtling past five feet from your left foot. You can taste blood, like someone's just punched you in the face, you're swimming in an ocean of pain, you want your mummy, you hate motorcycles, like really fucking hate them.

There's an old saying in racing: if you're not crashing, you're not going fast enough. Proof: The last rider to win a world championship without crashing was Sito Pons, who lifted the 1989 250 crown without once overstepping the mark. And here's another racing axiom, from three-time 500 king Wayne Rainey: 'If a rider's fast and he's crashing, maybe you can stop him crashing, but if a rider's slow, you're not going to make him fast.' In other words, there's no racing without crashing. And if you ever go racing, you'll be crashing too.

Crashes happens because racing is all about being faster than the next guy, which means you've got to bend the laws of physics to your own will and thus exist on the edge of a precipice. It's therefore inevitable that you'll fall over that precipice every now and again.

But what does crashing mean to a racer? Beyond the obvious physical agonies, what does it do to a rider's state of mind? And how do they keep coming back for more while they're still struggling with injuries and pumped full of painkillers? What follows is a veritable list of racing wreckers who really do know what crashing is all about: 1987 500 champ Wayne Gardner, former World Supers rider James Haydon, 1960s pile-up legend Dave Croxford, MotoGP star Carlos 'Chuckitaway' Checa and king of 'em all, 1993 500 champ Kevin Schwantz.

Wayne Gardner: the Digger who always dug deep

Some racers are always in the headlines, sometimes for all the wrong reasons. Wayne 'Digger' Gardner was one of them – if he wasn't grabbing daring 500 GP victories, he was usually incarcerated in Dr Costa's House of Pain, nursing another bunch of broken bones. That's how it went with WG: up or down, no in between.

Gardner epitomises the rough-edged Antipodean racer – frighteningly brave, always up for a fight and never one to say die. His career peaked at a time when 500s were seriously nasty pieces of work – horsepower dramatically outstripping tyre and chassis technology – which kind of suited his give-it-heaps-and-hang-on-for-dear-life riding technique.

'The NSR500 was a hunk of shit in the 1980s,' says Gardner, who won the 500 crown with Honda in '87. 'The suspension wasn't very good, the tyres weren't that good and the power came in hard, so it highsided a fair bit. There wasn't a lot you could do.' Not that this stopped him from giving it big handfuls: 'You're dedicated, you're committed, you're in that little world that all racers are in, so you have a go. Sometimes I was just trying too hard, other times there were riders who brought me down, other times I had machine failures.

'You've always got to analyse the crash and be honest with yourself – was it my mistake or what? If it's your responsibility you've got to accept it and learn from your mistakes. You've got to be pragmatic and work out why it happened, so you don't take your confidence away.'

'I was really scared, I thought I was actually dying, that really frightened me inside, that was the crash that brought me undone.'

But there were crashes that did spook him. 'The one that really shook me up was the Uncini accident at my first GP [Assen '83, when reigning world champ Franco Uncini crashed just ahead of Gardner, who collided with the Italian, putting him into a coma]. I went to see him in hospital and he was wriggling around in a coma, so I was bawling my eyes out saying: "Jesus, I've just nearly killed this guy", so I was quitting. Even though it wasn't my fault I kinda accepted some responsibility, but Franco got better and I had to get back out there and do my job, you've got to be cold blooded about it.

'The other one that really frightened the shit out of me was Assen in '92. I was trying to go round a slower guy into turn one and ran out of road, crashed and went into a post. I got knocked out and they carted me away, thinking I'd broken my neck. They put me in one of those full body scanner things, I was coming in and out of consciousness, I was really scared, I thought I was actually dying, I didn't know what was going on. That really frightened me inside, I mean mentally, and that confirmed I was over the whole bike racing thing – that was the crash that brought me undone.'

Six weeks later at the British GP Gardner announced that he was retiring, then went out and won the race. He quit bikes at the end of that season.

Kevin Schwantz: the ultimate floored genius

Revvin' Kevin Schwantz was king crasher of the late 1980s and early 1990s – the archetypal floored genius with tons of talent and a touch too much enthusiasm. He raced clip-on to clip-on with Wayne Rainey, Mick Doohan, Eddie Lawson and Wayne Gardner, and was generally recognised as the most naturally gifted rider of that remarkable era. But boy, did he crash a lot.

'I remember '89 was probably my worst year,' says the '93 500 champ. 'I was wearing Taichi leathers and I remember seeing racing suit number 19 – so I'm guessing 20 to 25 crashes that season.'

Schwantz is the first to admit that he did get carried away rather too often, but his machinery was also to blame. For nine years he raced Suzuki's notoriously fickle RGV500 which was never the quickest 500. Not only that, it had borderline chassis performance – get it right and it was the sweetest-handling thing out there, but go racing two clicks out on the suspension settings and it was a vindictive piece of machinery, apparently hell-bent on flinging its rider to the ground.

'Most times I crashed I was trying to figure a way to go faster and it just snuck up and got me. I'd be having problems getting the bike to do everything I wanted it to – to handle right and to finish the corner exactly the way I wanted – so I might try and go in a bit deeper to get the sharper part of the turning done early.' Cue front-end crash. 'Or maybe it wasn't finishing the corner, so I'd try to steer it with the back wheel coming out.' Cue highside crash.

'I only remember a few races where things worked really, really well. But for the most part it was such a fine line to get a grand prix motorcycle working right that I had to ride 100 per cent pretty much every corner, every lap.'

Whatever his bike worries, Schwantz was always unwilling to give in, which is why he was such a big hit with the fans. 'There were a lot of times when I was following somebody thinking: "God he's getting away, I gotta come up with something, I gotta figure something out", that can sneak up and get you too. You're tryin' to do something on newish tyres, where you've not really got to the limit and figured how much you can push the front or spin the rear. Then the thing spins, snaps sideways, snaps back and throws you off. I was just a little over-anxious.'

But however much he crashed, Schwantz never angered his bosses to the point where they gave him the flick, simply because they realised that no one could ride a motorcycle quite as hard as he could. 'I'm sure there were people in the team who got angry with me, but I think they realised that slapping my hand and telling me that if I ever fell again I wasn't going to race any more wasn't the way to solve the problem.'

And yet inevitably there came a time when the accidents did begin to gnaw at his confidence, though it was a single tumble which began the process – that scary pile-up at Donington 1993 when an out-of-control Doohan clipped him as they braked for the esses, precipitating Schwantz into a 130mph end-over-end prang. 'That knocked my confidence to the point where I may never again have ridden like I was riding before that. That season I'd been building the championship lead over Wayne (Rainey) and suddenly the lead had completely vanished. From a mental standpoint it was much harder after that because I was banged up and had that little bit of doubt in my head. Even after a crash that has nothing to do with you, it's still hard to get back on the bike and go back to that same level of performance.'

Just five weeks later came the spill that flicked the switch in Schwantz's mind once and for all. 'The one that scared me the most wasn't even one of mine, it was Wayne's. [Schwantz's career-long rival Rainey crashed at Misano in September '93, sustaining injuries that paralysed the Californian from the chest down.] I didn't see it, I don't know what caused it, but it was the result. Wayne was someone I looked up to, I used to say: "Man, that guy never crashes and when he does fall he's always okay, he never gets hurt", but all of a sudden Mr Invincible was hurt. To me that crash had the biggest effect on me.'

Schwantz continued racing until mid-1995 when lingering hip and wrist injuries forced him to stop. He had often raced hurt because he has an enormous tolerance for pain, but he was only storing up problems for later. (Doohan is the same, once rejecting pain-relief injections with the immortal words: 'I'm not a painkiller type of person'.)

'I never really used anything for pain, I think I was pretty good at blocking it,' adds Schwantz. 'I've just been to the doctor so he could look at my recently broken hand. He said: "You know what, I'm pushing on this bone and you're not even hurting, most people would have flipped over on the x-ray table by now. Your tolerance for pain is somewhat different to the average person." I don't know if that's a good thing – I probably rode some times I shouldn't have, but you've just got to get it into your mind that it's a 45-minute race and you've got to tough it out, then you'll have some time to heal and get better.'

That's what top-level bike racing is all about – it's not only about riding blindingly fast when everything's peachy, it's about riding blindingly fast when every twist of the throttle makes you wince, and not giving a damn, just keeping it pinned.

Dave Croxford: ol' rubber bones

Dave Croxford was a legend in his own launch time – he launched himself into the barriers no less than 203 times during a career that ran from 1962 to '76. Crox made his name racing the factory John Player Norton twin in an age when Yamaha's scarily fast TZ two-strokes were changing the face of racing. Remarkably he didn't break a single bone in those 14 seasons. That would be incredible these days, but back then, when riding gear was rudimentary and run-off often non-existent, it smacked of some kind of God-given immortality, or perhaps a pact with the devil. No wonder fans called him 'Rubber Bones'.

Now well into his 60s, Croxford is very aware that he got off lightly at a time when fatalities were commonplace. 'I'm one of the lucky ones, no aches or pains, I'm right as rain,' he says, recalling that racers used to take the risks more lightly back then and damn the consequences. 'It was real good fun in them days – if it rained you sometimes popped in the bar for a couple of pints of Guinness and then went out to race.'

Like any racer, Croxford does have reasons for his multitudinous get-offs, and not all of them involve the consumption of intoxicating liquor. 'The TZs were coming out then and they had loads of power, but the handling wasn't right, while the Norton was great in corners but slow on the straights, so I was always trying to make up ground.'

Many of Croxford's tumbles were comedy events. 'I crashed at Brands while battling with Bazza (Sheene), I was sliding along on my arse waving at him, and he was waving back.' Or one of his two TT crashes: 'This bloody great big pig comes out and it's running alongside me...'

Of course, Crox lost plenty of mates who weren't as blessed as him, but somehow he managed to blank it all out. 'Other blokes did get killed, which made you think "It could be bloody me", but it's no good being cautious because then you're not going to be up the front. No, it never used to worry me, I lived for racing, that's all I wanted to do – every Wednesday I'd bunk off from work to go down to Brands for practice. Sure, there's many times it could've happened to me and I'd think "God, I was lucky there", but I'd just pick meself up, bow to the crowd and that was that. Nah, don't think about it – just get back on and ride. And if Derek [Minter, famed Brands Hatch ace] crashed in front of me, I'd think: "Oh great, some extra prize money!"'

Croxford is still big into his bikes – he rides his VFR most days and loves watching racing on the telly. 'I thought I was the dog's bollocks when it came to crashing, but I tell you what, they crash more than I did. I think: 'God Xaus, you're worse than me!' Poor guy, he doesn't seem to know how to ride any more because he's crashed so much.'

Despite his rock-hard attitude, the west Londoner knows very well how too much crashing can mess with your head, even if fear's got nothing to do with it. 'I used to feel sorry for the mechanics. I crashed four times in one meeting and Frank (Perris, legendary Norton racer and team boss) was saying: "Crox, can't you please try and stay on?" So I said: 'I promise, I promise!', but of course you don't enjoy yourself when you've got to stay on.'

Carlos Checa: clank, crash, here comes careless chucker
Carlos Checa's Yamaha MotoGP mechanics sometimes did a kind of John Wayne swagger when they walked through the paddock, shouting 'Clank, clank, clank!' as they went on their way. In other words – the guy's got balls of steel, very big balls of steel.

The Spaniard was one of MotoGP's bravest hoons. In 1998 he crashed heavily during British GP practice and was helicoptered to hospital where he suffered a relapse – lying blind and partially paralysed for 15 hours. His surgeons told him they weren't sure whether he'd recover, but six weeks later he was racing, and crashing, again. The following season Checa quit Honda and joined Yamaha, falling 27 times before the year was out; an impressive achievement, but even more remarkable was his ability to limp back to the pits, take his number-two bike and continue at the same pace, or even faster. Checa was unique in this – most riders begin to ease the throttle shut after a dozen or so crashes. Well, you would, wouldn't you?

So what was different about Checa? 'I get a good feeling by fighting the limits within myself and breaking down barriers,' he says. 'When you do that and get a good result, you feel great. I know that crashing is part of my job, so if you want to make it in this sport you've got to really want to win, so you can fight with your rivals, with your bike's limitations, with your own mind, and if you do crash and get injured, you don't care, you'll recover. You have to have that instinct. When I came back from my Donington crash I was honestly scared, but I fought against that feeling.

'I used to go skydiving, even though my contract forbids this, but skydiving isn't risky, well you can die but you won't get injured, which makes things simpler. Anyway, when I was ready to jump and saw the ground so far away I had that really scary feeling, but I fought against it. Then, after you've jumped many times you lose the fear and start to feel many things you didn't feel when you were scared.'

Of course, Checa knows there are other consequences of crashing beyond inner feelings. 'Crashing is shit for you, shit for the bike, shit for the mechanics and shit for the set-up. It's a signal that you're heading in the wrong direction. You want to win but crashing is the opposite. It's like being in France when you want to go to England and when you crash you go to Spain. That way you'll never get to England!'

Checa admits that he has been freaked by some crashes. 'All riders have scary moments, except when you're on a confidence high. When people talk about riders losing confidence it's just that scary feeling affecting you, it's chemicals in your brain. The worst crashes are the ones you can't explain – because then you don't know what to change. If you know you braked too deep into a turn, then you can change that, or if the front end's wrong, you can change that, but if you don't know what went wrong, it's hard to get back on and go to the limit again.' Checa blames most of his crashes on his Yamaha's tendency to lose the front mid-corner. 'You get off the brakes and go to open the gas, which shifts weight to the rear tyre and suddenly you've got no front-tyre contact.'

James Haydon: 'There's been times I've over-ridden a bike'
James Haydon was one of those riders with a bit of a reputation for crashing too much, and like most other riders who carry the stigma, he doesn't think he really deserves it.

'I've crashed a bit but I've rarely been on the best equipment, which means you've got to push a bit harder,' explains the former BSB, WSB and 500 rider. 'Riding like that might've caused me a few crashes but it's also given me a few wins I wouldn't otherwise have had. The only time I've had a bike that matched everything else out there was the Red Bull Ducati in 2000. Getting on that thing was like "Wow!", I didn't have to over-ride it, so I hardly crashed it at all.'

Haydon cheerfully admits that he's one of those riders who doesn't know when to let his discretion get the better of his valour. 'I don't like getting beaten, but sometimes you've got to use the clever bit in your head, so if you're struggling to stay with someone because they've got a better set-up or a faster bike, maybe you should see that and settle for what you've got, rather than keep trying to outdo them on the brakes or whatever. But when the bike you're riding is 35 kays down, like the Foggy Petronas, you've no choice. If you don't try and take five bike lengths on the brakes, you're nowhere, so by the very nature of the package, you're more likely to crash.'

Not everyone is like this. Former 500 champ Kenny Roberts Junior and double 250 champ Luca Cadalora are well known for their lack of interest in pushing their luck on below-par machinery. It's not difficult to see their logic: after all, what's the point of risking your neck to finish 11th instead of 12th? 'Maybe guys like that are more clever than me,' adds Haydon. 'I want to do the best I can, so there's been times I've over-ridden a bike, but now I'm starting to look at it differently.'

Haydon had two crashes in his last few years of racing that alerted him to his own mortality – a crunching highside at Silverstone in 2001 and a terrifying get-off at Oschersleben in June 2003. 'The Oschersleben crash was absolutely petrifying, the worst I've ever had, just amazingly scary. I had a gearbox problem and went off at the fastest part of the track. The worst thing was that I knew I was going to crash, I was heading towards this barrier, my brain judging all the distances, and I knew I was definitely going to hit it. What made the crash really scary was that I was still on the bike and it seemed like an eternity, knowing I was going to go down, so I just had to jump off.' Haydon hit the gravel trap at 120mph, sustaining neck injuries and a displaced disc.

There's nothing worse for a racer than crashes caused by mechanical problems – they take a rider's destiny away from him, leave his life in the lap of the gods. And while most riders can bounce back from the worst of tumbles and injuries, even the strongest-minded racer struggles to get back on dodgy equipment and ride his hardest.

As Haydon says: 'It all depends on you knowing what happened in the crash – if I know I was a bit early on the throttle or I got in a bit hot, that's not a problem at all, because I know what to do to make sure it doesn't happen again. The mechanicals are the really scary stuff.'

Some guys bounce better than others
There's no doubt that some racers get hurt more often, even if they don't fall off a lot. But why? Quite simply, some guys bounce better than others, as injury-hit Kevin Schwantz explains: 'I think some riders have something

about them that allows them to tumble better. I think a taller person like myself, with longer arms and legs, has more opportunity to get a leg or an arm in a bad position and maybe break it, whereas a shorter person is going to bounce a little bit better. I think there's definitely a technique to falling – you've got to try and stay flat and not tumble. And when you hit the ground you've got to make sure that you've come to a complete stop before you try and stand up, that stops a lot of injuries.'

GP medic Dr Claudio Costa has plenty of theories on the subject. 'Some riders learn to crash well,' he says. 'But much of it has to do with the type of crash – if you lose the front, maybe you just slide off, but if you lose the rear, you may highside, and highsides are always bad.'

Costa's Clinica Mobile is staffed by a team of physios who attempt to minimise injuries before crashes even happen, administering daily massages to riders, ensuring their bodies are as flexible as possible. 'The human body is a machine – a thermodynamic machine,' Costa adds. 'So we need to prepare riders just like mechanics prepare bikes.'

MotoGP Mutterings: December 2003
Admit it, you've always wanted to know the truth about brolly girls...

Do you ever wonder where brolly girls come from? Because I think it's time you got told. MotoGP brolly girls are chosen by a panel of five or six top riders – Rossi, Biaggi, Gibernau, etc – during a secret pre-season selection process that lasts several days and takes place in a flash hotel in the Swiss Alps. This is an increasingly controversial event – there've been plenty of rumours of, er, palm greasing in recent years – and some people want it stopped. Anyway, the chosen few are then contracted to the MotoGP series for a full season, during which time they get ferried around Europe in a mirror-windowed tour bus, all white-leather sofas and glass-topped tables. This vehicle is never parked within the paddock, for obvious reasons, until Sunday morning when it deposits each girl outside the back door of her respective pit...

I'm lying, of course, but from now on I'll be straight up. Most brolly girls are either local lasses desperate for their 15 seconds of fame or professional models, usually taken from the books of local modelling agencies. I know two girls whose job it is to choose grid talent for several of the top teams. They contact modelling agencies looking for trick Sheilas who are happy to stand on the grid in bikinis, even though the nearest beach is 200 miles away. These women are usually gorgeous, but sometimes not gorgeous enough, or at least not mucky enough. Just recently some MotoGP teams have been complaining that they desire raunchier flesh next time around, so the two girls I know now surf porno websites to find the right chicks for the job. Shocking, eh?

But nothing new. Back in the late 1970s there was an Italian 500 GP racer called Walter Migliorati. He was a privateer, so he never won anything big, but his presence dramatically increased interest in the back row of the grid, where he'd sit awaiting the start, flanked by two, sometimes more, topless prostitutes. You couldn't get away with that kind of behaviour these days, what with global TV feeds and all. Migliorati was a bit of a player: he liked to race bikes, party and hang out with whores, and he always wore a pair of ho's panties (panty hoes?) under his helmet. No really, straight up. His racing career ended early when he went down in a major-league cocaine bust. Proper bad boy.

You may wonder what got me round to thinking about sex and motorcycle racing, because obviously they're not subjects that occupy the same head space. At the 2003 Czech GP I got invited to the launch of the International Roadracing Women's Association, presumably an organisation that had been established to look after the interests of the growing number of girls working in MotoGP, most of them in paddock PR, catering and hospitality. I imagined a few ladies discussing how to turn the macho-centric paddock into a more lady-friendly place. No chance. IRWA's launch party rocked –

'Migliorati was a bit of a player – he always wore a pair of ho's panties under his helmet'

Melandri and Rossi on the decks above a writhing mass of bodies, most of them IRWA members but a fair number of paddock blokes, looking worryingly pleased with themselves. I should've suspected something when the IRWA president handed me the invite along with a baseball cap emblazoned with the IRWA logo – a silhouette of a Vegas ho, all big hair, plastic tits and stilettos, waving a flaming chequered flag in the air. Shocking.

But I know what you really want to know – does any shagging go on in the paddock these days? Of course it does, but the goings-on are very hush-hush, not like the late 1980s when Wayne Gardner's missus got into all sorts of bother for (er, allegedly) shagging one of Toni Mang's mechanics. (She recently published a racy novel – called *Leathers* – based upon her paddock experiences.) And I know it still goes on, because I've done some middle-of-the-night-creeping-down-hotel-corridors myself (okay, it was only once), and a few weeks back a MotoGP team manager told me of a 3am fire alarm that had him leaping out of his hotel bed during British GP weekend. He emerged from his room to find several semi-naked couples, who weren't supposed to be couples, sprinting down the corridor with bath towels hurriedly wrapped around their torsos. It's a wonder any racing gets done at all.

CHAPTER 36

THE MADDEST RACERS IN THE WORLD, EVER

May 2004

You don't need to be mad to race motorcycles but it definitely helps, as these men bear testament

We should begin this top ten by reminding everyone that all motorcycle racers are nutters, if only because 'normal' society tends to regard them as such. But some are bigger nutters than others, and this lot, we reckon, are the nuttiest of them all. Each of these ten riders has a reputation for some or all of the following: crashing a lot, T-boning rivals on a regular basis or just generally riding out of control like they're totally immortal. Above all, they just scare the hell out of us.

Of course, these men are more than just nutters. If all bike racers are a wee bit crazy, those who make it all the way to the top have other stuff going for them. While every racer requires a certain disregard for his own safety and for the safety of others if he's to race competitively, he'll need the following characteristics and more to exalt himself beyond the ranks of club and national racing: riding talent, determination and intelligence (of a kind).

Perhaps we could distil those attributes down to genius and bravery, but we all know that genius is closely allied to madness, as bravery is to stupidity. All these riders have those four qualities in the mix. Kevin Schwantz was maybe three parts genius and four parts bravery to two parts stupidity and one part madness, Christian Sarron perhaps four parts bravery and five parts madness to four parts stupidity and three parts genius.

Finally, an important word of advice: never share a rentacar with a bike racer.

1 – Dave Croxford

Even Carlos 'Chuckitaway' Checa doesn't crash as much as Dave Croxford used to, and 'Crockers' raced in the days when the Armco was bare and rusty and body armour was something you found in the Tower of London.

Like Checa, 1960s and 1970s nutter Croxford was one of those riders to whom it never occurred that slowing down might be a bit of a plan. He just kept on crashing, from Brands Hatch to the Isle of Man, cheating death and broken bones in more than 200 tumbles. Sometimes he bounced well because he was pissed, other times it was just sheer London geezer luck. And Crox was always in the midst of any post-race piss-ups, which were very much the norm on Sunday nights back then.

But he was also known as a decent development rider. And he reckons he asked Norton to make a slipper clutch three decades before they became the must-have accessory on any race bike or supersports bike.

'That Cosworth Norton, it was so over-bored, with such a short stroke that it used to lock up the rear whenever you shut the throttle,' he recalls. 'I told them something was wrong, but they said "no, it's fine Crox". So we were testing at Snetterton and it was pissing down with rain. I told them "right, you stand by the pits, I'll come past, take my hand off the throttle to show I've shut the throttle, then you can see what it's like". So I come along, take my hand off the throttle, the wheel locks and I crash. I get back to the pits and say "there, told you so", but they did nothing...'

2 – Christian Sarron

The maddest racing nutters always inspire fear and loathing from their rivals. Christian Sarron did just that during the late 1980s and early 1990s when he was the only European 500 rider to regularly hassle the ex-dirt trackers from the USA and Australia.

Eddie Lawson and his ex-dirt-tracking peers hated racing with Sarron because (a) he was nuts and (b) his old-school riding style didn't fit with theirs. While they would enter a corner focusing on a rapid exit, Sarron would career up the inside on his Gauloises Yamaha, trying to make all his time on the way in, with predictable consequences. And on the way out of corners he was an accident waiting to happen, for this was the heyday of highsides. Sarron, who won the 1984 250 title before graduating to 500s, went over the top countless times, invariably knocking himself out in the process.

Fellow former 500 rider Niall Mackenzie remembers him well: 'Christian didn't mean to be dangerous, he just was. He'd come flying past, then crash at the next corner. Once he crashed in front of me at

Imola when I was catching him. I thought I'll just run over him and then this'll never happen again. If you ever spoke to him after a race he couldn't even recall what had happened – either too focused or too many bangs on the head.'

3 – Gustav Reiner

Not the most famous of our top ten, but without doubt nuts enough to qualify, Gustav Reiner was one of the leading 500 privateers of the 1980s who occasionally got the chance to terrify a factory rider on his Honda RS500. It was Arian blond Reiner who originated the fabulous racing saying: 'Rostrum or hospital'.

And he wasn't joking. The wild-eyed German was a regular in the Clinica Mobile throughout his GP career, quite capable of crashing both his bikes in one practice session, to the chagrin of lone mechanic Steve Blackburn who went on to work with the more restrained Nicky Hayden. And yet Reiner never made the podium in a GP, his best was a fourth-place finish in the riders' strike-hit '79 Belgian 500 GP.

'Reiner would be in Costa's after pretty much every practice session,' remembers fellow 500 rider Niall Mackenzie. 'He was hard and pretty mad, though he was another one of those guys on uncompetitive machinery.' And he was dead scary off a bike too: 'You wouldn't want to meet him in a dark alley,' adds Mackenzie.

Reiner's wonky knees and mangled knuckles told his story as he hobbled around the paddock doling out insults to his English mates. 'I hate you fucking English,' he used to say. 'You killed my dad in the war. Okay, so he was drunk and fell out of a lookout tower…'

4 – Kevin Schwantz

Our only nutter to have won the 500 world championship, Kevin Schwantz spent much of his eight-year GP career battling his crashing demons. But like most racers he was maddest in his early years. His earliest British outings – in the 1986 and 1987 Transatlantic series – were unforgettable displays of a burgeoning riding talent pumped to breaking point by dangerous amounts of it'll-never-happen-to-me lunacy; the old genius/madness interface.

'He was definitely a bit mental early on,' remembers former rival and team-mate Niall Mackenzie. 'Again, a lot of it was just pushing so hard on uncompetitive machinery.'

'There was blood everywhere, but we were all drunk so we didn't feel any pain'

Like most nutters, Schwantz surfed a wave of testosterone that didn't stop flowing when he climbed off the bike. He was famous for being king of après-race excess – half-drowning himself in a fountain during the notorious end-of-season party that followed the 1992 South African GP, crashing Porsches into ditches or playing knuckles with Mackenzie. 'There was blood everywhere,' Mackenzie grins. 'Kevin always came up with these painful games, but we were all drunk so we didn't feel any pain.'

5 – Carlos Lavado

It takes a very special brand of nuttiness to lead a race by a country mile, then fall off. Kevin Schwantz and Graziano Rossi were good at this but nowhere near as good as Carlos Lavado (Careless Bravado to his mates), winner of the 1983 and 1986 world 250 titles. Clutching defeat from the jaws of victory was Lavado's specialist subject – he tumbled out of first place three times in '84 alone. But that's not all, Lavado could do better than that, he could even lead a race, crash, get back up with the leaders and then crash again. No one ever picked up a fallen bike quicker, but then he had a lot of practice at it.

The lovable Venezuelan was certainly a nutter but he was also astonishingly talented, almost as if the bikes and tyres of his era hadn't caught up with his riding ability. In 1985 Lavado gave Freddie Spencer a seriously hard time in the 250 world championship, even though his Yamaha was way slower than Spencer's Honda. Spencer rarely admitted to the skills of his rivals, but he was moved to say that he was really quite scared of Lavado.

It should also be noted that it was Lavado who began the paddock fashion for wearing your helmet atop your head and backwards, a style now adopted by London scooter kids.

6 – Ron Haslam

This is not Ron Haslam the elder statesman of British roadracing whom we all know and love. This is Ron Haslam the long-haired loony from Langley Mill who put the fear of God into the British racing establishment during the late 1970s.

Haslam was a greasy, fearless teenager when he burst onto the scene in 1974, riding ratty, metalflake silver Pharaoh Yamaha TZ750s belonging to well 'ard car dealer Mal Carter, father of 250 GP winner Alan and former speedway world champ Kenny. Mick Grant, then a Kawasaki factory rider, remembers 'wild young Ron upsetting the old school, barging into me and Barry [Sheene] at Cadwell'. Haslam was indeed terrifying to behold as he crashed and burned his way to the top on Carter's TZs. The Pharaoh Yam set-up was from another age of Britain, when men still got dirty down the pits and serious glamour was a one-week package holiday in Torremolinos.

Haslam was so lairy that his decision to race the deadly Isle of Man TT circuit in 1978 was greeted with horror by some, though by that time he had been signed by Honda Britain. The factory-backed team smoothed off Haslam's rough edges, eventually propelling him into a reasonably successful career in 500 GPs.

7 – Jeremy McWilliams

Jeremy McWilliams carved a career out of racing uncompetitive motorcycles in the world's most competitive racing class, so it's not really his fault that he's in this top ten. If McWilliams had been blessed with more horsepower during his ten years in GPs, he might have been able to channel his undoubted talents into perfecting a smooth and gracious riding style. Instead he had no alternative but to develop a technique that's the racing equivalent of a military full-frontal attack – frighteningly late braking that occasionally employs rivals and/or their motorcycles as extra deceleration aids.

We can barely imagine what it's like to be at the receiving end of a McWilliams onslaught, but fellow MotoGP rider John Hopkins got a taste during their hard-fought duel in the 2002 Australian GP. 'McWilliams is an evil little rascal, some of the moves he pulled were a bit heavy,' said Hopper, with a tinge of understatement in his voice.

McWilliams' total commitment to winning the racing line, whoever might be in his way, has won him great respect from those people who appreciate riders with oversized crown jewels, like the Italians, which is why Aprilia were always keen to give him a job, and the hard-to-impress King Kenny Roberts for whom McWill rode in 2002 and 2003.

8 – 'Omobono' Tenni

Tomasso 'Omobono' (Italian for 'good man') Tenni was a nutter back in the days when world war seemed a reasonable way of proving that you were bigger and tougher than the next guy. In other words, he must've been seriously frightening.

Tenni made his name during the interwar years, dazzling fans with his fearlessness. They nicknamed him Death Defying Man but it didn't do him any good, for he was killed in an accident during practice for the 1948 Swiss grand prix.

From a poor peasant background, Tenni started racing and winning as a teenager, quickly gaining a reputation for riding with total abandon. After landing a factory Moto Guzzi ride he terrified the British on his TT debut. While the Italians loved his fearless, wall-grazing riding style, the more uptight Brits found it all too much and gave him yet another nickname: 'Black Devil'. Nevertheless Tenni became the first Italian to win a TT when he triumphed in the 1937 Lightweight TT. He also won three Italian 500 titles and two Milan–Naples roadraces, losing two toes in another attempt at Milan–Naples victory.

9 – Noboru Ueda

Racial stereotypes dictate that Japanese riders are inscrutable, obscure and scary. Noboru Ueda was definitely scary but he was neither inscrutable nor obscure. Nobby – as his European fans liked to call him – rarely stopped grinning during his decade on the GP scene, apart from those occasions when he was gnashing his teeth after throwing away another likely victory with another impossible manoeuvre gone wrong.

Ueda was the first breath of Japan's storm from the east that swept through 125 GPs during the early 1990s. Within a few years riders like Ueda, Kazuto Sakata, Haruchika Aoki, Takeshi Tsujimura, Tomomi Manako, Masao Azuma, Masaki Tokudome and Youichi Ui made Japan the third most successful nation in 125s, most of them also reinforcing the kamikaze stereotype on account of their out-of-control riding.

Ueda stayed faithful to the proper nutters' class throughout his GP career, probably substantially contributing to profits at the Honda Motor Company as he demolished one Honda RS125 after another. He came close to winning the 125 world title in 1994 and 1997, and suffered nasty hand injuries the following year that would've put lesser hard nuts out of racing for good. Instead Ueda had a special bionic glove made for his right hand with spring-loaded fingers, because he couldn't open the hand once he had clenched it.

10 – Toni Elias

Toni Elias would be the Tony Montana of bike racing, except that he seems a much nicer guy than Scarface. It is Elias' swarthy Latin looks, monobrow and don't-give-a-fuck riding style that liken him to Scorsese's seriously nasty cocaine baron, but Scarface never grinned as much as Elias does. Then again, maybe Elias' cheery complexion is that of the grinning maniac – he's just looking forward to the next time he stuffs someone really badly when he's out on the track.

Elias established his hard-man credentials early on, bashing fairings with 125 rival Manuel Poggiali in 2001 and proving that he was quite prepared to sort things out back in the paddock when he felt he'd been done over.

In 2002 Elias won his first 250 GP victory with an inspired final-turn manoeuvre over Marco Melandri that was five parts genius, two parts madness. In 2003 he trashed his title hopes with a berserk last-lap attack on Poggiali at Rio that was more like six parts madness, ten parts bravery and zero parts genius. But at least the boy gave it a go. We advise you to love this kid because he's a huge laugh and he's going far.

Dishonourable mentions: Wayne Gardner, Ruben Xaus, James Haydon, Alan Carter, Paul Lewis, Yvon DuHamel and anyone else who rode in the Yamaha Pro-Am series.

MotoGP Mutterings: May 2004
Celebrating 25 years of getting away with it

Four thirty in the morning, both of us still pissed, still stinking from the night before. Pushing the two ratty RD400s up the builder's plank and into the rusting Transit van. That bleary drive to Snetterton in bleakest early March, wondering how the snide pistons I'd just fitted would handle a Saturday and Sunday of heavy-handed abuse. Of course, they wouldn't even last through practice, but we were shockingly naïve back in 1979.

Things were different when I got into bike racing 25 years ago, life even smelt different. The mate with whom I shared that Transit was just starting out racing, like me, so he used to get a bit too nervous while waiting on the grid and end up pissing himself. I can still smell the drive home – piss-stained leathers hanging in the back of the van.

Oh yes, how things have changed. Nowadays it's sniffing champagne-stained leathers as I jostle for position in a MotoGP press conference, hanging on the every word of some goggle-eyed twentysomething who's high on the taste of victory and a few mouthfuls of champagne.

I suppose they feel the way I used to feel when I was their age. But not quite. While your average modern-day MotoGP star is wondrously talented and laser-guided by his management team, we were a bunch of terrifyingly inept morons, happy enough to spend our weekends charging into turn one, fuelled by a dangerous mix of blundering innocence, testosterone, punk rock and Harp lager. Getting stupidly drunk was all part of the deal, so we'd crash out on the floor of the Transit at 3am Sunday morning, gobble down a full English in the paddock canteen at nine and be on the grid for the first race at ten. Jesus Christ, what on earth were we thinking?

No wonder we crashed a lot. I distinctly remember a 250 proddie race at Snetterton that claimed more than half the grid in just six laps, that's about 20 crashes in less than seven minutes, after two restarts. I didn't even make it beyond the first corner, tumbling out in a six-man pile-up that smeared tyre marks across my helmet. My own personal record was four crashes in a weekend at Brands Hatch, two at Druids hairpin within an hour of each other. I lay the blame for this kind of behaviour firmly at Yamaha's front door. By manufacturing the 250 and 350LC they sent half of Britain's biking youth barking mad, launching a thousand racing careers and causing god knows how many thousands of broken bones. I'm sure the LC racing boom of the early 1980s was largely responsible for getting the NHS into such a mess – we clogged up hospitals from Norwich to Nottingham for years.

They called us the headbangers and with good reason. We were Northern nutters and London geezers, fighting pitched racetrack battles across the country as fiery riots raged from Brixton to Toxteth. There were dodgy Enfield types who financed their racing by nicking bikes and Durham miners who kept going by claiming on dodgy injury insurance policies. I was the odd-one-out public schoolboy but I was as crazed as everyone else so that was okay, I didn't get any hassle.

Things were no less out of control at home. I shared a house in west London with two racing mates, which caused all kinds of trouble with the suburbanites. Bikes, vans and caravans littered our street, mates turned up to give us impromptu wheelie displays on Z1300s, and when we painted the house in team colours the locals got up a petition to get rid of us, claiming we were running a quasi-commercial race team on the premises. When one neighbour complained that the rusting truck outside our front door 'wasn't very aesthetic', we replied: 'What colour would you like it painted then?'

Of course, we were too young to give a fuck, though an Interpol police raid did sober us up for a while. One of our gang had lent a bike to a mate who was touring Europe, but the guy got busted trying to get heroin into Sweden. Oops.

If we shared anything with today's MotoGP stars it may have been a demented belief in our own immortality. But that youthful conviction tends to fade as reality bites. So just as MotoGP got more serious after Daijiro Kato's death in 2003, so did we, as mates and loved ones fell victim to our foolish mania for going absolutely as fast as possible wherever we were. During less than a decade I lost six mates (including Howard Lees and Dave Chisman, with whom I'd shared that London house) and my brother. Cheating death stops being fun once it's death that's doing the cheating.

Howard and Dave were the prime movers behind Team Bike, a quasi-commercial race team (okay, so we can admit it now) named after British magazine *Bike* that started off as an excuse to get pissed in paddock bars across Britain and ended up as an excuse to get pissed in paddock bars from the Nürburgring to Suzuka. We were a bunch of middle-class hoodlums who spent our summers driving around the Continent doing the Bol d'Or and Le Mans 24 hours, fuelled by a heady mix of cheap French wine, strong weed and a desire for world domination. We had a habit of getting into trouble.

During the Barcelona 24 hours we triggered a mini-riot that ended with rifle-toting cops herding several of us into vans and off to prison. And after the Bol d'Or a gang of our maddest supporters got nailed by cops getting nasty with CS gas and truncheons; more broken bones and concussions. I'm not proud, but it did seem funny at the time.

I tend not to get into trouble with the cops any more. Instead I take my luncheon in fancy MotoGP VIP suites, surrounded by sponsorship fixers, CEOs and attorneys, making civilised conversation with PR flunkies and smiling hospitality girls. Things aren't any better now and neither are they any worse, they're just different. And a lot quieter. Thank fuck.

CHAPTER 37

THE YEAR THAT CHANGED ROSSI'S LIFE

July 2004

Arguably the greatest rider of all time, Valentino Rossi came of age as a racer and a personality during the 1997 GP season. Rossi, his mates and his rivals recall how he became a superstar overnight

Valentino Rossi was just another crash-happy teenage GP rider when he commenced the 1997 125 world championship. The kid had won just a single race in his rookie '96 GP season, so back in the spring of '97 no one had any idea of the greatness that lay ahead for the girlie-looking Italian. However, by the end of that year there was no doubt that Rossi was a bit special – at the age of just 17 he was already 125 world champion and a bona fide superstar.

During '97 he won 11 GPs from 15 starts on his factory Aprilia 125, all the while developing the talent that would allow him to go on to dominate every GP category – from 125s to 250s and from 500s to MotoGP.

But what really grabbed everyone's attention that summer were Rossi's hilarious post-race theatrics. One weekend he would take a blow-up doll for a ride on his victory lap, the next he'd arrive on the podium dressed like superman. These comic displays made him much, much more than just another fast man on a motorcycle. They turned all kinds of people on to Valentino Rossi, ultimately transforming him into the biggest bike racing star the world has ever known.

Thus the 1997 season made Rossi the man he is today. Here we look back at that crucial year with the help of six witnesses: Rossi himself, Nobby Ueda, Rossi's main rival for the '97 125 title, former Aprilia race boss Carlo Pernat who in 1995 had signed Rossi to a three-year deal, Uccio Salluci, Rossi's best mate and constant companion since they were five years old, dad Graziano, a three-time 250 GP winner in 1979 and myself.

Graziano: 1997 was a fantastic season, Valentino's first with a factory machine. There were ten or 12 very fast riders in 125s, so he had to fight very much. There were some very beautiful races.

Valentino: In '96 my bike was very slow, I had many good races but also some big, crazy mistakes. For '97 I had a good bike, so I knew in my heart I could win the championship, though winning 11 races and not making too many mistakes was a surprise.

Pernat: I signed Valentino the first time I watched him ride in '95. Graziano had been a friend for many years and he told me 'my son is very strong', so I went to see. Unbelievable. I made a contract that day for three years – '96, '97 and '98 – and I signed it with his father and mother because Valentino was only 15, too young to sign. We put him in a team with Mauro Noccioli as his engineer, because Mauro is very good with young riders.

Ueda: I already knew Rossi when he was 11 because I lived only one kilometre from him in Italy. On weekend nights we'd go to minimoto courses and enjoy racing together. I wasn't as fast as him. When he started GPs in '96, he stayed at my house in Japan. At first my friends thought he was a girl but I told them he would be the next world champion. Before '97 his riding style was so wild, he crashed many times. I think he was studying the limit and how he could control his machine 100 per cent. By '97 it was very difficult to beat him.

'A rider like Valentino is born every 20 years – he's similar to guys like Pele, McEnroe, Muhammad Ali or Maradona'

Oxley: It was obvious that Rossi was really good, but there've been plenty of great 125 racers who never made it in 250s, let alone 500s or MotoGP. It turned out that he was way, way better than most of us realised, in every possible way.

Pernat: A rider like Valentino is born every 20 years. For me he's similar to guys like Pele, McEnroe, Muhammad Ali or Maradona – people who tower over their sports. Two qualities make him special. First, his sense of balance on the motorcycle is unbelievable; I've never seen anything like it. Second, he has fun, he amuses himself by racing, that's all he does, he amuses himself. His other big skill is finding the limit so quickly. While most riders have to get there step by step, his sense of balance allows him to get there so quick. At first he crashed a lot trying to find the limit too fast, he was lucky not to get injured.

Ueda: His riding skill is about controlling his weight on the bike – through the footpegs, the seat, the tank, the handlebars. He moves so well, it's like he's dancing on the bike. This allows him to move traction between the front tyre and rear tyre, depending where he is in the corner, and it also helps turn the bike, especially when the tyres are finished. He can find side grip especially at the end of races by shifting backwards and pushing on the outside 'peg to put weight on the rear tyre.

He was fun to race, he never cut me up, but I knew I couldn't play with him, so I just gave gas all the time. The race I remember best from '97 was Austria, because I won! He made a small mistake at the last corner and I passed him just before the finish line.

Salucci: We have been friends since we were five. We used to race each other on minimotos, but I stopped after that and started going to races with him. I always knew he was very fast but I never imagined the future. In '97 we were too young to notice that he might be a really good rider.

Oxley: Rossi ran away with the championship. He won two of the first three GPs and would've won round two at Suzuka if he hadn't crashed on the last lap. That was when I first noticed he was a bit special as a person – he didn't pull a strop, but limped back to the pits, grinning and waving, then told us: 'At first I thought I could win, now I just think I'm an idiot'. He made us laugh. It was a breath of fresh air because GPs were pretty dull back then, Doohan was breaking everyone's balls in 500s and the paddock was so serious, like working in an office, a nightmare. The fun really started at Mugello.

Valentino: Mugello is always crazy. Up on the hill it's another world, the crowd is coming crazy: drink, naked people on motocross bikes... In '97 I went up in the evening and it was very dangerous, everyone jumping on me, shouting 'Rossi! Rossi!' There was this big wall of people and only one way out, through the shower block, so I rode my scooter through the shower block.

Oxley: Rossi won the race, then ripped the piss out of Biaggi by riding his victory lap with a blow-up doll called Claudia Schiffer. A few months earlier Biaggi had been putting it about that he had shagged Naomi Campbell but no one really believed him. The display had everyone in hysterics – we wondered what he'd think of next.

Graziano: These gags weren't so much for the fans, they were more for his friends and for his fan club, the people who were behind him, the people who loved him. I always knew what gags they were planning. My favourite was Jerez '98 when he won the 250 race, then climbed inside a marshal's Portaloo halfway round the victory lap.

Valentino: When I came to GPs all the riders were very, very serious. So when I started winning, me and my friends decided we should try to make some big fun.

Salucci: I was one of ten people who would meet on Tuesdays before races to organise the gag. Then I would arrive at the track on Wednesdays to find a nice place to do the gag. We bought the material for the 'Superfumi' cape and made it ourselves for Assen, but for Mugello we rang someone from the fan club to buy a blow-up doll from a sex shop.

Pernat: Valentino doesn't like Biaggi. They are different characters – Valentino doesn't like hanging out with movie stars, Biaggi is the opposite, he likes to be with famous people.

Valentino made a lot of theatre at this time – he entered the hearts of ordinary people who want to dream. And it was this that helped bike racing appeal to the whole family: the kids, the mothers, the grandfathers, the grandmothers.

But Valentino is clever, while he amuses himself, he always has a goal in mind. Some people say he has less ego than other riders but I think he has a bigger ego. He is very clever psychologically. Biaggi was always so mentally strong against any enemy but Valentino is stronger. For four or five years they've had this psychological war. Valentino has won it because he has fun; Biaggi doesn't have fun, he just gets angry.

Oxley: Valentino was totally unique. Not only did he do all this comedy on the track, he'd also spend Sunday evenings in the media centre, chatting and joking with journalists. No other rider does that. Sometimes it was hard to get any work done! Of course, he doesn't do it any more, these days he needs to get away from the media.

It was at Imola '97 that I realised he'd become a superstar – his fans covered half the hillside on the pit straight, so he was already more popular than Doohan and Biaggi. You'd go to his motorhome and there'd be 20 teenage girls hanging around outside, even though he had a girlfriend at the time.

Salucci: We really enjoyed having so many girls around! Maybe some top riders or superstars worry 'Is this girl coming to see me because I'm famous or does she really like me?', but Valentino didn't think like that, he always said 'I don't care why she's coming to see me, I'm just happy that she is coming!'

Pernat: I've never seen so many girls around a rider, maybe Sheene or Lucchinelli but never so many. Valentino doesn't like to stay with a girl more than two or three months. He lived like a kid then and he lives like a kid now, with the same friends, the same way of life. After the racing is finished it's impossible to find him, no one knows where he goes, maybe he's in London, maybe he's in a disco with some friends he's known since he was a boy. He never changes, he doesn't want to be famous, he doesn't want a movie star girlfriend, he doesn't want to be in the papers with famous people.

Ueda: Frankly speaking, I feel sorry for him now, his life is too busy – too many fans come to see him, too many journalists, too many cameramen. He just loves riding bikes, otherwise he wouldn't continue. At the end of '97 I went to the Milan bike show and was surprised there were so many girls after him. He had seven or eight security around him – big macho men – otherwise he wouldn't have been able to move. I was on the stand of one of my sponsors, who also sponsored Rossi, and he arrived saying 'Incredible, what can I do? I want to get away.' So I went out front to sign autographs until there was a crowd, so he could escape out the back.

Salucci: Valentino hated the security guys, so at the '98 Bologna bike show he wore a wig, dark glasses and a baseball cap. He was so happy that he could check out the bikes without getting mobbed.

Oxley: He wrapped up the title at Brno in August, then announced he'd move up to 250s in '98. He didn't see the point of hanging around to pose with the number-one plate the next year. He was world champion at 17, and still driving around Europe with his dad in a tiny camper van.

Graziano: I was very happy for him, my feeling was more joy than pride, I'm not a proud person. Valentino didn't change inside during '97 but by the end of the season we had seen too much of each other. We shared this camper all summer and were always fighting. It was terrible because he cannot go to bed before one o'clock, it's impossible for him – then I had to wake him up in the morning, the most difficult job in the world! I had to wake him once, twice, three times. In the end I got his engineer to do it.

Valentino: Maybe the best thing about going to 250s in '98 was that I could get out of bed later. I had to get up at seven for 125 practice, and that was a big problem. In 250s I could stay in bed until nine.

Salucci: As '97 went on I was amazed at what was happening. We had never imagined how big our adventure would become, but I was also very happy that Valentino had realised his dream. To this day our relationship has never changed, but he has changed in the way he relates to the media, the fans, the people who aren't around him all the time.

Oxley: Valentino was such a laugh in '97 that it was easy to forget how brilliantly he was riding. And we were only seeing the very beginnings of a talent and a character that has still got us transfixed. It's difficult to wonder what he will do next, he's always out for new challenges. He never wants to take the easy option and count the quids, he's always searching for something new to have a pop at.

Pernat: Every time Valentino does something new he surprises us and probably himself. Even he doesn't know how far he might go. I actually think that no one knows his absolute limit.

CHAPTER 38

RIDE LIKE
THE GODS

July 2004

**Valentino Rossi may well be the best motorcycle rider ever to
have walked this earth, so who better to ask for a few riding
tips? And for good measure Mick Doohan, Kevin Schwantz,
Kenny Roberts Junior, Garry McCoy and Jeremy McWilliams
explain a few of their riding secrets**

Valentino Rossi is a man in love with motorcycles. The seven-time
world champ is arguably the greatest bike racer in history, but that's
not all. While most pro racers shirk road riding, claiming that it's too
dangerous, Rossi is a regular on the streets, especially in his home town
of London where bikes rule. The Italian bubbles over with enthusiasm
when talking about street riding, just as he does when he talks about
riding on the track. So who better to ask for advice about how to get
more out of your motorcycle, whether you're riding to work or getting
your knee down at a track day?

'I still ride on the road always, I enjoy it but for sure it's not the
track,' says Rossi. 'The problem with the road is it's full of "stupids",
especially in cars, and also you never know the grip of the asphalt, so
you need to stay a little bit slower than on the track.'

Mental focus
Mental focus is everything when you're on a motorcycle, no matter
whether you're on the track or the street. There is nothing more
fundamental to good riding than focusing on the task in hand and
being aware of what's going on around you so you can be prepared to
expect the unexpected.

'When you ride you should try and forget everything else,' says
Rossi. 'Don't think about the rest of your life or the rest of the world.
Try to forget all that and think only of the road or the track and the

bike. It's not always easy to stay focused on the bike, sometimes you feel that one part of the brain rides the bike; thinks about the tyre, sees the road, but maybe the other part is thinking about a girl, a friend, a song.'

Breathing

Riding a motorcycle is a strenuous activity, and the faster you go, the more strenuous it becomes. Breathing is therefore vital, to provide enough oxygen for brain activity and muscle movement. This may sound obvious but many riders tense up when they're on board, which reduces their oxygen intake, just when they need to increase it. As a hugely experienced racer, Rossi's breathing technique comes naturally, but he still wears athlete's nostril flares to improve his oxygen intake.

'On the bike you need to stay concentrated and relaxed, and to do that you need to have enough air for the brain.'

Looking ahead

Looking and planning ahead are also fundamentals to fast, effective and safe riding, wherever you are. Racers usually think one corner ahead; you should use a similar technique on the road.

'When you ride a big, fast bike, everything happens very fast so you need to stay 100 per cent concentrated on what is going to happen next. You need to ride with your mind a little bit in front of the bike. On the track I'm always thinking about the next corner.'

Keeping it smooth

The best racers and riders work smoothly on their bikes, because getting vicious with the throttle, brakes and steering makes you slower, not faster.

'Riding is very much about all your movement on the motorcycle. The bike feels every move you make – the braking, the throttle and your movement to steer the bike. To have everything under control is better to ride smooth. Maybe with little bikes, like 125s, it's possible to be more aggressive. But on more heavy bikes – like a MotoGP bike or 1000cc street bike – you need to ride smooth by making all your movements very smooth. If you ride too aggressive you will lose stability.'

Making mistakes

Everyone makes mistakes, even Rossi. But how to make sure you don't make them again? When you're riding or racing, you're thinking about so many things that it's not easy to alert yourself to any cock-ups you make. Rossi has a simple way to ensure he knows he's made a mistake – he talks to himself!

'Yes, I very much talk to myself when I am on the bike. If I brake a little early for a corner and lose some time, I will say to myself 'Fack! Brake a little more deep next time!' I talk to myself more on the track than on the street. On the street I am always a little more nervous, because a car can exit from a street at any moment, so you need to be more relaxed.'

Man–machine relationship

Working as one with your machine is vital. You need to know your motorcycle, so you can understand what you can do to ride faster and more safely.

'The rider is a big part of the motorcycle, so you need to understand that you are a part of the bike. It's not the bike and the rider – both need to be like one thing. You also need to think about having a good relationship with the bike and making a direct rapport with it. Try to understand what she wants from you, so you can ride the bike differently, especially if you want to make good of different settings, different tyres and other modifications. You always need to arrive at this situation step by step. If you think well and go step by step, you should be able to have a 100 per cent feeling with your bike.'

Throttle control

When it comes to machine control, nothing is quite as important as throttle control. Working the throttle doesn't just make your motorcycle go faster or slower, it also affects how the bike steers and handles.

'For sure throttle control is the most important part of riding a bike. It's very difficult with a big bike, like a MotoGP bike or 1000cc streetbike, because you can spin the rear tyre even in the dry. The only way to learn throttle control is experience, riding as many bikes as possible in as many conditions as possible. A few years ago I made some training with a motocross bike with enduro tyres on tarmac, just to slide easy and to understand the slide. I think the dirt is the best place to start this training.

'But basically you need to make many kilometres because you need to understand the power delivery of the bike. When you understand how and when the power arrives, it becomes more easy with the throttle. When I'm racing, the slide can happen in the middle of the corner when I'm on the edge of the tyre. If you open the throttle when you don't have enough tyre on the ground you can start to spin and from that point you control the slide with the throttle. It's better to stay constant with the throttle, don't open, then shut when you get the slide, then open again because the bike becomes unstable. You need to feel the bike and stay with the throttle.'

Choose your gear
Choosing the right gear for the corner is crucial. Many riders tend to use lower gears than they need, making the bike unstable going into the corner and also coming out.

'If I need to decide between a lower gear or a higher gear, I always go for the longer gear. It's better to be in a slightly taller gear than a slightly lower gear. The important thing with the choice of gear is that you need to stay where the engine has the best torque, not before and not after.'

Braking
Braking is a very different deal on the racetrack and on the road. Whereas racers can use the full performance of their front disc brakes thanks to slick tyres and ultra-grippy racetracks, road riders have to be much more circumspect when braking. Ultimately it all depends on the road surface.

'I always brake very much with the front, road or track. I would say I use 80 per cent the front and 20 per cent the rear. Really, you only stop the bike with the front brake, doesn't matter if you're on the track or the road. You use the rear just a little, to keep the bike stable. The difference between the track and the road is this – on the track you can use the front brake all the way into the corner. But on the street you need to release the brake before you start to flick the bike into a turn.'

Using the tyres

Your tyres' footprints vary according to how much lean you're using. Generally, the further you're leaned over, the less rubber you'll have on the road, which is why racers work very hard to lift up their bikes as quickly as possible as they come out of a turn.

'If you have very much horsepower, you need to put more tyre on the ground for when you open the throttle. I didn't really do this so much in 125s but I started using the technique a lot in 250s, and the more power you have, the more important it becomes, so I use this very much in 500s and also in MotoGP. You need to put some weight on the outside footpeg, work the handlebars and also use your body weight to lift up the bike.'

Feeling for grip

Racers usually have a predictable amount of grip to deal with – they know how grippy the tarmac should be. But it's very different for street riders who are constantly changing from one tarmac to another.

'When I am on the street, I also use the rear brake very much to make the rear slide so that I can understand the level of grip. But be careful where you do this!'

Using your body

Some of Rossi's racing rivals reckon that he makes the difference on the track by using his body weight more cleverly than other riders. Rossi understands that you can increase traction at the front or back of the bike by adding weight accordingly. Likewise, you can reduce traction at either end if you need to. Perhaps this isn't so vital for street riding, but shifting your weight also affects the way your bike handles and steers.

'Moving on the bike is very, very important to weight the front and add traction to the rear. When braking you move over the front of the bike to weight the front, but not too much because then the rear end comes up. In the middle of the corner you need to keep some weight up front, so you stay over the front. This helps traction and helps the bike to turn. Coming out of the corner, when the tyre starts to slide under acceleration, you need more traction at the rear, so you need to push back into the back of the seat and also push on the outside footpeg.'

Changing direction

Being able to change direction fast is an important part of machine control, on road or track. You may not encounter many chicanes on the street, but you have to work your way through a lot of roundabouts, and the faster you can switch from left to right or vice versa, the more time and effort you can put into cornering.

'You use everything you've got to change direction – counter-steering on the 'bars, weighting the footpegs and using your body weight. But it is important to move your body before the bike moves, don't follow the way the bike moves, lead the way the bike moves. You'd don't have to move very fast either, just be smooth and ahead of the bike.'

Some more riding secrets

Garry McCoy: highside to get through chicanes quicker

'There's some esses or chicanes where I actually like to get the thing to highside me halfway through, to help me get steered into the next turn as fast as possible, because that's the kind of place you can make up half a tenth or two. If it's a left-then-right esses, I get the rear spinning up out of the left, then shut the throttle a bit sharpish, which makes the tyre grip suddenly and flicks me over the highside, laying the bike into the right, fast as you like.'

Mick Doohan: the do-it-yourself slipper clutch

'I always liked using the rear brake, which came from dirt tracking, jumping on the brake to get the rear kicked out into turns. Back then the four-strokes didn't have slipper clutches, so I found the engine-braking a problem because I preferred to use the brake to slow the bike. I'd heard that Gregg Hansford (1970s Aussie GP winner) used to disengage the clutch going into turns when he raced four-strokes and I thought it made sense.

'If you saw me going into a turn on the RVF you'd hear the engine shut down and there'd be not much noise at all. I'd shut the throttle and have the clutch in, instead of having the thing rpm-ing. Into the turn the clutch wouldn't be fully engaged nor completely out, then once the bike was settled in the corner I'd start to let the lever out, just smooth transition back into engaged, then get on the throttle, a smooth, seamless progression.'

Colin Edwards: how to save a front-end slide

'Nowadays losing
the front is normal,
I may have a little
"lose" every lap and
pick it up on my
knee'

'Nowadays losing the front is normal, I may have a little "lose" every lap and pick it up on my knee. When you're pushing just over the limit you're ready for it, so you've got your knee on the ground to pick it back up when you get into a turn a little too hot. It's like you've already seeing it happen before it's happened, so you're ready.

'It means you can go past the limit and not crash, which is cool! When you're on a bike that can do that it's beautiful, and a lot less expensive! The M1's front end is good, so it'll tuck but it doesn't extend [when the forks extend during a slide, taking too much weight off the front tyre, the point of no return has been reached]. You just put your knee on the ground and save it, the M1 is probably the best bike I've ever ridden for that.'

Mick Doohan: do-it-yourself traction control
'Back when I was racing 500s we didn't have traction control. You had to work out your own way so you didn't get chucked off, so my right wrist was my traction control, plus my left hand, too. On the way out of corners I'd have a finger on the clutch as I got on the throttle, so if the rear started to spin up, I could pull some of the power straight back out. The clutch is the quickest way to pull power out of the bike, much quicker and safer than shutting the throttle.'

Kevin Schwantz: spinning to turn
'Back when I came into GPs the thing that stood out was steering with the back tyre. Lots of times you'd do a corner good but it'd start to push and run a bit wide, so instead of shutting off or staying on neutral throttle you'd pour the coals on it to get it to steer with the back and finish the corner. Any time the bike's not steering the way you want it to and you think you're running out of racetrack, you don't worry about what more throttle will do, you just stick it on and make it steer. It takes a fair bit of bravery to make yourself do that.'

Kevin Schwantz: using the footpegs for grip
'Weighting the outside footpeg was a little trick I learned when I was

trials riding when I was a kid. Whether I was on an off-camber hill or on a greasy pavement I'd get some weight on the outside 'peg because it really helps the grip. Whatever the scenario, if it's raining or it's the end of the race, it's the thing to do when the grip's lesser. You can use the inside 'peg for the opposite scenario, so if she's pushing the front you get your weight off the outside 'peg and stomp it on the inside. That should make the rear slide and take some weight off the front to stop it from pushing.'

Garry McCoy: using the footpegs for control
'If I'm running wide and it's some place where I don't want to use the throttle to get the bike steered, I'll weight the inside 'peg to get the rear to slide and tighten the line. Or sometimes when the bike gets so sideways, to where it's almost on the full-lock against the lock stops, I weight the inside 'peg to help it spin a little more, which stops it gripping and highsiding me.

'Any place I'm looking for extra grip or drive I weight the outside footpeg. Sometimes it's when I get on the gas mid-corner, when the bike starts to wheelspin and I need a bit of extra grip. Other times I'll weight the 'peg a little later in the corner when I'm looking for drive coming onto a long straight. Generally I don't get so sideways through corners that lead on to long straights because I want to get some extra drive. '

Kenny Roberts Junior: how to slipstream
'It's a good feeling because it's the easiest way to pass someone. You just line 'em up on the straight and fire past. Once you're within three or four bike lengths of the guy ahead, you get into the draft and you start closing in, then you try to time your move when you're about half a bike's length behind. You pull out and as you go by you stay as close to them as you dare because if you give them too much room you get back out into the dirty air and you'll lose the draft effect. If your bike's quick enough, you just go right around them. But if you pull out and only get alongside, without flying by, that means both bikes are about the same. It can get pretty interesting because your bike's shaking around like crazy because the front end's hardly on the ground and you have to really yank the steering to manoeuvre at that kind of speed.'

Jeremy McWilliams: how to overtake
'Top GP riders don't mind riding into people. You want to pass as clean as possible, but if you're getting frustrated and it's the last lap, you ride into the guy. I've got into punch-ups and all kinds of hoohah doing that at British championship meetings but I don't think anyone's ever protested about that kind of thing at a GP, it's just part of racing at that level. Everyone's on the edge, with just an element of control.

CHAPTER 39

THE FASTEST BROOD IN THE
WHOLE WILD WEST

August 2004

Its midway through the 2004 MotoGP championship and there's three Roberts in the paddock – King Kenny, his elder son Kenny Junior and younger son Kurtis who's riding for dad's MotoGP team – wouldn't it be comedy to get them together to answer some questions?

King Kenny Roberts & Sons are MotoGP's royal family. Gathering together the three of them – former 500 champs Kenny Senior and Kenny Junior and former AMA Superbike winner turned Proton V5 rider Kurtis – for an interview isn't easy. And when we do get them together, the three of them are chaos, a bit like watching the Simpsons in action. The comedy starts the moment they gather in Homer's front room, sorry, the King's luxury lounge on the top deck of the Team Roberts paddock bus, the nerve centre of his struggling Proton MotoGP squad. There's a non-stop torrent of wisecracks, cussing and dick jokes, mostly from the King and Kurtis, while the more reticent Kenny Junior absorbs himself surfing the CNN website for a weather forecast. Then Kurtis suffers a minor panic attack when he realises someone's cleared away the plastic cup into which he gobs used chewing tobacco.

The quick-fire abuse that flows between them would embarrass the more prudish onlooker but does suggest that they are indeed a happy family, confident enough in each others' love and respect to know that they can rip the piss without anyone taking serious offence. Their contrasting characters are noticeable throughout, Kenny Junior always the quietest, wearing an amused, sometimes slightly embarrassed grin at his father's and younger brother's profane outbursts. And if Kurtis is the only one of the three who hasn't won a world championship, he is definitely the funniest, managing even to out-wisecrack his dad, a considerable achievement, and one of which he should feel very proud.

Who's the most stubborn?
Senior: I'm easygoing
Junior: Me too.
Kurtis: I don't know, I'll agree with the other two.

Do you ever think what would dad do in this situation?
Kurtis: It would depend on the situation. If it was relationships probably not, but if it was riding a motorcycle, probably.
Junior: It's such a loaded question. No.

Isn't nepotism fantastic?
Junior: What's the meaning of that?
Senior: No, it's not at all fantastic, but sometimes it's a necessary evil.
Kurtis: For sure my brother could've ridden for other people when he rode for dad and so could I, and my dad could've hired a lot of other people, it's not like it's all charity work here.

How competitive are you as a family? Have you ever come to blows over a board game?
Kurtis: Yeah!
Junior: Yup!
Senior: I've had to step into the middle of it to separate them, yes.
Junior: We were playing electric monopoly…
Senior: And table tennis, and…
Junior: I was selling Kurtis property. He had the game won but I was making the option go up on Kurtis' side by 10,000 bucks and he was choking the heck out of my stepdad.
Kurtis: I was only 'bout seven maybe…
Junior: I mean like really choking, him until he couldn't breathe.
Kurtis: Yeah, we've had some altercations.

Fathers always reckon they know best; is that true in the Roberts' household?
Senior: Yes, absolutely.
Kurtis: Yeah.
Junior: Sure.

Would the family fortunes fare better moving into Superbikes?
Senior: You what?

Junior: What are Superbikes?

Who's run up the biggest repair bill over the years?
Kurtis puts his hand up.
Senior: I've wrecked a lot of shit over the last few years, but Kurtis has wrecked more sitting on top of it. I've scrapped a lot of stuff, just saying 'this is junk', get rid of it.

Who's the safest rider on the road?
Senior: We don't ride much on the road. I probably am.
Kurtis: I'd say Kenny Junior would be the safest, especially when Rochelle (his wife) is behind him.
Senior: Little Kurtis can get going a little bit too fast on the Harley sometimes.
Kurtis: I slide them around a little too much.
Junior: Yeah, I've never slidden a Harley around a roundabout (laughing)… But I hardly ride on the road now, the more I do this job the less time I have.

Was it always inevitable that a world champion racer would have kids who became racers? Didn't anyone ever consider working in a bank?
Kurtis: I thought about robbing a bank!
Senior: Yeah, robbing one.
Kurtis: No I never thought about working in a bank but other stuff, of course. But I've been wanting to race since I was real young, four or five, I would always be watching reruns of dad forever, every day.
Junior: I had a lot of opportunity to do all types of things, all kinds of sports but never really got committed. Like in high school I never wanted to get hurt in football because it never felt like the right thing to do. But after I saw John Kocinski win a race in Sears Point, that's when I decided I wanted to race bikes.

How much pressure is there to live up to the Roberts name? And who feels it most – the kids or the old man?
Kurtis: I'd say us kids feel it the most because dad started the Roberts thing, so there's not a lot of pressure on him.
Senior: They have pressure.

Kurtis: There's quite a bit but I'd say I put more pressure on myself than anyone could put on me.

Junior: Yeah, that's the thing, it's the competitiveness inside yourself that drives with you.

Senior: I'm always looking at a glass that's half full. Even as much as I complain about things at the moment, I still wake up the next morning thinking: 'Okay, I've got this shit, I've got to fix it'. I'm not one to look at it and say I'm done. That's why I'm still here. I've been here a long time and I think you have to have something built into you because you get kicked around a lot and especially if you have a name people automatically think you should be up there racing Honda and we're not. We weren't doing that when we had Junior in my team and we aren't doing it with Kurtis. We're trying to cut a whole new thing, and that needs money and time and either you don't have enough time or you don't have enough money. But you know, we're still here, trying to make it right.

How long before we see a Roberts in the top five again? And that includes the manufacturers' championship.

Senior: Right now the championship has never been so clear cut equipment-wise. With the two-strokes, even with our little three-cylinder, at times we were very, very close to the podium, but with the four-strokes the equipment makes all the difference. This is a new adventure for us. We're less than a year and a half into it, so it's all new, we're still finding out stuff we should have known a year ago but we're not Honda. There's a lot of companies, even the one Kenny's riding for, that should be a lot better than they are. It's going to take another two or three seasons before everyone gets to grips with having everything they need to make them competitive. This year it happens to be tyres that are keeping us back. [Team Roberts ran Dunlops in 2004.]

Junior: Suzuki are starting to narrow down some things that are crucial to make the bike go around the track. We're already going round the corners as fast as if not faster than anyone else, so if we can improve 10kmh on the straight plus get the traction control fixed... It's up to the development people, the quicker they can do it, the quicker we'll be up there.

Kurtis: I wouldn't doubt myself to be in the top five if I had a Honda, maybe this year, maybe not, but more like next year. I think if Kenny had a Honda he'd be winning the championship right now.

Who's had the most success with the ladies – in their single days, of course?
Kurtis: Success? Is that getting rid of them all?
Senior: You can't even count me in this because I'm so much older.
Kurtis: Or is that having one girl for a long period of time?
Senior: Both my marriages – Patsy and Pamela – were the same, seven years, so Kenny would probably be the guy.
Junior: I guess I've been with Ro [his childhood sweetheart and now his wife] nearly ten years.
Kurtis: He's not a whore!
Senior: Well, one out of three ain't bad.

Who gets most nervous before the start of a race?
Senior: These days, probably me. As a rider I could sit and have a hotdog, wait for the race, throw the hotdog away, push off… But when you're in charge there's a lot more to think about.
Kurtis: How can you actually judge who gets the most nervous? Sometimes I'm very calm, when I have no problems.
Senior: It depends how practice has gone, if the thing runs and you feel good on it, those things make a difference…

Is the endless chasing of lost causes a family trait? How do you keep going? Are you mentally stronger than the average family?
(Incredulous laughter from all, especially Kurtis)
Kurtis: I think you might have to be mentally strong to be in our family.
Senior: We never met an average family, we don't know any average families.
Kurtis: Everyone's idea of average is their own, I guess.
Junior: What was the question again? Okay, if you're saying that what I'm doing is a struggle, I'd take it over most any other jobs, like getting shot at in Afghanistan or Iraq. I mean there's a lot worse things to do in life.

What does Kenny Senior think is wrong with the big factories? Do the boys agree?
Kurtis: Their bikes are too fast.
Senior: There's nothing wrong with the big factories, if you're a big factory. I just don't believe in working for nothing for a big factory.

(Kenny senior walked out of a hugely successful, sometimes stormy 25-year relationship with Yamaha at the end of 1996.)

Kurtis: I was with Honda for a while and I had quite a lot of friends there but sometimes it was a little too, er, corporate for a rider.

'Somebody needs to get everybody on the same tyres and start putting weight on the bikes that are faster. The racing would be a lot better'

Junior: I'd say somebody needs to step in and get everybody on the same tyres and start putting weight on the bikes that are faster. The racing would be a lot better. Take Sete [Gibernau] for example, he was on the Suzuki and he was having poor results in the grand scheme of things, then you throw him on a Honda and he's got a shot at this year's championship. Think how much better the sport would be if things were more equal. I mean if he wasn't Spanish, so he didn't have that opportunity to take the Telefonica money with him, he'd still be with Suzuki riding around back down the pack. I would like to see some kind of government in this sport.

Senior: Instead of the factories being the government. Basically, he's saying he thinks Nascar is better than F1.

Is Mick Doohan right that Kevin Schwantz could put the GSV-R on the podium? Or is it right to decide not to bust your arse for 13th place?
Kurtis: Mick's probably not right about a lot of stuff he's said since he quit racing.
Junior: I don't know. It's an impossible question to answer.
Senior: I never busted my ass for 13th place. You do what you can do on the bike on the day, then you go home and the next time you try and do it better. It's all a calculated risk, sometimes you've got to take a calculated risk on the last lap whether you're seventh or first but it's always a whole lot better when you're first. There's obviously little things in your brain that work different if you're racing for first place.

What's more important for a rider: luck, talent or a factory Honda?
Kurtis: a factory Honda right now.
Senior: All three.
Junior: All three
Kurtis: All three.

'The NSR500 was a hunk of shit in the 1980s, the power came in hard, so it highsided a fair bit. There wasn't a lot you could do.' Wild man Wayne Gardner on the misery of crashing, chapter 35. (Gold and Goose)

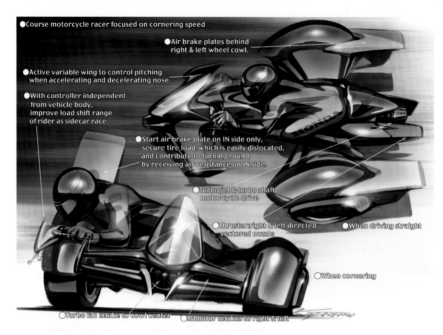

●Course motorcycle racer focused on cornering speed

●Air brake plates behind
right & left wheel cowl.

●Active variable wing to control pitching
when accelerating and decelerating nose.

●With controller independent
from vehicle body,
improve load shift range
of rider as sidecar race.

●Start air brake plate on IN side only,
secure tire load, which is easily dislocated,
and contribute to turning round
by receiving air resistance on IN side.

●Turbo jet & turbo shaft
motorcycle drive

●Thruster-right & left directed
vectored nozzle

●When driving straight

○When cornering

○Turbo fan intake to cowl center   ○Radiator intakes to right & left

ABOVE AND BELOW: *This is what Honda and Kawasaki would build if MotoGP was a rule-free zone. Honda's creation is blue-sky thinking to the max – it's got two wheels but not as we know it. Kawa's streamliner is very nearly as insane. See chapter 46.*

'Trick Sheilas who are happy to stand
on the grid in bikinis, even though
the nearest beach is 200 miles away.'
The mysteries of the brolly girl
explained, page 264.
(Gold and Goose)

ABOVE: *'If I regret anything it'd be what I did to my wrist in '94 to fix it quick. I should've got it fixed right and taken a year off.' Assen '94, this is the crash that ended Kevin Schwantz's career. See chapter 35. (Gold and Goose)*

ABOVE: *'The difference between us and the Japanese is we design and race the bike, while with them, someone designs the bike and someone else races it.' The secret to Ducati's success, chapter 30. (Gold and Goose)*

BELOW: *'Aprilia's RS3 Cube looks beautiful in a brutal kind of way. It looks like it may hurt you. Badly.' See chapter 24. (Gold and Goose)*

LEFT: *'My plan is to be world champion, pretty simple really, now I'm trying to put the pieces together, to understand the life, the circuits and the bike.'* How Nicky Hayden organised world domination, chapter 32 (Gold and Goose)

BELOW: *'Every year on the last lap of the last race, I used to say to myself in Ramsey, "just one more time over the mountain and thank fuck, that's it for another year".'* Steve Hislop on the TT, chapter 17. (Phil Masters)

ABOVE: 'Mick [Doohan] took so little pain medication, it's almost superhuman, it's like he's reset his pain thermostat.' But you can tell he still feels it. Hardest racers in the world, ever, chapter 41. (Gold and Goose)

OVERLEAF: 'Stoner isn't reticent, he never takes a step back, he is always on the attack, from the moment he leaves pit lane.' And he likes to use all the track and then some. Stoner's genius, chapter 49. (Gold and Goose)

Who's the rudest to their crew when things break?
Senior: Me probably.
Kurtis: I'm never rude to my crew, I just get frustrated if I've got problems with the motorcycle. There's things that break that aren't their fault.
Senior: No, he's not bad to the guys.
Junior: I'm never rude intentionally.

How smart is it to try to apply car thinking to bike racing? [King Kenny was always big on this, bringing F1 gurus like John Barnard into his operation, but without any success.]
Senior: I think it's another avenue. If you think about bike racing there's not a whole lot of avenues you can go down, so sometimes you've got to pick on the car people. It is all engineering. It may take a while to learn motorcycling engineering and to improve, but basically I don't see any difference.

What's Mrs Roberts like? How does she cope with you lot?
Kurtis: She's nuts, no, I'm joking, she's nervous, with us racing, of course. But she's got to deal with what we're going to do because she doesn't want to stand in our way. It's our life, we've got to live it, whatever happens.
Junior: From the safety side, sure, she has to cope with stuff, but other than that the things she copes with are fairly standard I guess.
Senior: I'm saying fucking nothing.

Who drinks the most when you go to a wedding?
Senior: I get totalled out the easiest.
Kurtis: He gets the loudest, does that count? He's definitely the most obnoxious, I might do a few accidents...
Senior: Yeah, like turning cars over, that kind of stuff. [A few weeks earlier Kurtis had turned Max Biaggi's garish Smart car, sprayed up with massive yellow and blue Max logos, on its roof in the Mugello car park – see page 310.]
Kurtis: But he'd offend more people than me.
Senior: I kind of watched the car thing and thought, well, it serves Max right, painting the damned thing like that...
Kurtis: I didn't even know it was Max's. The wind caught it or something...

Junior: I think we all celebrate as much as normal people, I think we enjoy life.

Kurtis: We're not at AA meetings yet, we're not alcoholics yet...

The madness of King Kenny

His Modenas/Proton KR MotoGP team recorded disastrous results over several seasons, but King Kenny Roberts insisted he ain't crazy, he just ain't a quitter.

Sometimes it's tough to figure out why King Kenny Roberts still runs a MotoGP team when he could be sitting on the porch back home in Montana, telling hilarious tales of ancient racetrack derring-do, annoying sportsbike riders on his hopped-up Harley or shooting up innocent wildlife. The man who won the last of his three 500 crowns a quarter of a century ago and scored his last world title as a team owner more than a decade back still lives a high-stress lifestyle at the head of his struggling, Banbury-based Proton KR outfit, which designs its own MotoGP bikes from the ground up in a hopelessly Quixotic attempt to compete with Honda in the world's fastest, richest bike racing series.

But then the King always was a bit crazy. He is one of those weird dudes who get their kicks from attempting the impossible, a have-a-go hero who's not afraid of anyone or anything. That's the way he was in 1978 – when he won the 500 title at his first attempt against all predictions – and that's the way he is now. Maybe that's not quite it though. The fact is that King Kenny is hopelessly addicted to the ritual of competition, even if nowadays that means weekly humiliation at the hands of Honda, Yamaha and Co, rather than more gongs and glory. And there's something else too...

'Why am I still here?' he ponders from behind mirror shades. 'Well, obviously it's a love of bikes – motorcycles have been a part of my life for a long, long time.' Now into his 50s, Roberts is still a real biker. When he's not hooning on his Harley, he's thrashing around the dirt aboard a Bee Em GS or motocrosser. And not for pure pleasure. 'I still can't ride and just have fun,' he says. 'I've got to ride it to where it's skidding the front and the rear. I'm not at the point where I can ride around slowly. That's why when I first came to Europe I knew I would die if I did the Isle of Man. And it's still my problem. Someone watched me ride a motocross bike the other day and said "what the fuck, you're going to kill yourself, crank it down", but that's the way I ride, I can't crank it down.'

In other words, he's a sucker for punishment, a stress junkie, as unable to kick back and chill out as you or I would be able to win a MotoGP race. And Roberts' love of speed and competition means that he sees beyond the miserable results recorded by his MotoGP team. During the first eight races of 2004 son Kurtis and Nobuatsu Aoki scored just seven points between them, while Valentino Rossi scored 139 points. But Roberts doesn't see it in those harsh terms because he is still fascinated by the technical challenges.

'I'm still interested in the engineering,' he continues. 'This year we've been way under where I estimated we'd be in terms of performance but it's a lesson, not the end of the world. When I started this project I didn't draw a line and say "okay, in two years we're going to be world champions". I had two choices when I stopped racing with Yamaha in '96 – quit racing completely or build my own motorcycle. I decided I wasn't done yet, and it wasn't a question of building my own motorcycle because I knew I could beat everybody, it was just that I couldn't deal any longer with the system that Yamaha had at the time.'

During 2003 and 2004 Roberts attracted some derision from within the bike world for hiring a bunch of F1 car engineers who were supposed to make the team's own V5-powered four-stroke racer competitive. In fact Team Roberts is less competitive now than at any stage since the King built his first bike, the two-stroke Proton KR500 (née Modenas) in 1997.

'Okay, so I went the F1 route. Now I'm looking at evaluating what that has done for me and then I'm going to make another adjustment to try and take it up another level. When you're a racer and you're not fast enough for a couple of years, you go and do something else, but it's not the same in team ownership, I still have 60 people to employ.' And that's another thing that keeps Roberts in MotoGP. 'I've been loyal to a lot of people in my career and it's just one of the things about me. The friendship, the camaraderie in racing, all that stuff has a weight of some sort.'

Despite his resolutely gung-ho approach to racing and his irrepressible desire to have a crack at the impossible, Roberts admits that there is one thing that will have him heading home to Montana for a well-deserved retirement – lack of an adequate budget. His Proton-backed squad is already one of the poorest in MotoGP and the recent falls in the value of the US dollar have hit hard. 'The dollar has dropped 30 per cent – that's two million dollars off an already not so healthy budget,' he explains. 'That can wear you down – you see shit that needs fixing and you don't have the money to fix it, that's the kind of thing that will send me home.'

Thankfully there are a couple of opportunities on the horizon that might keep the King in racing. First, Roberts has talked with KTM about taking over its stillborn V4 MotoGP project. And, even more alluring, Proton's Malaysian parent company (which already owns the Lotus car brand) has just bought legendary Italian marque MV Agusta. Now that would be cool – the King at the head of a team that used to be owned by an Italian count. Kind of makes sense…

Epilogue: King Kenny's outfit struggled on until the end of 2007, when it faded out of MotoGP due to lack of funds.

MotoGP Mutterings: *August 2004*
Forgive me, for I am traumatised

The word on the street is that my favourite MotoGP event may be scratched from the calendar. That's right, the Rio GP may be no longer. Brazil's world championship race is likely to be replaced in the calendar by bigger, richer, 'more important' nations like China and the USA. It almost makes me weep, thinking of swapping Rio's screaming chaos for the anodyne charms of a US GP.

I love Rio because it's a mess. It's a world away from the icy professionalism of the European circuits, where you can set your watch to the last plug chop of 125 qualifying. You would never dare do that at Rio. A few years back, moments after first qualifying had got underway, the entire circuit was blacked out by a power cut, forcing the organisers to red flag the session. But this wasn't some massive electricity blow-up, it was the local lekkie company cutting the circuit's power supply because they hadn't been paid for ages. Being Brazilian, they knew how to get their cash – they waited until the track's only world championship event of the year had started, then pulled the power. Needless to say, they got the money.

In 2004 there *was* a power cut. In fact there was a bloody great explosion when the media centre power supply went bang. We were all evacuated through choking smoke, waiting outside while a fleet of fire engines rolled up, just in case the building went up in flames. It didn't, so we were allowed back inside to continue fabricating our lies and deceits. To make sure there was no repeat of the meltdown, the organisers placed an elderly local electrician at the back of the press room where he hovered over the fuse box for the remainder of the weekend. Every time the system glowed red he'd trip a few fuses, extinguishing half the television monitors until things had cooled down a bit.

Of course, most paddock people abhor Rio for the same reasons I love it. Where I see its down-at-heel allure and smell its wanton party atmosphere, all they see is dirt and muggings and all they smell is, well, the smell. And, jeez, does the joint stink. But Rio's fetid stench isn't enough to stop some paddock people from sneaking out of their hotels under cover of darkness to indulge themselves in the local ladies of the night. For every dark tale of another MotoGP mugging (they're surely asking for it by promenading down Copacabana in team shirts) there's another story of shocking night-time debauchery. Like the factory MotoGP rider who had to wake his favourite mechanic from his slumber to ask for assistance in, erm, entertaining two hookers in his hotel room. (Obviously, I'm not advocating this kind of behaviour, but I do believe that racers are meant to live fast – it's their job.)

Please don't be appalled, for MotoGP is, after all, little more than an officially sanctioned home for testosterone-charged problem youngsters, neatly packaged to flog consumables via television. You see, that's why I love Rio because it perverts the all-pervading corporate professionalism that will, eventually, turn MotoGP into another Formula One: all multi-million-dollar deals, private jets, big-business wank and absolute zero tolerance for anyone even thinking about having some fun.

Not so long ago every GP used to be like Rio – racers, groupies, parties – total chaos on a Sunday evening, riders living on the edge by day, tipping over the edge by night. Nowadays MotoGP is too professional for all that, at least until the 747 screeches to a halt at the end of the Rio runway and everyone deplanes, sniffs that fetid air and realises that they are, after all, very much alive, so it's time to work a little less, play a little more. As British author John Fowles once wrote (during a frenzied attack on Hollywood): 'The absence of leisurely amateurism, from which all great art finally springs, is the most frightening thing here'. That's what frightens me about MotoGP – too many paddock people renouncing everything leftfield and anti-establishment that bikes are about (or is that just me fooling myself?) and prostrating themselves inside MotoGP's cosy bubble of corporate overkill. What's needed is less professionalism, not more.

The other reason I love Rio is that it gets back to racing's fundamentals – a bunch of riders and mechanics, some bikes, a racetrack and a big pot of pasta in a Portakabin – there's none of the suffocating corporate hospitality that has swamped the European paddocks, leaving little space for what really matters.

But amidst MotoGP's shameless headlong rush into full-on corporate cocksucking there are a few paddock people striving to keep it real, apart from the aforementioned anonymous star. Stand up Kurtis Roberts, younger son of The King, currently enduring a miserable debut GP season on dad's Proton KR5. I'm glad to say that Kurtis is brash, bonkers and very badly behaved, in other words a carbon copy of his father as a young man. Before telling this next tale, I should explain that Max Biaggi owns a Smart car which his motorhome driver uses to travel from the paddock to his hotel each night. Fair enough, but the self-styled Roman Emperor's Noddy car is sprayed up in Camel blue and yellow and emblazoned in huge Max logos. In other words it's asking to be done over. And, please forgive me Lord, I've been tempted myself, but Kurtis beat me to it at Mugello, turning the thing on its roof and spinning it round and round. Then when a bike cop rolled up to investigate, he jumped aboard the cop bike and rode a couple of laps of the paddock, blue lights flashing, siren wailing. Proper behaviour for a 25-year-old bike racer.

So please join me in proposing a toast to Kurtis Roberts Esquire and saying a fervent prayer to the Big G that Rio may be spared from MotoGP's death row. It's because it's worth it...

Epilogue: obviously Dorna didn't hear my prayers – they did indeed axe Rio.

CHAPTER 40

WHEN MEN WERE MEN AND THE MAFIA FIXED RACES

September 2004

From Triumph dirt trackers to Kawasaki KR750s, hell-raising American Gary Nixon raced across continents, decades and racing eras. And he would've won a world title if the mafia hadn't stitched him up

Gary Nixon's career straddled two great eras of motorcycle racing – from the good old days of rattling, belching Harleys and Triumphs to the bad old days of Japan's malevolent, stinking 750 two-strokes. 'Nickers', as his mate Barry Sheene used to call him, achieved success on them all in a career that spanned three decades. He was a tough racer, who experienced more than his fair share of hard knocks, and a hard partier, renowned for his nightlife exploits with Sheeney & Co. Amazingly, he was still racing at the time of this interview, well into his 60s and competing in veteran races here and there.

Nixon won his greatest successes in the late 1960s when he rode factory-supported Triumphs to back-to-back titles in America's multi-discipline Grand National championship. And he would've won the 1976 F750 world title on Erv Kanemoto-tuned Kawasaki triples if the mafia hadn't stitched him up…

A funny, rambling raconteur, Nixon has fond memories of both periods of his career, though his memories of racing those seize-prone 750 Kawasaki and Suzuki two-strokes are tinged with terror. He would almost certainly have become a 500 GP star in the mid-1970s if he hadn't got badly smashed up while testing Suzuki's brand-new RG500 square four in Japan.

'I rode a lot of great bikes,' he says. 'The Triumph 500s were great, the Triumph Cub was great, the bike they built me when Doug Hele came over in '67 was great and so were the triples they brought over in '70 and '71. All the bikes that Erv built me were special too, but the Kawasaki

they gave me in '72 was junk. The mechanic was a nice guy but he had
arthritis and couldn't tighten the nuts and bolts. Shit, the exhaust fell off
a couple of times, the gear shift lever too, the handlebar
came loose, the engine sprocket... Fuck, you were shell
shocked riding around on that thing!'

*'The mechanic was a
nice guy but he had
arthritis and
couldn't tighten the
nuts and bolts'*

Born in Oklahoma in 1941, just months before Pearl
Harbor brought the United States into World War II,
Nixon first got into bikes a full half-century ago, while
barely a teenager. 'I wanted to be a sports star, but I
wasn't big enough for football, wasn't tall enough for
basketball and I'd got hit in the head with a baseball
bat, so I figured I better find something else,' he says, recalling the events
that led to his first bike ride in the summer of 1954. 'My sister's boyfriend
had motorcycles, I used to steal them and ride around the block when
they went to the movies, then I conned my dad into getting me one.'

Nixon's first bike was a Harley 125, and pretty soon he was taking it
to the local drag strip. Weighing less than eight and a half stone at the
time, he won his first drag race title at the age of 15, started scrambling
on a Triumph Thunderbird the following year and commenced his
professional career in 1958, aged just 17.

His early years on the pro-dirt track circuit were anything but high
rolling. Nixon lived a Kerouac-style life on the road, barnstorming his
way from one town to the next, relying on the charity of rivals to get
through. 'I used to go to races and borrow two dollars to sign on, when
you have to do that you're fuckin' broke,' says the man from Maryland
who hooked up with AMA legend Dick Mann and fellow racer Neil
Keen for much of his travels. 'If my engine blew, Dick would lend me a
spare and I'd give him half my prize money. If it hadn't been for him
and a few other guys, I wouldn't have made it through the early sixties.
That's all I was doing – racing to put food in my tummy.'

The AMA circuit was indeed punishing in those days: 'One August I
rode 31 events.' Nixon would clock up 50,000 street miles in a season
– racing, driving, racing, driving, racing – Sante Fe one night, Granite
City, Illinois the next, someplace else the next – sleeping in his trailer,
in the workshops of friendly bike dealers or, on a good night, in a cheap
motel. The money was anything but great, Nixon would have to wait
for the 1970s for TV coverage and serious sponsorship to kick in before
he could enjoy some real octane-fuelled glamour.

'I made 600 bucks my first Grand National year. When I won my first AMA title in '67 I made 38,000 bucks, as good as an average baseball player, you could buy a house for 30 grand in those days. I bought a brand-new Shelby 500GT Mustang that cost six thousand; God, that motherfucker would be worth 200 grand now. But my best was '76, I did 70 grand that year.' Of course, those earnings are chickenfeed compared to a modern-day racer's income. 'Shit, Rossi makes 15 million bucks now. But maybe they don't have such a great time as we did, they're going too fuckin' fast to party. We didn't used to do all that training shit. We were drivin' all the time.'

Back in the days when Americans only raced two kinds of motorcycle – Harleys or Limeys – Nixon started out on Harleys but made his name on Triumphs. As is usually the case in racing, he didn't make the switch for any other reason than pragmatism – Harley were talking about offering him parts, Triumph a whole lot more. At first he raced for West Coast Triumph dealers, but in the winter of '62 he headed east to be closer to the Triumph importers, TriCor. It wasn't good timing: 'I loaded all my shit up and moved up there just as the Cuban missile crisis was happening. There I was driving towards Washington DC, right where they would've bombed if it'd happened.'

Once the threat of imminent nuclear conflagration had subsided, Nixon focused his mind on getting his career together as a fully fledged factory Triumph rider. In '63 he won his first national, lapping the entire field, including second-placed Dick Mann. Third overall in the '65 AMA series and second in '66, Nickers finally got his hands on the number one plate in '67, retaining it the following year. In '67 he also won the Daytona 200. (Closest rival and team-mate Dick Hammer might have beaten Nixon in the Florida classic but was slowed after a mid-race pit stop, when a wiping rag got sucked into one of his T100's Amals!)

Nixon's success on his sweet-handling T100 infuriated Harley bosses, especially race director Dick O'Brien who raged: 'We have the best machines, spend the most money... and that little red head comes out and blows off all of us, with 15 less horsepower.' Nixon's success on his Limey twin didn't meet with the approval of fiercely patriotic US fans either, not that it bothered him: 'They'd all boo and everything, but at least they were thinking about me.'

Of course, these years were the beginning of the end for four-strokes.

Ever the pragmatist, Nixon started racing a Yamaha TD1C 250 in '64, because it allowed him to contest 250 races as well as big bike events and because 'Yamaha gave me 1000 bucks a race when Triumph were giving me 300'. At the time it must have seemed like danger money – the TD1C seized not infrequently, throwing Nixon to the ground on one occasion and breaking the thumb on his throttle hand. 'One day we got through seven crankshafts.' Only Nixon's remarkable ability to withstand pain allowed him to keep racing towards his first AMA title.

In '69 Nixon suffered the first of several seriously injurious crashes, but this time a rinky-dinky two-stroke wasn't to blame. He was riding a Triumph dirt tracker at one of the many West Coast horse tracks that were 'converted' for bikes. 'This thing didn't have any midrange, so I punched it down a gear and ran it wide open, missed a gear and hit a four-by-four post. They didn't have any hay bales. I remember my femur bone sticking out of my leather pants, blood squirting everywhere.'

Nixon never won another national dirt track race, that injury forcing him to concentrate on roadracing because his left leg, now held together by an 18-inch steel nail, didn't like going round in anti-clockwise circles. His full-time move to the hard stuff was completed when he signed to Kawasaki.

Kawasaki's early H2 750s were evil pieces of equipment. Their fragile air-cooled motors required riders to focus much of their attention on engine noise, nervously listening for warnings of an imminent seizure amongst the cacophony of open spannies. And when the motors were running, they screeched out more power than their flexi frames and iffy tyres could handle.

'Hell, they were scary,' Nixon admits. 'But it was just something you had to do. You're a racer, you're out there trying to go faster, and the Triumphs were running 150mph when the two-strokes were running 180. That's a big difference. But that Kawasaki would wobble so bad at Daytona that Yvon [DuHamel] told me: 'Well, just cut an inch or two off the bars'. The thing still wobbled but your hands didn't go so far back and forth.'

Nixon's career on these Grim Reaper two-strokes was saved by Erv Kanemoto. 'Everybody was saying "that ol" Nixon is a has-been', then I signed with Erv and I was AMA roadrace champ the next year. But then Kawasaki offered me 5000 bucks for '74 and gave Yvon 100 grand, so I said "stick it up your ass" and rode for Suzuki.'

Nixon's two years running Kanemoto-fettled Suzuki 750s might have turned him into a 500 GP star if it hadn't been for a horror crash at the factory's Ryuyo test track. Sheene had talked Suzuki into entering Nixon in the '74 Dutch TT, aboard one of the factory's brand new RG500 square four. On his way to Europe Nixon stopped in Japan to test some TR750 chassis mods he wanted Suzuki to adopt.

'Our 750 was running a 24 degree head angle, their 750 was 30 or 31. First lap out Ken Aroaka (Suzuki's test rider) comes by me, and me being a dumb ass I passed him back. Going into this fifth gear corner I backed the throttle off and the thing seized. Ken clipped my back wheel and I went down. I woke up, noticed my arm was all bent over, then the pain hit. They put me on a workbench on the back of a pickup with a little Jap guy on top of me so I wouldn't fall off. I was screaming and yelling till they shot me up in the hospital. A few hours later I heard loud screams – Ken's on the little bench next to me with one of the Jap docs pulling his broken leg, while the other guy's got a foot-long drill going through his knee...'

Nixon broke both arms, three ribs and an ankle in that accident, but he still wasn't finished. In '76 he moved back to Kawasaki to have a crack at the inaugural F750 world championship, riding a KR750 that had been heavily breathed upon by Kanemoto. 'I guess the '76 Kawasaki that Erv built me was the start of what they have nowadays – it had cantilever shocks, chrome-moly frame, the right head angle, all the stuff like that.'

Nixon made a great start to the series – taking second to Johnny Cecotto at Daytona and winning round two at San Carlos, Venezuela. Or so he thought. 'The race was sponsored by the local Yamaha importers, so they fixed Steve Baker's laps so he won it on his Yamaha. I found out later that the race was run by the Mafia, so I was just fuckin' lucky I was still alive.' The row dragged on all year, the FIM eventually deciding to pretend the Venezuelan race had never even happened. If things had gone Nixon's way, he would've won the world title by a single point.

Nixon raced his last serious race in 1979, after a couple of reasonable years on Kanemoto-prepared Yamaha TZ750s. Since then he's carried on with his motorcycle parts business, more recently creating his own website that flogs the 'Gary Nixon Enterprises' T-shirts made famous by Sheene, who never raced without a Nixon tee after surviving his horrific '75 Daytona smash while wearing one. 'Shit, if I'd crashed wearing that I wouldn't have worn it any more,' Nixon opines, with some logic. 'I would've thought it's unlucky but I guess Barry thought he was lucky he didn't get killed. The guy did so much for me, some stuff I can't even tell people. We just hit off, we had some good times.'

In recent years Nixon has returned to the tracks and still isn't to be messed with – he can still make the podium at Daytona on his classic Honda CB750: 'We had it running good and I was running right along with Springer (Jay Springsteen, a recently retired AMA dirt track legend), I was screwing with him and he was screwing with me...' And there's no plans to retire just yet: 'If people like to watch me, I'll keep doing' it. I just go as fast as I can without crashing.'

To keep his aching body moving between races, Nixon gets himself along to the occasional MotoGP race to help look after Honda star Nicky Hayden. He's known the Hayden clan for years. 'I used to race with Nicky's dad in the 1960s, though I don't remember him. Then I ran into his dad when Nicky and his brothers were first racing. I remember talking to Nicky when he was 12. I asked him "how old are you?", he was like (Nixon raises his voice several octaves), 'sixteen!' I saw him doin' a dirt race or two and I thought this kid is unbelievable. Then he got on a roadracer, and when he got on a good bike he just took off. He's a great kid. At dirt track I'd say to him "You look a little high here or a little low there", then when he started roadracing I'd go out to corners to watch him. About the only real thing I ever said to him was "Hey, get all the money before you start drinking and partying". But he goes to church, he lives life right, he's just concentrating on being world champion.'

MotoGP Mutterings: January 2005
Some of the world's greatest minds also get off on a good blast of speed

'Speed, it seems to me, provides the one genuinely modern pleasure,' wrote Aldous Huxley back in 1931. Arguably the greatest mind of the 20th century, Huxley knew what he was talking about. During his life the author of *Brave New World* tried all kinds of different intoxicants in the pursuit of pleasure, having decided that modern man was going to need some kind of special buzz to make it worthwhile getting up every morning, whether it be a capsule of brain-bending mescaline or a 150mph blast down your local bypass.

After mph and mescaline Huxley tried LSD and God knows what else in his ultimately unsuccessful quest to find the perfect source of industrialised happiness. (If you're looking for the epicentre of today's let's-get-out-of-it-to-make-life-bearable culture, Huxley's your man, though his own intentions were honourable; he was no binge drinker, he consumed all his drugs in precisely measured quantities, then noted down the effects in full detail.)

Huxley was very impressed with the effect that straightforward miles per hour could have on the brain, at least until he discovered the warp-drive effects of designer drugs. 'The inebriating effects of speed are noticeable at about 20 miles an hour,' he wrote, explaining to his readers that 72mph is the speed at which life starts to get a bit scary: 'One begins to feel an unprecedented sensation – it grows intenser with every increase of velocity.' And Huxley was proper scared of going much faster than that: 'I have never travelled at much more than 80mph, but those who have drunk a stronger brewage of this strange intoxicant tell me that new marvels await anyone

'I am a slave to speed. On my tombstone they will carve: It never got fast enough for me'

who has the opportunity of passing the hundred mark. At what point the pleasure turns into pain I do not know, but two hundred miles an hour must be absolute torture.'

Thirty years after Huxley wrote those words a good chunk of humanity was already addicted to speed, none more so than American journalist Hunter S. Thompson, author of cult novel *Fear and Loathing in Las Vegas*, who rates speed as 'one of my finest addictions'. 'I am a slave to speed,' he once wrote. 'On my tombstone they will carve: It never got fast enough for me.'

Of course, speed alone has never been enough for Thompson; he also got off on handguns, high explosives, drugs, booze, political intrigue and under-age sex. While Huxley worried about the horrors of ton-plus travel, Thompson spent most of his life looking for a practicable equivalent of being loaded into an Apollo rocket and blasted into space, whether it meant popping pills in an armchair back home in Aspen or riding fast motorcycles down his favourite mountain highway. (The

Woody Creek Perverse Environmental Testing Facility, as he liked to call it.) Which is probably why a few years ago some sicko at American bike mag *Cycle World* had the bright idea of offering the gun-totin' acid casualty a Ducati to road test. That's a bit like asking some blingin', tooled-up rapper from So Solid Crew to test drive the latest Ferrari on a zigzagging Alpine road. Just asking for trouble.

At least Thompson did fully understand the dangers involved in riding bikes too fast. 'The final measure of any rider's skill,' he wrote in summing up the big red Duke. 'Is the inverse ratio of his preferred travelling speed to the number of bad scars on his body.' He did nearly crash the v-twin, of course: 'I felt nauseous and I cried for my mama, but nobody heard... This motorcycle is simply too goddam fast to ride at speed in any kind of normal road traffic unless you're ready to go straight down the centreline with your nuts on fire and a silent scream in your throat.' He also found the bike's ergonomics unsuited to his substance-abused body: 'I was hunched over the tank like a person diving into a pool that got emptied yesterday'.

But however much Thompson suffered for his speed addiction you just know that the world's number-one expert on growing old disgracefully never went soft and bought a steady old Harley: 'Some people will tell you that slow is good – and it may be, on some days – but I am here to tell you that fast is better. I've always believed this, in spite of the trouble it's caused me. Being shot out of a cannon will always be better than being squeezed out of a tube. That is why God made fast motorcycles, Bubba...'

Years before HST, years before Huxley even, another literary genius was getting into the joys of speed. Irish author James Joyce wrote these words a whole century ago, after watching a road race rattling into the streets of Dublin: 'Rapid motion through space elates one; so does notoriety; so does the possession of money'. That sentence blows me away, in 15 words written in 1905 Joyce exactly describes the forces driving every MotoGP star: speed, fame, money. In the same chapter of *The Dubliners* he adds (referring to a big, blue Citroën racer): 'The journey laid a magical finger on the genuine pulse of life and gallantly the machinery of human nerves strove to answer the bounding courses of the swift blue animal.' So nothing's changed – all racers and road riders make themselves feel more alive every time they yank open the throttle and challenge their nerves to keep up.

MotoGP Mutterings: February 2005
All the world's a stage, or in our case, a racetrack...

It's a funny old world and it's a funny old world championship. All human life is right there in the MotoGP paddock; there's good guys and there's bad guys, a microcosm of the world itself. Except that motorcycle racing tends to attract the more extreme forms of homo erectus, and the most extreme form of motorcycle racing tends to attract, well, some serious nutters.

I've known a few in my time, though not all MotoGP riders are nutters. There's all kinds, driven by all kinds of inner forces. There's those racked by insecurities and a wretched desperation to succeed and, at the opposite end of the racers' psychological spectrum, there's those who just happen to be very, very good at doing something they really, really love. Over the years you tend to fall out with the arseholes and maintain a distant respect for the nice guys, trying your best not to be their mate because there's nothing worse than a journalist who pretends the riders are his mates.

So who are the arseholes and who are the good people? I never really got on with former world 250 and Superbike champ John Kocinski. JK (or the 'little shit', as his team boss King Kenny Roberts sometimes referred to him) was a very weird racer. His attitude to life was as obsessively compulsive as his attitude to winning. You'd end up interviewing him while he painstakingly picked the lint from his socks. During his time with Team Roberts he was banned from using a motorhome because he'd be up half the night polishing the kitchen fittings, so he'd be worn out come race day. On returning home to the States one summer Kocinski got arrested for hoovering his three-piece suite on his front lawn at 3am. Not long after he had been spurned by GP racing he accused me of having been paid to destroy his career. Hell John, I'd have done it for free if anyone had asked...

I had a few run-ins with Max Biaggi too. Years back I worked for one of his sponsors and the self-styled Roman Emperor always made my life as unpleasant as possible, just like he did for most people around him. He was always agonisingly desperate to win and wanted everyone working with him to be similarly tortured, which is why, in the end, no one in MotoGP wanted to work with him, even though he is still a very fast rider. To be honest I felt sorry for the guy, his mum left him when he was a kid, so maybe it's no surprise that he doesn't seem like a happy person. Then again, it was hard to feel sympathy for someone who used to hire a couple of muscled Roman gladiators to follow him around at the Italian GP.

Then there's Eddie Lawson. The guy once threatened to set his attorneys on me after I'd written some story about his defection from Yamaha to Honda in 1989. In fact the four-time 500 champ hated most of the press. I was never really sure what to make of him until I read something he said a few months ago: 'I've always had the utmost respect for the US military'. That made up my mind.

Lawson seemed to feed on his dislike for people, using its heat to power him on the racetrack. That's not uncommon in racing. Valentino Rossi certainly had more fire in his belly in 2004 and 2005, stoked by his burning desire to make his former Honda bosses look like fools. But I've no doubt that Rossi is a reasonable human being, though he's definitely got a dark side which he betrays so easily that it's funny. When Rossi gets the hump his face darkens, his eyes seem to sink into his skull and you know it's time to get out of his way. We saw him get nasty on Sete Gibernau at the end of 2004 after he accused the Spaniard of behaving like a classroom sneak, getting Rossi sent to the back of the grid at that year's Qatar GP.

At least Rossi and Gibernau behave like normal human beings when given half a chance (though you don't see them getting drunk together any more). They are able to compartmentalise their racing selves from their non-racing selves; which is the whole point, you need to be evil on the track, not off it. Some riders never get the hang of that concept. Your ultimate MotoGP or WSB Jekyll and Hyde would have to be Troy Bayliss. A total animal on the motorcycle, Bayliss is a charming family man in the paddock. I've found him in his motorhome, five minutes after crashing out of a GP, quietly mucking about with his kids, calmly suggesting they might clear up their bombsite of toys. And he likes a beer or ten on Sunday nights, too.

Bayliss is funny when he's pissed but the best Bayliss moment is Sunday mornings, when you'll find him in the team VIP unit, addressing the breakfast buffet, selecting a bowl of muesli and some croissants to take back to his motorhome where he gives his wife Kim her breakfast in bed. Now there can't be many blokes who fix their wives' brekkie on their way to work. A proper family bloke for sure, Bayliss is very aware that he's got a raging animal inside him, which is why he's recently found himself in a dilemma. Him and Kim had their third child a few years back, so Bayliss has been considering getting the snip, only he's terrified that a vasectomy might rob him of his Rottweiler-style aggression, like some castrated dog transformed from snarling beast to cringing mutt. 'So I won't get the snip till I retire,' he finally decided. I'm guessing Bayliss never bothered with biology classes at school but somehow I couldn't bring myself to tell him that vasectomies don't involve having your bollocks chopped off...

MotoGP Mutterings: *March 2005*
Do we like speed for its own sake or are we chasing after something more complex than that?

We love speed. You, me and Valentino Rossi are the same in this respect – we all get a kick out of moving rapidly through space, from feeling ourselves rocketing across the landscape like some master of the universe.

But is it really as simple as that? Is it purely the miles per hour that gets us going or is it something more complex than that? Rossi says this about going really fast on a motorcycle: 'At high speed everything becomes more difficult and more beautiful'. Obvious enough maybe, but the world's greatest bike racer is suggesting that it isn't merely speed that turns him on, it's the difficulty of achieving a certain speed that delivers the real buzz.

My own personal take on the speed thing is that it's degrees of throttle opening that really count, on the street at least, rather than pure miles per hour. Seventy miles per hour can be a yawn or a scream, depending on what you're riding and how you're riding it. When speed comes too easily, on a mere whiff of throttle, it's not so much fun, but when every mph is hard won at the end of an over-stretched throttle cable, you really begin to enjoy the sensation. So 70mph on a 'Blade can be seriously underwhelming while 70mph on a knackered 125 is teetering on the brink, about as tricky and therefore as rewarding as attempting to re-enter the earth's atmosphere in an Apollo rocket. It's like anything in life, really, the more you put into something, the more you get out of it.

Okay, I guess this means I'm going to be singing the praises of crap motorcycles here. Consider this: if you want to regain the careless rapture of your first teenage rides, don't go out and buy a brand-spanking new R1, go out and buy a CG125 with a bent frame and an intermittent misfire. With a cracked, quirky machine like that you will be able to rediscover that long-lost sense of adventure on every journey you take, indeed on every corner you take.

My own personal crock of biking shite is a dirty, four-year-old Burgman 400 (okay, so it's a scooter but don't tell anyone) which rarely fails to make me laugh, or at least snigger, whenever I ride it. It isn't that fast but it is fast enough to hurt. This hideous hunk of steel and plastic can surpass 90mph and when you go into a corner at that speed you really feel like you're living, though you feel even more alive when you make it out the other side. You see, that same corner taken on a 'Blade or a 999 would be a non-event – in and out, no doubt. On the Burgman it can make you feel like Valentino. You're heading into the turn, feeling the under-damped suspension seesawing back and forth, transferring too much force to the pressed-steel frame which begins to twist and flex like a drunken lap dancer. You're holding your breath, wary that you may be about to push things an nth too far, your muscles tautened and ready to do whatever it takes if she does get too far out of shape. So it's up to your skill, talent and judgement to keep this floating marshmallow hovercraft on the road. Brilliant.

(And not only that, because the enjoyment I derive from riding this sorry mess is multiplied by my lack of concern for the thing – I can park it anywhere without a moment's worry because I don't really care if it gets scratched or nicked.)

Now you may think that wrestling an ill-handling heap through corners is a perverse way of getting your motorcycling thrills but I'm not the only one who feels this way. Rossi is the same: he knows that you get what you give, that's why he quit Honda for Yamaha. During 2003 Rossi had found racing Honda's RCV too easy, too boring, and if his YZR-M1 isn't exactly a bent, misfiring CG125, it certainly required the world champ to dig a little deeper into his goldmine of talent. Rossi likes to dig deep, to accept challenges from which others might shy away because he's man enough to know that going out on a limb can be a whole lot of fun and he realises that the risks of failure are far outweighed by the rewards of success. 'I knew that if I could win on the Yamaha it would bring me great joy,' Rossi said. 'That overcame any fears and doubts I'd had about making the move.' It's the same with my Burgman, honest.

Of course, back on the streets there are some pleasures that a crap motorcycle can never provide. If the proliferation of Gatsos, speed traps and nobbers in cars ensures that you're never able to keep your R1, 'Blade or whatever pinned for more than a few brief moments, it doesn't really matter because those few seconds are all that's required to have you mainlining enough adrenalin to keep you high for the next 45 minutes.

That's the true attraction of modern superbikes – they're so outlandishly fast that it's possible to achieve the most disgracefully inappropriate speeds in the shortest of distances, in between the Gatsos, if necessary. It's these little moments of madness that can make any two-hour ride worthwhile and memorable, the fizz of adrenalin still trembling through you as you sit on the kitchen floor taking off your leathers. Even so, I still reckon that every garage should contain at least one crap motorcycle.

CHAPTER 41

THE HARDEST RACERS IN THE WORLD, EVER

April 2005

Most racers are hard by normal standards. But some defy the rules of medicine and good sense to force their battered bodies back into the saddle and ride just as fast as they did before. It's time to pay homage to bike racing's hardest men

Motorcycle racing is populated by hard nuts. There's a good reason for this – you don't get far in bikes if you can't shrug off bone-crunching, stomach-churning pain like you or I might shrug off a mild cold. Pain is such an inevitable part of a racer's life that he must learn to live with it, or as legendary racetrack medic Claudio Costa believes, make it his friend.

'By mutating pain's dimension the rider can make it his friend and carry it with him into the race to complete his enterprise,' says the Italian doctor who has spent the last few decades putting broken MotoGP and WSB riders back together.

But what drives racers to torture their bodies so? What made King Kenny Roberts defend his 500 crown with a broken back, Mick Doohan return to racing with a leg bent like a banana or British Superbike champion John Reynolds start the 2005 BSB series just 38 eye-watering days after breaking a leg? Money and machismo, mostly, the lust for gongs, gold and glory...

Reynolds amazed many people when he began his title defence at Brands Hatch in April 20005, just five weeks after breaking his right leg while testing at Valencia in February. But all he was doing was continuing a rich tradition of motorcycle racers overcoming the medical odds.

Racing injured is the dark side of bike racing, when it all starts getting a bit ugly. Really, you shouldn't be racing but you're out there because you're scared of losing your crown, scare of losing your ride, scared of losing your income. To a racer, ignoring the agony of injury is simply the flipside of quaffing the ecstasy of success.

Reynolds knows the deal, which is one reason he raced at Brands, seven weeks earlier than doctors deemed reasonable. 'If you're going to race bikes you've got to be aware that you're not always going to be racing pain free,' says Reynolds, who turned 40 halfway through the 2005 season. 'A lot of the time you're racing in pain – there were eight or nine guys riding injured when I came back at Brands. Most of the time I've got the best job in the world but sometimes it's one of the worst, like when you're on the third row with 35 hungry riders around you, when you know you're going to get swallowed up and you know you've got a broken leg. It's not pleasant, mentally and physically it's hard to get out there.'

Reynolds scored two ninth-place finishes at Brands for his pains, even though he'd been uncertain of his ability to control a bike. 'The first two sessions I was making mistakes, running wide, scaring myself, because it was the first time I'd ridden more than a few laps in anger since October. In the races I was riding 99 per cent but my right boot was dragging on the floor, that was the biggest issue with lap times.'

And yet Reynolds doesn't think he's hard or heroic. 'I'm no hero, it's just grit and determination. And I'm not hard, like I don't go around the streets looking for fights. But I am hard on myself because if I say I'll do something for someone, I'll give 100 per cent to make sure the job's done and I'd agreed to do a job for Rizla Suzuki.'

But what really drives Reynolds to do these things? It can't all be for a pat on the back from his team. 'I wouldn't want people to say I'm a wuss,' he says, possibly getting to the crux of the matter. 'If anyone ever told me I'm a scaredy cat I'd be devastated.' And what about the money? 'If you start thinking about money, it's game over.' Then he thinks again. 'In fact money does matter, racing is my living, but money doesn't make you go faster, it just makes you work harder at it.'

On this occasion, working harder at it meant thrice-weekly sessions locked in a hyperbaric chamber, followed by laser and magnetic treatment. And it meant racing at Brands knowing that another crash could finish the leg. 'I've often wondered how much slower I'd go if I rode around naked, and that's how I felt, very vulnerable. Every time I went into a fast corner I was thinking I don't want anything to go wrong here.'

Reynolds admits that pain wasn't a problem with this injury, but he couldn't have ridden without his tailor-made Alpinestars boot, featuring a rigid carbon-fibre inner that straps to the shin, taking weight off the still-healing tibia and fibula. 'The only problem was that the boot cuts of the blood supply, so I got pins and needles. Riding wasn't so painful, more clumsy than anything. I didn't have to go through a massive pain barrier, even though I had no painkillers because the boot strapping was so good, comfy and tight.

'It would've been so easy to sit at home watching Brands on TV, thinking I'll race when I'm fit, but if you want to defend a championship you've got to be out there doing it. At the end of the year I may need those points, so I'm pleased I rode.' [In fact he didn't need the points, because six months later he was an ex-racer. Reynolds decided to quit immediately after smashing himself up at Brands in October, breaking a collarbone and four ribs and puncturing a lung. 'When I hit the barrier it was like a switch in my head flipped,' he said. 'Instantly I knew it was time to stop.']

JR's story is enough to make your normal bloke on the street squirm and wince, but it's nothing out of the ordinary in the cruel, hard world of bike racing. The list is as long as a badly broken arm...

King Kenny Roberts is probably the only racer to have won a world title with a broken back. The American claimed his second 500 crown in 1979 despite a massive smash during testing at Yamaha's lethal Fukuroi track (or in this case 'Fuck you, Kenny').

'Daytona wasn't so bad but Silverstone was major – my left leg was hanging on by the femoral artery'

After slamming into a barrier at 90mph he felt the numbness flow through him. But he was racing again nine weeks later. A few years before that Roberts had an agonising motocross crash after which surgeons removed one of his testicles. Three weeks later he was racing at Daytona, with a hole cut out of his Yamaha's seat to relieve pressure on his still-tender scrotum. King Kenny also has a bullet lodged in his left leg from a shooting accident.

Roberts' former sparring partner, the late Barry Sheene, was famous for three things – winning two 500 world titles, shagging a top model and returning, Lazarus-like, from prangs that would've ended any normal human's career. As Dr Costa says: 'Barry had so many accidents that he became a walking encyclopaedia of traumatology for my staff'.

Sheene took just six weeks to come back from that notorious 1975 Daytona smash that left him with a broken femur, wrist, forearm, collarbone, six ribs and compression-fractured vertebrae. And he returned from an even more disastrous pile-up at the 1981 British GP, after which surgeons used 28 screws to fix his legs. 'Daytona wasn't so bad but Silverstone was major,' Sheene said later. 'My left leg was hanging on by the femoral artery.'

If that makes you feel a little bit icky, Mick Doohan's tales of pain and suffering have made grown men weep. The teak-tough Aussie was notorious for his ability to withstand the most horrendous agonies. After breaking a finger during qualifying for the 1995 German GP, Mighty Mick refused pain-killing jabs with the immortal words, 'I'm not a painkiller type of person,' then went out to grab pole position. But that was the least of it. In '92, Doohan nearly lost his right leg after a crash at Assen. Dr Costa sewed his legs together to save the mangled limb and he was racing again within seven weeks, narrowly missing out on that year's 500 title to Wayne Rainey.

The next winter Doohan bent the still-mending bone while training too hard but was winning GPs again within a few months. Surgeons later fitted an Ilizarov gantry to straighten the leg. All Ilizarov patients take morphine, except Mick who existed on an over-the-counter painkiller. Californian surgeon Kevin Louie says: 'Mick took so little pain medication, it's almost superhuman, it's like he's reset his pain thermostat.'

Racers are used to dealing with physical injuries – breaking bones, tearing flesh, getting so beat up it's like they've been badly done over outside a nightclub – but brain damage is something that strikes fear into every one of them. Perennial World Superbike runner-up Aaron Slight had already bounced back from his fair share of knocks – including a deforming hand injury – when he suffered a stroke before the 2000 World Supers season. He was rushed into hospital where neurosurgeons fixed a burst blood vessel in his brain. Medics said he might never race again but the Kiwi was back on board his Castrol Honda within two months.

Even more scary was Carlos Checa's comeback from a life-threatening accident at the 1998 British GP. Careless Chucker was MotoGP's most crash-happy racer, once crashing 27 times in one season, but accidents never slowed him down. At Donington he crashed at Craner Curve at 120mph, staggered back to his motorhome and collapsed with massive internal bleeding. He was helicoptered to hospital where surgeons removed his spleen. But Checa suffered a relapse, going blind and partially paralysed for more than 15 hours. Seven weeks later he was racing, and crashing, again. 'Honestly I was scared,' he recalls. 'But I fought against that scary feeling to prove to myself that I was well again.' Not as easy as it sounds.

Carl Fogarty was famous for gritting his teeth during the years he battled for his four World Superbike crowns. But Foggy had already been through the mill before he'd even made it onto the world scene, twice breaking his right femur while racing 250s in Britain. In fact that's why he moved to Supers, because he could no longer fit on a 250. But his hardest day's racing came at Sugo in 1995 when he came back from a stratospheric race-one highside to win race two. Only later did x-rays reveal that the crash had broken bones in his right hand and ankle. After that the Italian media nicknamed Foggy 'Lionheart'.

The list goes on and on and on: Supers hero Chris Walker, always an ace at crashing in race one and winning race two, 1987 500 champ Wayne Gardner, the man who narrowly avoided semi-castration after a nasty tankslapper at Suzuka and Kevin Schwantz, who rode half his career with broken bones. Nutters! We salute you all...

The science of pain – do heroes really exist?
Pain exists for a reason. It's there to tell you to stop doing whatever you're doing or risk damaging yourself. The hard racer ignores those warnings – he feels pain from his broken wrist, forces himself to ignore it and insists on racing next Sunday. He can race despite stinging pain because he's desperately determined, because he's high on dopamine (the body's natural painkillers) and maybe because he's undergone a course of pain-killing injections.

Of course, the tricky thing about pain is that it's impossible to quantify objectively. We all feel it differently, so the exact same pain might leave one victim whimpering in the corner while another shrugs it off with ease.

But what's the difference between a wuss and a hero? Genetic make-up, if recent research is to be believed, which means that Schwantz, Doohan, Reynolds et al may not be heroes after all, they've just got genes that make them less sensitive to pain. It's all down to how many mu opiate receptors you've got, according to neuroscientist Dr George Uhl: if you have loads of mu, you've got good resistance to pain, if you haven't, life's gonna hurt. Then there are the researchers who believe that pain is a bio-psycho-social phenomenon (ouch!), influenced by factors ranging from neuroanatomy to social and economic issues. But it would hurt all of us too much to go any deeper into that.

One final question – are today's racers harder or softer than their predecessors? Difficult to say, but there's probably no difference. Racers will always be racers and the hard nuts will always do just about anything to win.

But some things do change. Motorcycles are much more physical today than they were 10, 20 or 30 years ago. They have sharper brakes, grippier tyres, better chassis and more powerful engines, which means far greater stresses and strains on an injured body. And modern technologies, like special boots or special brakes, can allow riders to ride when they never could have done a few decades back. Just as well that pain-killing technology has come on some too.

Tricks for the sick – how racers race when they should stay home

Papa's left-hand throttle
There are times when a racer's determination becomes desperation, and so it was with Italian 500 rider Marco Papa at the 1994 Malaysian GP. Papa had suffered a broken right wrist during pre-season testing and was determined to race, so he reversed his Yamaha's controls – clutch on the right, throttle and brake on the left. It took just three scary laps for him to realise that this wasn't a clever idea.

Doohan's thumb brake
When Mick Doohan broke his right leg in the summer of 1992 he also damaged the ankle so badly that he couldn't operate a conventional rear brake. So his engineers fitted a thumb-operated brake to the left handlebar of his NSR500. Within months Doohan was winning races and went on to claim five world titles.

Ueda's glove
When Nobby Ueda crashed out of the 1998 French 125 GP, badly breaking his right arm and suffering nerve damage, some said he'd never race again. But within four months he was back on track, thanks to a robo-cop glove, created by Spidi. The glove had spring-loaded fingers which allowed him to open his hand when the muscles and nerve tissues weren't up to it.

Mesotherapy
This is the most common form of painkiller used by top racers but mesotherapy can be pretty agonising in itself. As MotoGP champ Valentino Rossi says: 'I have very much fear of the mesotherapy needle.' Each course requires dozens of micro-injections around the injury. The advantage of mesotherapy is that it's locally very effective but doesn't dull the rider's brain, as do many painkillers.

Other therapies
Apart from straightforward physio, riders can speed their recovery by undergoing laser and magnetic treatment. These therapies accelerate bone growth by increasing blood supply and decreasing inflammatory reactions. Very much the rage these days, hyperbaric chambers help oxygenate the blood supply to speed healing. Brian Simpson's Ipswich hyperbaric has been used by many racers including Reynolds and MotoGP rider John Hopkins.

MotoGP Mutterings: May 2005
MotoGP is haulin' ass, but where to, exactly?

Please excuse me for being the prick who bursts the MotoGP bubble. You think I'm crazy, I know. Surely, no bike race series has ever looked better than MotoGP: lairy, scary 210mph four-strokes, Valentino Rossi, live BBC coverage, global corporations apparently hosing cash at the championship? Yup, the sun is shining on Valentino and his supporting cast but I see dark clouds gathering on the horizon.

Some day soon MotoGP may just become a victim of its own success. Jolted into action by the championship's booming popularity, the larger factories are investing big, triggering a desperate technology race. Sounds great but isn't. What do you really love about MotoGP? Perhaps enjoying the sight of riders wrestling 250 horsepower motorcycles into submission? Not for much longer. You may already have noticed that you don't see many MotoGP riders backing it into turns or getting gloriously crossed-up on fistfuls of throttle anymore. And in a few years you won't see any of that.

The quickest way around a racetrack isn't sideways, so fast-improving electronic engine-braking and traction-control systems will consign the rip-snortin', tyre-burnin' MotoGP bike to extinction, replacing human ability with computer trickery. As Marlboro Ducati rider Loris Capirossi says: 'A few years ago the rider was 70 per cent important and the bike maybe 30 per cent, now it's more like 55 per cent and 45 per cent. There's more electronic cables on the bikes than engine: I think it's too much.'

Curiously enough, we've already seen this happen. F1 car racing has been headed down this road for some years, with the most terrifying of consequences – worldwide outbreaks of narcolepsy every other summer Sunday afternoon. Less and less fans truly respect F1 drivers, because they're perceived as overpaid PlayStation operators, not cavalier risk takers sticking the pedal to the metal and sawing at the steering wheel. And MotoGP isn't so much lurching blindly down this same alley as hooning down it at full throttle, cackling maniacally into a howling 210mph gale.

The problem is this: MotoGP is effectively run by Japanese factory bosses, who treat the championship as an R&D laboratory rather than as an entertainment arena, so when the four-stroke rules were originally thrashed out, no one wanted to ban electronic rider aids. That would've been Luddite heresy. 'For us MotoGP is an experimental field, we don't want any restrictions,' says HRC boss Suguru Kanazawa. Which means that before long MotoGP riders will also be enjoying the benefits of automatic gearboxes, semi-active suspension and god knows what else. The hi-tech genie has been let out of the bottle and there's not much chance of putting it back.

'Call me a prophet of doom, but I see MotoGP becoming a two-wheeled F1'

There's another problem. MotoGP bikes may one day become too rider-friendly but they are already too fast, knocking on 220mph now, so the factories decreed that from 2007 engines would be shrunk from 990cc to 800cc.

Indeed MotoGP has already started limiting performance: bikes must now run with 10 per cent less fuel than they had in 2004, but, inevitably, they are already faster and, ironically, harder to ride. 'They're more aggressive because we're running leaner carburation,' explains world champ Rossi. 'So they aren't more safe, they are more unsafe.'

Excellent, I hear you say, so we will get to see Rossi and his peers seriously sideways again, after all! Nah, engineers will quickly fix that with more traction control. In the longer term, the 800cc motors will be much more peaky than the grunt-tastic nine-nineties and thus massaged into usability by yet more electronic controls. They may also end up being slower than Superbikes, to begin with at least. And the higher-revving 800s – 18,000 or 19,000rpm perhaps – will be more stressed than the 990s and thus require replacing much more often, adding dramatically to MotoGP's already frightening costs.

These two factors – ever-increasing complexity and spiralling costs – will only benefit the richest and most clever factories, in other words, Honda. So far Yamaha is keeping up, largely thanks to the genius of one young man, Ducati too, but Suzuki and Kawasaki are still unable to attract serious sponsorship because they show no signs of even beginning to trouble Honda. Meanwhile Aprilia has been forced out of the series and Team Roberts is down to a one-rider team and still struggling.

Call me a prophet of doom, a techno-reactionary or just a balding ol' fool, but I see MotoGP becoming a two-wheeled F1. Which isn't good.

Epilogue: Told you so…

CHAPTER 42

Mainlining the Greatest Drug Known to Mankind

June 2005

The Isle of Man TT. Nothing like it. In 1985 I jumped on a Honda NS250R and won the 250 proddie TT, thanks in part to some clever tactics (skulduggery, if you prefer)

Until yuppie City traders on six-figure bonuses arrived, the 1980s were pretty skint in Britain, which is why production racing was British racing's mania of the moment. The traditional 250 and 500 GP classes had become too costly, while Superbike, Supersport and Superstock had yet to be introduced, so bog-stock racing made sense, especially since the race-replica craze had just kicked off.

The 1980s was the age of the R: Suzuki's GSX-R750 and 1100, Yamaha's FZR750 and 1000, Kawasaki's GPz900R and Honda's VFR750, big four-strokes that were built as much for the racetrack as for the road. And then there were the GP replicas, for the 1980s were simultaneously the golden age and the last hurrah of the high-performance two-stroke, bikes like Suzuki's RG250 and 500, Honda's NS250R and NS400R, Kawasaki's KR-1, Yamaha's TZR250 and RD500LC, all following Yamaha's 250 and 350 LCs that had taken biking by storm in 1980 and 1981.

For once the Auto Cycle Union (UK racing's governing body) had its finger on the pulse, announcing the return of production racing to the Isle of Man TT in 1984, a decade after Triumph's Slippery Sam Trident triple had won the last proddie TT. Production bikes on the Island seemed a perfect fit: the world's fastest road bikes on the world's greatest road circuit.

During the spring of '84, when I was a spotty *Motor Cycle News* road tester and Pro-Am racer (Pro-Am was an insane Yamaha race series for up-and-coming British youngsters), I was summoned into the editor's office. 'We're sponsoring the production TT, fancy a go?' No, I said. Two heroes of my teenage years – Pat Hennen and Tom Herron – had been done in by street circuits (Hennen suffered career-ending head injuries on the Island while Herron died in Ireland's North West 200), plus I was a bit of a crasher. Then I thought about it, two weeks on the Island, all paid for and not much work... I got on the phone to Suzuki and blagged one of their latest RG250s. I wanted something nice and slow because I'd already decided that all big bikes are too fast for the TT – imagine full-throttling a GSX-R1100 down your favourite mountain road, in sixth gear – and that full-blown racers with lightweight this and that aren't engineered to be jumped off humpback bridges at 80 miles an hour.

I headed to Douglas, the Isle of Man's capital, a few days before practice began, driving endless laps of the 38-mile course in a van with my TT tutors, fellow journalist Mac McDiarmid and classic racer Anthony Ainslie. With over 200 corners to learn, most of them fast and lethal, with zero run-off, you need all the help you can get because your first mistake will most likely be your last. To be honest, the place terrified me. I didn't want to race, so I decided I'd do one practice lap, then go home. But my first sun-blessed early morning practice had me hooked. Flat in top through a sleepy little village? Just superb!

> 'My first sun-blessed early morning practice had me hooked. Flat in top through a sleepy little village? Just superb!'

I finished that year's race in third, behind winner Phil Mellor's suspiciously quick power-valve 250LC. When I returned in '85 I'd used *MCN* clout to secure one of a batch of Japanese-market-only NS250Rs that Honda UK had imported for the race. It was a big leap forward from the RG and RD but the competition was intense, with Robert Dunlop (Joey's brother), Gary Padgett and other young hotshots also on NSRs. In an effort to find an advantage we all rode Pro-Am-style, in other words, pretty much out of control. The 250s were too slow to allow you to make up time through the fastest sections, because you were already flat out, chest bruised blue by the fuel tank, so you made the difference scratching through slower corners. Or jumping the infamous Ballaugh Bridge at speeds that had the local commentators complaining that we were being too dangerous.

Of course, there were some quick areas where you could make a difference. I'd mentally prepare for these miles ahead, knowing that if I got through without easing off I'd carry that extra speed for the next mile or two. Rhencullen was the best – the buzz of getting that just right, flat in sixth, front wheel airborne, hedgerow to dry-stone wall, was what the TT was all about. Mainlining the greatest drug known to mankind.

Then I found another way to gain an advantage. Most of us felt the NSR wouldn't make the three-lap race without a fuel stop. None of the other riders tried three laps in practice because they were busy with other bikes, but I had a go and hatched a dastardly plan. We filled the fuel tank upside down, through the tap aperture to ensure it was totally full, then refitted the tap. I rode three flat-out laps, stopping as I came down from Creg-ny-Baa for the third time, pretending I'd run dry. Then I completed the lap at speed, as if I'd begged some fuel from a spectator. The news went round that the NSR couldn't make three laps, but back in our Douglas shed we discovered I'd still got two litres left. It was worth the risk.

I led the early stages of the race but slowed too much for a downpour, my old Pro-Am rivals Padgett and Graeme Cannell (on a Yamaha RD) sneaking past as we headed up the mountain. Both had started ten seconds behind me, so my hopes seemed doomed (the TT course is so dangerous that riders are started at ten-second intervals, with race results decided on corrected time). We spent another lap together, colliding once or twice, Cannell's riding verging on the homicidal. Usually these hard nuts beat me on short circuits, but that day I had something in me. I pulled ahead on the final lap, despite nearly losing it when the NS snapped sideways on a damp patch at the 33rd, banked hard left, flat out in sixth gear. Cannell finished ten seconds down, Padgett (who hadn't fallen for my fuel ruse) crashed at Governors' Bridge.

Post-race celebrations were a panic. I'd planned to skip the podium ceremony because I had a flight to catch. I had a road bike parked by the pits to ride to the local airport to fly over the Irish Sea to Liverpool, where I'd parked a GSX-R750 to ride to London's Heathrow airport, then fly to Milan, where I was competing in that weekend's Monza Six Hours race. But I couldn't resist the podium where me, 750 winner Mick Grant and 1300 victor Geoff Johnson were greeted by leather-clad tarts from soft-porn mag *Club International*. Classy. Then I lost my trousers (nothing to do with the girls). I was late for the flight, but they kindly held the plane. I sat down, the air hostess gave me a glass of champagne and I started blubbing. The whole thing hit me, my brother

Julian had died a few weeks earlier and I'd promised myself that if I did win I'd dedicate it to him. But I forgot. Twat.

I was back again in '86, this time on a TZR250, with promises of fat win bonuses from bike manufacturers and tyre companies. The proddie TT had got big because success sold a lot of bikes and tyres. I was wined and dined at the Island's smartest restaurants by marketing types anxious for me to use their stuff. People were taking the racing much more seriously, so riders were riding harder, taking more risks.

I never got close to winning in '86 or '87, then rode my last TT in '89, contesting the new supersport 400 class, riding a reverse-cylinder TZR250 with factory expansion chambers. The jetting was all over the place. Coming into Ramsey, my mind occupied with the carburation conundrum, I ran way too fast into the Schoolhouse left-hander, wheels in the gutter, heart in my mouth. Nothing unusual, but the sense of invincibility that had stayed with me since my first TT evaporated. There and then I realised I didn't want to do this any more. A few days later I was at the Salzburgring, covering the Austrian GP and listening to news of the Tianenmen Square uprising, when someone told me that Mellor and Steve Henshaw had been killed in the 1300 production race. And that was the end of TT proddie racing.

MotoGP Mutterings: July 2005
Rubbing shoulders with the Shanghai glitterati on the eve of the first-ever Chinese MotoGP race

Battered by the Desmosedici's demented roar, the crowd jostles for position at the side of the racetrack, peering over each others' shoulders for a glimpse of the first contender. And here she comes, up the steps and around the slow right-hander, keeping it tight and looking oh-so-stunning in a Ducati leather jacket, denim mini-skirt and Manolo Blahnik stilettos. The crowd screams its approval. Nope, this isn't a MotoGP race, this is the launch party for a high-rolling' Ducati clothing outlet in downtown Shanghai on the eve of China's first-ever bike GP.

We're stood on the top floor of a glittering fashion emporium, gawping at a skyline that's straight out of *Bladerunner* and watching models parading along a mini-racetrack that curves around the terrace, sashaying to a pounding soundtrack laid down by a renta-cool DJ, who mixes Desmo snarls with dope beats. We're surrounded by fashionistas, fat financiers and ferociously fit females. Factory Ducati riders Loris Capirossi and Carlos Checa have long departed for their hotel rooms. The air is filled with a curious whiff – the seductive scent of Chanel No 5 mixed with the stench of serious money.

'We're stood on the top floor of a glittering fashion emporium, surrounded by fashionistas, fat financiers and ferociously fit females'

In case you hadn't already heard, China is boomtown. The dragon has awakened from its half-century Communist snooze to strike terror into western economies. The figures are jaw-dropping stuff – the country already produces 48 per cent of the world's motorcycles (at 16 million units a year, though most are Honda CG125 rip-offs, the automotive version of a snide Louis Vuitton bag), built more miles of motorway in 2003 than we've ever built in Britain, while consuming more than half of the global output of steel and concrete.

The Shanghai circuit, where Valentino Rossi scored his first wet-weather victory for Yamaha, is similarly awe-inspiring. It's like the *Starship Enterprise*, which would make Donington Park a 14-foot dinghy with a leaky hull. The gargantuan grandstand/pit complex is a national statement of intent: check us out, see what we can do: 'Look on my works, ye Mighty, and despair'.

So China has a world-class racetrack and tens of millions of rinky-dink motorcycles. Next is a MotoGP bike. China's Zongshen factory is now planning to enter MotoGP with its own V4. One of the most go-ahead names in China's dynamic bike industry, Zongshen produces 1.2 million motorcycles annually and is soon to launch its first hi-tech streetbike.

The man behind this headlong rush into bike racing's big time is, curiously enough, a Frenchman. Michel Marqueton came to China ten years ago after marrying a Chinese lady who just happens to be a senior official in the military. An endurance racer in Europe, he was soon spectating at illegal Chinese street races – wild affairs involving serious gambling, rider fatalities and the inevitable arrival of truncheon-wielding cops. Itching to get back into the sport, Marqueton adopted the quickest street racers and trained them on go-kart tracks until they were unbeatable in the nascent national championships. The Chinese Motorsport Association got interested and helped Marqueton thrash out a four-stage plan for world domination.

Stage one: establish a team to win China's first world title. Job done – Marqueton's Zongshen-backed, GSX-R1000-equipped squad won the 2002 world endurance crown with western riders. Stage two: create a Chinese world champion. Marqueton currently has a couple of teenage Chinese contesting several 250 GPs. Stage three: build an all-Chinese motorcycle to win MotoGP. Stage four: create a Chinese world champ on the same bike.

Anyone who laughs at these ambitions should recall how people guffawed at Soichiro Honda's little 125s when they first arrived on the Isle of Man in 1959. And anything Japan can do, China can do better, not least because its workforce is ten times as big. The economies of scale are obvious – brand-new 50cc scooters were on sale near our hotel for £150.

China's industry seems unstoppable. Globalisation was born to allow corporations to shift money around the world in search of cheap labour, and since Chinese factory workers earn £15 a week, why would a businessman build a factory in the west where he'd have to pay workers 10 or 20 times as much? Tragic as it is, that's why it's so over for Rover. For many westerners globalisation will mean you can buy a dirt-cheap microwave or motorcycle, but you don't have a job.

As the Ducati party reaches its climax, the DJ slips in a few tunes of which the Armani-clad new masters of the universe wouldn't approve – some Sex Pistols and Ian Dury's sex and drugs and rock and roll. But the ex-pat bankers don't seem to notice, they've already got their arms around the local lovelies…

MotoGP Mutterings: September 2005
Idiot racetrack designers are spoiling our enjoyment of racing, what to do about it?

'There are only three sports: bullfighting, motor racing and mountaineering; all the rest are merely games,' said hard-drinking writer Ernest Hemingway. I'm assuming that the original 20th century man's man would've included bikes within motor racing because bike racers are at least as rough 'n' tough as matadors, mountain climbers and motor car racers.

Hemingway's words came to me during MotoGP's long-awaited and much-hyped return to Laguna Seca for the 2005 US GP. Laguna is a scary racetrack, way more dangerous than anywhere else that Rossi and Co ply their trade. It's America's Brands Hatch, plunging up and down like a rollercoaster, a proper Wild West ride in pretty Californian scenery, some of which is way too close for comfort. It's the kind of place where you feel proper awe watching riders do their thing, because you know the consequences of a mistake would be very messy. Winner Nicky Hayden was genuinely awesome to behold through Laguna's notorious Turn One – a 160mph left-hander over the brow of a hill – drifting both wheels at full lean, regardless of the cliff face a few yards away.

I feel a little uneasy that I'm so entertained by watching riders attack that kind of corner, which tests their skill and even more so their bravery to the very limit. I hate to admit it but I find that much more fun than watching the world's fastest, most fearless riders perfectly execute Valencia's Turn Two, or Three, or Four, or Five, or Six, or Seven, or pretty much any other second- or third-gear corner at Losail, Shanghai, Motegi, Rockingham, Oschersleben, Lausitzring or any other recently constructed glorified go-kart track.

So what am I on about, taking the British GP back to the Isle of Man? Obviously not. But I reckon someone needs to do something before all racetracks are soulless ribbons of tarmac, dominated by identikit slow-to-medium-slow corners that are merely a game of technique and technology, rather than the sport of balls and bravery. What do the designers of these places think they're doing?

Well, the German architects who laid out Shanghai created the circuit in the shape of the Chinese character Shang (meaning 'above', which is the origin of the port city's name, Shanghai or 'above the ocean'). Lovely concept, guys, but they've ended up with a mind-numbing layout. There's not one corner at Shanghai you'd ever look forward to riding around. Same with Losail (in Qatar), which the designers created by linking together a dozen different corners from other tracks. Again, nice idea, but they've built a soulless, formulaic track where the corners are indistinguishable from one another. You can spend a whole weekend watching practice and racing at Losail and still not recognise one corner from the next. I feel we should condemn these people to purgatory, where they shall ride laps of their own sorry creations for eternity, forever forbidden to take a leak.

Ironically, a lot of riders agree. They want safety but they also want a challenge and a thrill, as Neil Hodgson says: 'I hate tracks like Valencia, places like that are glorified car parks.' British 250 rider Chaz Davies also likes 'ballsy corners, the stuff you've got to really grit your teeth for, that's what you get the biggest adrenalin rush from.' Mick Doohan was the same – his fave corner was at the old Salzburgring – a daunting 180mph right–left twister with zero runoff, Armco one side, mountainside the other. 'I know it's dangerous,' he said. 'But to me it's everything racing is about.'

'I know it's dangerous, but to me it's everything racing is about'

Yes, racing is about speed, which doesn't mean a second gear corner, shift to third and then fourth, back to second for the next turn, up to third then back to first for the hairpin. It means a few slowish turns, plenty of medium-to-fast corners and a long straight. And shite racetracks aren't just boring to ride around, they also promote processional racing because they don't have the kind of corners where riders can stay close and they don't have long enough straights to allow slipstreaming. You always get the closest, most exciting racing at fast, open and epic tracks like Phillip Island, Mugello, Catalunya and Sepang. Those last two are both modern venues, designed in the '90s, which proves that inspired, intelligent track designers can still produce fast yet safe layouts. Sadly I haven't got a clue how we stop this pox of humdrum racetracks spreading across the globe. Have you?

CHAPTER 43

GOD'S GREAT
LEVELLER

November 2005

Some racers call it the great leveller – when it pours, the rain lets some riders really shine. Here's three of the finest wet weather rides in bike racing history

Christian Sarron sinks Fast Freddie, Hockenheim, 19 May 1985
When Christian Sarron beat Freddie Spencer in the rain-soaked 1985 German GP it was a big deal. Fast Freddie was at the top of his game, on his way to winning a unique 250/500 title double and revered as some kind of riding god. On the Continent they called him ET, the Extra Terrestrial.

Sarron's 500 career is remembered for that single victory and a multitude of scary crashes. The all-dominant Americans – Spencer, Eddie Lawson and Randy Mamola – loathed him because he was so dangerous.

Wet-weather racing is more about risk than dry-track racing, which is why Sarron excelled, the nutty Frenchman usually prepared to push further into the danger zone. This was especially true at Hockenheim, where blinding spray hung over the 190mph autobahn-like straights, unable to escape through the surrounding forests.

'I couldn't see where I was going and suddenly I was on the grass. Oops!'

'You couldn't even see where you put your wheels, you just knew the track from practice,' recalls Sarron, who had got his usual bad start. 'I was 24th and I was passing guys without even seeing who they were. I passed Lawson without noticing but there was less spray up front, then there was Freddie. I carried on riding my rhythm, on the edge, sliding everywhere, and passed him. I saw my pit board and thought "is this really true?"'

Of course, Sarron has his own theories regarding his winning wet-weather prowess. 'The rider can make more difference in the wet,' he says. 'It's always hard to find the limit in the rain, you need to find the front limit on brakes and into corners. Most riders don't have front confidence, it's easy to find the rear limit.'

At Hockenheim Sarron also enjoyed a tyre advantage because his stock Michelin wets were harder than Spencer's trick development tyres, so they didn't get shredded by the long straights.

A few weeks later Sarron pissed off Spencer again, too keen to repeat his German GP success at a rain-lashed Assen. 'I couldn't see where I was and suddenly I was on the grass. Ooops, that's bad. By the time I was back on the tarmac it was too late for the brakes into the next corner. I took Freddie's front wheel with my footpeg. I was very cross with myself. I'd been 20th at the first corner, then sixth after half a lap, maybe it was a little crazy...'

Rossi walks on water, Donington, 24 July 2005

For a man who once said 'I don't like riding under the water', Valentino Rossi usually makes a pretty good fist of walking on the stuff. His winning ride at the 2005 British GP was one of his most awe-inspiring, indeed he rates the race as one of the most difficult of his career, simply because conditions were so appalling. Donington was so badly flooded that riders had to deal with both ends aquaplaning.

'That race was not like riding a bike,' says Rossi. 'It was like riding a boat because there was a lot of water between the wheels and the track, so always spinning the rear and locking the front.' [See also Chapter 53.]

His secret was to wait for his rain tyres to warm up, then suss out the conditions before pushing to victory. 'Biaggi crashed in front of me, then Gibernau, there were a lot of people making mistakes, also me, so I preferred to wait.' At half-distance, after several scary moments of his own, Rossi put the hammer down, clearing off from nearest rivals Kenny Roberts Junior and Alex Barros by more than two seconds a lap even though he had no tyre advantage.

Although Rossi was a ropey 250 wet-weather rider, he got much better when he graduated to 500s, preferring the bigger bikes' fatter tyres and torque curves. Indeed he scored his debut 500 GP win at a wet Donington in 2000 and the first-ever MotoGP race at a soaking Suzuka, 2002. Like everything else, he puts it all down to practice.

'Riding on water is not easy, to go fast in that condition is important to have a good feeling with the bike. In one year we make almost 25,000 kilometres, maybe 24,500 in dry, maybe 500 in the wet, so you need to arrive step by step for have a better feeling with the bike.

'At the start of 2004 the M1 was a disaster in the wet, so we make some practice, then the bike coming better and now we are fast. I don't like the water but I'm a racer so I need to go fast in any condition.'

Crew chief Jeremy Burgess doesn't reckon Rossi has any particular wet-weather skills: 'What makes Valentino good in the wet is probably what makes him good in the dry – maybe his reflexes and motor neurons are quicker than the other guys'.'

Michael Rutter makes a splash with WSB podium, Brands, 3 August 1997

When Brummie Michael Rutter turned up for the 1997 Brands WSB round he was a little-known BSB rider. By the time he left the Kent circuit he'd beaten Carl Fogarty and John Kocinski to the chequered flag in front of 100,000 fans, thanks to a British summer downpour.

Just 24 at the time, Rutter had already gained a reputation as a rain rider. 'I enjoy the rain because I know everyone else probably doesn't, so it's like, great, it's raining!' he says. 'My dad (multiple TT winner Tony) was the biggest help, he enjoyed the wet too, so that rubbed off on me, plus he helped me set up the bike so it's nice to ride, just making it a lot softer so you've got feel. It moves around more but you've got a gauge.'

Rutter wasn't expecting much from Brands, just sneaking into the top ten aboard his V&M-prepped RC45 would've been an achievement. He finished race one in twelfth and was in a similar position in race two when the heavens opened. The race was stopped and restarted, with the eventual result to be decided on combined times.

'After the restart it was pissing down. I'd started from the third row and just picked my way through. It was nice passing some of the big boys, then I got up behind Foggy. That was a fantastic feeling because he was a bit of a superstar to me, but I was thinking "God, I don't want to take him out", so it took me a few laps to pluck up courage to pass him. After that, it was good to do Kocinski because he was on the factory RC45 and the thing I was on was a piece of scrap.'

Rutter took the chequered flag in first, combined times putting him third, and he looked overawed as he joined Fogarty and Kocinski on the podium. 'We were all using Michelin wets, though I didn't get the trick stuff they had. But maybe my bike was better than theirs in the wet. After riding the HRC Fireblade the last couple of years I reckon factory bikes are bloody hard to ride in the wet, just because they've got so much power.'

Rutter has straightforward advice for wet-weather riding. 'Be smooth and relaxed, don't hold on too tight, the bike will move around but you've just got to flow with it.'

CHAPTER 44

'RON WOULD ROCKET PAST, HANGING ON FOR GRIM DEATH

December 2005

Like a Phoenix arising from the ashes of the British motorcycle industry, the JPS Norton rotary and riders like Ron Haslam scored some of the most unlikely successes in racing history

When Imperial Tobacco returned to bike racing in the late 1980s it swapped the red white and blue of its 1970s John Player brand for John Player Special black and gold. The colours weren't as patriotic but that didn't matter because the JPS Norton rotary was a more successful motorcycle than its twin-cylinder predecessor. The bike won three British championships and dozens of races over four seasons, its success hugely magnified by the fact that it was so unexpected.

When JPS Norton riders Trevor Nation and Steve Spray lined up for the RCW588's first serious season in 1989 the British bike industry was presumed dead and buried. Nation, Spray and later Robert Dunlop, Terry Rymer and Ron Haslam proved otherwise and in doing so brought crowds thronging back to British circuits in a patriotic ferment. Everyone, from the fans to the riders, seemed touched by the success of this super-fast British underdog that ate Hondas, Suzukis, Kawasakis and Yamahas for breakfast.

'I'd never dreamed I'd be racing a competitive British bike but I was and it was a bloody big thrill – I was so bloody proud'

'I'd never dreamed that I'd get to race a competitive British bike but I did and it was a bloody big thrill – I was so bloody proud,' recalls Nation, who won the RCW588's first big race in August 1988, shortly before JPS got involved. 'I remember one of my first wins at Mallory. I'd just got the lead and as I came through Devils Elbow the whole flipping bank seemed to move, everyone was shouting and cheering, they all got sucked along by the Norton, it was something British. I mean, I hate cricket but when

England are doing well I watch, so if you're half interested in bikes and there's a British bike doing well...'

The drama was only intensified by the fact that the JPS Norton seemed to come out of nowhere. British racing had been dominated by Japanese machinery for almost two decades and all of a sudden Norton was winning again. The RCW588's unlikely existence was thanks to the vision of Brian Crighton, who joined Norton to look after its rotary police bikes, the fruit of a licence bought from NSU in 1972.

'I told Norton this engine could go really well in racing but they thought I was mad,' says Crighton, who began tuning a scrap police bike in his own time. 'I couldn't get anyone interested until it did 170mph at MIRA. It all went from there, they kicked the caretaker out of his house and let me have that as the race shop.'

With a tiny budget from Norton's new owner, investment banker Philip Le Roux, Crighton got Spondon to build a chassis and, following the bike's first victories, started hunting for serious sponsorship. 'We thought we'd try John Player because the link was already there. They came to Brands when Steve won his first two races on the bike, they saw the crowd go mad and that clinched the deal.'

Over the next four years the JPS Norton was British racing's jewel in the crown, even when it wasn't winning. Of course, not everyone loved the bike. There were various theories about how to measure a rotary's capacity, and plenty of rivals believed that Norton was cut too much slack by the ACU and FIM, who fully realised its value to bike racing.

'It was mental fast,' remembers Yamaha rider Rob McElnea, who raced against the rotary for several years, beating Haslam to the '91 title. 'When you were racing you thought "that fucking thing shouldn't be on the track, it's not legal". You'd be squeezing behind the screen and Ron would come rocketing past, hanging on for grim death, laughing like mad. But you put up with it because it dragged in the crowds. British racing was on its arse, then the Norton came along and got everybody into it again.'

It wasn't just the bike's amazing speed that made people jealous – JPS pumped in proper money and ushered modern-day sponsorship practices into British bike racing with a very glitzy operation. McElnea again: 'They had double the set-up anyone else had and they put as much money into promotions as they did into racing. They were the first to have replica bikes in spectator areas and take the whole show to shopping precincts.'

So how much money did JPS spend? It was certainly a significant investment. 'Their contributions more or less kept Norton going, apart from the aircraft engine sales,' reckons Barry Symmonds, who managed the team from 1990. One source reckons Imperial Tobacco spent £1 million over the first three years.

Unfortunately, the money didn't always make for a happy, united team. Crighton and Symmonds clashed badly, prompting Crighton to quit and develop other rotary racers. 'The whole thing was tainted by a lot of silly squabbles,' remembers Nation, who was dropped at the end of 1991. 'I always said what I thought and maybe I wasn't tactful enough, but a spade is a spade – I don't know what else you're supposed to call it. The worst thing was the converted Koni car shock, I was never a fan of copying the front of a Formula Ford and sticking it on the back of a motorbike.'

The final 1992 Norton rotary was almost certainly the most effective. It used a new motor from the F1 road bike and was renamed NRS588 (for Norton Racing Services), for the simple reason that Norton needed a logo that looked like JPS, because tobacco logos had been banned from the BBC-broadcast British championship.

JPS enjoyed massive media coverage from its Norton adventure but missed the rotary's most famous victory. Island genius Steve Hislop signed to ride the bike in the '92 TT but JPS weren't involved because they were frightened by the TT's safety record. Hislop rode an all-white NRS to victory in the Senior, Norton's first TT success since 1961.

JPS pulled out at the end of '92. 'The deal had run its course and anti-tobacco restrictions were getting tougher,' says Symmonds. Imperial may also have been concerned by allegations of fraud within the Norton Motors group, which triggered a Department of Trade and Industry investigation that resulted in convictions for Le Roux and several of his coterie.

Despite the marque being sold once again in 1993 (and on myriad occasions since), the Norton name continued to enjoy racetrack successes, Ian Simpson winning the '94 British title on a Crighton rotary. But the Duckhams-backed machines never excited the British crowds like the JPS bikes had done.

MotoGP Mutterings: *December 2005*
What have Biaggi's hairpiece, Gibernau's voodoo curse, Phillip Island and Led Zep got in common?

Assen, as you may know, used to be MotoGP's fastest, most hallowed ribbon of biking tarmac – outrageously fast, totally challenging. But not any more, not since the day after September's World Supers round when bulldozers rumbled in to desecrate the place, turning half the Dutch track into an entertainment mall and car park. Way to go, dudes.

'Looks like we need to call Ghostbusters'

Which means Phillip Island is now MotoGP's fastest venue and the best place in the world to watch motorcycle racing. Perched off Australia's south-east coast, a bit like they took the old and insanely fast Silverstone and dragged it to a clifftop on the north coast of Cornwall, Phillip Island is a wide-fucking-open primal scream of a racetrack. If it were a band it would be The Ramones, Led Zeppelin and The White Stripes all rock 'n' rolled into one. Which would make the emasculated Assen The Ramones unplugged, with Ronan Keating on vocals.

Bike racers love Phillip Island because it's crazy fast – just gas it up and bank it over. As Nicky Hayden says, 'it's got a lot of fast corners and that's what we like to do – go fast around corners', while Colin Edwards admits 'it scares the shit out of you'. This year the place claimed Capirossi (chest injuries) and Roberts Junior (broken wrist) but Valentino Rossi looked more relaxed than ever – all tangly Medusa hair and bad-boy swagger – because he knows that this is the ultimate rider's track and therefore his track. No one else stands a chance on the Island. Rossi has won every year since 2001.

In the middle of the Island's Portakabin paddock, we're in one of Rossi's media chat sessions. We get to asking him about the curse he allegedly inflicted on Sete Gibernau at the 2004 Qatar GP, where Honda notoriously had Rossi sent to the back of the grid, since when the Spaniard has apparently lost the ability to win. At first Vale hasn't got a clue what we're going on about, he's looking at us like we're nuts, then his face brightens into a big, evil grin as he mimics the act of stuffing needles into a voodoo doll. Poor Sete, what can he do, his deadly rival isn't just superhuman, he's actually supernatural. No wonder Aussie fans call him Sete GiveItUpNow.

Personally, I think it may have had less to do with wicked witches and more to do with hair crimes. Like some kind of 21st-century Sampson, the more out of control Valentino's hair gets, the more invincible he becomes, while the more 'Hollywood' Gibernau and Max 'Roman Emperor' Biaggi preen themselves, the slower they become. Biaggi, for example, now wears a hairpiece to hide his balding pate. I kid you not. As far as I'm aware he's the first GP racer with a rug, though Mike Hailwood did hang out back in the '60s wearing a hippie wig and Lennon shades, just for a laugh.

Whatever, Gibernau's Tory boy locks may be a lesser tonsorial crime than Biaggi's rug but they have been punished mercilessly. His 2005 season was an accursed summer of doom, less Hollywood, more Hammer House of Horror.

He crashed out of five races, which makes Kevin Schwantz at his most crash-happy seem steady and circumspect. And when Gibernau wasn't eating dirt, he seemed equally doomed. At Jerez Rossi rammed him into the gravel after he'd led the whole race. In Germany he lost the lead after being distracted by his team extravagantly applauding him from the pit wall, with one lap still to go. At Brno his RCV ran dry on the final lap while he contested the lead with his tousle-haired nemesis. In Qatar he threw away victory with another gravel excursion. Gibernau's crew chief Juan Martinez knows something sinister is afoot: 'Looks like we need to call Ghostbusters,' he says.

So what killed Sete Gibernau GP winner? Was it Rossi voodoo? Or did he just get too worked up about needing to beat his bitterest rival? Or did his head really go to Hollywood? Or was it the hair? Whatever the reason, Gibernau's disastrous 2005 proves how easy it is for riders to lose that winning edge. Winning racers don't stop winning because they forget how to ride, they stop winning because something's disturbed their psyche, destroying their mental focus. Only Gibernau knows what's gone wrong in his head, or maybe even he doesn't.

Epilogue: In 2006 Gibernau had a Ducati, the fastest bike in MotoGP, but he got hurt. At the final race Casey Stoner knocked him off, breaking the Spaniard's collarbone again, then nicked his Ducati ride for 2007. Tough luck, huh?

CHAPTER 45

CROZ, LAST OF THE GREAT ALL-ROUNDERS

March 2006

Graeme Crosby was the last racer to successfully combine the contrasting demands of GP racing and the Isle of Man TT. He was also the man who introduced Superbike-style racing to Britain.

Back in the old days, looking cool and going fast was all about the racing tuck. You weren't part of café-racing society unless you were crouched over the front, hanging onto a set of low-slung clip-ons or ace 'bars. At least that's the way it was until New Zealand nutter Graeme Crosby turned up at Brands Hatch in May 1979.

The inimitable Croz turned British racing on its head, beating the nation's best on his ratty, US-style 'sit-up-and-beg' Moriwaki Kawasaki and showing British bikers a whole new way of going fast. Fans adored him for his speed on the track and his devil-may-care antics off it.

The lairy Kiwi may have been Britain's Superbike revolutionary but he was so much more than that. In an international career that burned bright but short, Croz became the only rider in history to win the Isle of Man, the Daytona 200 and the Suzuka Eight Hours. He was also the last man to successfully straddle the increasingly different demands of TT and GP racing, winning TTs and scoring GP podiums within weeks of each other in 1981. And although he never quite won a 500 GP, he finished second in the 1982 world championship, ahead of Freddie Spencer, King Kenny Roberts and Barry Sheene. And all this while enjoying a reputation as a carouser who could start a party anywhere and strike terror into the hearts of rentacar staff the world over.

Of course, Croz never planned to do most of this, his career just evolved organically. And when he was at the height of his powers at the end of '82, he went and quit. For a naturally talented racer who just wanted to have fun, the sport's icy new professionalism had no attraction.

Crosby was an overnight sensation at Brands in 1979, driving into the paddock an unknown, leaving as the talk of the track. Fans could hardly believe what they'd seen – some guy in scuffed, oil-stained leathers hassling Ron Haslam's pristine factory Honda and beating everyone else.

'I think the British crowds were looking to get into an underdog away from your Sheenes and [Mick] Grants,' says Croz, who remained a firm favourite with British fans until he tangled with Barry Sheene in 1981. 'But we only had the high 'bars because we were aiming towards the new Daytona Superbike race and because proddie racing was big at home – all clanging handlebars, scraping side covers and lots of crashes, that's what the audience liked. When we turned up at Brands, Phil Read told me he'd buy me a set of clip-ons. I said I'd rather have the money so I could eat!

'That way of riding was so natural to me. I'd look at bikes like the P&Ms which were nice but they didn't have that feral-ness for short-circuit scratching. The English set up their bikes traditionally, so they didn't have that ability to flick left and right. Our bike was unstable towards top end but more manoeuvrable at lower speeds, so it was well suited to shorter circuits.'

'I was the worst at piss drinking and partying, I don't know how Suzuki put up with me'

Typically, Croz hadn't even planned to be in the race that changed his life. 'I came over to do the Isle of Man and then someone suggested I do Brands,' he recalls. 'I'd always wanted to do the TT, it's an icon race. I didn't feel it'd be too dangerous because I'd always been street riding and street racing. It was Mike Hailwood who helped us get a start. He was living in New Zealand and used to watch a few races. I was just a hairy-assed kid, but we use to go to his place, talk about the TT and spill red wine all over the carpets, much to his wife's dismay.'

Crosby finished his first TT in fourth, behind Alex George, Charlie Williams and Haslam, but ahead of Mike the Bike, the man who kickstarted his international career! Many TT old-timers thought Croz was riding too fast and told him so, but he insists he always treated the circuit with great respect. 'I didn't learn the track the traditional way, lining up those two lamp posts and so on, I got to know where everyone had killed themselves. It was macabre but it demanded I had a helluva lot more respect for the circuit.'

Croz cancelled his return flight after the TT, realising he could make a wage out of British racing. Living out of the back of vans or dossing on mates' floors, 'like most Aussies and Kiwis back then', he hung out with fellow Antipodeans and factory Suzuki mechanics Mick Smith and Dave 'Radar' Cullen, though this wasn't the only reason Suzuki GB signed him for 1980.

Partnering Randy Mamola in Texaco Heron colours, Croz did it all that year. In March he won the Daytona Superbike race on a Yoshimura GS1000, in May he made his 500 GP debut, in June he won his first TT, (the F1 race, then a one-race world championship), in July he won the Suzuka Eight Hours (beating Kawasaki's Eddie Lawson and Gregg Hansford) and in August he scored his first 500 GP podium. Such versatility came naturally, he says: 'where we came from we raced on street circuits, short circuits, GP style circuits, the lot'. Nevertheless, Suzuki were so impressed they doubled his pay for 1981, to £25,000.

Continuing his two-stroke and four-stroke duties, Croz was just as successful in 1981, winning two more TTs, taking his first GP pole positions and four podium finishes. But the doubts were already creeping in. That year's TT was marred by death and controversy – Honda and Suzuki got involved in a nasty wrangle over Croz's F1 win, Honda famously protesting by wearing all-black livery for the Senior, in which Aussie privateer Kenny Blake died.

'It was a big Honda versus Suzuki fight, a lot of controversy, which took the edge off the enjoyment. And then we lost Kenny. I will always remember leaving the paddock with Kenny's van still parked there, clothing hanging on the line, that had a huge impact. That's why I decided not to go back – I'd won three races and that was enough.'

Croz also found himself embroiled in a messy tabloid wrangle with Sheene, after he had crashed out of the lead of the British GP, taking Sheene with him. 'I was a bit naive on how to deal with that; I was being told by various people what I should be saying and it backfired.'

And then he was axed by Suzuki, because Mamola didn't want him as a team-mate, which may or may not have had something to do with Croz flushing Mamola's head down the toilets in the Pukekohe paddock when the snotty youngster first raced in New Zealand during the mid-1970s.

Croz was lucky to start 1982 with Giacomo Agostini's Marlboro Yamaha team, or so he thought. He won the Daytona 200 on a TZ750 and was a podium regular in GPs but something wasn't right. 'I was falling behind, not from a riding point of view but more from an organisational point of view. I guess I needed a manager.'

The early 1980s were a period of massive transition for GP racing – big sponsors rolling in, riders forming themselves into unions, increasing professionalism – and fun-loving Croz found himself all at sea. Then when the factory Yamaha and Marlboro Yamaha teams merged for 1983, Croz once again found himself without a ride. It was the only excuse he needed to head home. 'All of a sudden racing lost its appeal; I'd taken up flying and that was consuming for me.'

Over the next three seasons Croz rode occasional races for Suzuki in Japan, though his heart wasn't in it. 'I'd be halfway through a race and I'd go "what the fuck am I doing here?", every lap was a real wrong one, then all of a sudden it'd click in and away I'd go and 20 laps would disappear without me even thinking and I'd be "shit what happened there?" It was then that I decided enough was enough.'

Now 50, Crosby isn't too worried that he never achieved his full potential. 'You always have regrets but I'm still alive and I only ever broke one collarbone, so I came out of it remarkably well; there's so many other people who aren't around.' Since retiring for good, Croz has run his own motorcycle shop, sold cars and become a builder. He married his second wife, Helen, in the summer of 2006.

Crosby, beer and rentacars, a lethal combination
Crosby's international career coincided with a period of huge transformation, with gung-ho amateurism replaced by shiny professionalism. But none of that stopped Croz from partying hard.

'I used to be the worst at piss drinking and partying, I don't know how Suzuki put up with me,' he says with a guilty grin. 'I used to be so bad, there'd be times I probably would've failed a breathalyser test racing at the TT. I'd have a few beers and some wine the night before and in the morning I wouldn't eat anything because my stomach would be churning around. I'd just get out there and do it.'

Croz was also infamous for his rentacar antics in the days when no self-respecting racer would return a hire car in one piece. 'I remember meeting some Irish guys on the beach at Daytona at two in the morning. We were hooning up and down in my car and got kinda bogged down and that was it. The tide came in and by the time we were rescued there were waves coming in one window and out the other...'

I was the butt of one of Croz's jokes at Suzuka in 1985. Me and my team had broken into the circuit swimming pool in the early hours after a session at the legendary Mama's bar. We stripped off for a skinny dip, then realised someone had stolen our clothes. No need to guess the culprit...

Croz's factory beating rat bike
Crosby may have won TTs on factory Suzukis and Daytona on a factory Yamaha TZ750 but he's best remembered for the rat bike with which he first made his name in Britain.

The yellow and blue Moriwaki Kawasaki Z1000 was a wolf in grubby sheep's clothing, ratty as hell and yet as fast as the factory Honda RCB1000s. Built for the USA's new Superbike series, both engine and chassis had been breathed on by Mamoru Moriwaki, Pop Yoshimura's son-in-law.

In addition to the usual – hot cams, pistons and so on – the 120 horsepower Zed Thou had also been strengthened with Z650 valve buckets, replacing the stock tappets, and solid cam chain tensioners, replacing the standard auto tensioners. Carbs were 31mm Keihin smooth bores, ignition came from a total-loss system and the crank end was sawn off for extra ground clearance. The chassis was also strengthened and tweaked, with revised geometry, Z650 triple clamps, lengthened Moriwaki swingarm and Kayaba racing forks and shocks.

The bike was sold to racer Gordon Pantall who recently carried out a full restoration – it looks tidier now than it did in 1979!

CHAPTER 46

MotoGP RACING WITH
NO RULES

March 2006

When you ask a group of top MotoGP engineers what kind of bike they would build if there were no MotoGP regulations there's bound to be some extraordinary creations...

What kind of MotoGP bike would you build if there were no rules? That's the question we asked the sport's top designers. We asked MotoGP engineers from Honda, Ducati, Kawasaki, Suzuki and Yamaha to start with a clean sheet of paper, with only one aim in mind – to go as fast as possible.

Not everyone welcomed this breath of freedom, this escape from MotoGP's myriad technical regulations. Pit-lane engineers spend their lives shackled by rules so that some of them seem unable to envisage anything beyond those rules; they simply find the concept of thinking outside the box too scary to contemplate. Yamaha's M1 project leader Masahiko Nakajima said: 'No rules is nonsense!' Ducati said simply they were too busy designing their very real 800cc GP7 to create a fantasy MotoGP bike.

No surprises there, really. Race engineers tend to be busy people and also realists, not dreamers. That's the stereotype anyway, but this story proves that some engineers have dreams just like the rest of us, except they tend to be wilder than anything we'd ever dream. Both Honda and Kawasaki embraced the no-rules idea with enthusiasm, creating sensationally radical motorcycles which beg the question: who's been putting what in their green tea?

'Honda and Kawasaki created sensationally radical motorcycles which beg the question: who's been putting what in their green tea?'

Suzuki crew chief Tom O'Kane and former GP-winning engineer Hamish Jamieson also dreamed up their own race bikes, created with one idea in mind, to cut the fastest lap times ever. Amongst the features desired by these cutting-edge designers are jet power, two-wheel drive, variable wheelbase, supercharging, nitrous-oxide, hub-centre steering, ABS braking, active suspension, semi-auto gearshifters, Bonneville-style streamlining, 14-inch barrel-shaped tyres and, most bizarrely, a two-track motorcycle with its wheels side by side, not in line. Now that really is blue-sky thinking…

Honda: two-wheel drive, active triple

Honda came up with two designs, one for now, one for ten years hence. Their dream machine for now is a 250 horsepower, 834cc four-stroke inline triple with pneumatic valves, hub-centre steering, active geometry, part-time two-wheel drive, linked brakes, shaft drive, 16-inch tyres, active suspension and a semi-automatic gearbox.

They reckon the bike would rev to 19,000rpm, surpass 350kmh and beat most MotoGP lap records by about 10 per cent, which would equate to an improvement of around ten seconds at a racetrack of average length. And all performance factors – both engine and chassis – would adjust actively according to weather and track conditions.

'We chose hub-centre steering because we wanted to make a bike with active wheelbase and geometry, which would adjust itself for cornering, and this would be impossible with telescopic forks,' explains Honda Racing Corporation managing director Satoru Horiike. 'We also think two-wheel drive is a good way to go in the future, very useful for both front- and rear-end traction. But this is just an idea; so far HRC doesn't have any two-wheel drive prototypes.'

The bike's geometry – wheelbase, ride height and so on – would adjust automatically for each corner and straight. During acceleration and deceleration the bike would be long and low for stability, but during cornering the wheelbase would shorten from 1430mm to 1390mm and the centre of gravity would rise for quick steering and greater manoeuvrability. HRC won't say how they'd achieve this adjustment but it'd take gyroscopes, sensors and plenty of electronics. The triple's front wheel would be driven by an electric motor during corner exits to improve traction and turning.

Honda: way-out two-wheeler

Is it a bird? Is it a plane? Hang on, is it a motorcycle? If you think HRC's 834cc active triple is radical, its vision of MotoGP racing in 2016 is about as far out as you could possibly imagine. In designing his dream MotoGP bike of the future, Satoru Horiike took our 'no rules' concept to the limit, changing the entire dynamics of the motorcycle in search of ultimate cornering grip and therefore ultimate lap times. He has designed a two-track machine, which still fits the *Oxford English Dictionary's* definition of a motorcycle as 'a two-wheel vehicle that is powered by a motor'.

'The only stipulation of a motorcycle is that it must be two wheels, that's all,' Horiike smiles. 'This kind of bike wouldn't necessarily be safer but it would be much faster. With an inline two-wheeler you can't achieve more than 1g but if you put the wheels side by side you can achieve more g. This would mean more grip and lap times closer to Formula One cars. At the moment MotoGP lap times are much slower than F1, even though top speeds are quite similar. I think it would be possible to build this kind of machine in ten years. Already Segway (the self-balancing two-track scooter) has done something similar. It's simple, you just need a giro and some electronics. I first had this idea in 1989; I've already made the patent.'

The two-track Honda uses the company's jet-plane know-how with a turbojet engine that would produce massive horsepower with a smooth delivery. Like something out of *Star Wars*, the machine harnesses the jet's thrust by using vectored nozzles to help steer the machine through corners. Air brakes would also play an important role in cornering, helping the bike to tilt, developing extra downforce and therefore grip for the inside tyre. An active-controlled wing would control pitching during acceleration and deceleration. But it's not all computer trickery, the rider would also use his body weight to improve cornering speed, just like bike racing and, er, sidecar racing.

One wonders if this was the bike that Valentino Rossi was talking about when he said: 'When I was racing for HRC I kept hearing that in Japan, in some secret drawer, there were projects that would revolutionise motorbikes...'

Kawasaki: Bonneville-style streamliner
Kawasaki want MotoGP bikes to be super-radical, much less like supersport bikes than they are currently, so they'll be unique machines which will fascinate fans. That's why Team Green MotoGP engineer

Kenichi Furuhashi has come up with a semi-tilting, streamliner with hub-centre steering, supercharged motor and enormous rear tyre which he believes will be super safe and crazy fast.

Like Honda, finding extra grip was a key factor in their design. Their solution to this issue was creating a super-fat, super-low-profile 800/10-14 rear tyre and a two-part carbon-fibre monocoque chassis that is, quite literally, hinged in the middle. The rider sits in a reclined 'armchair-style' sitting position in the front section, which leans fully during cornering while the rear rolls slightly through centrifugal force, the barrel-shaped rear tyre delivering a massive footprint. The 400 horsepower supercharged 800cc engine is housed in the rear section. Wheelbase is 1500mm.

Kawasaki believe that this machine – with huge horsepower, massive grip, very low centre of gravity and ultra-slippery aerodynamics – will deliver lap times that would give an F1 car a run for its money.

And Furuhashi didn't stop at designing a motorcycle. He believes MotoGP needs more than just radical new bikes. 'We propose that racetracks should be shorter, so spectators can see all the course at once, like the Valencia MotoGP track or like Supercross,' he says. 'We would also want all teams to run engines of the same specification, so the rider becomes the main player of MotoGP, which will produce very close and exciting races.'

Only one problem: HRC's Satoru Horiike reckons he patented a very similar idea some years ago!

Tom O'Kane: bat-mobile (with rocket launchers)
Chris Vermeulen's Suzuki crew chief Tom O'Kane has worked in GPs since the late 1980s, first on Team Roberts' factory Yamahas, then on the squad's own two-stroke triple and four-stroke V5. He joined Suzuki in 2005.

Like some engineers, O'Kane struggled with the concept of total engineering freedom. 'I tried to work on the basis of "let your imagination run wild", but after wracking my brains to come up with a two-wheeled bat-mobile, I gave up. Motorcycles simply don't work that way. So what I've come up with is a wish-list of what I think is achievable, given a no-rules situation with maybe a few bat-bike parts.'

O'Kane's creation is thus a lot less wild than those dreamed up by HRC and Kawasaki. He reckons a V5 four-stroke would be the ideal power plant, but with nitrous-oxide injection. 'More power is always nice,' he adds. 'In the lower gears, the important thing is to limit the power to what the rider can use and provide good throttle connection. But on long straights, in the higher gears, we could benefit from the use of nitrous oxide, controlled by the ECU.' And to improve corner-entry performance O'Kane's bike would have anti-lock brakes. 'I believe in keeping computer control to a minimum,' he adds. 'But an ABS system that allowed the rider to keep both brakes on *hard* up to mid-corner would be worth its weight in silicon chips.'

Because O'Kane works in the pits he's also keen to create a bike that's not merely user-friendly for the rider. 'The bike would be easy to work on,' he explains. 'The designers would have to practise common tasks such as wheel and shock-absorber changes, then redesign the bike accordingly. The designers would also be on a parts-count bonus scheme. That is, every time they reduced the parts count without reducing the bike's performance, they would receive a pay bonus. Performance in this sense means lap-time, reliability and how easy the bike is to work on. Every time they managed to make one part (or system) do two jobs, they would receive a double bonus.'

Safety is also a priority for O'Kane. 'Materials should be chosen for safety. Billet parts, particularly those subject to stress cycles, will be made from 2024-T3 or T4 aluminium. Although 7075-T6 is a little stronger, 2024 is less notch sensitive and more fatigue resistant, that is, fatigue crack propagation is slower. Motorcycle parts should not fail within their design lifetime, but materials must be chosen so that if they fail, they should do so progressively, not catastrophically. Brittle materials and materials which do not show outward signs of impending failure have no place on this bike.'

And O'Kane has one final trick up his sleeve. 'Finally, if weight wasn't too much of a problem, and only to be used as a last resort, a couple of heat-seeking missiles would be nice...'

Hamish Jamieson: super-light and turbocharged
Hamish Jamieson was the man who adapted Yamaha's YZR500 so that wild-sliding Garry McCoy could win GPs. After that the Scot worked on

Kawasaki's MotoGP project before taking time out in Africa, working for the Riders for Health charity.

His dream concept is a small and light bike that delivers excellent feel. 'The overall ethos of this machine is feel and weight, both static, hence the small-capacity engine and dynamic, hence my choice of carbon-fibre wheels.' The engine is a 300cc inline four-cylinder four-stroke with twin turbochargers, water injection and a very low inertia crankshaft rotating backwards. The frame is a Ducati-style steel trellis unit with a swingarm made from cast magnesium. The bike would weigh just 115kg.

Jamieson reckons feel is crucial in allowing a rider to extract the bike's full potential over a 17-race season. 'The machine needs to be kept at its maximum feel, that is why I've chosen carbon wheels, which are 20 per cent lighter than forged magnesium, allowing the suspension to be better tuned, which helps give the rider more feedback.'

Adjustability will be another key feature. 'The rider will be able to adjust the power output via the turbo waste gates, especially important considering the high power output, and the suspension, allowing optimum use of available grip. The ECU will take care of other functions like traction control. Engine braking won't be such a big issue due to the turbocharged engine's low compression.'

His only concern is running costs. 'The engines would be of the throwaway variety. The light materials and the huge stresses imposed by the performance would render them junk in a very short time, about 500km. Thus a team of two riders would need about 80 engines for a year of racing and testing.'

No Rules MotoGP bike specs

Honda's triple
Engine: 834cc inline triple four-stroke with pneumatic valves
Bore: 93 x 40.9mm
Fuel system: PGM-FI
Engine management: 32-bit processor ECU
Gearbox: semi-automatic
Top speed: over 350kmh
Horsepower: 250bhp at 19,000rpm
Aerodynamics: optimised for rider compatibility

Frame: Frameless, carbon suspension supports on engine
Wheelbase: actively variable, 1390 to 1430mm
Weight: 125kg
Suspension: Showa single shocks, front and rear
Brakes: linked Brembo system
Wheels: carbon dish
Fuel capacity: 18 litres

Kawasaki's streamliner
Engine: 800cc four-stroke with supercharger
Fuel system: direct injection
Gearbox: semi-automatic
Top speed: over 350kmh
Horsepower: 400bhp
Aerodynamics: streamliner
Frame: two-part carbon monocoque
Wheelbase: 1500mm
Weight: 180kg
Suspension: single shocks, hub-centre steering
Brakes: rim disc front, conventional disc rear
Wheels: 16inch front, 14inch rear
Fuel capacity: 30 litres

O'Kane's bat-mobile
Engine: 75.5 degree 990cc V5 with nitrous oxide in higher gears
Bore: 72 x 48.6mm
Fuel system: 10 injectors, 5 upper, 5 lower
Engine management: 32-bit processor ECU
Gearbox: six speed
Top speed: about 360kmh
Horsepower: 245bhp, 325bhp with N_2O
Aerodynamics: optimised for handling, then cooling, then drag
Frame: conventional aluminium beam frame
Weight: 145kg
Suspension: Öhlins
Brakes: carbon front, steel rear
Wheels: forged magnesium
Fuel capacity: 30 litres

Jamieson's turbo
Engine: 298.45cc, 16 valve, four-cylinder four-stroke with 180 degree firing
Magnesium cases incorporating cylinder block, beryllium cylinder head
Bore: 54.5 x 32mm
Fuel system: Marelli twin injector system, two KKK turbos
Engine management: ECU-controlled water injection and waste gates
Gearbox: six speed
Top speed: about 360kmh
Horsepower: 300bhp at 15,000rpm, depending on boost
Aerodynamics: optimised for handling, then cooling, then drag
Frame: steel trellis
Wheelbase: 1420mm
Weight: 115kg
Suspension: Öhlins
Brakes: carbon front, steel rear
Wheels: Marchesini carbon-fibre
Fuel capacity: 26 litres, plus 3 litres water

MotoGP Mutterings: *April 2006*
I have seen the future of MotoGP and it's electro

Marco Melandri is stood in the back of the Mugello pits looking a bit
unsteady on his pins. He's leaning heavily on a walking stick but still
looks like he might teeter over at any moment. No wonder really
because the former MotoGP world champ is 77 years old. It's 2059 and
old man Melandri is watching intently as grandson Fabrizio eases out
into pit lane to commence his debut season in motorcycle racing's
premier class, ElectroGP.

Fab made his name winning the 100kW scooter world championship
in 2052, before moving on up to conquer the 200kW supersport class.
Oh yes, GP racing has changed a lot in recent years. The stinky 125cc
and 250cc two-stroke categories were axed in 2010, replaced by 200cc
and 400cc four-strokes. Then internal-combustion engines were run
out of GPs in 2046. Petrol now costs 40 quid a litre, if you can get your
hands on any, because the world's shrinking oil reserves have either
been commandeered by the military or bought by China and Russia,
who have become firm friends with oil-rich nations like Venezuela and
Kazakhstan, Iran and Iraq.

Fab Melandri rides for the Panasonic team, which is due to launch a 200kW street version of its 300kW ElectroGP bike at the Milan show later this year. Meanwhile Honda are working on a 250 watt Electroblade…

A fanciful scenario? Possibly, but oil is a finite world resource, it's going to run out one day, probably within the next half century, and there are plenty of people already preparing for that moment.

'Electric-powered vehicles aren't slow – the White Lightning streamliner has reached 245mph'

HRC recently built their first electric competition bike, US company Electric Moto Corp are already racing a hyper-trick leccy Supermotard in the States and Mitsubishi are developing a Lancer-based electric rally car (with a motor in each wheel, making three times the torque of a conventional engine at very low rpm). Electric-powered vehicles aren't slow either. Fastest so far is the White Lightning streamliner which has reached 245mph at Bonneville. Powered by two 150 kilowatt motors, this warp-speed cigar buzzes out 400 horsepower.

Only one slight problem, the 420 volt arsenal of batteries inside White Lightning fill the same space as a V8 engine and last for just two minutes at full chat. As HRC's current MotoGP electronics geek Makoto Tanaka says: 'Motor is easy, battery technology is problem'. But as anyone who's used a mobile phone over the last 15 years will know, batteries are always getting smaller and lasting longer. And anyway, there are already sun-powered electric vehicles nudging 100mph in Honda's annual solar race at Suzuka.

Sadly, HRC's first electric competitions bike is a trials tool and not a roadracer, but it's a start, and Tanaka reckons the bike is amazingly easy to ride. Well, it would be, it's got perfectly linear power, which is exactly what racers need to give them the control to rear-wheel steer. Tanaka's only concern is wet races: 'These bikes produce over 100 volts,' he adds. 'Maybe big problem if you crash in the rain…'

So electric racing bikes will be fast, exciting to watch and, most importantly, dangerous too. And don't worry, they'll be loud as well, as loud as you like and making whatever noise you like – some electro, obviously, Wagner's *Ride of the Valkyries* perhaps or maybe Madonna's 389th top-ten single. (Well, I never said the future was going to be perfect.)

If all this still sounds far fetched, then consider this cautionary tale. When I was a teenager, me and a mate doorstepped the drummer from

Seventies orchestral rock band *The Moody Blues* (sad, I know, but we'd just bunked off school and were bored). Amazingly, the guy didn't set his dogs on us but instead invited us indoors, gave us tea, proudly showed us his gold discs and then ushered us into this big room where he was working on new music technology. Inside was what he called an electric drum machine – miles of cables and boxes full of valves, transistors and other electronics – which took up half the room. The awe of being in the company of a rock star evaporated, I couldn't have thought the man was more of a clueless moron if he'd shown me a bicycle which he planned to ride to the moon. Nowadays, of course, the whole world moves to an electronic drum beat, which just goes to show, you never know what's around the corner…

CHAPTER 47

'HE JUST FUCKED OFF AND I DIDN'T EVEN KNOW HOW HE WAS DOING IT'

June 2006

Top racers are never easily impressed by other racers, so what kind of a ride does it take to blow the mind of a racetrack hero? Valentino Rossi, King Kenny Roberts, Nicky Hayden, Jamie Whitham, Steve Parrish, Jeremy McWilliams and Rob McElnea recall the rides they'll never forget

Jamie Whitham, former Superbike nutter and all-round raconteur: Giancarla Falappa shows the world how to walk on water, Brands Hatch 1993
'I've always seen myself as a bit of a wet-weather man. I didn't have any particular skill in the wet, I just knew I could always go as quick as anyone else on the day and, if I stayed on I did all right, and if I fell off I fell off. I never believed Falappa had any great skill on a bike, he was just rock hard and prepared to push himself beyond what he should've done.

'At Brands Hatch in '93 it was really pouring down, there were puddles everywhere, just stopping on your bike was an achievement. We had a good bike with good tyres and I knew how to ride it in the wet. But he just fucked off and I didn't even know how he was doing it; I could see him for maybe three-quarters of a lap, then he was gone.

'I remember seeing him through the gloom going into Druids, he just went bing, bing, bang, down the gears and threw it onto his knee. I thought that just cannot work, it can't work for three corners, let alone the whole race. A few laps later I fell off coming out of Clearways, pinged myself through the 'screen and got up. As I'm walking back to the pits, he's coming around doing the same thing every lap, so he's 30 seconds ahead, then 40 seconds in front and he's still doing it. At that point I'm thinking he's mad, because he could slow down but then I'm thinking, well, he's doing it and it's working, so if he slows down he might actually make a mistake. I've done it myself, you're in the groove, knowing exactly how far you can push, and if you back off you may end up on a different line and hit a puddle or something. He was so fucking impressive that day, I used to think I knew how to ride a bike in the wet but apparently I didn't.'

Nicky Hayden, former dirt-tracker, 2006 MotoGP champ: Scott Russell's crash-and-win ride at the 1995 Daytona 200
'I would say the big memory that's always stuck with me is Scott Russell crashing and winning at Daytona in '95. I was there at the first horsehoe turn, standing on this other dirt-track kid's box van. Russell crashed early in the race, right in front of me, then ran and jumped over the bike and picked it up, they made a big deal about that in the US.

'The thing I remember more than anything is when he came by the next lap. I mean this was Russell, he owned Daytona, everyone loved him there and he was cocky, he'd told everyone he was going to win. So when he came back by the next lap, the whole place went wild. Then he was just charging through the pack, picking them up and laying them down, it was impressive. He wasn't hurt too much but his bike was torn up.

'I must've been about 13 at the time, in eighth grade, so about halfway though Friday school I said I needed to go home because I wasn't feeling too good, so then me and my older brother drove down from Owensboro to Daytona to watch the racing. Of course, I had school on Monday morning so we couldn't stay for the whole race, we had to beat the crowd and get home, so we were listening to it on the radio as we were leaving the track and I just remember thinking, man, this is unheard of, some guy crashing and still winning the thing. Sure, he got some help from the pace car later in the race, but the way he was coming through the pack is still right there in my memory, I can still see it all.'

Jeremy McWilliams, rock-hard former GP winner: Wayne Rainey's Lazarus-style comeback at the 1991 Japanese GP
'Valentino Rossi's ride at Phillip Island in 2003, when he beat a ten-second penalty to win, is right up there in my mind but the one that really blew me away was Wayne Rainey in Japan in 1991. I'd started racing a few years before though I wasn't a race fan, I wanted to race,

I just never thought it was that important to sit down and watch races. But I'd come over from Ireland to do the British championship in '91 and that gave me a big kick up the backside because I could see what racing was all about.

'At the time some riders had an influence on me and Rainey was obviously the man. That race was at Suzuka, he was on Dunlops while everyone else was on Michelins. He was up there but then he made a mistake and dropped way back. Then he starting coming through, he was smoking the Dunlop around the left-hander at the top of the hill (Dunlop curve) and you didn't see that kind of thing back then. He was smoking the thing up and I was thinking no way, that can't last, he can't sustain that, but he went on and won it.

'From that point, that was it, Rainey was set in stone, as far as I was concerned he was the god. That ride had a big influence on me because you see what can be achieved, you think that's it, he's not going to do it, but then you see the determination, he just rode the wheels off the thing. I saw so many things in 12 years of GP racing, so my memory is clouded, but that ride had such an impact that I remember it from even before I got into GPs. It's absolutely the most awesome race you could watch, I still tell people to get the video.

'Rainey reckons he had an out-of-body experience at Suzuka and you only get that when you're really in the zone, when you're riding and you can do no wrong. It probably only happened to me once in my whole career, when I beat Rossi and Capirossi in Germany in 1998. Rossi was having a go at me on the last lap and I had a major moment in a fast left, I lost the front and I remember thinking, that's okay I've got it, and you're never in control of a front-end slide. Rossi reminded me on the podium, he said how did you save that?'

King Kenny Roberts, three-time 500 champ, bike builder, motor mouth: Makoto Tamada's Japanese runaway MotoGP win in 2004
'It'd be when Makoto Tamada ran away with the race at Motegi, just because of how much sidegrip he actually had. I just sat there going, wow, this guy is not going to finish this race and I was amazed that he did. It was just that his Bridgestones had so much grip, I couldn't believe it. That was the first time I'd seen that and Valentino [Rossi, who took second place, six seconds down] commented afterwards that it was like Tamada was on qualifiers.

'I guess you could say I more pay attention to the technical side of what happens than to anything else. At this level everybody has natural ability and some pull out more than others, but the differences are so minute that I can't think of a ride where I was, like, wow, that's unbelievable. At Motegi it was just impressive that Tamada could achieve that much grip and I remember thinking at the same time that if this is the way racing is going, we don't have much hope for good racing anymore. As guys get more mid-corner grip they use more corner speed, which means they'll all be on one line, which means there will be a lot less passing, a lot less manoeuvring. It's pretty close to that already, these bikes are like big 250s and I think the 800s will be worse.'

Valentino Rossi, seven-time champ and maybe the greatest racer ever: Going head to head with 250 rival Loris Capirossi at Assen in 1999
'I think I'm very good at understanding when another rider is fast and there have been a few times when some rider has impressed me, for sure more at the beginning of my career, because when you arrive from the European championship to world grand prix, you say, fuck, for me it will be impossible in all my career to go like the guys up front.

'I suppose Capirossi has impressed me many times, Barros for a short period in the last races of 2002 and sometimes Gibernau has been very, very fast. Also, Pedrosa impresses me a lot now because he's a different rider because he is so tiny, so he needs to ride different.

'Maybe the most impressive was Capirossi at Assen in '99. Usually another rider impresses you when you are in good shape, with a good bike, and he's still able to beat you. That day I was very fast and Capirossi was faster than me, he was in fantastic shape. He amazed me at the last chicane; what he did that day was impossible! That race wasn't a race, it was a battle. That sometimes happens, you stop with the right lines and just fight, like remove one chip from your brain and put in another.'

Steve Parrish, British champ and GP racer turned BBC commentator: Bayliss v Edwards, Imola, final round of World Superbike 2002
'I can't think of a race I've enjoyed more than when they were going head to head for the title. The stakes were so high, it was the final round and whoever won would be world champion. Troy had been

romping away with the championship until he crashed at Assen, and Colin won eight races on the run after he got new parts from the Suzuka Eight Hours.

'Race one was a huge, huge battle, it seemed like it would come down to who fell off, but Colin beat Troy by a bike's length to go six points ahead. What made race two even better, the most enthralling race I've ever witnessed, was that it was another enormous battle, but also because Troy's only chance for the title, if Colin didn't crash, was to back Colin down, because Ruben Xaus (Bayliss' team-mate) was coming through. The plan worked to start with because Xaus was catching, catching, catching and got to within two seconds. We thought the shit was going to hit the fan, because who would want Xaus in the middle of it all? Then Colin bit the bullet and passed Troy, then Troy went back past him, they were clashing fairings and pushing each other wide.

'Seeing those two duking it out for a championship with three laps to go was quite extraordinary; it's one race I'll never forget. The gloves were off, nothing was being held back. I'm surprised that Colin didn't just take Troy out. Maybe I would've done that because it was the short way of winning it. The hot tip would've been to smash into Troy under braking when they were crashing into each other and take him out. You wouldn't have blamed Colin and he could've got away with it.'

Rob McElnea: former TT winner, GP rider, now Virgin Yamaha BSB boss: Kevin Schwantz destroys Rainey, Lawson & Co, German GP 1988
'The race I'll always remember is Schwantz nearly lapping everybody in the wet at the Nürburgring. The sidecars had fucked the track, it was like ice, lethal. I was his team-mate and I knew I was witnessing something special; sometimes you don't realise that until afterwards, but all through those Schwantz and Rainey years I knew I was lucky to be there.

'Winning any race on that shitbox Suzuki was amazing, but to destroy everybody like that! All the riders had so much respect, like how the fuck did you do that? It was a shite bike, an absolute joke bike, without him Suzuki were doomed.

'And it was a shite weekend. We sat there half the weekend in thick fog, unable to ride, it was hideous, like being in Hitler's playground, but he turned it into something special.

'He could ride like that because he always rode like that, he was so far on the edge all the time, it'd be on his knee, he'd roll the front round and just save it. He rode like that all day long in the dry, so when the rain came he'd ride the same. It was normal for him to have a moment every corner and save it. Normal people have a couple of big moments and think, fuck me, that'll do, but he'd just have another one at the next corner.

> 'Schwantz was so far on the edge all the time, it'd be on his knee, he'd roll the front round and just save it'

'It was front tyre stuff that he was unbelievable at. He rode the bike so weird, pushing on the front so hard, but he had such a mega feeling for it, the thing would roll around underneath him and he'd keep it going. So when it came to shitty conditions he had such a natural feel for where he was at that he was prepared to keep pushing it and keep saving it.

'I remember the party at the team hotel afterwards. We did all the normal juvenile stuff, like pinching Shirley's (Schwantz's mum) camera and taking photos of my schlong in the toilet and filling her handbag full of cutlery.

'Suzuki brought me into the team to look after him. Then the first time we went to Ryuyo (Suzuki's test track), he broke his wrist after six laps, so it was left to me to do all the testing. At the end of three days the Suzuki engineers sat me down and asked me what I thought. I told them maybe they'd make the top ten at the first race at Suzuka. They were pretty shocked. So Schwantz didn't do any more testing, came to Suzuka with the wrist all fixed up and won the race. But that was all him, it wasn't the bike.'

MotoGP Mutterings: *June 2006*
On the passing of MotoGP's oldest and only truly unique racetrack

I write to tell you of the sad loss of an old and much-loved friend. We visited GP racing's old dame during June and although she is not quite dead, she may as well be, for she has been hideously mutilated by brutal thugs.

Assen was once a thing of great beauty, a unique racetrack that offered unique challenges to both man and machine. But no longer, she has been dismembered, her northern loop hacked off to make room for 'TT World', an entertainments complex with hotel, car park and shops, because the world needs more shops.

Yes, I am a sentimental old git and a Grumpy Old Man too, but I mourn not so much for the sacred tarmac nor for its history but for the loss of seeing even the world's greatest riders thrown headfirst into another whirling dimension by Assen's tricky, cambered curves and forced to ride like they ride nowhere else.

The mean little kink that replaces the butchered one-mile northern loop simplifies the circuit no end (dare I say, dumbs it down) but racers don't go racing because they want an easy life. They loved the old Assen because it forced them to dig deep inside themselves to find a whole new way of riding, reformatting mind, body and motorcycle to unlock the secrets of its insanely fast sweepers, uniquely crowned in the middle like a public road.

'Assen was once a thing of great beauty, a unique racetrack, but no longer, she has been dismembered, her northern loop hacked off'

Around normal racetracks, racers essentially go left or right. But around the old Assen riders negotiated corrugations of camber while zigzagging back and forth at crazy speeds, like riding the back of a giant, wriggling snake, swerving right and left over the centre crown, positive camber one instant, negative camber the next, then positive, then negative, the slightest slip and you were gone. That's why riders used to variously call Assen bike racing's university, its cathedral, temple or Mecca. Racers were in awe of the place. Even Mick Doohan.

'The camber has bitten some of the best riders in the world,' said Colin Edwards a few years back. 'It makes you feel so comfortable, then you get to mid-corner and the track drops away, so if you're not careful it's "Sayonara!", you're out of there! And man, it's so fast, every time you go there you have to adjust your eyes because everything goes by so quick.' This is what Edwards had to say at the 2006 Dutch TT. 'The new circuit is crap, it's just like anywhere else, it's lost the challenge and the history.'

In fact Assen is still heavy with history. In between the whiff of chip fat and weed smoke you can almost taste the sweet old smell of Castrol R. Mike Hailwood won races there, so did Barry Sheene, King Kenny Roberts,

Giacomo Agostini, Freddie Spencer, Kevin Schwantz, Mick Doohan and Valentino Rossi (Graziano too). There is no other GP track in the world where you can say that because Assen is the sole survivor from GP racing's inaugural 1949 season. But Assen is no longer unique, so even though it's better than some GP tracks, it's only half the place it used to be.

You may wonder why I consider racetracks to be so important, why I get excited rolling up somewhere fast and open, like Mugello, Phillip Island and Istanbul, but become strangely depressed when I turn up at mean little layouts like Losail, Motegi and Shanghai. I feel like that because great circuits promote great racing, with riders mugging each other at every other turn, while poor layouts encourage F1-style processions. That's why circuits matter, possibly even more than bikes and riders.

CHAPTER 48

PEDROBOT:

SMALL MAN, BIG TALENT

August 2006

They call him 'Pedrobot', so what is the secret of success inside MotoGP's tiniest superstar?

First of all, an apology. I once referred to Dani Pedrosa as a cheerless midget. On closer inspection I realise I was wrong, or at least half wrong. Pedrosa is miniscule but he's not miserable, he just takes his job very, very seriously. Although he is now mentioned in the same breath as Freddie Spencer, because he's the first rider since Fast Freddie to achieve such success in a rookie premier-class season, Dani Boy is more like Eddie Lawson or Mick Doohan in his attitude to the sport: first of all, racing is a job, second, it is a science and must be treated as such, third, if people enjoy watching the racing, so be it, though this is not really his concern.

These are not good times to hold such dangerous beliefs, Valentino Rossi has seen to that. Nowadays every MotoGP star is expected to be a party clown – as you sit on the grid preparing to get nasty with the world's greatest riders you are expected to wave daftly at the cameras, like you've just spotted your neighbour's five-year-old son on your way to the corner shop. Most MotoGP racers now indulge themselves in this sad ritual, doing their damnedest to tell the world that they are really fun characters but ultimately failing. Pedrosa doesn't mug up to the cameras before races, nor after races, even when he's won. He has copped some serious flak for having the audacity to behave in such a manner – how dare he not enjoy what he's doing? – when really he is just a bit too shy, a bit too nervous when he's in the public eye. Nevertheless, some critics have nicknamed him 'Pedrobot', others call him 'Minnie Mick' (after relentless winner Doohan).

So does bike racing's puniest superstar – all five foot three of him – really enjoy racing or would he be just as happy/unhappy working at

McDonald's? 'For sure I enjoy racing, that's why I'm here,' he says with a quiet assuredness that characterises his answers throughout this interview. 'The thing I enjoy most is the feeling I get in myself when I finish a race, when I see my guys are happy because the team is very important to me.'

'I am not worried if Rossi retires and then my style isn't the same as his and people don't like it'

So why doesn't he smile more? 'Just because I don't always smile doesn't mean I'm not enjoying myself. I think some racers smile but they don't enjoy racing as much as me. I don't feel I'm much different to the others, I just feel that some of them show another face when they are off the bike.'

The former 125 and 250 world champ is almost certainly correct in his assumption that many racers are only acting when they play up to the crowd. They are not being real, they merely feel that it's part of their job to salute the fans and do the occasional burn-out. There is no doubt that Rossi enjoys his victory celebrations, but the Italian also knows that these shows are an investment that pays rich dividends. Barry Sheene was the same, he happily signed thousands of autographs, each and every one of them part of a career-long brand-building exercise.

Pedrosa will sign autographs and wave to the crowd but he's definitely not in the business of showbusiness. 'If making a show was natural to me, then maybe I would,' he explains. 'But when something doesn't come naturally I don't feel I have to do it to give enjoyment to other people. I am not worried if Rossi retires and then my style isn't the same as his and people don't like it.'

Quite simply, Pedrosa prefers if people appreciate him for what he does during a race, not after it. 'It is a big emotion to feel that people like you for what you do, but I like it more when I feel they like me because I have ridden a great race, not because I make a great party on the podium.' In this respect he is very similar to Lawson and Doohan (his all-time racing hero, which explains a lot), though he is less brusque and more polite than GP racing's biggest winners of the 1980s and 1990s.

And yet the 20-year-old has a big following, especially in Spain, where gangs of teenage girls throng round the back door of the Repsol Honda pit, screaming: 'Dani! Dani! Dani!', just like the Valenteeniboppers at Mugello. Pedrosa is an unlikely sex symbol and he certainly doesn't feel comfortable in the role. I ask him how he feels when he hears those strident cries. He grins widely and says: 'Suspicious!'

Not one for the groupies, then, which brings us onto the subject of girlfriends. Pedrosa reveals that he does have a girlfriend but laughs uncomfortably when I ask if she's Spanish or English. He doesn't want to answer that one. The Catalan lad is one of many MotoGP stars who choose to live in the UK to take advantage of complex EU tax laws. He recently moved into Notting Hill, London's luvvie central, and some twisted part of my mind wants to see him out on the town with the local glitterati, perhaps dating Kelly Osbourne. But the celeb circuit isn't his scene, he's more likely to be seeing a checkout girl from Tesco Metro in the Portobello Road. (Subsequent research reveals that his lady is Spanish, not English.)

'I am a simple man,' he insists. So what would be his ideal night out? 'Maybe take supper with my girl or with friends, go to the cinema, then go out and talk about the movie or anything. I mainly don't drink, except on the nights when the situation tells you this is the night to do it, but by two o'clock I am finished.'

Pedrosa is indeed an old man for his 20 summers. His racing career got serious when he was just 13, so he never enjoyed a normal, carefree adolescence. A few years ago I spotted him dining on Phillip Island with his mentor Alberto Puig, Dorna boss Carmelo Espeleta and two other fiftysomething suits. That is not a normal way for a 16-year-old to spend his Saturday nights – the poor kid looked bored to death – but that's the price you pay for doing a dream job.

He is aware that the lifestyle he has lived over the last seven years makes him somewhat abnormal but he has strategies to deal with that. Like Rossi, he prefers to hang out with old mates who treat him like Dani the childhood friend, not Dani the teeny-weeny superstar. 'People I've known since I was little don't look at me any different, so that's when I don't feel different, this is a good thing,' he says. 'But sometimes other friends make you feel different because they look at you with other eyes.'

If Pedrosa is wary of star-fucking mates and gold-digging girls, he is even more distrustful of the media. Puig has instilled much of this suspicion and rightly so, because the media is a ferociously fickle beast, bigging you up one moment, knocking you down the next. This is another reason why Pedrosa enjoys living abroad where he is relatively safe from the Spanish tabloids: 'In London I cannot read the Spanish press, which is nice'.

So this is one rider who counts no journalists among his paddock mates. In fact Pedrosa is in no hurry to make any friends in the paddock, whether they be journalists, rivals or members of his own team. 'I don't go out fishing or anything with my mechanics, we do our jobs, they go home, I go my home.' Casey Stoner, a rival in 125s, 250s and now in MotoGP, is stunned by Pedrosa's chilly paddock persona. 'He won't communicate at all or make any eye contact,' says the Aussie. 'Maybe he's got a problem with me.'

This is my second one-on-one interview with Pedrosa since he arrived in GPs in 2001. When I first interviewed him in 2002 he hardly got a word in edgeways, Puig answering most of the questions. This time Puig is again present in the interview room, along with two Repsol Honda media personnel who hover on the sidelines, apparently nervous that the interview might prove all too much for their treasured charge. In fact Pedrosa seems to enjoy the chat, absolutely confident but never cocky, sometimes funny, sometimes raising an eyebrow if he thinks I'm getting a bit too tasty with my line of questioning.

Not surprisingly, the subject of Rossi comes up several times. He is aware that MotoGP's long-time ruler has taken a few swipes at him, most famously at Donington 2006, where a journalist asked Rossi if he was excited about sharing a podium for the first time with MotoGP's up-and-coming star. 'Oh yes,' beamed Rossi. 'So excited I pissed myself!'

Pedrosa is more oblique when talking about his most famous rival, perhaps because he knows he could never win a war of words with the globally popular Italian who has been premier-class champ five times since Pedrosa arrived in GPs. I ask him if he's impressed by his MotoGP rivals. 'I think they have good talent but for sure I know other people with more talent,' he replies, referring to his childhood heroes Ayrton Senna and Lance Armstrong. Even Rossi? 'I don't know if it's talent or experience, or the team and the whole package, I just feel he's very strong and he always tries to win.' And you know Pedrosa is a real racer when he implies that Rossi's god-like status is just another target: 'For me he is a good opportunity to prove my ability as a rider.'

His abilities have so far taken him to the 125 world title at his third attempt (Rossi managed that in his second season), to the 250 title in his debut year (Rossi took two seasons to win in 250s) and to his first

MotoGP victory after just four races (Rossi took nine races to win his first 500 GP). But all he wants to say about his remarkable success is this: 'I feel very fortunate to have what I have – the bike and the team – to help me get where I am.' He doesn't want to talk about what he's good at, only what he's bad at. 'I still need to improve my riding in the rain, also my overtaking, just because these bikes are quite big and difficult to manage, and also because of the speed.' Oh yes, the speed, so how did it feel graduating from a 170mph motorcycle to a 210mph machine? 'Once you are riding full-on you forget it, but the first time you arrive at the track where you are used to riding a 250 you feel a big difference, like whoa!'

Pedrosa has adapted seamlessly from 125s to 250s to MotoGP bikes. He still uses the same spot-on, inch-perfect technique he used on 125s and 250s, maybe because he's just too small to muscle a bike around. His crew chief Mike Leitner believes he succeeds by using brains, not brawn. 'Dani is very intelligent. He is quite small so he has to ride the bike in a different way to the others. A MotoGP bike is too big and too heavy for him but he thinks and then adapts to the situation.'

No doubt Pedrosa is a thinker. But the MotoGP bullies who taunt him with cries of 'Pedrobot' don't worry him. After all, in bike racing it's probably more of a compliment to be called a robot, because that is the state that racers spend their lives working towards – being able to hit the same braking points and the same lines lap after lap after lap.

And how long before the batteries run flat on this particular robot? 'I don't know, because many things can happen,' says Pedrosa. 'But maybe my mid-30s would be a good moment to retire.' Which takes us to 2020 or thereabouts. Love him or loathe him, better get used to him...

MotoGP Mutterings: August 2006
Ducati celebrated its 60th year of motorcycle production in 2006. Big up the Bolognese!

'War, what is it good for? Absolutely nothing,' sang Edwin Starr, among others. He was right, of course. Well, up to a point. Because if it hadn't been for the US Air Force bombing the hell out of the Ducati factory in 1944 we would never have got to see the

'If the US Air Force hadn't bombed the hell out of the Ducati factory in 1944 we would never have got to see the wondrous 916'

wondrous 916 or watch Loris Capirossi grappling with his loopy Desmosedici.

Until the USAF appeared over Bologna 62 years ago, Ducati had no interest in bikes. Inspired by local electronics genius Guglielmo Marconi, the Ducati brothers manufactured radios, electric shavers, cameras and condensers. Mussolini was well impressed when he visited the factory in 1940, so much so that Ducati was pressed into manufacturing military equipment, first by Mussolini, then, after the Italians surrendered in 1943, by the Nazis. Hence the 1944 visit by hundreds of Flying Fortresses in the aptly named Operation Pancake.

With their factory flattened and the war over, the Ducati brothers decided to build a new factory and have a go at making motorcycles to get war-ravaged Italy back on the road. Their first bike, Il Cucciolo (the Puppy), was no more than a bicycle with a tiny 1.5bhp engine attached, very similar to Soichiro Honda's first bike, the Putt Putt, also created in 1946.

Strange beginnings for a company now nicknamed 'the Ferrari of motorcycling', the only biking brand outside Japan capable of humbling the mighty Honda. Ducati's achievements in racing – both in MotoGP and World Superbike – are remarkable when you consider the size of the company. In a good year the Bolognese production lines make 40,000 bikes, while Honda churns out several million.

But to fully understand Ducati's racetrack prowess you need to look at some different numbers. Of Ducati's 1000 staff, 100 (or 10 per cent) work at Ducati Corse, while 125 engineers toil at Honda Racing Corporation, around 0.4 per cent of Honda's 30,000 workforce. And if you can't understand why Kawasaki Heavy Industries can't kick arse in MotoGP, try these numbers for size – Kawasaki's race shop numbers just 30 souls, or 0.075 per cent of KHI's 40,000 workers. So Ducati's commitment to racing is 25 times greater than Honda's and 130 times bigger than Kawasaki's.

In other words, Ducati is a large race shop with a smallish production line attached. And the company lives or dies by its race results. Few people remember that just two decades ago Ducati seemed doomed to collapse. Two things saved it from those dark days – the seminal 748cc eight-valve v-twin built by Massimo Bordi, understudy to the legendary Fabio Taglioni, and the creation of the World Superbike series. Bordi's 748 begat the 851 which begat the 888 which begat the 916, while WSB provided the stage upon which Ducati showed the world what it could do. And World Supers success allowed Ducati to dare to dream that they might also humble biking's Japanese overlords in MotoGP.

During its 60-year history Ducati has been through more ups and downs and ins and outs, through more hairpin bends and multiple pile-ups than an Italian autostrada or parliament. And it may well always be so, because while Ducati bosses talk in public about passion ('Our company is glued together by passion,' says CEO Federico Minoli, which sounds a bit messy), behind closed doors they probably talk more about private equity. The factory has just changed hands again, back in Italian ownership after some years with US backers.

Coincidentally, Ducati's museum was completed at about the same time. The final piece of the jigsaw – a 1956 triple camshaft desmo 125 GP bike – was recently discovered in the corner of a French garage where it had been for four decades. The museum – almost certainly Europe's best collection of race bikes – is worth a visit, packed with everything from Cucciolos to Hailwood's TT-winning 900SS, half a dozen Foggy Superbikes and Capirossi's MotoGP machine. The museum is cool, dark and quiet, like a chapel, and crammed with relics and icons, including the very drawing board at which Taglioni worked.

It is perhaps odd that Ducati has only recently awoken to the value of its history, because while machines like the Desmosedici RR convince the world of its technical brilliance, perhaps its financial saviour will be bikes like the Sport Classics which emulate the Harley model of building low-tech bikes that command premium prices.

Let's just hope, however, that Ducati doesn't cheapen its legend too much by copying Harley in flogging cratefuls of Harley shaving cream at Tesco. I'm not optimistic, however, because Ferrari has already started selling its own brand of aftershave called, wait for it, 'Passion'.

CHAPTER 49

STONER: 'I EXPECTED IT TO TAKE TWO YEARS, NOT TWO RACES'

August 2006

Casey Stoner's debut MotoGP campaign proved he had the speed to race with the best, but problems with his equipment also caused him to crash, so what went right and what went wrong for MotoGP's hottest new star in 2006?

Aussie youngster Casey Stoner has always had the mark of genius about him and now he's made his mark on MotoGP. The 20-year-old qualified on pole for the 2006 Qatar GP, making him the second youngest premier-class pole-sitter after American legend Freddie Spencer. 'I expected it to take two years to get a pole, not two races,' said the former 125 and 250 GP winner who went on to lead that race until leg cramps and a dose of the 'flu slowed him. Eventual victor Valentino Rossi was stunned by the new boy's speed: 'He was racing like he's been in this class for ten years'. Stoner's secret? An even earlier start to his career than Rossi: 'I was doing the throttle of a Pee Wee when I was 18 months old, my cousin sitting on the back.' Youth may be wasted on the young, as nineteenth-century Irish wit Oscar Wilde once opined, but not always.

So Stoner and his LCR Honda made their mark with impressive speed during 2006, though they also made a few dents in MotoGP's surrounding scenery. But like the feisty Australian says, people shouldn't criticise him for trying too hard. And Stoner always tries hard. He is the exact opposite of former 250 rival Dani Pedrosa. He is not reticent, he never likes to take a step back, he is always on the attack. His style is all-action, from the moment he leaves pit lane to when he returns. And he's the same off the bike, happy to fire off a volley at anyone who dares criticise his riding. Excellent, the paddock needs people like that!

Do you enjoy MotoGP more than you enjoyed 125s and 250s?
It's a little bit more my style, what I've grown up to deal with, which is

dirt track – sliding and moving the bike around. That way of riding is a little more enjoyable for me, so I feel more relaxed on these bikes.

So your dirt-track training is now coming into play?
With MotoGP bikes it's not so much to do with the settings. Of course, you've still got to get the best setting you can, but it's not all to do with that. At the end of the day you can ride what you've got and still be competitive, whereas with 125s and 250s it's very hard to make up the time if your settings aren't any good.

We have more time to work on set-up in MotoGP but if it's not perfect going into the race you can still get a good result out of it. If you don't have the setting pretty much perfect in 125s and 250s you're pretty well buggered for the race. In MotoGP it's a little easier to pull it out of the bag if the bike isn't perfect, as you've seen Rossi do many times. He qualifies terrible, then wins the race.

In MotoGP the main thing you've got to do is get the power to the ground and towards the end of the race is when that gets real important. If you've got the riding style and a good feeling to get the power to the ground, you can pretty much make whatever you want out of the bike.

Does your style change much during the course of a race?
Yeah, at the start of the race you trust the tyres a little bit more and you push the bike into the corners a little bit more because the tyres are there. Towards the end of the race you take it a little easier, you just try and concentrate on getting the rear grip to hook up and that makes a lot of time.

Is that easy with traction control?
I don't know what the Yamaha and the other bikes are like. With the Honda the traction control is there to a certain degree but it doesn't help a heck of a lot. Yeah, when the tyres are terrible at the end of a race then it can help because it saves you energy and you don't have to concentrate so hard on keeping the thing hooked up. But the bikes are a lot more powerful than anything else around so they need traction control, if you didn't have it the tyres would be buggered in a few laps, so it definitely helps when the tyres aren't great.

In practice at the Sachsenring my traction control wasn't working but I was only a couple of tenths off what I was normally doing. It's no big deal; personally I just think it stops a lot of highsides and, yeah, instead of the tyre constantly spinning when it steps out, it only lets it go to that certain place and it's still hookin' you up.

Are you impressed by the riders in MotoGP?
Yeah, definitely. I'm impressed by the fact that every week they're up front and they're always fighting hard, there's no easy race. In 125s or 250s, if you have a good set-up and some people are having a bad day, that's it, they're nowhere to be seen. In MotoGP everyone has a good day at every race pretty much, they're always running up front. That's the hardest thing to get your head around.

Who impresses you the most?
Valentino, of course, and I've got a lot of respect for Dani. What Dani has done this year is very impressive, I'm kind of proud to step up to MotoGP at the same time as him. He is running second in the championship in his first year; he can't really be too upset about that. If I had finished the races I hadn't finished I'd be in a lot better place as well, but we didn't come in this season to even think of running where we are running, so I've got to be happy with what we are doing.

Do you gauge yourself against Dani?
Not really, because we're racing so many more people. Last year in 250s it was kinda just us two consistently running up front. In MotoGP the top five are always running up front, it's a lot harder work, it's not just between me and him.

Are you mates?
We used to be until we were in the same class. He doesn't seem to communicate with me, at all, or make any eye contact. I've never had a problem with him and I respect him as a racer, but maybe he's got a problem with me. I don't know why, maybe because we came through at the same time. We both came through Alberto Puig's schooling. But I've got no problems with him and at one stage we got on pretty well.

Are you sad you never got to race 500s?
I'm sure Dani's got the same opinion as me. I'm a little frustrated with what some other riders have been saying, like we wouldn't be going

anywhere near as well as we are now if we were on 500s, that you've got to ride the 500s differently, stand them up more and all the rest of it, but at a lot of the tracks Dani and I are standing our bikes up more than the seasoned guys, so they can't really tell us we wouldn't have been good on 500s. I think everyone should keep their opinions to themselves until they're proven. I would really have liked to stayed two-stroke and raced 500s. I mean, I'm impressed with the four-strokes and what their power is like, but I would say that they are a lot easier to rider than the 500s. I would've liked to have tried the savage power of the 500s, I suppose.

Who is your coach these days?
I just do my own thing, I have been for a few years now. I'm getting along really well with my chief mechanic, we have a lot of the same opinions and we're doing a good job. Nobody coaches me now, when I know I'm doing something wrong, I sort it out. I don't like it when a few people in the team are afraid of telling me what they really think, I'd like people to be more honest with me and also people to understand what I'm going through a little bit more.

You didn't used to enjoy life on the road, but is it different now you're an adult?
I've been on the road since I was 14 and that aspect of my life has definitely improved. It's nice when I go home to chill out and relax a bit. I definitely wouldn't have it any other way, I love my racing and being in this class, especially because I can be up front week in, week out because I'm on a good bike that's consistent. Every time I go on the track it's the same.

Do you drive now?
No, I don't have a car now. I've had a licence since I was 16. I can drive in Europe but I don't have a car because I'm on a plane every week. Next year I'll have my fiancée over here, she'll be my wife by then, and then we should drive to a few races.

Where do you live?
Since the beginning of last year I've lived in Monaco, basically because it's near Lucio's workshop, plus it's very central for Europe, so it seemed a good option. I've also bought a house back home near my parents' place where I stay when I go home, it's a really nice spot.

What do you do with your time off?
Nothing. Well, I either train or do nothing. It should be a lot better next year. With my wife over, we'll be able to trip around and see a bit of Europe.

Do you go out?
I'm more of a stay at home and watch a movie guy. Party life has never really been mine. I tried it for a bit but absolutely hated it. I tried it a few years ago when I was travelling around with friends from the paddock. But I never really liked it because I don't drink so I ended up holding the drinks for everyone else and keeping an eye on them, that was about it.

What's your dream scenario for 2007?
I'd like to stay where I am, maybe on a bit better machinery, then have a real shot at a top three in the championship, that would be a realistic aim. I might not get there but it would be a good thing to aim at.

'I'd like to have a real shot at a top three in the championship. I might not get there but it would be a good thing to aim at'

Who is your manager now?
My dad, always has been. We seem to be doing an alright job to get where we are by ourselves.

You've had a few crashes this year; why?
To tell you the truth the last couple of crashes I've had I've been very disappointed with. They all seem to be losing the front end and I haven't been very happy with the way I have been riding from that aspect. At the beginning of the season I wasn't too worried when I had a few spills in practice and qualifying but now I've been getting a bit frustrated that I've made those mistakes in the last few races. Hopefully we can make some better results without the mistakes in the last part of the season.

You also crashed a bit in 125s and 250s?
I was running up front quite consistently and I didn't have a factory bike. I made some mistakes but it also got me to where I am today, so no one can point a finger at me for what I did wrong.

What's happening with the front-end crashes?
It's quite hard to lose the rear with these bikes just because of the throttle control you've got and how much wheelspin they've got. So I suppose what you've got left is to push the front end to get the time out of the bike. The last few front-end crashes I've had I can't really understand exactly why they happened, so it's something I need to learn. I just need to spend a bit more time on the bike. I'm sure I will find where the limit is in those areas and draw back from it a little bit. Like I said, we have been doing a lot better than we expected and now I know I'm capable of running up front and that's all that matters, so we can't be unhappy.

What have been your most memorable crashes?
There have been a couple that have hurt me a bit. Just like a horse, you get bucked off and you get back on and you don't let it beat you. A lot of people when they crash it goes straight to their heads and they're a bit wary for a while but it doesn't bother me too much. I know what mistake I've made and try not to do it again.

You're always fast from the get-go, at Laguna you were fastest for a while in your very first session at the track. How's that?
A lot of people criticise me for going too fast, too early. Yeah, I might be a lot faster than people at the beginning of practice and maybe everyone thinks I'm going too fast but we were still a good two or three seconds from the eventual pace so I'm really not going that quick. I just go quicker sooner but it's never at that stage of the weekend when I'm crashing. People should stop criticising me for that as well. I just learn the tracks a lot quicker, I learn naturally, it's no big deal to do those times so soon.

CHAPTER 50

THE JB MANTRA:
KEEP IT SIMPLE, STUPID

November 2006

Jeremy Burgess is the most successful GP engineer of the modern age, winner of 11 premier-class crowns with Valentino Rossi, Mick Doohan and Wayne Gardner. This is how JB learned his legendary problem-solving skills

Engines and engineering would seem to run in Jeremy Burgess' blood. A century before JB won his first world championship with Wayne Gardner in 1987, his great-uncles David and John Shearer were creating Australia's first motor car, a wood-burning, steam-driven vehicle equipped with a differential, a decade before Henry Ford's seminal Tin Lizzy featured a diff. The Shearer creation now takes pride of place in Australia's national motor museum, near Adelaide, JB's hometown.

'The car looks like anything that Benz built in the first days when all those guys realised that trains ran on rails and that a smaller steam engine would drive something on the road,' says Burgess, a self-taught engineer who isn't so sure that engines do run in his blood. He reckons his love of engineering is a factor of nurture, not nature, of his growing up on the family farm, surrounded by agricultural machinery.

'My father always insisted that my mechanical knowledge came from the Shearers but my brother is a lawyer and my sister is a doctor, so I'm not so sure,' he adds. 'I think any young bloke growing up on a farm in the Adelaide hills with machinery all around would've picked up on all of that.'

What seems more certain is that the rough and tumble of rural Aussie life and then of the Aussie bike-racing circuit equipped JB with the ability and the resolve to get stuck in and solve problems quickly. Where others get sidetracked by the bullshit and complexity of modern racing, JB always gets to the nub. It is this no-nonsense attitude and a straight-forward intelligence that has made him bike racing's most successful engineer of the past two decades. Burgess followed Gardner's 1987 500 title with a further ten premier-class world championships between 1994 and 2005, five with Mick Doohan and five with Valentino Rossi.

JB started his love affair with internal combustion engineering at eight years old, in 1961. 'I was driving at eight and bought my first car at 12. The idea of buying the car, as the old man saw it, was to tinker with it, but my idea was to get it going as fast as we could and milk his tank for petrol.'

At 15 he got his first bike, an ancient Velocette scrambler. 'Someone had converted it to run on alcohol and it kept bending valves, so we played around with that.' He didn't know it at the time but he was getting sucked in. He bought his first road bike, a Suzuki T500 twin, a year or so later, and then a Kawasaki 750 triple in 1972. 'Your first years out of school you never really know what you're going to do and I don't know why I suddenly went out and bought a Mach 4 but I did and as soon as I got it I was racing it. I suppose my mates were doing it, that was the starting point, then you realise you enjoy it. Some things just take over your life.'

'I was exceptionally close to getting conscripted for Vietnam, but I was going to dodge it, anyway'

It might all have ended there if JB had been conscripted to join the Australian army, which was mired in Vietnam with the Americans. 'I was exceptionally close to getting conscripted. I had to register by December 31 1973 to come up for the draft in the first six months of the next year, but fortunately our government changed in December and we didn't have to worry about it. I wasn't going to register anyway, I was going to dodge it. My father had always said he didn't raise two sons to have them killed in a stupid war.'

Saved from Vietnam, JB got serious about racing. He bought two TZ350s to go with the Kawa triple, then in 1976 traded them in for one of Suzuki's new RG500s. He was earning good money working for a drilling company and the local brickworks, winning plenty of races and driving plenty of miles – 26 hours to Perth, 23 hours to Surfers Paradise on the Gold Coast. 'Racing consumed me. I felt I was pretty good at it, I made it all the way to A grade pretty quickly, where I was up against guys like Gregg Hansford, the Willing brothers, John Woodley and Kenny Blake, all the guys who went on to Europe.'

JB decided he needed more horsepower to stay with this remarkable generation of Aussie riders, so he sold the RG in 1979 and bought a TZ750. 'It wasn't the smartest thing I ever did. Compared to the Suzuki the TZ didn't have the calibre, it just wasn't a purebred racing motorcycle like the RG, it was cheap, but they made bucket loads of them and they did a good job.'

By now JB was starting to dream about joining Hansford and the rest in Europe. But in the end he made the trip as a holidaymaker, not as a racer. His own racing career lost momentum after his travelling companion got killed in a streetbike crash. 'I never retired, I just stopped doing it!' At the end of '79 JB sold his race bikes, took six weeks off work and headed to Europe, part holiday, part recce, just in case he decided to continue racing. Inevitably his savings ran out sooner than expected and he applied for a job as mechanic to racing prodigy Randy Mamola, who had just signed for Suzuki.

JB's bike preparation in Australian championship racing had always been immaculate and it was this reputation that got him the job working on Mamola's factory RG500s. 'The guys at Suzuki knew my RG ran when others broke,' says JB, who still works by his father's axiom, the five Ps: perfect preparation prevents poor performance. So his fascination with all things mechanical was starting to pay big dividends and had put him on the road to world-class success. 'When I was racing back home, mates would drive up the driveway with their girlfriends and I'd be up to my elbows in a TZ gearbox or an RG rotary valve or whatever. They'd hang around for half an hour and then go off, but I never felt compelled to drop the tools and go with them, I was doing what I wanted to do.'

Burgess fettled Mamola's bikes for three years, winning five GPs, then when Suzuki downsized to a one-man team in 1983 he got a job with HRC, spannering for Ron Haslam. He worked with Freddie Spencer during the American's unique 250/500 title-winning year in 1985 and got his first crew chief job with Gardner the following season. In 1987 JB and the Wollongong wild one defeated reigning champ Eddie Lawson to win the 500 title. In 1989 Burgess was assigned the task of honing Honda's new signing, the fast but scary Doohan. The pair won five back-to-back titles from 1994, then when Doohan quit in 1999, HRC signed Rossi and put him to work with Burgess. Some critics suggest that JB has been lucky to work with genius riders, but that's nonsense; HRC understood his talent for getting the best out of both man and machine and thus gave him their most valuable riders.

JB's winning secret: don't complicate things

Burgess is famously blunt ('When you say I'm blunt, do you mean rude?') because he believes there's no time in racing for cloaking what he's got to say in diplomacy. If something's not right or someone's not doing their job properly, he calls a spade a bloody spade. His insistence on always standing his ground – even when he's working with a superstar rider – gets him respect and results.

But it is his problem-solving abilities that have contributed most to his success, and JB believes that this talent comes from his days of making do. 'When I worked for that drilling company we were always in the bush. So you're 500 miles from the city and you can't get a new part, so you've got to fix what you've got, so you heat it, weld it, cut it, whatever. The mentality is there – how can we keep it going?'

Although the make-do mentality no longer applies in top-level racing where parts mileage is automatically logged by computer and everything is replaced in good time, the process of thinking your way through problems does still count. JB's approach is always straightforward, unlike many engineers who seem to get too caught up in the complexity of it all, and it is ironic that the more complicated racing becomes, the more vital it is to have a simple approach. Burgess is a big picture man, always determined to simplify and demystify, so here comes another favourite maxim: the KISS principle – keep it simple, stupid.

'It's the same in all sports,' he says. 'Look at soccer, there are three sides to the game – when they've got the ball, when you've got the ball and when no one's got the ball. How much more difficult than that can it be? It's the same in motorcycle racing, everything on a motorcycle is mechanical, so it either works or it doesn't. Every rider is going to have problems, and problems are only questions that don't have answers, so you find the answer. And when your rider comes into the pits he's always going to speak about his biggest problem first, otherwise he's a complete nitwit. It's that simple. Maybe I'm so dumb I can only see the big things but I think you should fix your bigger problems first and then you move on. A lot of people get wound up about small things.'

JB's job is to oversee the weekend's work, making sure that a dozen Yamaha engineers, a Michelin tyre engineer, an Öhlins suspension technician and Rossi's mechanics are all working together to get the best result. 'If I was to describe myself, I'm the non-specific guy,' he explains. 'A modern racing motorcycle is so sophisticated that it's impossible for one or two or even three men to work on it, it demands much more than that, but there has to be someone who has an understanding and a feeling for what the rider is trying to explain. Over the years I've become Valentino when Valentino goes back to his motorhome because the data engineer taking the information off the computer needs someone there to tell him what Valentino was saying. There's a lot to be done, so someone has to organise and prioritise how much time we can give between one practice and the next on a particular problem and what steps we're going to take to reduce that problem.'

JB'S dream garage

Like most people in MotoGP, Burgess thinks much more about the future than the past: 'We're always pushing into the space age, going faster and faster,' he says. But when he finally retires in a few years, he's all set to take a little trip down memory lane.

'Currently all I've got in the shed is a CB1100RC (legendary early 1980s superbike) and a KE175 trail bike but in the next few years I'd like to pick up one or two pieces that are of interest to me. My dream garage would start off with a car, a Mk2 Jaguar. It wouldn't be difficult to do one of them in cherry condition. Then a '69 Bonneville, I've always wanted one of them. And I wouldn't mind putting together a bike that no one ever talks about anymore, the T500 Suzuki, because I had one years back and the bike's got a lot of history. Any more than that and you're in trouble.'

Typically, JB refuses to get excited about the exorbitant prices currently being achieved by old race bikes. 'Both my TZ750 and my RG have been restored by others and sold. The RG went the other day for $33,000 and the 750 went for similar money. But if I'd put the money in the bank when I sold the bikes, with compound interest it'd come up to almost 30 grand anyway. These bikes sound expensive but they aren't really.'

MotoGP Mutterings: *November 2006*
Two-strokes were banned from MotoGP at the end of 2006 – a good thing or a bad thing, depending on which way you look at it

So it's goodbye to the 990s – the fastest race bikes ever seen on this planet are to be dumped in the dustbin of racing history. No doubt Valentino Rossi was on the money when he said: 'Maybe we are lucky to be racing these bikes, because soon they will become legend'.

The 990s aren't the only monsters being regulated into extinction. While robbing us of wondrous machines like Honda's RC211V, the powers that be (that's the Motorcycle Sports Manufacturers' Association) have also taken the chance to quietly rid MotoGP of two-strokes from 1 January 2007. That's right, for the first time in more than half a century of GP racing, two-strokes are to be banned from the premier class. As Rossi's crew chief Jeremy Burgess says: 'You only ban things when you're scared of them'.

Of course, the writing had been on the wall since 2002, when the MSMA welcomed back four-strokes with a 98 per cent capacity advantage over the 500cc strokers. But while the two-strokes have been living on death row, I've liked to dream that some rogue cell within HRC was secretly toiling away on a wildly updated NSR500 that would humble the 990s, bankrolled by some Yakuza drugs baron who goes all watery-eyed on recalling his teenage years spent popping wheelies on his RD350LC through the Tokyo night. Perhaps my dream was more than mere fantasy, however, because some Japanese engineers strongly protested against favouring the four-strokes so heavily. If the 'diesels' get 990cc, so should the 'stinkwheels', they argued. Rough calculations suggested an NSR990 would make 420 horsepower…

But we may as well stop dreaming because it isn't going to happen. Two-strokes have now been banished to the cheap end of the GP paddock, away from the high-gloss MotoGP pits and VIP units to the 250 and 125 ghettos. No bubble-wrapped motors air-freighted from Japan for these people, only blood, sweat and riffler files.

There is definitely a romance that hangs around two-stroke GP bikes. Engines are still stripped after every practice session (despite detonation sensors and endoscopes) so that mechanics can pore over pistons, carefully examining burn patterns, like gypsies reading tea leaves. And then these 21st century sorcerers open caskets of strange treasures – main jets and needle jets – and put their hands upon bizarre devices – reed valves and rotary valves – as they chase performance nirvana. No wonder mechanics love them. 'I enjoy two-strokes more,' says Brit Trevor Morris who used to work on Nicky Hayden's RCVs but now looks after Yuki Takahashi's Honda RS250s. 'Even my kids notice it because I come home with a smile on my face. It's more demanding, it's more involved, you feel like you're a mechanic, not a parts fitter.'

And there is more. Two-stroke advocates argue that the acute nature of the two-stroke race bike – both in its set-up and behaviour – educates racers better. This is why, they say, MotoGP is packed with former 125 and 250 riders, not ex-Superbike or Supersport men. 'Top MotoGP guys come from categories in which you don't just use the bike, you must know about set-up,' says Harald Bartol, KTM's 125 and 250 engineer. 'To me, 600s is donkey racing. A 600 is not a race bike, it's not a race-horse.' The ACU, who axed the 250 British series in favour of 600s, should ponder Bartol's words as they consider the lack of British talent in MotoGP.

But perhaps it won't always be so. Racing technology is getting so good that a two-stroke education may soon be unnecessary. Burgess adds that MotoGP engines are already largely 'self-adjusting'. And Morris admits that while changing a gearbox ratio by less than 2mph can crucially affect a two-stroke's performance, 4mph either way is fine on a MotoGP bike. So who needs the finely trained ear of a two-stroke racer? Then there is Bartol complaining that some KTM GP rookies who don't even know when an engine has seized. But there's good reason for this. Massive improvements in lubrication, carburation and metallurgy mean that youngsters may never have experienced a seizure, so they don't have ears tuned to anticipate the stroker's death rattle or the gunslinger clutch-hand reactions that may have saved their lives a few decades ago.

The 250s and 125s aren't set to disappear from GPs any time now (250s are safe till 2012, 125s to 2014) but they will go eventually, which will be a tragedy because there is nothing more graceful on a racetrack than a 250 GP bike. But as for two-stroke romance? Try that on someone stuck in, say, rush-hour Jakarta surrounded by a thousand ancient mopeds belching poisonous smoke, their throats on fire and all but blinded by tears…

CHAPTER 51

PRO-AM: THE PRODUCT OF A SICK AND TWISTED MIND

March 2007

Yamaha's infamous one-make 350LC series stunned TV viewers with its scary on-track violence and made stars out of young British riders

Yamaha's Pro-Am championship was Britain's most notorious race series of the early 1980s, a crazed one-make championship apparently created by some sick and twisted mind to cause maximum mayhem and carnage for sensation-hungry TV viewers.

Pro-Am was dreamed up by the British Yamaha importers to promote a motorcycle that needed no promotion – the company's race-developed RD250LC and RD350LC were the nation's most lusted-after motorcycles even before the series made it onto ITV's *World of Sport* during the summer of 1981.

Of course, Pro-Am wasn't just genius lowbrow TV entertainment, it also played a significant role in building our racing stars of the 1980s. In 1987 Britain had five factory riders in the 500 world championship – Niall Mackenzie, Rob McElnea, Kenny Irons, Roger Burnett and Ron Haslam – and all but Rocket Ron had cut their teeth and sharpened their elbows in Pro-Am.

One-make racing championships weren't anything new. France's Coupe Kawasaki had bred stars like Christian Sarron and Patrick Pons during the 1970s, and British club racing was already effectively a one-make affair with LCs dominating from Knockhill to Brands Hatch. But Pro-Am was unique because the specially chosen riders, supposedly the cream of young British talent, turned up at each race and were allocated bikes by lucky dip, the riders picking ignition keys out of a helmet. Tuning and cheating were thus impossible, so the racing was always stupidly close.

Pro-Am was motorcycling's bastard offspring of the movie *Rollerball*, a kind of *X Factor* with GBH: take 25 of the nation's most promising,

most desperate under-24 racers, give them free motorcycles and tell
them they don't have to fix them when they crash, offer them foolishly
generous prize money and broadcast the racing on national TV at a
time when very little bike racing made it onto the box. It was a recipe
for disaster and great television with crashes aplenty and ten-rider
dogfights for the lead. They even used to get Barry Sheene to do the
commentary. 'Blimey,' he'd say. 'You need a Valium to watch this.'

'You were racing against criminals, drunkards, bike thieves...'

With no way of gaining a technical advantage over
your rivals, Pro-Am came down to knees, elbows and
some of the dirtiest riding ever seen on a racetrack. The
organisers did their best to keep it clean but roadracing,
and especially production bike racing, were already
pretty loose at that time, just like life itself with Britain
in a state of high anxiety, experiencing desperately high
unemployment, nationwide inner-city rioting and the
death throes of punk rock. As Mackenzie remembers: 'Proddie racing was
really aggressive back then, everyone was completely mad, you were racing
against criminals, drunkards, bike thieves and good people as well.'

I got a Pro-Am ride in 1983 after a successful season of LC club racing,
by which time the more experienced riders had sharpened their ferocious
tactics to a knife point. I was one of the Ams, baby-faced hopefuls
embarking on national careers after success at club level, while the Pros
were established national riders like Mackenzie, Irons and Ray Swann.
So I was the kid moving up to big school, gawping wide-eyed at the
badness of the older boys. And they were bad, very bad; I'd never
experienced such murderousness and vindictiveness on the racetrack.

You were never safe in a Pro-Am race. Into corners, through corners
and out of corners there were always a few homicidal maniacs to your
left, a villainous fool or two to your right. Even the straights were free-
for-alls, you'd be riding along, stretching the throttle cable to breaking
point when the revs would drop and the bike would break into a weave
because some idiot you'd just outbraked into the previous corner had
snuck into your draft, grabbed hold of your LC's pillion grabrail and was
in the process of hauling himself past you, with a speed advantage of,
oooh, maybe half a mile an hour. And that was the nice bit. If he did
manage to maintain his momentum despite you getting busy with your
knees and elbows, he might nudge your kill switch as he sneaked ahead,
not good if there's another half dozen riders chasing your slipstream. Or

he might just give you the old front-end chop, swerving violently into your path as he slipped ahead, forcing you to momentarily shut the throttle to avoid impact or risk a potentially disastrous high-speed collision. Mackenzie again: 'I remember a big one coming onto the start-finish at Donington. I cut the nose off Steve Chambers and had a bit of a wobble, he crashed and slid halfway down the straight...'

The fact that the bikes were so slow only made things worse. Most Pro-Am men were up-and-coming 250 riders, plying their trade on Yamaha TZs or Rotax 250s (I had a Waddon, a tandem-twin Rotax with a length of curtain rail for a chassis that seized frequently, hurling me over the handlebars), so they felt invincible at the LC's top speed of 110mph. There were other, less savage ways of squeezing more speed out of the two-stroke twins – some riders were convinced they could gain a few mph by lying flat on the bike, feet dangling past the tail light.

Often the leaders would speed down a straight five or six abreast, taking long, hard looks at each other, psyching themselves up for another game of chicken that would begin when the first rider took fright and hit the brakes. The latest brakers would hurtle towards the corner, forks fully bottomed-out and juddering madly, rear ends yawing crazily and only when it seemed far too late would they dare tip into the turn, tyres sliding, bikes bucking, handlebars tangling. In such close encounters it wasn't unusual for the leader to slip four or five places in one corner, then regain the lead a few corners later.

For this reason Pro-Am wasn't the greatest of racing schools. The LCs were slow and very easy to ride, so classy riding techniques were always vanquished by naked aggression. Of course, the fastest way round a racetrack was nice and smooth with big arcing lines but you never got the chance to ride like that. There was always someone trying to come up the inside or around the outside, so you had to ride tight, defensive lines or cruel, vicious attacking lines, depending on the situation.

True, Pro-Am did teach racers plenty about overtaking but it was more useful for promotional purposes. It gave wild young men the chance to prove themselves in a high-profile championship that enjoyed massive TV coverage, though there were downsides to the live broadcasts. 'I was bunking off work to go racing at Donington,' recalls Mackenzie. 'ITV were showing the Pro-Am race live, so my boss was sitting watching me on telly while I was meant to be digging holes for the electricity board. My cover was blown.'

Riders like Mackenzie used Pro-Am as a shop window to woo sponsors and they also survived on the championship's generous prize money. First place paid a dazzling £500 at a time when ninth or tenth place in a British TT F1 race would pay £10. Mackenzie reckons that the Pro-Am booty helped him to quit digging holes and turn professional in 1983.

Such was the championship's success that it inevitably spawned spin-offs, including pan-European Pro-Am finals and a Two–Four challenge consisting of an LC race and an MG Maestro race (this was indisputably the funniest motorsport event ever, with Pro-Am riders trashing a dozen Maestros and possibly contributing to British Leyland's ultimate demise). I never got to race a Maestro but I did make the five-strong British team for the 1983 European final as top-placed Am, thanks in part to a third-place finish at Snetterton behind Mackenzie and Irons.

The '83 Euro final at Hockenheim was Pro-Am insanity on an international scale. Mackenzie, Irons and Graeme Cannell ganged up on the French favourite during practice, hunting him down on one of the German track's autobahn-like straights and running him onto the grass at high speed. He returned to the pits a tearful, gibbering wreck and never bothered them again.

Obviously the bad boys of the British crew behaved just as disgracefully off the track, getting drunk, crashing hire cars and devising ever more mendacious ways of dealing with their rivals. With the fastest Frenchman out of the running, their main concern was fifth Brit Steve Chambers, a quiet, well-behaved racer who steered well clear of his ne'er-do-well compatriots. They messed with his head by slipping a local hooker into his hotel room at 3am on race day. That afternoon Cannell beat Chambers by a fraction, Mackenzie fourth, me nowhere.

The British series enjoyed its final year in 1984. Since then there have been several other one-make race series but none has ever caught the imagination quite like Pro-Am.

How Pro-Am helped build Britain's stars of the 1980s
The Pro-Am entry list reads like a who's who of 1980s and 1990s racing stardom. Niall Mackenzie, Rob McElnea, Kenny Irons and Roger Burnett all went on to contest 500 GPs on factory bikes, while Alan Carter went one better and actually won a GP and Damon Hill went on to win the 1996 Formula One car title, 14 years after he had thrashed a humble LC around Cadwell and Snetterton. Then there were Graeme

Cannell, Andy Watts, Kevin 'Mad Dog' Mitchell, Steve Chambers, Ray Swann, Mark Phillips, Neil Robinson, Alex Bedford, Gary Padgett and Pete Wild, all great racers, several of them sadly no longer with us.

But what role did Pro-Am play in building the careers of these youngsters? 'The championship was certainly good, it really set me up,' says Mackenzie, who began his Pro-Am career in 1981 as an amateur. 'But it may have only been coincidence that so many of us made it into 500 GPs.'

McElnea, who contested the inaugural Pro-Am season as a pro, is convinced the series did help the amateurs make it big. 'It was just a bit of a laugh for the pros but it really did help the ams, it put them in the shop window and the money was big,' says Rob Mac, who now runs Yamaha's one-make R6 series. 'Pro-Am was perfect for them because they were desperate to make a name for themselves and they did exactly that because they were racing on a premier-league stage.'

The RD350LC: 'You could get away with murder'
The real star of the Pro-Am championship was Yamaha's RD350LC, the liquid-cooled successor to the air-cooled RD400 and loosely based on the factory's TZ race bikes. The 350LC and its 250 sibling were the perfect proddie race bikes and dominated British club racing for years. In Pro-Am form they were pretty much bog-standard, fitted with number plates and Dunlop TT100 tyres. And there was no chance of cheating because riders weren't even allowed to touch the bikes allocated to them for that race.

'The LC was way ahead of its time,' says Niall Mackenzie. 'I ride one now and it's still an okay road bike. Back then the LC had good suspension, good grip and handled well. They were really forgiving so we could stay on board, most of the time, anyway.'

'I would ride hard for a few laps till the tyres went all funny and then go "fuck this!" It was mental'

Rob McElnea adds: 'We used to thrash the fuck out of them all the time, it was terrible. They were a mega bike, but they were all over the shop as soon as the tyres got warm, they were really scary going down Craner at Donington. I'd never raced on road tyres so I would ride hard for a few laps till the tyres went all funny and then go "fuck this!" It was mental. But you could ride them so hard and they'd just float all over the place, you could get away with murder on them.'

CHAPTER 52

'EVERYTHING NOW IS SYNTHESIZED – THE TT IS THE REAL THING

May 2007

British racer Nick Jefferies – who experienced both joy and misery during four decades of racing in the Isle of Man TT – explains why he has never stopped loving the world's most dangerous race

Nick Jefferies only scored one Isle of Man TT victory but for many years he was Mr TT. Always a staunch defender of racing on the Island, he raced the Mountain circuit every year from 1975 to 2003, starting 18 Manx GPs, 67 TTs and scoring 18 TT podiums, including that F1 win in 1993. During those years he rode pretty much everything – from official Yamahas and Hondas to the Britten and a BMW K100 proddie bike.

Jefferies, now in his 50s, comes from a Yorkshire family in the north of England that is inextricably linked to the event, through both glory and tragedy. His father Allan rode his first TT in 1933 and finished second to Geoff Duke in his last, the 1949 Clubmans Senior TT. His brother Tony won three TTs in the early 1970s and his nephew Dave became an Island great by scoring three consecutive hat tricks from 1999 to 2002 before losing his life in a high-speed crash during practice for the 2003 races. Remarkably, Jefferies was back on the Island just a couple of months after DJ's death, doing the Manx GP classic race aboard a Manx Norton.

You grew up in a TT family; what made it so attractive?
It's the nearest thing to riding your road bike on that imaginary road you had in mind when you were falling asleep at night, that road in Wales or Scotland or wherever, where you could really have a go. The TT did all that for me. Before I started racing, when I was trials riding, I was always tear-arsing around the Yorkshire roads. I had my own imaginary TT course, of similar length to the TT, and I used to go out in

the early mornings or late evenings and time myself around this route. I was probably a menace to all road users. So when I first rode the TT, the circuit was so good compared to what I'd been doing on the Yorkshire roads that it didn't seem that hard. Not to say it was easy.

I did all the road circuits – Macau, the North West 200, Scarborough, and I won the Ulster GP. I used to find Donington and other short circuits a real challenge and I loved them but I got a bit dizzy and it was all a bit frenetic. The TT was all more gentlemanly, they line you up one at a time, then they come to your number and it's 'Right, Mr Jefferies, it's your turn to go, off you go now'. I felt it was a more gentlemanly way of racing. I wasn't a very good dicer, I wasn't good at pushing the front wheel underneath other riders. I wasn't good at that, it didn't suit me. I just love the Isle of Man, being given the freedom to ride at my own pace, it just suited me. I'm not suggesting that it's the only way to go racing.

And what was your own pace?
I used to ride damn hard. I used to go as fast as I could. Phil Read once said to me in the early 1990s, I think it was the year I won the F1 in 1993, he said 'The problem you've got is that you enjoy it too much, you want to stop enjoying it, you'll go a bit faster then'. So I did and I won, it was merely down to Phil Read!

How did you stop enjoying it, just get more businesslike with your riding?
Yes, more businesslike. I used to have a comfort zone. I was happy with the speed I was going but I wanted to win and to do that you have to go that bit harder.

What was it like when you went faster, any scary moments?
You still have those inbuilt limits. You should never get to the point where you're coming out of a bend so hard that you're hitting the kerb on the exit. I was just riding the bike a bit harder, really racing it. I was always kind to bikes because you want the thing to last six laps.

John McGuinness [current TT star and 13-times winner] says they are really motoring hard now and they must be riding damn hard to do a 130mph lap, even if the course has got a bit easier and the bikes have got faster. I did just short of 122mph on a 750.

You must've had a few big moments.

Not the day I won it. I've been off five times round there, three big ones, bad news. The first big one, I had just been passed by Carl Fogarty, it was in the wet 1990 Senior TT. He passed me and I was on a slick rear and treaded front. I just rode it too hard on the wrong tyres trying to keep up with him. I lost it after Sarah's Cottage, going onto the Cronk-y-Voddy straight. I knocked myself about a bit: bad ankle, bad shoulder, bad lots of things.

The other one was when I had an experimental gearbox seize on a CBR600 in morning practice. I'd just caught Joey Dunlop going into Greeba Castle and that was the last thing I knew. I was quite poorly from that, lost all the ligaments in me knee from that one, that was an unconscious job.

The third one was when the suspension collapsed on my RC45. It was our fault, we'd modified the shock. The whole back end collapsed before the left hander after Ballacraine. I was off the bike before I got to the bend. That was another airlift [helicopter] job. I lost the ligaments in me other knee, broken toes, broken arm, broken shoulder, I broke quite a few things. But they're not serious injuries compared to what you can have on the Isle of Man at those sorts of speeds. I always got back on again, I didn't want to finish on a low.

Apart from the win, what's your best TT memory?

It was a privilege for me to ride in teams alongside Carl Fogarty, Steve Hislop and Joey Dunlop. Bearing in mind that I started life as a trials rider, I used to pinch myself that I was actually riding alongside these giants of the sport. Believe me, to follow these legends around the TT course or Macau or the Ulster or the North West 200 was a sight to behold and will live with me for the rest of my days. The things they could do with a motorcycle, and I would highlight Hizzy [Hislop] here, beggars belief.

What's important when you ride the TT?

To accomplish what I call a clean lap – it might not be absolutely the fastest you can do, but it's a bit like a good round of golf, you're trying to aspire to the best you can do. If you can achieve a lap where your braking points are right, you put the power on at the right place, your apexes are clipped and you come out of the corners on line, on the power and in the right gear, if you just do all that without trying too hard and if you know exactly where you're going, it'll still be a very good lap.

How long does it take to learn the line?
They always said three years; Dave (Jefferies) had a triple win in his third year, so I think that's still true. Once you've done six years you should be right on it, there shouldn't be much more to know about it. But then as the bikes get better and the tyres get better, the lines change.

What did you most love about the TT as a whole?
I think the Island atmosphere is a bit special, that does something for me. And the variety of the course does something for me, it's not all one thing like so many circuits. There's so much variety, it's smooth, it's bumpy, there's tight twists, there's late apexes, early apexes, brows, your bike's airborne a lot, there's steep descents, steep ascents, hairpins, there's everything. I was brought up in my own mind as a true motorcyclist, so I had a feeling of accomplishment in getting around the course.

The thing about the Isle of Man is that you're not always back round again where you were a minute ago, you're still on your journey, an adventurous journey. When you're lining up on the Glencutchery Road and it's a six-lap race it's quite a journey, quite intimidating.

The TT atmosphere used to bring out the best in me. There is something about being on the Glencutchery road, looking across Douglas Bay at the shimmering sea. And there was something about those early morning practices that was extraordinarily special to me. When I was a schoolboy I was over there for practice week, it was first light, I looked out of my hotel window and there was an MV mechanic bringing an MV four along the prom for morning practice, where else are you going to see that? I've never lost that. There's more legends and stories about the Island than about any other race circuit.

'There's a feeling of camaraderie, I wouldn't be at all surprised if a First World War trench was a similar thing'

But the stories are about tragedy as well as triumph.
We've all sat in the paddock, looking across at each other before a race, knowing that triumph has touched us, that tragedy has touched us all. We've all had that mix of emotions; no one is singled out for special treatment, everyone knows they could be prone to it. There's a feeling of camaraderie, I wouldn't be at all surprised if a First World War trench was a similar thing. It's a very tough paddock

when people are getting hurt but everyone knows that somehow you've got to keep going on.

Why do you have to keep going on?
I think if someone was going to invent the TT now – okay, it's going to be a race on public roads and each lap is 38 miles – they would be laughed out of bed. Because it's there is why we have to carry on going. Life is dangerous. I'm not condoning death, injury, tragedy, but how many die each day on British roads? That doesn't justify the TT but life is a risk, we must get off our backsides and do things, you can't take risk out of life.

Just recently a lad got killed riding a quad on our local dump. People have been riding bikes over that dump for 40 years and now the council is talking about closing it down. If they do close it down the kids will still want to go and take risks, they'll find them somewhere.

What are the rewards, what does the TT make you feel like?
Believe me, if my circumstances allowed, if age hadn't done a bit of damage and if I didn't have a family, I'd still do it. Apart from bringing children into the world it's the best thing I've ever done, from a selfish point of view. It was my injection, my drug, the TT did it for me. I can just about cope with not riding there now but I still miss it. Sadly, golf has taken its part in my life!

The TT was everything within your family; is it still?
Not with all of us.

You raced there just weeks after DJ's death, that can't have been popular.
The reason I went was that I was committed to riding. My daughters were a little upset, there was a little bit of family pressure not to ride but I'd promised my sponsor. Once I was on the bike, I was loving it. I love being on the track, screwing a bike to the limit.

Have you always been a supporter?
Even in the darkest days. I can hold my hand up with a clear conscience and say I've never knocked the TT, never. When I was riders' representative for 18 years I used to fight the inequalities and inconsistencies; I'd fight like crazy over all kinds of issues. But I am an ardent supporter of the

overall principle of the TT and the Manx grand prix [an 'amateur' race over the same 37¾ mile circuit]. I think the concept of racing a bike around 38 miles of closed ordinary roads is quite simply a sensational thing. Everything now is synthesized and shrink-wrapped, like Donington Park and so on. The TT is still the real thing. It has stone walls, you just mustn't hit them because if you do it'll hurt.

How do you deal with the risk?
On the morning of a race I was bad because I was trying to control my emotions; there'd be quite a few visits to the loo. I used to hide the fear by laughing and joking, which is commonplace I suppose, but underneath I was shitting myself. Waiting for the start on the Glencutchery road is surely like nothing else in the world. It's terror.

There was that terrible morning practice on Friday 31st of May 1996 when we lost Mick Lofthouse and Robert Holden, both good pals. I remember going back to bed to my wife and having to tell her the news. We sobbed our hearts out but next day was the F1 race. I'm stood there lining up to race, I've got a badly damaged foot from the North West, I'm on funny pills and I'm feeling crap. I've lost two friends and I went and finished second to Phil McCallen [11-times TT winner between 1992 and 1997], feeling like shit. Once I'd jumped on the bike, despite feeling diabolical all morning, I was absolutely fine.

We're the selfish ones because it's the ones left behind who do the worrying. The wives, the girlfriends, the parents must go through hell. We're the lucky ones because we know we're okay.

Do people like McGuinness do it for money or because they love it?
They do it for the money and because they're good at it. Jim Moodie [eight-times TT winner between 1993 and 2002] did it for the money, McCallen did it for the money. I did it for the money and I loved it as well, I think you've got to love it. I think very few of the top TT riders hate it, they have to love it. But none of those guys, hand on heart, could earn proper money in World Superbike or British Superbike. In many ways it's a different skill, it's like squash and tennis.

I think the fans appreciate all the riders on the TT course. The races bring in a lot of income for the Isle of Man. A lot of ordinary people, not the offshore bankers, benefit from the TT. It's a fabulous event and long may it continue.

MotoGP Mutterings: *June 2007*
The notorious Isle of Man TT races celebrated their centenary in June 2007. Time to salute the world's greatest biking event

'The TT is the manifestation of every human emotion of victory, of triumph, but sometimes of tragedy and pathos. Here one learns some of the basic truths of human experience, of human struggle and rivalry, of exultancy and despondency.'

When Norton boss Gilbert Smith spoke those words in the 1930s the TT was the world's most important motorcycle race and several riders had already died chasing fame and fortune on the Island's treacherous roads. Nowadays the TT is no longer the world's biggest bike race; it is but a meandering country lane a world away from the eight-lane motorways of MotoGP and World Superbike. Riders still die at the TT every year: the death toll now stands at over 200, and by the time you read this maybe more will have lost their lives chasing their Island dreams.

The TT is pretty impossible to defend. Some years ago I argued that it should be shut down. I'm no longer of that opinion. The TT is as insanely dangerous as it ever was, so maybe it's me who's changed, or the world itself. In fact the TT has changed, it's of much less importance to the motorcycle industry, so no one is coerced into racing there to get a factory ride, which used to happen all the time. In other words, riders race there because they want to, because they can't resist its unique and sometimes deadly charms. Like nutters who climb Everest.

'You have to be totally at ease with yourself, know exactly what you're doing, and accept that you might be going home in a box'

The adrenalin rush of a fast TT lap is like nothing else on earth: it's mainlining the greatest drug known to man, your synapses on fire as you burst into a sleepy village at five times the speed limit. No buzz that big comes risk-free.

Obviously, no one who races there is unaware of the enormous dangers they face each time they rocket down Bray Hill, bouncing from gutter to manhole cover, fighting the mother of all tankslappers. Poor old David Jefferies was bang on the money when he gave this upfront assessment of racing on the Island: 'You have to be totally at ease with yourself, know exactly what you're doing, and accept that you might be going home in a box.'

The TT fascinates racers who should know better. Some years ago Wayne Rainey watched an on-bike TT lap and didn't stop talking about it for days. The former 500 king was genuinely awed by the reality of racing around the streets at 190mph – he couldn't believe it's still allowed to go on.

The TT is a relic from an age when most racetracks were similarly lethal, roped-off public roads. But while dozens of other street venues have been shut down the TT survives because it sits on a self-governed island which is very fond of the millions generated by the races. If anyone else was in charge – Westminster, Brussels – it would be just another piece of bike-racing history.

And perhaps this is where the world and I have changed (please excuse me as I enter Grumpy Old Git mode). It seems to me the world has been taken over by puritan megalomaniacs and I don't like it. These crusading cretins pretend they care about people but they don't, they want us to stop riding motorcycles (why else would they keep tightening the bike test?) and quit smoking, but they start wars. The TT is a wild anachronism in an increasingly controlled society; it's barking at the moon, a big fingers up to those who want us all to lead safe, obedient, mortgaged lives under the all-seeing eye of the CCTV camera, obeying the command of dayglo-clad security gorillas with an IQ of 50 and tranquillised by the government's looped mantra of 'your safety is our primary concern'. Bollocks to the lot of them.

I don't defend the TT. The only people who have that right are those who race there. All I will do is salute their right to do what they want with their own lives, unconstrained by government health-and-safety muppets who think they know best. That said, I wouldn't want my best mate doing it.

CHAPTER 53

ROSSI: WHAT MAKES HIM SO GOOD?

June 2007

Casey Stoner made a brilliant job of dismantling the legend of Valentino Rossi during 2007, but there's no doubt that the former world champ is one of the greatest riders of all time. So what makes him so good?

Not very long ago Valentino Rossi was bike racing's King Midas, the golden boy who could do no wrong. He was a genius motorcycle racer and it seemed he was even more than that, because while his talent won him dozens of races and a pile of world titles he seemed to have an almost supernatural power to make things go his way, even when the odds were stacked heavily against him.

Not any more, though. Things have changed over the past year and a half; Rossi has lost the crown he had made his own, proving that he is in fact only human. 'Unbeatable superheroes only exist in movies, real life is different,' he said after losing the crown in 2006.

So Rossi is human and a fallible human at that. Nowadays bad things happen to the former MotoGP king, he makes mistakes and he loses races, so the glitter is tarnished. But despite the bike problems, the tyre woes and the crashes, there's no doubt that he is one of the greatest riders of all time. So what's so great about the seven-time world champion's methods, his psychology, his talent and his racecraft? We decided to ask the people who really know, those who get to watch him up close, both on the track and in the pits: the man who made him king, his crew chief Jeremy Burgess, the man who first stole his crown, Nicky Hayden, and his Yamaha team-mate Colin Edwards.

This trio of paddock personalities call Rossi a lot of things – foxy, sly, vicious, crazy, serious, focused, aggressive, clean – but perhaps it's Burgess who gets to the root of it all. The straight-talking Aussie believes that Rossi's genius is a factor of good biology. JB reckons he's got very high-performing motor neurones that give him the ability to process information remarkably quickly. Comes in handy at 200mph.

So, first and foremost, it is his intelligence that makes Rossi so good. He is a very clever young man, and he could succeed at pretty much anything he wanted to turn his hand to, because he would work out how to do it right. Perhaps JB helped format Rossi's racing brain to work unerringly logically, but Rossi would probably have worked it out anyway. His intelligence is obvious to all – you see it in his eyes, hear it when he opens his mouth, witness it at work when he cuts another masterful manoeuvre on the track.

This brain power is also the most vital ingredient in his talent, because he has the ability to decode what he feels on the bike, either to ride faster or to make the bike better. This isn't easy; many riders get lost in the labyrinth of machine settings – they focus on the wrong issues, give confusing feedback to their technicians, waste time trying to fix problems that can't be fixed. Rossi isn't like that, he knows where he wants to go, he gives crystal clear feedback and never expects the bike to be 100 per cent perfect. This is hugely important because motorcycle racing is a technical sport, it involves ultra-high-tech machinery so it requires a scientific mind. As his Öhlins suspension technician Mike Norton says: 'Valentino is very good because he's very methodical... he doesn't dwell on problems... he's very black and white, very clinical. It's very rare he can't tell you what's going on but if he can't feel any difference, he'll say so.'

True, Rossi does appear to have an amazingly natural feel for motorcycle riding but that comes from a combination of brainpower and miles covered, which seems to have created some kind of information superhighway between the tyres, his brain and everything in between. Rossi and his motorcycle are apparently wired together, so they work as a single unit.

Rossi's psychology is also very strong, though it'll be interesting to see how he reacts in the long term to Stoner's current domination. He really enjoys what he does and that's another major factor in his success. Racing isn't only a job, it's something he loves, he loves it all, from poring over computer data readouts with his engineers to playing mind games with his rivals, to sticking it up the inside of those rivals at the hairpin. As Edwards says, he is sly.

His upbringing probably has a lot to do with his psyche. His dad was a wise, open-minded teacher who didn't bring Valentino up as a racer first and a human being second. Many modern-day racers who've been racing since they were four years old aren't rounded human beings because they've never had the chance to become rounded human beings. Rossi is mature and worldly wise, that's why he is so good at dealing with people, which helps him excel in pit lane and outside in the everyday world.

He seems an objective person, aware that there is a bigger world out there, so he fully understands that he is only playing a game, albeit a game he plays to win. Many other riders are apparently engulfed by the enormity of what they're involved in – they truly believe that what they're doing is the most important thing in the world. Rossi's make-up is the opposite of the standard template for modern sporting success – the no-life sports star who eats, breathes and sleeps his sport to ensure he is always one step ahead of the competition. Rossi does work incredibly hard at his racing, but he's got a life beyond it, which is a vital counterpoint to his brilliance on the racetrack.

Rossi is also very brave, incredibly brave. In fact he is a bit of a nutter, prepared to win pretty much by any means necessary. We have seen his dark side in action on plenty of occasions, most memorably when he rammed the hapless Sete Gibernau off the track at Jerez in 2005. Troy Bayliss called him a maniac, which is pretty rich. Edwards calls him vicious, which is fair enough, because however nice you might be off the racetrack you need to be very nasty on the track if you're going anywhere. As George Orwell wrote: 'Serious sport has nothing to do with fair play. It is bound up with hatred, jealousy, boastfulness, disregard of all rules and sadistic pleasure in witnessing violence. In other words, it is war minus the shooting.'

So if you want to be another Rossi, this is what you need in your character make-up: plenty of brains and bravery, a bit of ebullience and a certain viciousness. Couldn't be easier, eh?

The team-mate: Colin Edwards
Colin Edwards first partnered Rossi in the 2000 Suzuka Eight Hours and he's been his full-time MotoGP team-mate for three seasons.
'We started as team-mates at the Suzuka Eight Hours in 2000. It's cool, we get along great and I have the luxury to go in the garage and look

at the computer to see exactly what he's doing. I enjoy that and I've learned a lot. There are times when I feel like I'm hitting my head against a wall, it's like "Why am I losing so much time in section three? Or whatever". It's pretty easy, you overlay the data and you go "Ah, all right, now I see how fast you can go through that corner", so it helps out. And nowadays with GPS you can even look at what lines he's taking. Sure, it's not as easy as that, you don't just hold the gas on for another second, you have to analyse it and work out how.

'My own assessment of Valentino is that he's like a 16-year-old who never grew up. He's always having fun and he's fun to be around. He looks at riding a motorcycle like my daughter looks at riding her bicycle – it's something fun to do. It's a little bit different to the approach of most guys on the grid who are maybe gritty, hard faced and determined. Valentino has got all that, he just has a different way of showing it, he goes out there and enjoys the battle.

'I've never really felt like he gets enough credit for how hard he works, there's always that myth that he always has the best bikes and so on. But until I arrived at Yamaha I'd never seen anybody work as hard as I do, so I was like "Wow, he does work hard as well". I don't think many people realise that. There's no in between, he does it all to the max.

'He's very clever, how would you say it… he's sly. He's very undercover, foxy, sly. It's cool, he's not real blatant about some of the mind games. To him it's big and to the person he's playing it to it's big but not many people will catch onto it, because he's real clever about it. I don't know how much of it he thinks up on his own but maybe most of it. It's pretty funny, you see a little sticker on his bike or you see something he does and you go what's that all about? He's always got an explanation, it's always subtle little things. He's done a good job to make a lot of people think he's Jekyll and Hyde, if you know what I'm saying. His whole personality is not so much that, he's just normal. But on the track he's pretty vicious!

'What are his strongest points? Well, apart from his ability to make up 20 bike lengths in two or three corners, which is a pretty good ability if you ask me, I don't know. I guess he's just so smooth, he's aggressive but he's making lots of time and it doesn't look like it. If you're behind him you're working your balls off and he's easing away from you, bit by bit. You're going "I'm doing everything I can", but he looks pretty easy. I don't know if there's one thing he's got that really impresses me on the track… just everything, the whole package.

'Something he is really good at is recovering from mistakes. When he makes the kind of mistake that would have most people sliding on their asses into the gravel, he seems to somehow gather it back. Occasionally he'll overcook it but the way he gets away with it makes you go "how the hell?".

'Like Donington 2005, that really wet race. I locked up the front a couple of times and it scared the shit out of me, so I was cruisin' with the pack and the next thing you know he just pisses off. I looked at his data and it was scary. That guy was locking the front in the rain on a shitty track that was slicker than snot, every other corner he just had it locked. I said to him "Was your front locked?"and he said "Oh yeah, a couple of times pretty bad". Then I looked at the computer and it was like, a couple of times? Fuck, it was every corner, this guy's crazy! That was probably the most impressive ride, I could look at the computer and actually see how much locking was going on, it was crazy. I almost crashed a couple of times and my locks weren't as bad as his. I was like "oh fuck!" and he's just like, sssrrrcccccchh, that'll be all right, yeah! (Edwards mimes the act of flicking the bike into a turn with the front end ploughing sideways.)

'I looked at his data and it was scary – his front was locked every corner – this guy's crazy!'

'I really don't think he's got any weaknesses. Guys keep saying he's gonna go F1 or rallying and I say "no way". He looks at all that stuff as fun, he gets an opportunity to drive the cars, it's just fun. He's smart, he plays the part so people think this is what he's thinking about. He loves and enjoys rallying and maybe later he may do that but I don't think he'll give up motorcycles the way it is at the moment.

'To him motorcycle racing is a puzzle. If you put it into climbing terms he's got to work out how to get up the wall. As far as making the pass and pulling away, that's the crux, he has to figure out that puzzle, where he needs to pass before the three or four corners where he knows he can pull a little gap and demoralise the guy, that's what he's doing the whole time. Valentino doesn't make unnecessary passes. Even at Qatar in 2007 he was passing Stoner to play with him, to see what he had. He doesn't do anything too hasty, except maybe the first lap or two when he'll do some hasty things to get up front.'

The rival: Nicky Hayden

Hayden is the man who finally brought to an end Rossi's run of premier-class successes by beating him to the 2006 MotoGP title.

'I can't say it's just his approach that makes him good. Some guys take their racing real serious, others are really laid back, it's whatever works for that rider. But regardless of whatever he does he definitely gets around the track fast, that's what's most important.

'One thing I noticed when we were team-mates is that he looks like it's fun, fun, fun; he definitely cuts up a lot, but once you're in the garage that dude is so serious, so focused. Everything seems perfect, right down to the windscreen sticker and the colour of his boots. He doesn't overlook anything and I think that's a big part of it.

'More than anything it's the racer in him that makes him so strong, it's obvious the guy wants to win. He's got a lot of natural talent but I know a lot of guys with natural talent and it gets some guys in trouble. It's the whole package that makes him strong: the desire, the focus, the talent.

'I think sometimes maybe he's not as laid back as he comes across. He knows what to say and when to say it to make it look like things aren't really getting to him. He knows how to play it, on the bike and off the bike.

'It's hard to say what he's like with mind games because I can only comment on how he's been with me and I've never seen him play any games with me, especially in 2006 when he was taking chunks out of my points lead. The guy didn't really change, maybe he just knew that I wasn't going to roll over. Maybe some of the guys he can break down mentally, maybe he knew it wasn't going to get to me.

'Him and JB (Jeremy Burgess) haven't won all those titles just through his riding, they know how to play people, they know how to play their cards, when to show their hand, when not to show their hand. I don't think he plays as many games as other guys – you don't need to play a lot of games when you can ride like that.

'On track sure he's aggressive but he's totally clean and he definitely has a lot of tactics. He knows when he wants to race just one guy, how to separate groups, how to slow down. Like Phillip Island in 2005 I was on him the whole race and he eventually saw that he wasn't going to get away, so he slowed down, brought the next group up to us to get me caught up with them, then tried to make another break. He's got a lot of racecraft.

'I'd say his biggest strength is that he can adapt. If the tyres go off and he needs to slide he can slide, when the bike need to be ridden in line he can ride in line, he can definitely adapt to situations. I can't say there's one area of his riding where he just kills guys. It's not just braking or corner speed or this or that, I'd just say that when he's in a rhythm and putting those laps down he can break a guy. Like at Jerez this year he broke Pedrosa by about half a tenth a lap, he just kept putting those laps down, riding on that edge. He doesn't ride 95 per cent, he rides on that razor edge for a long time.

'I don't know about weaknesses, it's hard for me to point out a guy's weakness when he's won all those championships. In fact I'm not going to say he's got any weak points because I don't need to motivate the guy! That's why I don't want to say anything negative. I'm a big believer in not motivating these guys any more, that's why I don't talk trash.'

The crew chief: Jeremy Burgess
JB has worked full-time with Valentino since the end of 1999, so probably knows him better than anyone else in the paddock.
'Racing is like anything in life – you have to have a plan and you have to work through the plan. Clearly the methods we used to use on 500s and now use in MotoGP differ somewhat from the methods he used at Aprilia, the basic is to understand that the bike won't be exactly how you want it when you wheel it out of the trailer, so you have to set about attacking the problems in a logical order in a given amount of time. In the early days we identified what we want him to tell us when he returns to the pits and that's what we get – he has worked very well with us.

'He enjoys his job and I think everybody in this team enjoys their work. There are days when it might grind you the wrong way and I'm sure there are days when Valentino would rather be in Ibiza. But as long as he enjoys the challenge of his employment on most days, that's all we need.

'He only uses mind games when people make a serious challenge, then he pulls out that extra tool in his armoury, which he did with Max, with Sete and to a lesser degree with Marco. Then there's Loris, who is also a serious challenge, but there's a different understanding between them, there's a respect. When I first worked with Valentino he was mates with Marco. Whenever there was a dinner or a party, Marco was always there.

When Marco came to MotoGP it was still fine, then when there was any sort of a challenge their friendship cooled off a bit.

'As for talent, whether it's Valentino, Roger Federer or Tiger Woods, these guys have a very special ability to process information, so they can correct mistakes as they're happening, before we would even realise we've made a mistake.

'When Valentino goes rabbiting around the track he enters a corner and knows he's six inches too much to the inside and he starts correcting that long before anyone can see he's made a mistake. In his own mind he's made a little mistake which he gathers in a long way before anybody even realises he's made the mistake. It's the ability to process information so fast and so accurately. Whether the little electric pulses in his brain fire a bit better than yours or mine, I don't know.'

And finally, a word from fellow legend Giacomo Agostini
Legend of the 1960s and 1970s, Ago still holds the records for the most premier-class wins. He won 68 500 GPs, all with MV Agusta.
'I think it's no secret, I remember when Ago go very fast and I first race Mike Hailwood and he was also very, very fast. But we don't know why, it's difficult to know because it's something inside. When I race with some other rider and I crash, I say "why do I fucking crash and you don't crash?", but I don't have the answer. It's something that God or my mother give to me, same with Valentino, Hailwood, Barry Sheene or Michael Schumacher. I go fast but why? Maybe you crash at 45 degrees and I crash at 47 degrees, it's something inside and it's difficult to find the reason, in Italian we say *regalo dalla natura*, it's a gift from nature.'

CHAPTER 54

TOWERING MOUNTAINS AND RAGING RIVERS OF RIDING TALENT

October 2007

How did men like Casey Stoner, Mike Hailwood, Freddie Spencer, John Surtees and Valentino Rossi manage to reach the very pinnacle of their sport when barely out of their teens?

Casey Stoner was a fresh-faced 21 years and 342 days old when he won the 2007 MotoGP championship, making him the second youngest rider to have conquered biking's dizziest peak. Four others have managed the feat at similarly young ages: Freddie Spencer won the 1983 500 title at 21 years and 258 days, Mike Hailwood secured the 1962 500 crown aged 22 and 160 days, John Surtees took his first 500 championship in 1956 at 22 years and 182 days and Valentino Rossi wrapped up the 2001 500 title when he was 22 years and 240 days old.

Those five title successes must rank amongst the greatest achievements in racing history; I mean, what do most of us achieve by that age? A first proper job, passing your bike test, maybe getting through university, certainly nothing as grand as climbing to the summit of one of the world's most vicious sports.

So what makes the young Stoner, Rossi, Spencer, Hailwood and Surtees so different from the young you and me? Why were they on top of the world when you were maybe festering in student digs, dispatch riding on a shagged-out Honda NTV, on the dole or simply getting pissed up and shagging around? And what makes them stand so high above other racers who also started young?

Riding talent, for a start, towering mountains and raging rivers of the stuff, plus intelligence and unfaltering dedication, or, as Surtees called his own brand of world-beating determination, 'the inherent Surtees family cussedness'. That's all downright obvious, but where did their talent come from and how was it applied so successfully and so early? In short, it's all nature and nurture, the two factors that control all our destinies. Nature is your genes, the stuff that's passed down from your parents, while nurture is how your upbringing developed your character. In other words, a lot of it's down to parents, and fathers in particular.

Stoner's dad reckons his son's skill is in his DNA: 'Like a lot of kids it was obvious from an early age that Casey has the skills level required,' says Colin Stoner. 'He was doing things on a bike aged six you wouldn't believe. Plus he's got the mentality to go with it. He's very, very mentally strong. And like all the others, he comes from a petrol background.'

> *'Casey was doing things on a bike aged six you wouldn't believe, plus he's got the mentality to go with it'*

Stoner, Rossi, Spencer, Hailwood and Surtees share several characteristics and life factors in common, but perhaps most important of all, their dads were all into bikes and into speed. More than that, in fact, their dads all raced. Colin Stoner started riding on Australian roads when he was 14, borrowing his brother's streetbike, and became a very handy roadracer and kart racer during the 1970s, though he admits 'I didn't have a clue what I was doing', which is why he got involved with his son's racing, to help him avoid the pitfalls. Rossi's father Graziano was a top GP racer and won three 250 GPs in 1979, the year Valentino was born. Freddie Spencer Senior was up for racing anything with an engine – dirt bikes, drag bikes, sprint cars and eventually powerboats. Hailwood's old man and Surtees' dad raced sidecars before the Second World War, pop Hailwood later earning the nickname Stan 'The Wallet' as owner of a chain of motorcycle shops, while Jack Surtees was at one stage the UK's biggest Vincent dealer.

So bikes and racing loomed large in the gene pools of these thrusting youngsters, but that doesn't mean that their dads or their upbringings were the same, far from it. Take Surtees, Rossi and Stoner and you could hardly imagine more different backgrounds: Surtees, the grubby-kneed kid growing up during the Blitz, scraping together enough cash to go racing on a weekly apprenticeship wage of £2.50, Rossi the firstborn of a beaming GP star, motorhoming it around Europe with Barry Sheene and King Kenny Roberts in an age of vivid sporting glamour, Stoner growing up the Aussie way in the big outdoors, a few minutes from the beach, mucking about in boats, on horseback and on dirt bikes.

Their childhoods span generations, during which time the world changed a great deal. Europe was transformed from war torn, bombed and exhausted to rich, bangin' and economically united, while Australia boomed and became arguably the world's sportiest nation. In the meantime society's attitudes were turned upside down, not least its attitude towards youth, while sport metamorphosed from a game for moneyed amateurs into a form of dynamic advertising.

Back in the 1940s kids didn't even get out of school shorts until they were well into their teens. Surtees had to wait until he was 13 for his first bike ride and a further three years before his first roadrace, having spent the previous ten learning to put bikes together with little more than a screwdriver and a piece of string.

Stoner and Rossi grew up in an age obsessed with youth, when teenagers can do things they never dreamed of doing half a century earlier. Stoner was sitting on the back of a minibike working the throttle when he was 18 months old and riding around the garden at three. A year later he competed in his first dirt track race and aged six he won his first Australian title. Rossi rode his first minibike aged two and a half, was Italian champion by the age of 15, contested his first GP at 16 and was a multimillionaire before leaving his teens.

There are similarities in their upbringings, however. Surtees, Stoner and Rossi didn't have pushy fathers. Colin Stoner, Graziano Rossi and Jack Surtees were delighted that their kids got a kick out of bikes, just as they did, but there was never any question of their sons being pushed into racing. Dad Surtees was still pursuing his own racing career when John first got into riding, so the young teenager was merely happy that his father showed 'no resentment, just lots of encouragement'. Years later Stoner wanted nothing more than to go racing. During his schoolboy racing days he saw many kids being pushed into racing by their fathers, but as he says: 'the good riders have always wanted to do it all their lives'. Rossi was also the driving force behind his own entry into competition, initially in go-karts. 'But the problem with go-karts is that they cost very much money,' he recalls. 'So I said to my father "Maybe it's better we race with a bike," and he say "Ah, bo, really?"'

Anyway, all that really mattered was that Stoner was out there at the youngest-possible age, as were Rossi, Surtees, Hailwood and Spencer before him, learning the art of machine control, as well as strategy, technical aptitude, coolness of head and how to deal with the downs as well as the ups. But most of all, having fun.

If Rossi's and Surtees' casual rise to greatness lacked any grand plan, things were a little different for Hailwood, arguably the most naturally talented of all, and Spencer, whose fathers seemed more intent on their offspring achieving success. Stan was a hard-nosed businessman who threw serious money at Mike's career from the outset; he was determined his boy would succeed. He bought the best bikes and harangued the media to get Mike the best coverage; in that sense Hailwood Senior was way ahead of his time.

Although Hailwood wasn't legally allowed to start racing until 17, when he was working his apprenticeship at Triumph (making the tea), his father gave him a hand-made miniature motorcycle at the age of seven, to ride around the grounds of the family's Oxfordshire home. That creation, powered by a 100cc Royal Enfield two-stroke, gave Hailwood something of a head start in an age when no one had even thought of mass-producing minibikes.

Like Surtees and Stoner, Hailwood and Spencer were also made in different eras and different cultures. While minibikes didn't exist when Hailwood was caning his little Enfield around his dad's garden during the 1950s, Spencer grew up in the 1970s, when minibike racing was exploding across the United States. Spencer's father dedicated himself to helping Freddie make it in the gritty world of US dirt track, collecting his son from school on Friday evenings and spending the weekend driving thousands of miles across the States. They'd do a dirt track Friday night, drive to another state to roadrace on the Saturday, then maybe another dirt track before heading back to school. By the time he was 12, Freddie was already a renegade pro-racer, competing in 'outlaw' dirt track events against real pros at rodeos, and then sharing the drive home with his exhausted dad.

Stoner's dad put in the hard yards too for his son, driving thousands of kilometres across Australia. And all that effort surely had some effect on the kid's determination to do well. Stoner is renowned for never doing a lazy lap and his dad thinks that goes back to his interstate dirt-tracking days. 'We'd drive 2000 kays to a dirt track race and Casey would get five laps of practice, so he had to make every lap count,' says Stoner senior.

Perhaps the Stoner family made the biggest sacrifice of these five bike-mad families, selling up Down Under to bring 14-year-old Casey to

Europe. But Colin Stoner doesn't see it like that. 'The way I look at it there were no sacrifices,' he says. 'We set off on an adventure just to see where it ended up. The adventure really started when he was four years old and we went racing. The trip to Europe was another adventure, it wasn't going to kill us if we failed but we were determined not to fail.'

Nineteenth-century Irish novelist and wit Oscar Wilde jokingly observed that youth is wasted on the young, but not, apparently, on men like these, though you could always argue that Stoner, Surtees, Hailwood, Spencer and Rossi never really had their childhoods. While normal boys are out and about necking alcopops, puffing on cigarettes and putting their hands up girls' skirts, these youngsters were getting stuck in early, learning how to do a real man's job. Maybe that's cheating but everyone's at it these days; bike racing, tennis, golf, football and car racing are all ruled by former child prodigies. As former 500 King Kenny Roberts, says: 'If you start as a three-year-old and you've got a lot of talent, you're going to beat the guy who started as a 15-year-old with a lot of talent. Stoner and Rossi are natural-born motorcycle racers, like Tiger Woods is a natural-born golfer.'

In other words, it's both the blood and the guts, passed down by your dad, and Roberts knows that better than anyone, for he was the first world champ to father another world champ, Kenny Junior, who won the 500 crown in 2000. So don't be surprised if Stoner sires a child who brings home the world championship around about 2035.

History's youngest premier-class kings

John Surtees
Born: 11 February 1934, Surrey, England
500 world champion 1956, 1958, 1959, 1960
350 world champion 1958, 1959, 1960
Surtees rode roaring MV Agusta multis to four 500 crowns, later switching to cars and winning the 1964 F1 title with Ferrari. He's the only man to have won world titles on two and four wheels.

Son of a sidecar racer, Surtees grew up in the London suburbs during and after the Second World War, riding a bike for the first time when he was 13. He competed in his first race a year later, as a last-minute sub for his father's regular passenger, only to be disqualified because he was under age. At 15 he made his grass track debut and then started roadracing, quickly amassing wins on a Vincent Grey Flash, then factory Nortons before the MV call came. Surtees won a total of 22 500 GPs and also took three 350 titles for MV.

Mike Hailwood

Born: 2 April 1940, Oxfordshire, England
500 world champion 1962, 1963, 1964, 1965
350 world champion 1967, 1968
250 world champion 1961, 1966, 1967

Hailwood is generally considered to be the greatest racer ever. Supported by his rich father, Mike the Bike made amazing progress through the British racing ranks after his debut in 1957, winning three national titles the following year.

During 1959 he won all four British titles and his first GP success. Two summers later he leased a factory Honda 250 four to win his first world title and was quickly signed by the then-dominant MV factory, for whom he won four back-to-back 500 crowns, before returning to Honda. He won four more titles for the Japanese but ill luck prevented him from giving Honda-san his first 500 crown. Hailwood then went F1 car racing, before making a fairytale return to bikes in the late 1970s. He died in a road car accident in 1981.

Freddie Spencer

Born: 20 December 1961, Louisiana, USA
500 world champion 1983, 1985
250 world champion 1985

A dazzling natural talent, right up there with Hailwood, Spencer was one of the first modern generation riders who started not long after they could walk. The Bible Belt kid made his dirt track debut at the age of six and was roadracing by 12.

Honing the art of sideways riding, Spencer was soon signed by Honda, with whom he won the US Superbike title before embarking on a full-time GP career in 1982. That year he became the youngest-ever winner of a 500 GP, at 20 years and 196 days, claiming the championship the following season after a titanic duel with Kenny Roberts. In '85 he became the first, and still only, man in history to win the 250 and 500 titles in the same season, but his later years were dogged by injury and ill luck.

Valentino Rossi

Born: 16 February 1979, Urbino, Italy
500 world champion 2001, MotoGP world champion 2002, 2003, 2004, 2005
250 world champion 1999
125 world champion 1996

If Surtees and Hailwood were rare teenage winners in their era, Rossi was one of a whole brood of teen stars when he burst on to the GP scene in 1996. He rode his first minibike aged two and his first minimoto race at 11, after starting his career in karts. Italian 125 sport production champ at 15, he was ushered into the Euro 125 series by Aprilia in 1995 and then into the world series the next year, when he won his first GP.

The following season Rossi walked the 125s, establishing a pattern he'd repeat on 250s and 500s: learn the first year, dominate the second. He switched to 250s in '98, becoming the youngest-ever 250 champ in '99, aged 20 years and 250 days, then graduated to 500s in 2000, winning the final 500 title in 2001 and the first four MotoGP crowns.

Casey Stoner

Born: 16 October 1985, Kurri Kurri, NSW, Australia
MotoGP world champion 2007

Stoner, like Rossi, belongs to the modern generation of kid racers who get serious about racing before they can even read or write. By the age of three he was riding a minibike around the garden, a year later he had competed in his first dirt-track race and he won his first Australian dirt-track title aged six.

By the time Stoner was a teenager he knew he was ready for the tarmac but Australians aren't allowed to roadrace till 16, so his family moved to the UK soon after his 14th birthday so he could start roadracing, and he won a national title in his first season. In 2001 he made his GP debut. Casey won his first GP victory in 2003, finished second in the 2005 250 World Championship, scored his first MotoGP pole position in 2006 and his first MotoGP win in March 2007.

CHAPTER 55

COMPUTER SAYS NO

July 2007

MotoGP is turning tame – these days there's less sideways action, riding styles are getting more samey and races are more spread out. So are computerised control systems taking the nuttiness out of the world's maddest motorsport?

Valentino Rossi and Casey Stoner are neck and neck, rocking out of a slow right-hander, wrenching their machines upright as they grab big handfuls of throttle and take aim at the next corner. They are out of sight in an instant, gone in a blaze of sound, leaving only a lingering stench of hot metal and scorched rubber. But, if I'm not mistaken, something was missing from this assault on the senses. No wheelspin, no wheelies, no sideways silliness. Just mind-boggling speed.

In case you hadn't already noticed, MotoGP has changed. Fast-accelerating technology has transformed the bikes from unruly monsters to machines that hardly ever put a wheel out of line. If you are an engineer, you would be justifiably proud of this achievement, but if you are a fan, you may be a teeny-weensy bit disappointed. Perhaps you used to enjoy watching MotoGP riders employ increasingly outrageous techniques to wrestle their 250 horsepower missiles into submission. I know I did.

But they call this progress, and progress is a road along which we are always travelling. In the 1980s 500 GP bikes were made more manageable by the perfection of reed-valve technology. In the 1990s they were further tamed by the introduction of the big bang firing configuration. In 1998 they were emasculated a bit more by the switch to 'greener' unleaded fuel, which made them 'like big 250s', according to 500 master Mick Doohan. Then in 2002 they fully had their bollocks chopped off when the sport shifted to 990cc four-strokes. As former

500 winner Christian Sarron said: 'The four-strokes are nice bikes…
for girls.'

So MotoGP's new 800s aren't anything revolutionary, they are merely
the product of where we are at on the road of technological progress.
They are very manageable motorcycles because they are very well
managed motorcycles.

But is engine management – traction control, wheelie control, launch
control, engine-braking control – really sucking the glory out of MotoGP,
just like it did with F1 cars? Yes, if you listen to the riders. Even 800s
genius Casey Stoner thinks so. 'These things should be 1500s, not 800s,'
he says. 'In fact I'd rather be on a 500 two-stroke, they weren't stacked
out with computer control systems. These 800s, everyone can ride
them'. Valentino Rossi thinks the same: 'I prefer the 990s because the
latest control systems make it harder for the rider to make the difference.'
In other words, the most talented riders want nastier bikes, so they can
use their rare skills to beat their lesser rivals.

Rossi's 2007 Fiat Yamaha team-mate Colin Edwards agrees that
electronics have taken some of the talent out of MotoGP. 'You go into a
turn, you take your line, you open the gas and the bike somewhat takes
care of itself,' he says, which doesn't sound very difficult at all. 'In the
old days you used to come out of a turn, get on the gas and you'd go
"Man, I could've got on it five metres earlier", next lap you're on it five
metres earlier and then you're flying to the moon, so that's where
traction control really helps.'

Riders fully rely on the technology to keep them out of trouble. At the
start of 2007 I eavesdropped on Stoner debriefing his engineers after
practice. The Aussie had been flicked over the highside when he had got
too eager with the throttle, and he was angry. 'I should never have
crashed,' he told his crew chief. 'The traction control should have taken
care of it.' So Stoner believed that the electronics should have translated
his greedy fistful into exactly the correct amount of power that the rear
tyre could handle at that moment. This would seem to be irrefutable
evidence that traction control does take the skill out of riding.

And yet if electronics trickery has stolen something from MotoGP
with one hand, it does at least give something back with the other
(when the technology works, that is). 'These days we start a lot of GPs
with full and healthy grids,' says Edwards. 'In years past I don't know
how many times guys like Schwantz, Rainey and Doohan rode with

broken arms and legs. The technology definitely makes it safer, so you don't have so much of that ass pucker going on.'

Chris Vermeulen's Rizla Suzuki crew chief Tom O'Kane agrees. 'I see it solely as a safety issue,' he says. 'I don't care what kind of traction control you've got, if you open the throttle on one of these things at maximum lean you better know what you're doing, or it'll spit you off. I think traction control has been overestimated by people who don't ride the bikes.'

Traction control may make a rider's life easier and safer but it doesn't necessarily make him any faster around a racetrack. In fact, it may even make him slower, as Stoner says: 'The engine cuts reduce the power.'

That's why most riders prefer minimum traction control, so the electronics cut the power just in time to prevent a highside. Edwards: 'I've tried Valentino's traction control set-up and I didn't like it, because I couldn't get the bike to spin to finish the turn, it kept running me off the track. You don't spin the 800s like the 990s, but you still need some spin.'

Since traction control does allow riders to be braver with the throttle the fastest guys must find another part of the corner in which to make the difference. Edwards again: 'Now it's all about how you get into the turn, and that is only something a racer can do. The bike can't get you in the corner any better, it can't load the suspension for you, so that aspect of getting into the corner really is 100 per cent rider, plus a bit of bike set-up and engine-brake management.' So the emphasis has changed from how hard and how soon you can jump on the throttle to how fast you can get into a turn and how far you can lean over through the turn.

But not everyone is sure that it's hi-tech electronics that are responsible for the dramatic increase in cornering speeds and the loss of corner-exit dramas. O'Kane suspects it's much more basic than that.

'It's the 800s that have changed the emphasis to corner entry,' he says. 'The 990s had so much excess power that you could give them an ideal torque curve. With the 800s you can't afford a big fat torque curve, you've got to use the engine's capacity for peak power, otherwise you'll get hosed on top speed.' So with no big wave of torque available to kick them out of turns, riders now use smoother lines for higher corner speeds to get out of turns at the fastest possible rate, just like 250 riders.

And it seems like there's no other way to ride the 800s. The 990s could be ridden wheels in line, sideways, any which way, but the knock-on effect of the 800s' specific demands has been to morph riding styles into one. With the glorious exception of Spanish nutter Toni Elias, everyone rides the 800s pretty much the same because they are all about finesse. Kicking them sideways doesn't work, which is why 990 champ Nicky Hayden, veteran nutter Loris Capirossi and former 500 champ Kenny Roberts Junior have struggled with the smaller engines. 'The 800s have boxed in the riders as well as the engine designers,' O'Kane explains. 'The drop in engine power has removed some of the riders' options, so they have to ride the bikes more like 250s.'

And there's a knock-on effect to that knock-on effect. If everyone rides the same and uses the same lines, how do they overtake? With difficulty. Most riders agree that passing is less easy with the 800s, and not only because it's difficult to find an alternative line to get a way past. The 800s have shorter braking zones because they are slower down the straights and faster into the turns, so it's more difficult to overtake on the brakes.

This has required MotoGP engineers to change their focus on chassis setup, proving that changing riding styles can affect technology just as changing technology affects riding styles. 'Braking stability has become more important,' says O'Kane. 'And turning has become much more important, so the rider can carry speed into the corner when he gets off the brakes without the thing picking itself up and running wide. For bike setup, the 800s are a different set of problems.'

The end result of the samey riding styles and reduced overtaking opportunities is less close racing. MotoGP used to be renowned for ultra-close battles up front, but the 800s are spreading out the action. During the last three 990 seasons the average winning margin in dry races was just 2.07 seconds. During 2007 the gap from winner to second place more than doubled to 4.54 seconds.

This isn't simply because the 800s are one-line motorcycles which make overtaking so difficult – new tyre regulations have also played a part. Riders are now limited to the number of tyres they can use during a GP, which must be chosen before practice starts. Inevitably, some riders choose more suitable batches of tyres than others, so the competition is less equal than before (though some argue it's fairer because Michelin can't rush in specially tailored tyres on the eve of European races).

'Now it just seems like so much of your race is decided on Thursday afternoon, when you choose your tyres,' says Nicky Hayden. 'If you choose the wrong batch it's hard to dig yourself out of that hole. I think it's hurt the racing, whereas before, come Sunday, everyone was pretty close because during practice you'd eventually try a tyre that worked. I was never a big fan of the new rule, when they were kicking around the idea I said I don't like it, just because everyone was real close as far as tyres went, so the racing was real close.'

So there's no doubt that the 800s have changed MotoGP in ways that weren't predicted, or desired. And with teams already struggling with sponsorship, MotoGP bosses Dorna should be worried that the bikes are less fun to watch, because presumably fewer people will bother to turn on their TVs. But MotoGP's technical rules are looked after by the factories, not Dorna, and the factories want more technology, not less, because that's why they're there in the first place, to develop new technology. So there's zero chance of MotoGP diverting from its current path.

Which might just give World Superbikes a chance to get one over on its glitzier rival. If WSB boss Paolo Flammini bans traction control by equipping bikes with a 'control' ECU, he might be able to offer a spectacle that MotoGP has wilfully denied itself. Then the final decision will come down to you lot sitting at home in front of the TV: do you want high-brow technology, like F1 cars, or lowbrow fun, like Nascar? You decide...

MotoGP Mutterings: January 2008
I've smelt the future of MotoGP, and boy, it don't half pong

Smell is the most evocative of all the senses, which is why I'm immediately dragged back to my schooldays – in a wibbly-wobbly movie memory kind of a way – upon entering the cavernous Red Bull Rookies awning within the MotoGP paddock. The atmosphere is thick with that bitter, nose-puckering stench I remember permeating the locker room after each mean and downright vicious game of rugby I played in my teens. Except that in Red Bull Rookies' world the reek of teenage sweat and testosterone is turbocharged with a malodorous soup of fetid leathers, smouldering rubber and acrid two-stroke smoke. Excuse me while I go outside, I think I'm going to puke...

The Rookies awning is populated by 23 of the world's fastest 13- to 16-year olds, chosen from a nerve-jangling tearjerker of a global selection process that aims to fast-track these youngsters – via a series of races at MotoGP events aboard identical KTM 125 race bikes – to MotoGP fame and fortune. And perhaps that's what really makes your nasal hairs stand on end: it's the heady stench of youthful ambition intermingled with the odour of fear of failure.

There are futures at stake here, big futures for the riders (and for the parents) who only have to let their eyes wander a few yards up the paddock to see what ostentatious thrills might one day be theirs: the palatial motorhomes of MotoGP's gilded elite, gleaming Ferraris and Porsches and a coterie of silver-tongued managers and fixers, grinning hangers-on and girlfriends with ten-thousand dollar smiles and plastic tits. What wide-eyed pubescent wouldn't risk it all for a stab at that?

The Red Bull recruits have already made it this far, from a list of more than 1100 applicants from 60 countries, and from here on in every gear change is going to be the most important gear change of their lives. These kids' minds are set on their futures like most kids' never are when they're just 13 or 14. I was getting severely beaten for smoking Number Tens down fag alley and dreaming of riding an RD400 when I was their age, not focusing on becoming champion of the whole wide world.

You can see it in their faces, hear it in their voices as they describe each and every moment of their latest race with a glorious intensity that only someone relatively new to this life can feel. It almost makes me want to be an adolescent again. Their eyes aren't quite rolling around in the backs of their heads from all the adrenalin, but it's not far off. Ironically, the last people on this earth who would actually need a can of Red Bull are these 22 boys and one girl. They're already flying, they don't need wings. Not so the affable Red Bull marketing reps, dashing around making this dazzling enterprise happen while enthusiastically quaffing can after can of their speedy brew and hoping that somehow this show will add to the three billion cans they already sell each year.

The Rookies races are usually hugely entertaining, if only for the wild displays of reckless teenage braggadocio and out-of-their minds optimism that characterise so many of the overtaking manoeuvres. And the sense of fraternity among the 23 riders is refreshingly warm, none of the dead eyes and dead legs I remember from my days in schoolboy sport. But then I can't help but feel a nagging sense of moral unease about the whole thing – allowing a bunch of schoolchildren to tear-arse around a racetrack at 120mph, flogging energy drink and entertaining a hundred thousand trackside fans and a few hundred million TV viewers.

Isn't 13 a bit young to be sucked deep into the drive train of the corporate motorsport machine? Shouldn't the youngest of these stars of the future be back home swapping ringtones, bullying teacher, doing some heavy petting, some studying, maybe even a bit of schoolboy motocross or minimoto? Or maybe it's time to allow 13-year-olds to do all the other supposedly adult things we currently don't allow them to do – like driving on the road, drinking in pubs, working in factories, going down the mines, owning guns, voting, smoking, joining the army and having sex. Just a thought.

INDEX

Figures in italics refer to illustrations